ROUTLEDGE LIBRARY]
THE AMERICAN N

G000160921

Volume 13

WILLIAM FAULKNER'S
ABSALOM, ABSALOM!

WILLIAM FAULKNER'S
ABSALOM, ABSALOM!
A Critical Casebook

ELISABETH MUHLENFELD

Routledge
Taylor & Francis Group

LONDON AND NEW YORK

First published in 1984 by Garland Publishing, Inc.

This edition first published in 2018
by Routledge
2 Park Square, Milton Park, Abingdon, Oxon OX14 4RN

and by Routledge
711 Third Avenue, New York, NY 10017

Routledge is an imprint of the Taylor & Francis Group, an informa business

© 1984 Elisabeth Muhlenfeld

British Library Cataloguing in Publication Data
A catalogue record for this book is available from the British Library

ISBN: 978-1-138-09946-3 (Set)
ISBN: 978-1-351-25544-8 (Set) (ebk)
ISBN: 978-1-138-50510-0 (Volume 13) (hbk)
ISBN: 978-1-138-50519-3 (Volume 13) (pbk)
ISBN: 978-1-315-14643-0 (Volume 13) (ebk)

Publisher's Note
The publisher has gone to great lengths to ensure the quality of this reprint but points out that some imperfections in the original copies may be apparent.

Disclaimer
The publisher has made every effort to trace copyright holders and would welcome correspondence from those they have been unable to trace.

WILLIAM FAULKNER'S
ABSALOM, ABSALOM!
A Critical Casebook

Elisabeth Muhlenfeld

GARLAND PUBLISHING, INC. • NEW YORK & LONDON
1984

Library of Congress Cataloging in Publication Data

Muhlenfeld, Elisabeth, 1944–
    William Faulkner's Absalom, Absalom!

    (Garland Faulkner casebooks ; v. 4)
    Bibliography: p.
    1. Faulkner, William, 1897–1962.   Absalom, Absalom!
—Addresses, essays, lectures.   I. Faulkner, William,
1897–1962.   Absalom, Absalom!   II. Title.   III. Series.
PS3511.A86A676   1984   813'.52   82-48497
ISBN 0-8240-9227-9

Printed on acid-free, 250-year-life paper
Manufactured in the United States of America

Contents

Preface

William Faulkner is the most studied American author of our time. And of all his works, his ninth novel, *Absalom, Absalom!*, has received more critical attention than any other, with the possible exception of *The Sound and the Fury*. Some three hundred critical essays and chapters in books have examined this dense, powerful novel in which Quentin Compson in the early twentieth century seeks to know and understand the events and motives surrounding Thomas Sutpen and his doomed family in the nineteenth. Much of the criticism which has, in the nearly fifty years since its publication, attended to *Absalom, Absalom!* seems to have little merit today; some has become dated, some superseded, some was never very helpful in the first place. But a wealth of valuable criticism of the novel remains—articles and essays which deepen our appreciation of Faulkner's most demanding work, teaching us to read the novel better, to see more clearly its complexities and to consider its myriad implications. It has been the present editor's task to choose only a few of these essays for inclusion in this volume.

It should be said at the outset that many of the best treatments of *Absalom, Absalom!* do not appear here. No essays have been included which are readily available in book form elsewhere or which have been anthologized repeatedly. Certainly, a starting point for any study of the novel should be the work of Cleanth Brooks in *William Faulkner: The Yoknapatawpha Country* (1963) and *William Faulkner: Toward Yoknapatawpha and Beyond* (1978), and Michael Millgate's fine chapter in *The Achievement of William Faulkner* (1966). Several other critics besides these two preeminent ones have contributed dramatically to our understanding of the novel, among them John T. Irwin in *Doubling and Incest/Repetition and Revenge: A Speculative Reading of Faulkner* (1975), Albert J. Guerard in *The Triumph of the Novel: Dickens, Dostoevsky, Faulkner* (1976), John T. Matthews in *The Play of Faulkner's Language* (1982) and, most recently, Hugh M. Ruppersburg in *Voice and Eye in Faulkner's Fiction* (1983). Each of these books is in print; therefore, none is represented in the present volume.

The essays which have been included, however, are for the most part made easily accessible here for the first time. Taken together, they illuminate one of our richest literary works. Arrangement is chronological, so that the reader may observe and interpret for himself the development of criticism and scholarly response to *Absalom, Absalom!* since its appearance in 1936. Numerous critical approaches are represented; among them are theme studies, close readings, psychological studies, source studies, structural studies, and analyses of style and narrative technique. The editor's "Introduction" traces the development of *Absalom, Absalom!* from its inception as the short story "Evangeline," examines Faulkner's changing conception of the novel, attempts to sort out the long composition process, and discusses the publication history of *Absalom, Absalom!*

At the end of the anthology, readers will find an annotated bibliography which consists of a highly selective listing of the best and most useful criticism published through 1973 (and therefore included in the secondary bibliographies of John Bassett and Thomas L. McHaney), and a more inclusive listing of scholarship published since 1973.

E.S.M.
The Florida State University

INTRODUCTION

When William Faulkner completed the manuscript of *Absalom, Absalom!* in January, 1936, he handed it to a friend with the unequivocal statement, "I think it's the best novel yet written by an American."[1] Early reviewers did not share the author's enthusiasm; many found the novel hopelessly confused, and some even mocked it as a remarkable specimen of bad writing. Selling only respectably, this first of Faulkner's works to be published by Random House was a financial disappointment, eclipsed by the publication that same year of Margaret Mitchell's wonderfully melodramatic blockbuster, *Gone With the Wind*--a work far more accessible to the general reader and one which painted the years immediately before, during and after the Civil War in comfortably familiar hues. Nearly fifteen years elapsed before critics began to appreciate in print the artistry and depth of Faulkner's novel. Not until the 1950s and early '60s did essays in books and scholarly journals seriously begin to explore the intricacies of the work and to debate its themes and meaning. As critical attention to *Absalom* increased, so did our understanding of this most difficult of Faulkner's works. Today, almost fifty years after its publication, *Absalom, Absalom!* is regarded by many readers as Faulkner's greatest book; indeed, scholars and critics throughout the world celebrate its status as a masterpiece of twentieth-century literature. Thus Faulkner's initial assessment of his newly finished novel may be seen not merely as a euphoric response to just completed work, but as an expression of the artist's utter confidence in his genius and his full awareness of the greatness of his achievement.

Regardless of his confidence at its completion, *Absalom, Absalom!* did not come easily to Faulkner; its writing required more than two and a half years, from early 1934 until mid-1936. This was a period of remarkable productivity, on the one hand, and extreme financial, domestic and emotional difficulty, on the other. Just prior to beginning work on *Absalom, Absalom!*, Faulkner had been working, apparently simultaneously and unsuccessfully, on two novels: one, the first book of the Snopes trilogy, was completed three years after the publication of *Absalom*; the second, *Requiem for a Nun*, was set aside to begin the story of Sutpen and not published until 1951. During the almost three years which produced *Absalom, Absalom!* as its undisputed masterpiece, Faulkner also completed Snopes material--"Mule in the Yard" and "Fool About a Horse"; the short story "This Kind of Courage" and the novel developed from it, *Pylon*; and except for its final episode, "An Odor of Verbena," all of the stories that would comprise *The Unvanquished*.

As he was beginning *Absalom*, Faulkner was also readying his second collection of short stories, *Doctor Martino*, for publication; further, his production of fine short stories in the following three years is impressive: "Golden Land" from his Hollywood experience; three Mississippi stories unconnected with the Snopes saga, "That Will be Fine," "Uncle Willy" and "Lo!"; several stories apparently revisions of earlier attempts, including "Pennsylvania Station" and "The Brooch"; and two hunting stories, "A Bear Hunt" and "Lion." Interestingly, of these two, "A Bear Hunt" uses an unnamed narrator, possibly Quentin and certainly a young man with Quentin's kind of background and boyhood experiences, and "Lion" uses the young Quentin Compson himself as narrator. Because of financial strain, Faulkner was forced to spend a considerable part of this period in Hollywood, and thus, in addition to his own fiction, he worked on at least four movie scripts: *Sutter's Gold*, *The Road to Glory* (earlier called "Wooden Crosses" and renamed "Zero Hour"), *Banjo on My Knee*, and *Gunga Din*.

All of these accomplishments came at a time in his life marked by considerable stress. Most appalling to him personally was the death of his brother Dean; annoying professionally was the financial collapse of his publishers, Smith and Haas, and the necessity to establish new editorial and publishing relationships. Faulkner was in such serious financial difficulties by 1936 that he contemplated selling some of his carefully preserved manuscripts. His relationship with his wife Estelle was tenuous and at times violent, and his marital difficulties were exacerbated by the early stages of an intense love affair with Meta Carpenter, a young woman he met in Hollywood in the fall of 1935. The variety of problems with which Faulkner was forced to deal during the composition of *Absalom, Absalom!*, and the variety, quality and sheer quantity of the writing that he produced in addition to the major novel are difficult for the critic to assess--how could a work so broad in scope yet so intricately conceived and tightly controlled come from such a difficult, sometimes frantic time in the author's life? A brief look at this period suggests, perhaps, that the intricacy, force and sustained intensity of *Absalom*,

with its relative lack of humor and its overriding tragic
vision, may be due in part to the very elements in Faulkner's
life during the writing of the novel which he had to confront,
to endure, and ultimately to control, at least to the extent
that he was not shackled or defeated in his role as artist.

Despite the staggering amount of critical material written
to date about *Absalom, Absalom!*, few scholars have dealt in
any detail with the history of its composition. Robert Knox,
in a 1959 dissertation, attempted to give a brief summary of
its composition, but was hampered by the lack of reliable
biographical data.[2] Michael Millgate's chapter on *Absalom*,
in *The Achievement of William Faulkner*, appearing in 1966,
gave the first careful look at the origins of the novel.[3]
Millgate's chapter is particularly useful for the information
it provides about the final revision and editorial process,
and for its discussion of an earlier story which contained
elements of Sutpen's background. In 1971, Gerald Langford's
Faulkner's Revision of Absalom, Absalom!: *A Collation of the
Manuscript and the Published Book*, though seriously flawed,
described the manuscript at the University of Texas and provided scholars with information about the novel at completed
manuscript stage.[4] However, Langford's work, marred both in
conception and by the mistranscriptions which are perhaps
inevitable when dealing with Faulkner's hand, had to be ap-
proached with caution. Since Faulkner's practice was to revise his manuscripts extensively as he prepared a typescript,
and since the *Absalom, Absalom!* typescript was edited heavily
before being set in print, Langford's book did not actually
provide scholars with an accurate way to examine the author's
revisions. Because Langford's study ignored the typescript
version at the University of Virginia, it was extremely
limited in its usefulness. Noel Polk, in a 1972 review-essay
of the book, examined these problems associated with textual
studies of *Absalom* and further elaborated upon Millgate's
discussion of the changes made in the typescript by heavy-
handed editors.[5] None of these studies, however, concerned
themselves primarily with the genesis and development of the
novel.

Fortunately, today's scholar has far more material to work
with as he struggles to piece together the process whereby
Faulkner conceived and developed *Absalom, Absalom!* than was
available as recently as ten years ago. The publication of
Joseph Blotner's *Faulkner: A Biography* in 1974, with its
wealth of detail, made possible a much closer look at the
1934-36 period than had been available before.[6] Meta Carpenter
Wilde's 1976 memoir of her relationship with Faulkner in Hollywood, aimed at a general readership, enabled us to understand
more fully Faulkner's emotional life during the last stages of

the composition of the novel.[7] Finally, two recent volumes
edited by Blotner, *Selected Letters of William Faulkner* (1977)
and *Uncollected Stories of William Faulkner* (1979) provide
still more material of interest to the student of *Absalom*.[7]
Included in *Uncollected Stories* are two previously unpublished
stories essential to *Absalom* studies: "The Big Shot" and a
later reworking of the same story with the self-fulfilling
title "Dull Tale"; and "Evangeline," an early version of the
Judith-Bon-Henry story, discovered in 1971 among a group of
papers in Faulkner's home but unavailable to most scholars
until 1978.

In 1977, Estella Schoenberg, who had been granted access to
the newly-discovered Rowanoak Papers, published *Old Tales and
Talking: Quentin Compson in William Faulkner's* Absalom, Absalom!
and Related Works, the first serious attempt to deal with the
relationship between "Evangeline" and *Absalom*. Schoenberg provided a thorough summary of the still-unpublished story and identified elements within it which were later incorporated into the
novel. In addition, she examined Quentin Compson and Quentin-
like narrators as they appear throughout the Faulkner canon,
speculated provocatively on the chronological relationships between Quentin's various appearances, and analyzed with care several other stories, published and unpublished, which prefigured
characterizations and motifs in *Absalom, Absalom!* Schoenberg's
study raised many of the right questions for students interested
in the genesis of the novel, but her focus was on Quentin rather
than *Absalom* itself, and this focus led her away from the novel's
origins.[8]

A look at the composition of *Absalom, Absalom!* must begin
long before Faulkner started writing it or even conceived of
Sutpen's story as a novel. When he began writing it in early
1934, he had experienced nearly two years of comparative
difficulty with his work. After finishing *Light in August*
in March, 1932, Faulkner had been unable to focus on any sustained literary project. Much of the remainder of 1932 had
been spent in Hollywood, and the year 1933 saw Faulkner immersed in repairs to Rowanoak, flying lessons and the birth
of his daughter Jill. Although he worked sporadically on
short stories during this period and had tried to begin both
the long-planned Snopes novel and *Requiem for a Nun*, he was
clearly dissatisfied by the fall of 1933 with his work and
was chafing at his lack of productivity. When his editor
Harrison Smith proposed, probably in October, a book of short
stories, Faulkner replied that he had not written "anything
original or even thought in such terms" for more than fifteen
months, but that he would give some thought to a collection:
"I dont know what I have in short stories. I will take a day
off soon and go through them and see if we can get a book we
wont be ashamed of."[9] In the process of going through the

material he had on hand, Faulkner had occasion to look back
at several stories which had been set aside years before. In
all likelihood, it was this review of unpublished stories
which ultimately gave birth to *Absalom, Absalom!*

The most important of the stories at which Faulkner looked
again sometime in the fall of 1933 was "Evangeline," the story
of Judith Sutpen, her brother Henry, and her suitor and then
husband, Charles Bon. Faulkner had almost certainly written
the story shortly before its submission to the *Saturday
Evening Post* in July, 1931.[10] "Evangeline," whose title
evokes the devoted watching and waiting for her lost love by
the heroine of Longfellow's poem, had probably been inspired
by a tale connected with the antebellum home Faulkner had
purchased a year before. Local legend held that Judith, the
beautiful daughter of "Colonel" Robert B. Shegog who built the
house in the 1840s, had died during the Civil War while trying
to elope with a Yankee officer, and that her frail form still
haunted the house. Faulkner loved the story, and throughout
the rest of his life recounted it, suitably embellished and
changed over time, for the children close to him.[11]

In "Evangeline," Faulkner invented a tale he thought
likely to sell to the mass market--a story laced with bigamy,
miscegenation and murder, but suitably redeemed by honor,
selfless heroism and remorse. The story was seasoned with
elements of mystery, and set, somewhat mockingly, against the
magnolia-scented grandeur of the old South and the desolation
and poverty brought by civil war. In this version of the
Judith-Bon-Henry triangle, there is no suggestion either that
Bon is Sutpen's son or that Bon is part Negro, though Sutpen's
mulatto daughter, Raby (who narrates much of the action),
seems to be holding back a vital piece of information. Indeed, Henry's objection to Bon is that he is already married.
Placed at the end of the story and thus offered as the final
and sufficient reason for what has only been hinted at, that
Henry was Bon's murderer, is the dramatic discovery that a
metal case which had once contained Judith's picture, given
to Bon, now holds instead a picture of Bon's first wife, obviously Negro.

Most of the characters in the story are sketchily developed.
We know little about Henry, for example, except that he is
naive, a slave to a system of honor so unyielding that he refuses to divulge to his father and sister the truth about Bon,
because to do so would be to dishonor Bon himself. Bon is an
unrelieved scoundrel who lies to Henry about his mulatto wife
in order to marry Judith, who conceives a child by that wife
after his engagement to Judith (and possibly after he and
Judith are "married"), and who clearly prefers his black wife,
an insensitive, supercilious and thoroughly materialistic
woman. About Sutpen himself we know even less--only that he
is "a florid, portly man, a little swaggering, who liked to

ride fast to church of a Sunday."[12] Sutpen got his land by
unscrupulous means, built a house and laid out a park and
gardens with the aid of an imported French architect, and at
some unspecified time before the war had travelled in Germany,
bringing home two vicious police dogs. He serves as an officer
in the war, but returns a ruined man, dying in 1870.

Although most of the characters in "Evangeline" remain
flat, two are vividly developed: Judith Sutpen Bon and Raby
Sutpen, an aged former slave who tells the tale to the narrator
in time present. Judith, who died in 1885, emerges in Raby's
telling as anything but the pale, wan victim of tragic love
in the Shegog legend. Very much the stereotypical Southern
belle before the war (although stubborn enough to marry Bon
despite her brother's unexplained insistence that she break
her engagement), Judith is "solidified" by the experiences of
war and widowhood, which strip her of her beauty and coquetry
and leave in their stead consummate strength. Throughout the
war it is she who keeps the household together; afterwards,
she raises chickens to bring cash into the house, nurses and
ultimately buries her father, sends whatever money she can
to Bon's New Orleans widow and child, and even invites them to
visit, never revealing her own relationship to Bon.

Raby has witnessed all these events and has, since Judith's
death, hidden her half-brother Henry at the Sutpen house for
thirty-five years, The matriarch of her own multigenerational
family, she is now a wizened crone, described almost word for
word as Clytie would later be in *Absalom*. But unlike Clytie,
she breaks her long silence to tell the narrator the tale on
the eve of Henry's death. Having finished her tale, she rejects any help from the narrator, in words which prefigure
not only Clytie but also Molly Beauchamp at the end of *Go
Down, Moses*: "I dont need no help.... You go on away from
here and write your paper piece."[13]

There is some evidence to suggest that having reread
"Evangeline," Faulkner toyed with the idea of developing it
into a novel. Fragments of two précis found among the Rowanoak
papers discovered in 1971 sketch what seems to be a novel-
length work patterned very precisely on "Evangeline."[14] The
earlier is entitled "Dark House," used first as a working title
for *Light in August* and then in 1934 for *Absalom, Absalom!*;
the latter, probably written immediately after the first but
untitled, is simply a slightly expanded version, exploring
somewhat more deeply the characters of Henry and Bon and the
relationship between them. Both fragments break off after
two manuscript pages, so we can only speculate about the full
scope of the contemplated novel; however, there is no hint in
either of these drafts that "Dark House" would focus on Sutpen,
or that the relationship of Bon to Sutpen would be anything
more than that of suitor to prospective father-in-law. In any
case, the idea of a novel in this form seems to have been put
aside for the time being.

A second story at which Faulkner looked in the fall of 1933 as he contemplated putting together a collection of short stories was "The Big Shot," which contains elements anticipating several later works. Probably written in the late 1920s (before Faulkner began work on *Sanctuary* in January, 1929), "The Big Shot" is told by the same I-narrator and his friend Don who would later narrate "Evangeline" and who had already appeared in "Mistral" (first published in *These 13* in 1931, but almost certainly written in the late '20s). Of major interest in "The Big Shot" is a five-page background incident that the narrator, here given the full name Don Reeves, relates to his listener about the central figure, Dal Martin. Martin has experienced a rejection at the door of a "big house" much as does Sutpen in *Absalom*, and his reaction is not very different: he runs away, throws himself in a ditch and comes to grips with his loss of innocence. Like Sutpen would later do, Martin discovers that the message he had been sent to deliver was unimportant; like Sutpen's, his feelings for the owner of the house are confused but do not include overt hatred. The years between this experience and his subsequent success are vague, almost non-existent, and Faulkner comments explicitly on Martin's strange metamorphosis from boy to man in a passage which might well apply to Sutpen.

Martin is not, of course, an early Thomas Sutpen. In fact, there are elements in his characterization which suggest Wash Jones and Flem Snopes as well. Martin has less intelligence, stature and dignity than has Sutpen, but there are other elements in "The Big Shot" which suggest that the story offers a sketch of a Sutpen-like man. Martin runs a crossroads store, has a wife merely for convenience and seems not to grieve at her loss, and has a daughter through whom he hopes to achieve social recognition. Finally there is, in "The Big Shot," a suggestion of the kind of attitude the people of Jefferson have for Sutpen in the aloofness maintained by the townspeople toward Martin.

Very likely, the circumstance of having recently reread both "Evangeline" and "The Big Shot," coupled with the fact that he had been working with the Snopes material which would eventually appear in *The Hamlet*, accounts for the writing of "Wash," the story of a poor white who cherishes his relationship with the brave Colonel Sutpen, symbol of a lost, grand, almost feudal world.[15] As the story opens, Sutpen has seduced Wash's fifteen-year-old granddaughter and, on the morning after she gives birth to Sutpen's child, insults her grievously. When he can no longer ignore Sutpen's inhumanity, the sixty-year old Wash loses the innocence which has prevented his full adulthood and kills the object of his former worship.

As the evidence of the two "Dark House" précis suggests, when Faulkner wrote "Wash" in the fall of 1933, he had perhaps

already conceived of the idea of turning the Evangeline
material into a novel. He may, then, have used "Wash" to
work out an episode intended eventually for the longer work.
More likely, however, the character of Wash was not initially
associated with Sutpen, but occurred to Faulkner separately,
inspired by the poor whites of the Snopes material and by the
background experiences of Dal Martin in "The Big Shot," whose
response to his discovery of his own status in a plantation
society had been awe and a desire to emulate the very plantation owner who had barred him from entering the big house.
For the second character, the plantation owner, Faulkner
simply used a convenient character he had recently noticed,
one ready to hand in his "lumber room." Sutpen, undeveloped
in "Evangeline," worked well in "Wash." In fact, as the short
story evolved, Sutpen changed from a "florid, portly man" to
an imposing figure, arrogant, crude, but with elements of
the tragic hero fallen from power and, hence, grace.

Once Faulkner's creative energies focused on Sutpen, he
must almost immediately have conceived the possibilities of
a Sutpen novel which would combine the events of "Wash,"
"Evangeline," and Dal Martin's childhood rejection from the
big house in "The Big Shot." Evidence suggests, however,
that this more elaborate idea for the novel that would ultimately become *Absalom, Absalom!* was set aside for use at
some time in the future. In January, 1934, Faulkner still
expected his next novel to be either Snopes or *Requiem for a
Nun*, and debated in a late January letter to Harrison Smith
which of the two he might reasonably expect to complete
sooner.[16] He planned to turn to whichever novel he settled
on in March, when he anticipated a temporary easing of his
financial situation and thus time to work on serious fiction.
But as he contemplated these two novels-in-progress, the Sutpen story must have seized his attention. In early February,
1934, he set aside other projects to experiment with an appropriate opening for "A Dark House."

Faulkner initially intended to frame the Sutpen novel
precisely as he had done the Evangeline story, using two contemporary narrators, now named Burke and Chisholm, in place
of Don and the unnamed I-narrator of "Evangeline." The
earliest extant draft of an opening to the novel, written
on or before February 11, 1934, begins almost word for word
as does section I of "Evangeline." Burke has summoned his
friend by telegram, breaking a silence of six years: *"Have
ghost for you come and get it leaving myself this week."*
Both men assume the flippant approach to a "ghost story"
that the narrators of "Evangeline" had affected:

    "It seems that this bird—his name was Sutpen—"

    "—Colonel Sutpen." Chisholm said.

"That's not fair," Burke said

"I know it," Chisholm said. "Pray continue."[17]

As Burke tells his friend Chisholm the bare outlines of his
discovery, it becomes clear that Faulkner intended to use
"Wash" as a focal point on which to build:

"[Sutpen] walks out of the house that a.m., with Wash
probably watching him all the time, hid off somewhere
behind the garden fence with his whiskey jug, waiting
for him to come out--"

"Wash?" Chisholm said.

"Yes, the bird that killed him. Whose daughter old
Sutpen had betrayed as I usually say."

"You mean Wash was fooling with Sutpen's daughter, only
he got the plot wrong and shot Sutpen by mistake."

No. I mean it like I said it. That Wash shot Sutpen
because Wash's daughter was down home at the moment
with a 3 hour old baby, who didn't have any husband
to mention."

"Oh." Chisholm said.

"I believe you." Burke said. "An old guy who should
have been a grandfather only he had not only driven
his son away from home but apparently had had something
to do with widowing his daughter in time to leave her
a wife in name only, as I always say too."[18]

Burke and Chisholm continue to discuss the Sutpen story,
but they are more interested in their vaudevillian routine
of quips and one-upsmanship than in the story itself. Chisholm, a writer, has come for a week to "get a story for Mac's
agony page next Saturday." Burke's interest is that of the
tourist, gawking at the peculiarities of the natives. He's
fascinated by the moonshine whiskey he and Chisholm are
drinking ("'This seems to be the reason for the existence
of the Washes of this country,'"), and mocks the Southern
heritage of his friend Chisholm:

"--But am I telling you? I forget you were born in
this country too. That you are a southerner, too,
descendant of long lines of colonels killed in Pickett's
charge, at Steer's Gap."

"Gettysburg." Chisholm said without humor.[19]

When Chisholm asks how Burke has gotten so much information,
Burke's answer reveals that Faulkner had already decided to
use multiple narrators, among them an unnamed old man and an
elderly lady who seems to be an early conception of Rosa
Coldfield:

"Oh," Burke said. "You'll find it out too. But it
wont be from the young people here. The ones under 60.
They were born and raised here with it; they're not
supposed to know anything about it. There's one old
bird that sets all day on a chair in front of the store
that told me some, and there's one old lady that you
are going to talk to. She--"

"Oh, am I?"

"You bet," Burke said. "She's got the lowdown. She
was engaged to Sutpen. He had come back from the war
with his sword and plume and a citation from Joe John-
stone and not much else, including a widowed daughter
and a half-ruined home and one family of negroes that
had stayed on for some reason. And they were engaged
to be married: the old guy in his fifties and this
old lady who was a girl of 16 then. Nobody knew why.
And then it was broken off, and nobody knew why again
until Wash told them. Showed them."[20]

After another line or two, this draft fragment breaks
off. In a second and third fragment (the second also titled
"A Dark House," the third untitled but dated 11 February
1934), Faulkner departs from the "Evangeline" opening for
several paragraphs, and instead expands the setting in which
Burke and Chisholm find themselves. Here the two young narrators are strangely affected and temporarily sobered by
their environment:

It was hot in the room because the room was small and
built to rent for a dollar a day (with meals) to people
who would never return, and not for comfort. It was
12 feet square and walled and ceiled and floored with
the same [*illegible word*] tongue and groove plank and
painted the same brown The pictures on the walls were
lithographs made to arrest the eye like a red traffic
light long enough for the intelligence to assimilate
the printed descriptions of [*illegible word*] and auto-
mobiles and patent medicines beneath them. It contained a single unshaded bulb on a cord, a washstand,
2 chairs, a bed. And tho through the thin walls sounds
of life came from other parts of the house, the room
itself seemed to hang in the hot, weary, unfocused
country darkness like one of those cells in which
scientists let themselves down to the bottom of the
sea.... [Burke] turned and took his discarded sheet
from the bed and mopped his face with it. "You dont
do anything for fun in a room like this." He looked
at the bed quickly, quietly.

"I dont believe anybody ever even had any fun in that
bed."

> "Maybe they didn't ever try it." Chisholm said as
> quietly. "I dont believe I would have. I have that
> much respect and regard for the delusions of love."[21]

Although Burke and Chisholm shake off the effects of their
boardinghouse room and enter into the banter of the earlier
draft, they have nevertheless begun to take shape as narrator-
characters, involved in the atmosphere of the story and concerned with the "delusions of love" with which, ultimately,
Quentin would be obsessed in *Absalom*.

Faulkner had now established the striking image of two
young men sitting bare-armed across a table, in a stifling
and characterless room, drawn together by a telegram sent
unexpectedly after a six-year silence. One of the young men,
Burke, is northern born. The other, Chisholm, is a Southerner,
and therefore capable of comprehending the tale that Burke
can relate but never really understand. Unsatisfied, Faulkner
now tried a mirror image of the Burke/Chisholm setting: a
cold room, no longer in Mississippi but instead in remote
Cambridge, Massachusetts, and two other young men, still a
Southerner and a Northerner, but now Quentin and Shreve.
Instead of the jaunty telegram which had brought Burke and
Chisholm together, Faulkner uses a letter from Quentin's
father, describing the death of Miss Rosa Coldfield:

> Overcoatsleeved and snowpowdered, Shreve's arms got
> away: and now the blurred sharp mechanical *Jefferson
> Jan. 10 1910 Miss* and then the *My dear son*[22]

In three manuscript fragments, at least the earliest two
written on February 11, 1934, Faulkner considered beginning
his novel with a draft of Mr. Compson's complete letter, the
text of which varies only slightly from the printed text in
Absalom, Absalom! bracketing Chapters VI through IX.

Just why or how Faulkner settled upon Quentin and Shreve
as narrators of the Sutpen novel is impossible to say. The
two roommates seem a remarkable choice, most obviously because
Quentin's suicide in June, 1910, had formed the core of *The
Sound and the Fury* six years earlier. (Curiously, Quentin
is twenty-one in an early conception of the novel--perhaps
simply a slip of memory on Faulkner's part, but possibly a
daring intention on the author's part to have his character
in the later novel two years older than he was at the time
of his suicide in *The Sound and the Fury*.)[23] In a recent
essay, "'A Cosmos of My Own': The Evolution of Yoknapatawpha,"
Michael Millgate examines Faulkner's early use of Quentin and
concludes, in a brilliant piece of speculation, that prior to
and perhaps even after the composition of *The Sound and the
Fury*, Quentin (or a Quentin-like narrator) was "at one stage

intended to function as the essential recording figure ...
deployed through a whole series of otherwise separate narratives. In looking back from the perspective of adulthood
upon the tales he had heard as a child, he was presumably
to have learned to appreciate not only their intrinsic human
significance but also their particular meaning for him as a
boy and man of his place and time--to recognize, in short,
that they were quintessential expressions of that regional
world, past and present, which had made him what he was."[24]
Millgate's assessment of the evidence leads him to suggest
that Faulkner had once seen Quentin as "a focal point--though
not necessarily the only one--for the Compson material, the
Surratt/Snopes material ... and for what subsequently became
the Sam Fathers/hunting/McCaslin material."[25] If Millgate
is right--and his argument is both elegant and persuasive--
then perhaps Faulkner's use of the Quentin-like narrator in
"A Bear Hunt," written in the fall of 1933, had served as a
kind of creative resurrection of Quentin Compson, which
touched off once again Faulkner's earlier sense of Quentin's
structural, narrative and thematic potential.

In any case, the juxtaposition of Quentin and Shreve
with the Sutpen/Evangeline material provided Faulkner with
the final catalyst he needed to shift the tone of his novel
firmly from comic-melodramatic to tragic and its scope from
regional to universal. By emphasizing Quentin's fragmented
personality, Faulkner was able to cast even the absurd opening
banter of the "Evangeline" narration in a profound light.
In one very early draft, for example, this banter is between
two sides of Quentin's self, and represents his desperate
attempt to affirm his sanity. Here, in a passage still very
close to the wording of "Evangeline," he imagines hearing
the story told jokingly as at least part of him would like
to be able to tell it, but his imagined scenario lacks strength
sufficient to distract him from his own anguish. As he begins
to tell the story himself to Shreve, his attempt at a light,
sarcastic touch sounds only exhausted and defeated:

> *Continue, Quentin says*
> *--be a fitten setting for his lone jewel, a--*
> *--daughter named--Quentin says*
> *Wait; that's not--*
> *--Azalea, Quentin says*
> *Now, we're even*
> *I meant Syringa, Quentin says*
> *Now I'm one up. Her name was Judith*
> *That's what I meant, Quentin says--Judith*
> *All right   You tell, then*
> *Pray continue, Quentin says*   That's what it would be
> like, which no one says. But why tell me? Why must

> she tell me? And the other one saying. Because you
> are a dead part of the dead South the same as she is;
> the very fact that you are preparing for Harvard only
> means that you are getting a little [*illegible word*]
> and [*illegible word*] out of living. So Shreve was not
> the first at Cambridge to say, "What do they do? Why
> do they live at all? Why do they hate to die?" So
> I said,

> "Listen. It seems that he had a son too, as well as a
> daughter--a florid, portly man, a little swaggering,
> who liked to ride fast to church on Sunday....[26]

Once he had hit upon using Quentin and Shreve as narrators
and the letter from Mr. Compson as a framing device, Faulkner
apparently began to expand his conception of Rosa's role in
the novel, for Mr. Compson's letter touches off in Quentin's
memory a "long still hot weary dead afternoon" in Rosa's "office,"
listening to her recitation of the Sutpen story. In the
earliest draft fragments in which Rosa figures, she seems to
be an involved narrator, once engaged to Sutpen, but by no
means the haunting, dominant character of the finished novel.
The figure of Rosa seems to have developed from much the same
narrative needs as those resulting in the use of Quentin.

In "Evangeline," most of the narrative centers around the
recollections of Raby, the wizened ex-slave who eventually
reveals herself to be half-sister to Henry and Judith and
thus the living symbol of the miscegenation with which the
story deals. Raby's proximity to the actions about which she
tells allows her to function as a reliable, involved narrator,
but that very proximity works against the complexity Faulkner
wished to bring to the novel-length work. As long as Raby
remains silent, the mystery of the "ghost" at the Sutpen
mansion can be shrouded in uncertainty and speculation, but
once she is persuaded to tell her story, her tale is straight-
forward and virtually complete. Her role as servant allows
her, like Nelly Dean in *Wuthering Heights*, to see much that
could have been seen from no other perspective; nevertheless,
hers is the passionately private and personal view of an intelligence severely limited in education and scope. Sutpen,
seen only from the vantage point of his own family--extending
no further than Raby's cabin in the slave yard--must remain
a petty tyrant.

Grandeur, heroic stature required distance, even while
the necessities of plot required a narrator related closely
enough to the action of the story to be able to report first-
hand experience. Hence, for the novel, Faulkner split the
dual functions of Raby into two characters. Now, Clytie,
who performs essentially the same actions in the novel as

Raby does in the story, could by her very silence carry the
symbolic weight of all the tragic ramifications of slavery
far better than the more voluble Raby. And Rosa, the old
maid whose childhood had been clouded by Sutpen, whose adolescence had been encapsulated in the shadowy figure of Bon,
and whose adulthood had been consumed in hatred for the man
who had denied her humanity, could carry much of the narrative burden which had been Raby's.

   One result of the development of Raby into Clytie and Rosa
was a doubling and redoubling between Clytie, Judith and Rosa,
doubling that would survive in remarkable ways in the finished
novel, but which in early drafts was less than subtle. For
a time, Faulkner even toyed with having Clytie and Judith
born "at the same hour of the same day,"[27] although by the
time he had worked far enough into the project to begin Chapter III, he had modified this detail somewhat. An early
description of Clytie by Mr. Compson places great thematic
emphasis squarely on the relationship between the three women,
and in particular on Rosa's jealousy and resentment of Clytie.
According to Mr. Compson in this draft, Clytie

> was older than Henry and therefore at least 5 years
> older than Judith, tho I agree with Miss Rosa here
> (there is a sense of theater, of literary form, to
> hatred as well as to anticipation and desire) that for
> the sake of dramatic value Clytie and Judith should
> have been born at the same hour of the same day, tho for
> that to be true would be to hope for a little too much
> even from that perverse daemon which according to her
> Sutpen possessed. But at least she was Judith's half
> sister. Miss Rosa never forgave Ellen for this....
> It was between herself and Ellen that the fact of
> Clytie's life and breath seemed to be an outrage ...
> who had Sutpen's eyes as perfectly as Judith did....
> Perhaps it was because Clytie was being bred up to be
> Judith's personal handmaid and hence practically ate
> and slept with Judith.[28]

The implications of the blood relationship between Clytie
and Judith, then, appear to have been fully realized long
before Faulkner even conceived of Bon as Sutpen's rejected
son and hence the half-brother of Judith and Henry.

   Although Faulkner's conception of the novel was not yet
complete, he had by late February become sufficiently committed to the project that he described it in some detail to
Hal Smith, closing with a projected completion date:

> I believe that I have a head start on the novel. I
> have put both the Snopes and the Nun one aside. The one

I am writing now will be called DARK HOUSE or something
of that nature. It is the more or less violent breakup
of a household or family from 1860 to about 1910. It is
not as heavy as it sounds. The story is an anecdote
which occurred during and right after the civil war;
the climax is another anecdote which happened about
1910 and which explains the story. Roughly, the theme
is a man who outraged the land, and the land then turned
and destroyed the man's family. Quentin Compson, of
the Sound & Fury, tells it, or ties it together; he is
the protagonist so that it is not complete apocrypha.
I use him because it is just before he is to commit
suicide because of his sister, and I use his bitterness
which he had projected on the South in the form of
hatred of it and its people to get more out of the story
itself than a historical novel would be. To keep the
hoop skirts and plug hats out, you might say. I believe
I can promise it for fall.[29]

Nevertheless, after his burst of creative activity in mid-
February, the novel progressed haltingly for several months.
Faulkner's problems with it were three-fold. Perhaps most
important, he continued to struggle with financial difficulties and with consequent demands on his time; it was necessary
to turn to more lucrative projects. Within the next few
months, he wrote several short stories, among them "This Kind
of Courage," inspired by his attendance at an airport opening
in New Orleans in February; "Mule in the Yard," an outgrowth
of the Snopes material; and "Ambuscade," "Ripost" and "Raid,"
the first three stories which would ultimately make up *The
Unvanquished*--themselves almost certainly the product of his
having turned his serious attention to the period just before
and during the Civil War. By the end of June, he was forced
to work for several weeks in Hollywood on Howard Hawks' movie
Sutter's Gold. From Hollywood he wrote to Estelle that he
had "[d]one a little on the novel from time to time,"[30] but
immediately after his return to Oxford in late July, he reported to his agent Morton Goldman that in order to produce
some income, he would have to work another month on the movie
script and perhaps write more stories before he could return
to the novel in earnest.[31]

Yet Faulkner knew full well that his financial pressures
did not really account for his lack of progress. To Hal Smith
he wrote in August that he simply did not know when the novel
--which he had finally decided to entitle *Absalom, Absalom!*--
would be finished:

The only definite news I can tell you is, that I still
do not know when [the novel] will be ready. I believe

> that the book is not quite ripe yet; that I have not
> gone my nine months, you might say. I do have to put
> it aside and make a nickel every so often, but I think
> there must be more than that. I have a mass of stuff,
> but only one chapter that suits me; I am considering
> putting it aside and going back to REQUIEM FOR A NUN,
> which will be a short one, like AS I LAY DYING, while
> the present one will probably be longer than LIGHT IN
> AUGUST. I have a title for it which I like, by the way:
> ABSALOM, ABSALOM; the story is of a man who wanted a
> son through pride, and got too many of them and they
> destroyed him....[32]

Evidence culled from early manuscript drafts of *Absalom* suggests that Faulkner was still having serious conceptual and
technical problems with it in the fall of 1934.

Interestingly, Faulkner had envisioned most of the controlling images and several of the crucial tableaux of the
finished novel very early in its composition. As we have already seen, Mr. Compson's letter was composed in February,
1934, virtually word for word as it would finally appear.
Stage and theater imagery had been incorporated as early as
the Burke/Chisholm drafts, as had the image of the two young
men across a table, the naked torsos, the late night inquiry,
the outsider's lack of comprehension about the South. The
earliest of the Quentin/Shreve drafts used the odor of wistaria
to summon up the late-summer evening in Mississippi and the
image of the crucified child in connection with Rosa. Several
early fragments are drafts of the scene in which Judith and
Clytie observe Sutpen's "raree show" from the stable loft;
others prefigure Clytie's confrontation with Rosa at Sutpen's
Hundred. Shreve's "Wait" halts and punctuates Quentin's
monologues in numerous early draft fragments. Perhaps most
significantly, the crucial question "Why do you hate the
South?", in the final version the last (and ultimate) question
in the novel, appears as the *first* important question in
several early drafts.[33]

But juxtaposed against these images, tableaux and narrative devices which would be used to such striking effect in
the finished work were plot remnants from "Evangeline" which
marred the high seriousness of the work its author gradually
envisioned. Rosa had, for example, been almost fully developed
(even to details such as her arrangement for Judith's tombstone and her relationship with Judge Benbow, symbolized by
his portfolio of racing forms) well before Faulkner decided
that Bon would be killed at the end of the war. Early drafts
record Bon's date of death on his tombstone as April 19, 1860,
and his age as twenty-three. For at least a time, Faulkner
intended Henry and Bon to be the same age.[34]

It was also well into the composition of the novel before Judith achieved the dignity she would evince so steadfastly in the final draft. In one early fragment, Charles' death evokes an almost hysterical response, a flood of laments (which ultimately would re-emerge, transformed, as Judith's speech to Quentin's grandmother) that Rosa and Clytie have difficulty stemming: "Because even after Miss Rosa and old Clytie got her to bed, she would not be still. It seems that old Clytie had to hold her there and Judith shaking her head from side to side as a child does, screaming 'Pity us. Pity us. Pity us.' for a long time."[35] In this draft fragment, it is Clytie herself who has told Mr. Compson of Judith's wild grief. Several draft passages retain the collection of children and grandchildren which surrounded Raby in "Evangeline," now Clytie's, and Clytie's daughter Sibey is a source of considerable information.[36] Minor details (the mysterious police dogs, for example)[37] were retained from "Evangeline" long after Faulkner had decided to use Quentin and Shreve as narrators, and at least one major motif, Quentin and Shreve's consumption of whiskey throughout their "investigation," was slow to be abandoned.[38]

Furthermore, trial drafts of the novel suggest that in addition to such uncertainties about plot, Faulkner had not yet made some basic decisions about narrative voice. Numerous false starts reveal the author experimenting with persona, point of view, and more basic questions of the characterization of his narrators and the extent of their knowledge. In one fragment, Mr. Compson has, twenty years before the novel's time present, heard the whole story from Judith.[39] In another, Rosa knows that Bon was Sutpen's son.[40] In yet another, Sutpen announces unequivocally to Quentin's grandfather that his wife "who they had told me was Spanish had had some negro blood" and leaves no doubt that at his Christmas confrontation with Henry, he had told his son that Bon was his brother.[41] Similar passages appear as late as the completed manuscript draft, on which, finally, Faulkner has cancelled them, deciding at last to leave obscure the details of Bon's parentage.

Some drafts proceed in the present tense in Quentin's voice; in others Quentin speaks in past tense. In one important experiment, an omniscient third person narrator shifts to Rosa, speaking in the present tense to the dead Sutpen:

> I am 67 years old: I am a virgin: yet for 45 years now
> I have slept with a man every day and night of my life,
> and now after 45 years the only way I know to escape
> you is in talking to a child whom I must force to listen
> to me.[42]

In this, as in most of the extant manuscript fragments found among the Rowanoak Papers, Faulkner shifts points of view,

alternates back and forth between dialogue and thought, and
signals movements into and out of Quentin's consciousness with
italics.

After struggling with these problems off and on for at
least seven months, Faulkner had not yet achieved artistic
mastery over the *Absalom* material by late summer, 1934. With
financial pressures increasing and the end to the novel in
sight, he continued to turn away from *Absalom* periodically to
write short stories, finishing three more of the *Unvanquished*
stories ("Unvanquished," "Vendee" and "Drusilla") and "Golden
Land," set in California, between late summer and the first
of October. With these stories completed, he sensed a need
to turn to another major project for relief from the difficulties he was having with *Absalom*; too, he felt increasing
obligation to deliver a novel on which he had been advanced
money more than a year before. Accordingly, he began a novel
set uncompromisingly in the twentieth century, about a quartet
of barnstormers. From Morton Goldman he requested the return
of "This Kind of Courage," the story he had written in the
spring inspired by the February opening of the New Orleans
airport. Using "This Kind of Courage" as base, Faulkner wrote
Pylon at "forced draft" between early October and early December, 1934, and had finished reading proof by mid-January,
1935.

Critics have generally divorced *Pylon* from *Absalom*, considering the "air story" little more than an interesting
diversion as Faulkner worked on the Sutpen novel. Most regard
Pylon as failed art. Recent critics, however, have begun to
accord it careful attention and to consider at least briefly
its relationship to *Absalom, Absalom!* Although on the surface
the shorter novel is almost antithetical in theme, subject
matter, time and setting to *Absalom*, it is possible to view
the two novels as functioning together contrapuntally almost
as do the dual plots of *The Wild Palms*: the Civil War rural
triangle of Henry, Judith and Bon can easily be seen as a
kind of distorted and inverted mirror image of the Roger-
Laverne-Jack affair in the mechanistic, unrooted world of the
barnstormer; too, the similarity between Quentin's role and
that of the reporter and of Shreve's role divided in *Pylon*
between Hagood and Jiggs is indisputable. *Pylon* offered
Faulkner a chance to experiment technically with an involved
and impotent narrator, and to work through some of the epistemological questions at the heart of *Absalom*, most strikingly
questions of knowability and of the chasm between fact and
truth. Thematically, *Pylon* explores as does *Absalom* the
tangled and tragic ramifications of a human love played out
in the shadow of a magnificent obsession. Certainly, Faulkner

began *Pylon* because he had been unable to progress satisfac-
torily with *Absalom*; just as certainly, the date of publication of the "air story" (March 25, 1935) coincided almost
precisely with the beginning of the manuscript of *Absalom*
(March 30, 1935) which led to the final typescript of the
book.[43] Some insight or process, then, in the writing of
Pylon enabled its author to try again with *Absalom*, and to
come to it sure, finally, of his basic structural approach,
his style and his themes.

Still, though, Faulkner lived under financial pressure;
he had scarcely mailed the last chapter of the *Pylon* typescript before he had to turn again to projects likely to
earn some money. His first task was to revise "Drusilla,"
the sixth of the *Unvanquished* stories, and then to write
"That Will Be Fine" and "Lion," narrated by Quentin Compson
and inspired at least in part by the police dogs in "Evangeline" which had proved so problematical in *Absalom*--one
more example of Faulkner's reluctance to waste good material.
When in late March he turned back to the major novel, he apparently started with a fresh conception and a clear vision
of the entire work.

Once Faulkner began the novel again, his progress was
rapid and, except for a two-month lapse, undeviating. Having
begun page one on March 30, he was able to send Hal Smith a
first chapter in April. Chapter II was received in New York
on June 29, Chapter III on July 22, and Chapter IV on August 9,
1935.[44] His steady work during this period almost belies the
extreme financial strain under which he was working. In
April he had reported to Goldman that "I am writing two
stories a week now. I dont know how long I can keep it up."[45]
Most of the stories in question were rewrites of early, unpublished pieces; many would remain unmarketable. Faulkner's
work on them suggests not only that he desperately wanted to
make enough money to work full time on the novel, but also
that he was unwilling to turn his imagination to entirely
new material, thereby lessening his concentration of creative
energies on *Absalom*. By July, he was concerned enough about
money to consider selling some of his manuscripts. After
completing Chapter IV in late August, he decided to go to
New York, hoping to take a hand in selling his magazine rights
to the new novel. He was unable to do so, but finally persuaded his publishers, Smith and Haas, to loan him an amount
of money barely sufficient to cover his operating expenses.
In exchange, he agreed to spend two months in California
earning enough to repay the loan.

Immediately upon his return to Oxford in mid-October, he
began Chapter V, only to have the death of his brother Dean on

November 10th rock him so severely that, uncharacteristically, he felt compelled to discuss it with a complete stranger, Nunnally Johnson, in Hollywood seven weeks later.[46] Nevertheless, chapter followed chapter in a steadily accumulating manuscript, the final page of which he dated 31 January 1936.[47] Thus the final five chapters of the novel must have been written in about three months--an astonishing feat even without the devastating event of Dean's death. Certainly the work on *Absalom* served to alleviate his grief and guilt about Dean, who had crashed in Faulkner's own plane, leaving behind a young wife several months pregnant. Indeed, Carvel Collins has reported that Faulkner took the manuscript with him to his mother's house immediately after the fatal plane crash and there worked on it by candlelight.[48] Though probably apocryphal, the incident is suggestive when considered in light of the last half of *Absalom*, which proceeds with a sustained concentration and intensity possibly unequaled in any other Faulkner novel.

Yet another element in Faulkner's life at this time may well be reflected in the final intensity of *Absalom*. One month to the day after Dean's death, Faulkner went again to Hollywood, to honor the arrangement he had made in New York in October. For more than five weeks, he worked on *Absalom* in the early morning hours and on a Howard Hawks film, *The Road to Glory*, then entitled "Wooden Crosses," by day. While there, he found himself strongly attracted to Hawks' young secretary, Meta Carpenter. Soon Faulkner was spending every evening with Meta, and by the time he returned to Oxford in early January, he had begun a romantic and passionate relationship which would continue for several years--apparently the first and perhaps the only deep and reciprocal love affair of his adult years. The course of the affair plunged Faulkner into a cycle of emotional highs and lows, but at its best, in its early stages, it seems to have imbued him with renewed creative energy and increased insight into the intricacies of mutual romantic love.

After his return to Rowanoak in late January, he quickly finished reworking the manuscript and recorded on the last page the notation: "Mississippi, 1935/California, 1936/ Mississippi, 1936." The process of revision and typing took several months, during much of which he was back in Hollywood, working with Nunnally Johnson and then David Hempstead on *Banjo on My Knee* and spending evenings and weekends with Meta Carpenter. A final version of Chapter I was received in New York on April 6, shortly after he had signed a six-month contract as a screenwriter to begin August 1. The entire typescript was complete and in the hands of his editors by summer.[49]

Faulkner's revisions from manuscript to typescript testify
to the painstaking care he took with this novel. Revisions--
abundant on literally every page--ranged from the fine-tuning
of individual phrases and sentences and the sharpening of
imagery to frequent rearrangement of material (most often by
delaying passages for introduction into the text at a later
point). Some passages were shortened or omitted; others
amplified. (Faulkner added, for example, the long parenthetical
passage in Bon's letter.)[50] While most of the revisions are
of greatest interest because of the stylistic nuances they
achieved, several important kinds of revisions pertained to
the plot itself. First, as he revised, Faulkner consistently
heightened suspense and intensified atmosphere, often by de-
leting or postponing information. Faulkner ended the manuscript of Chapter III, for example, with Wash hollering to
Rosa, "Henry has done shot that durn French fellow. Kilt him
dead as a beef." On his typescript, he first decided to delay
the announcement of Bon's death and typed, "I reckon you better
come on out yon to Sutpen's.... I reckon you better hurry."
Still not satisfied, he added in ink the sentences with which
the manuscript had ended. A third revision, again in ink,
reflected his final decision, a single question: "Air you
Rosie Coldfield?"[51]

A second major area of revision relates to Bon's parentage
--how much was known, by whom, and at what point. Discarded
manuscript drafts from the final chapters suggest that Faulkner
did not decide until very late in the writing of the novel
that the fact of Bon's taint of black blood would remain
speculation. Consider this false start for Chapter VIII:

> "So Henry and Bon knew about the incest ... but not
> about the miscegenation," Shreve said....
>
> "Yes," Quentin said. "They didn't know that. Just the
> incest. Folks said that Colonel Sutpen believed that
> that would be enough, sufficient."[52]

Here, not only have Quentin and Shreve "discovered" that Bon
is part Negro, they are discussing it as a fact, and Quentin's
mention of what "folks" said suggests that Bon's parentage
had come to be known by the community. This discarded manuscript pages goes on to develop the image of "not 2 but 4 of
them" in the cold dormitory room, entering into the imaginative recreation of Bon and Henry's wartime interview. It was
clearly written in the last intense month or so of the composition of the manuscript. Thus, it was in the process of revision that Faulkner made the changes which would submerge
forever these "facts" beneath a tangle of speculation and
uncertainty, leaving the past finally unknowable.

A third type of revision took place principally after
the typescript was complete: the revision of dates to accord,
more or less, with the chronology which Faulkner almost certainly worked out after he had finished typing the novel.
Inasmuch as the dates in the novel are often inconsistent
(and sometimes fail to accord with the chronology--which
itself differs from the genealogy), we may speculate that
Faulkner made these changes only when he noticed inconsistencies; he did not, apparently, search for every instance of a
date or character's age. Likewise (perhaps after having drawn
the map of Yoknapatawpha County which would be included in
the published novel), Faulkner changed the distance from Oxford
to Jefferson.[53]

The editing of *Absalom, Absalom!* presents a somewhat confused picture. When the novel was originally contracted,
Faulkner's publisher was Smith and Haas. Working with Hal
Smith as his principal editor, he received advances from the
firm as well as at least one loan. Smith and Haas, however,
ran into financial and personal difficulties, and on January 31,
1936 (ironically, the day the *Absalom* manuscript was finished),
an announcement was made that Bennett Cerf's Random House had
bought the firm. Hal Smith went to Random House for a trial
period of one year. By the time Smith moved to Random House,
he had seen most of *Absalom* and had done a good deal of work
on early versions of the typescript. In May of 1935, he had
returned Chapter I to Faulkner with a number of comments.[54]
When Faulkner sent the final typescript to Smith, his publisher
was now Random House, which held out high hopes for Faulkner's
new novel to launch the firm successfully as a publisher of
works of real artistic merit. Bennett Cerf had long been an
ardent admirer of Faulkner.

Noel Polk, who notes that there are approximately 1,400
variants between the typescript and the book, asserts that
Absalom was "the most heavily and worst-edited" of Faulkner's
novels.[55] The typescript reveals that Hal Smith, Evelyn
Harter (primarily a book designer but here used as copy editor)
and Saxe Commins worked on the novel. The remarks made by
hands other than Faulkner's on the typescript indicate that,
particularly in the early chapters, his editors found the work
difficult, confusing and needlessly repetitive. And Faulkner's
responses to such remarks reveal a running battle between
author and editors. Time and again, editors questioned a line
and omitted or changed it, only to have Faulkner reject the
change or restore the omission. Nevertheless, he allowed many
deletions to stand in the early chapters--often passages of
several lines. Marginal editorial notations of "I don't get
this" or "Too much!" abound on the typescript. At one point,

where Faulkner had written "Yes. Henry: not Bon," an editor wrote, "I don't think one can wait for 2 1/2 pages to find out what Henry (+ not Bon) did," and changed the passage to: "Yes, it was Henry who seduced Judith; not Bon."[56] Such "minor" changes often did significant damage to the text, dulling Faulkner's intended effects.

By the end of Chapter IV, however, editorial comments (especially those of Commins) became less frequent, as if the editors had finally attuned themselves to the tone and rhythm of the prose. In the middle of a description of Jefferson's preparation for war, one editor wrote in the margin, "Magnificent," a clear indication that the novel's power had finally touched its earliest and most businesslike readers.[57] Type was set during the early summer of 1936, and Faulkner finished reading galley proof by September 1st. There is evidence that he was much interested in seeing that his revisions had been made; he asked Hal Smith twice to send him copies of the corrected galleys and made further correction on page proof in late September.[58] The publication of *Absalom, Absalom!* had been planned for October 6th, with a limited signed edition of 300 copies. Actual publication was on October 26.[59] The book received mixed reviews and, in addition, was a financial disappointment; after the initial first printing of 6,000 trade copies, a second printing of 2,500 on October 23 and a third of 1,400 on November 19, it faded into obscurity.

The failure of *Absalom, Absalom!* to achieve recognition as the finest novel "yet written by an American," which Faulkner had called it in January, 1936, was only one more bitter pill in a year which had been characterized personally for him by illness, depression, financial desperation and marital misery. Immediately after the completion of the manuscript in Hollywood, Faulkner fell ill, apparently exhausted physically, by the demands he had placed upon himself, and mentally, by the still-vivid memory of his brother's death and his relationship with Meta Carpenter. Again, in Oxford in early February, he lapsed into a drinking bout that ended with a stay in a sanitorium. By June, he had become so desperate about both his financial situation and Estelle's spending that he ran an ad in the Memphis *Commercial Appeal* and the Oxford *Eagle* to the effect that he refused to assume responsibility for any checks signed by her—an action doubly unfortunate because it precipitated a row with his father-in-law and attracted the attention of the national press, thus inviting the hated intrusion into his private life. When he returned to California in August, he took his family with him, and several incidents reported by Blotner and Meta Carpenter Wilde reveal the violent despair which at this time marked his relationship with his wife, now apparently alcoholic.

   Acclaim for the newly published *Absalom, Absalom!* might
have alleviated a painful passage in his life, but the novel
was, in the main, damned with faint praise. The important
reviews of *Absalom* were perhaps more ludicrous than those of
any other Faulkner novel. Some reviewers prefaced their
discussions of the book with an acknowledgment of the talent--
even genius--of its author (hardly an insight about one who
had in the last eight years published *Sartoris*, *The Sound and
the Fury*, *As I Lay Dying*, *Sanctuary*, *Light in August* and
Pylon). But most moved quickly to attack *Absalom* as turgid,
morbid, inchoate, repetitious, ridiculous or downright insane.
Clifton Fadiman's *New Yorker* review began in high comic mockery,
but modulated to a serious scorn:

> I do not know what to say of this book except that it
> seems to point to the final blowup of what was once a
> remarkable, if minor, talent. I imagine that many of
> my respected colleagues will see in it a tragic master-
> piece.... Perhaps they are right. For me, this is a
> penny dreadful tricked up in fancy language and given a
> specious depth by the expert manipulation of a series of
> eccentric technical tricks. The characters have no
> magnitude and no meaning because they have no more
> reality than a mincepie nightmare.[60]

Bernard DeVoto's "Witchcraft in Mississippi," in the *Saturday
Review of Literature*, was only slightly less caustic:

> All the prestidigitation of his later technique rests
> on a tacit promise that this tortuous narrative method,
> this obsession with pathology, this parade of Grand
> Guignol tricks and sensations, will, if persevered with,
> bring us in the end to a deeper and a fuller truth about
> his people than we could get otherwise. And it never
> does.... Meanwhile the talent for serious fiction shown
> in "Sartoris" and the rich comic intelligence grudgingly
> displayed from time to time, especially in "Sanctuary,"
> have been allowed to atrophy from disuse and have been
> covered deep by a tide of sensibility.[61]

And of those reviewers who praised *Absalom, Absalom!*, none did
more than touch obliquely its major themes. Few readers were
unmoved by the novel's control and intensity, but few understood it. Random House sold its last copy of *Absalom,
Absalom!* in February, 1940, and quietly allowed the novel to
go out of print.[62]

   Twelve years after the publication of the novel, Faulkner
was offered a chance to specify which of his works he would
like to have reprinted, and he chose *Absalom, Absalom!*[63] He
had apparently never lost the pride in it which he voiced to

David Hempstead in 1936. And in a letter to Robert Haas in February, 1949, he submitted a typescript passage intended for insertion into *Intruder in the Dust* in which he discussed a remark of Shreve to Quentin at the end of *Absalom*, implying that the novel would come to be regarded as a classic.[64]

Faulkner had been right from the beginning. The work which would become *Absalom, Absalom!* had had a compelling quality from the first, set in motion, perhaps, by the narrative tensions in "Evangeline." On the surface simply another of the Don-and-I stories in which two young men explore an event in the past, "Evangeline" actually differed markedly from earlier Don-and-I stories. Here, after he had passed along information, Don disappeared, and the narrative pattern of the story became one in which the burden of knowledge which Raby carried was passed to the I-narrator. Through this process, Raby experienced release, and her life achieved meaning. The I-narrator had moved from a curious, callow observer to a participant so involved that he accepted Raby's burden and thus became a living owner of the pain, sacrifice and pride of the past.

This is communication of a profound order--and it is the triumph of *Absalom, Absalom!* that Faulkner intensified and heightened this narrative pattern in the novel. As we have seen, much of this struggle with the novel in its early stages was precisely to create characters and circumstances strong enough to carry communication at such an intense level. At three major points in the novel, the pattern of passing along knowledge to achieve release, to insure meaning, to involve future generations is repeated. Judith does precisely this when she gives Bon's letter to Quentin's grandmother; Rosa does this in the focal fifth chapter of the novel. And Quentin, like the I-narrator of "Evangeline" reluctant to be drawn in, finally assumes the burden of his heritage and makes it live as he and Shreve create their remarkable reconstruction in Chapter VIII. At the novel's haunting end, Quentin, who can no longer carry the burden, passes it to us, as readers. As the essays which follow suggest, careful readers of *Absalom, Absalom!* will continue to find it compelling for generations to come.

NOTES

1. Joseph Blotner, *Faulkner: A Biography* (New York: Random House, 1974), p. 927.

2. Robert Hilton Knox III, "William Faulkner's *Absalom, Absalom!*" (Harvard, 1959).

3. *The Achievement of William Faulkner* (New York: Random House, 1966).

4. *Faulkner's Revision of* Absalom, Absalom!: *A Collation of the Manuscript and the Published Book* (Austin: University of Texas Press, 1971).

5. "The Manuscript of *Absalom, Absalom!*," *Mississippi Quarterly*, 25 (Summer, 1972), 359-367.

6. The present essay relies heavily on the data in Blotner's biography.

7. *A Loving Gentleman: The Love Story of William Faulkner and Meta Carpenter* (New York: Simon and Schuster, 1976); *Selected Letters* (New York: Random House, 1977); *Uncollected Stories* (New York: Random House, 1979).

8. *Old Tales and Talking: Quentin Compson in William Faulkner's* Absalom, Absalom! *and Related Works* (Jackson, Miss.: Univ. Press of Mississippi, 1977), pp. 16-69.

9. Letter to Harrison Smith, "something October [1933]," *Selected Letters*, p. 75.

10. James B. Meriwether, *The Literary Career of William Faulkner: A Bibliographical Study* (Princeton, N.J.: Princeton University Press, 1961), p. 172.

11. Dean Faulkner Wells recounts the story in *The Ghosts of Rowan Oak* (Oxford, Miss.: Yoknapatawpha Press, 1980), pp. 13-35.

12. *Uncollected Stories*, p. 584.

13. *Ibid.*, p. 604.

14. Found among the Rowanoak Papers, now in the William Faulkner Collection of the Alderman Library of the University of Virginia (accession number 9817), Item 1. Grateful acknowledgment is made to Faulkner's executrix, his daughter Mrs. Paul D. Summers, for permission to quote from these materials, and to Edmund Berkeley, Jr., Curator of Manuscripts.

15. In a letter to Malcolm Cowley dated "Thursday" [August 16, 1945], Faulkner discussed the genesis of *The Hamlet*, mentioning several Snopes stories. "This over about ten years, until one day I decided I had better start on the first volume or I'd never get any of it down. So I wrote an induction toward the spotted horse story, which included BARN BURNING and WASH, which I discovered had no place in that book at all." Malcolm Cowley, *The Faulkner-Cowley File: Letters and Memories, 1944-1962* (New York: Viking, 1966), p. 26. "Wash" was first published in *Harpers* in February, 1934.

16. Letter to Harrison Smith, received January 31, 1934, *Selected Letters*, p. 78.

17. Rowanoak Papers, Item 7, p. 1 of 3 MS pages.

18. *Ibid.*

19. *Ibid.*

20. *Ibid.*

21. Rowanoak Papers, Item 7, page 2 of 3 MS pages.

22. Rowanoak Papers, Item 6, page 3 of 3 MS pages.

23. See Rowanoak Papers, Item 4, reproduced in Blotner, *Faulkner*, p. 891.

24. *Fifty Years of Yoknapatawpha*, Doreen Fowler and Ann J. Abadie, eds. (Jackson, Miss.: Univ. Press of Mississippi, 1980), p. 31.

25. *Ibid.*, p. 32.

26. Rowanoak Papers, Item 3, p. 1 of 2 MS pages.

27. See Rowanoak Papers, Item 10, unnumbered page [33] of 48 MS pages.

28. Rowanoak Papers, Item 7, 1 p. MS headed "III."

29. Letter to Harrison Smith, probably written in February, 1934, *Selected Letters*, pp. 78-79.

30. Letter dated "Friday" [July 20, 1934], *Selected Letters*, p. 83.

31. Letter to Morton Goldman, July 29, [1934], *Selected Letters*, p. 83.

32. Letter to Harrison Smith dated "Thursday" [August, 1934], *Selected Letters*, pp. 83-84.

33. See, for example, Rowanoak Papers, Item 10, unnumbered page [43] of 48 MS pages.

34. Rowanoak Papers, Item 10, page numbered "9" [13] of 48 MS pages; Item 10, unnumbered page [45] of 48 MS pages.

35. Rowanoak Papers, Item 10, unnumbered page [47] of 48 MS pages.

36. See Rowanoak Papers, Item 10, unnumbered page [23] of 48 MS pages.

37. Rowanoak Papers, Item 10, unnumbered page [23] of 48 pages, contains material about the police dogs which would later be incorporated into "Lion":

> Nobody in this country had even seen a German shepherd until Sutpen brot the pair back with him. The male--it

would ramble a good deal at night--was shot at more than
once, until at last a legend grew that Sutpen had brot a
[*illegible word*] animal home with him from England and
that it could not be killed with powder and lead....
Perhaps it was just after sport, for it was a year before it killed again--a pig. The next day Sutpen led
it back to the [*illegible word*] and from a distance
shot it with a shotgun, knocking it down. He carried
the dog back home and isolated it in a pen to itself,
with a negro designated to thrust food and water in to
it with a long pole (the pole was the negro's own idea)
until it recovered. When it was up and about again,
Sutpen entered the pen. The dog retreated to a corner
and crouched watching him until he was within a yard or
so. Then it sprang at him, sprang for his throat without a sound. The negro with the pole struck from across
the fence and killed it in midleap.

38. Rowanoak Papers, Item 10, unnumbered page [42] of
48 MS pages. This page contains a wonderful exchange in
which Quentin digresses from his story about Wash and Sutpen's
death to explain to Shreve the ritual of obtaining moonshine
whiskey. The dialogue, clearly related to the Snopes material,
is interesting in light of Faulkner's later statement that
"Wash" had originally been a part of the Snopes novel.

39. Rowanoak Papers, Item 10, unnumbered page [47] of 48
MS pages.

40. Rowanoak Papers, Item 10, unnumbered page [7] of 48
MS pages.

41. Rowanoak Papers, Item 10, page numbered "121" [30] of
48 MS pages.

42. Rowanoak Papers, Item 10, unnumbered page [7] of 48
MS pages.

43. See Langford, p. 43.

44. Blotner, *Faulkner*, pp. 893, 896, 898, 900.

45. Letter to Morton Goldman, probably April, 1935,
Selected Letters, p. 91.

46. Blotner, *Faulkner*, p. 923.

47. Langford, p. 362.

48. Knox, p. 7.

49. A telegram from Harrison Smith to Faulkner in California,
June 11, 1936, asked for the manuscript, but correspondence in
early July suggests plans for typesetting and design were well

along. The book was in proofs by August 25, 1936. Random House Correspondence with Faulkner, Manuscripts Division, Alderman Library, University of Virginia.

50. William Faulkner, *Absalom, Absalom!* (New York: Random House, 1936), p. 131; Langford, pp. 147-148; typescript at the University of Virginia, pp. 155-156.

51. Langford, p. 110; typescript, p. 102

52. Rowanoak Papers, Item 10, page numbered "130" [36] of 48 MS pages.

53. See typescript, pp. 17, 151; numerical changes in dates occur in Faulkner's hand throughout the typescript.

54. Blotner, *Faulkner*, p. 896.

55. Polk, p. 361.

56. Typescript, p. 114; *Absalom*, p. 97.

57. Typescript, p. 144; *Absalom*, p. 122.

58. Letter from Harrison Smith to Faulkner, October 2, 1936, Random House Correspondence.

59. In June, arrangements had been made to publish a version of Chapter I in *American Mercury*, where it appeared in August. Meriwether, p. 26.

60. "Faulkner: Extra-Special, Double-Distilled," *New Yorker* (October 31, 1936), pp. 62-64; included in *Party of One* (New York: World, 1955), pp. 110-115.

61. October 31, 1936, pp. 3-4, 14.

62. Memorandum, Albert Erskine to Sidney Jones, December 3, 1965, Random House Correspondence. The book would not become available again until it was issued in a Modern Libarry edition in 1951, using the plates of the first edition.

63. Patrick Samway, S.J., "A Textual and Critical Evaluation of the Manuscripts and Typescripts of William Faulkner's *Intruder in the Dust*" (University of North Carolina at Chapel Hill, 1974), p. 53. See also Blotner, *Faulkner*, p. 168 notes.

64. *Ibid.*, p. 60.

"STRANGE GODS" IN JEFFERSON, MISSISSIPPI: ANALYSIS OF *ABSALOM, ABSALOM!*

Richard Poirier

Almost without exception, existing criticism of Faulkner has ignored *Absalom, Absalom!* or has examined it either as a naturalistic novel full of Gothic horror and romantic attitudinizing or as little more than a curious source book, significant only for what it can tell us about the problems of Quentin Compson in *The Sound and the Fury.* The only notable exception of which I am aware is Malcolm Cowley's essay "William Faulkner's Legend of the South."[1] But the commentary on *Absalom, Absalom!* which is included in that essay is not meant by Mr. Cowley to be extensive, and it only partially succeeds, it seems to me, in suggesting the true character of the novel.

An understanding of the environment which we see conditioning Quentin in *The Sound and the Fury* is of course helpful. We can perhaps better appreciate his response to experience in *Absalom, Absalom!* if we have learned from the earlier book that Quentin's disillusionment, the vacuity of purpose which plagues him, cannot be divorced from the spiritual dead end which his mother represents and which his father pathetically articulates. The latter, summing up his view of life, tells Quentin that "Time is your misfortune."[2] The remark is characteristic of Mr. Compson's teaching throughout *The Sound and the Fury.* In terms of it, his son has been deprived of the possibility of abstracting human values from a historical context. The father has slowly undermined for Quentin the myth of any spiritual transcendence of what seems to be the mechanism of historical fact. This is in great part the problem faced by Quentin in *Absalom, Absalom!* as well. It is a problem which makes Quentin, as an organizer of Thomas

From William Faulkner: Two Decades of Criticism, *Frederick J. Hoffman and Olga Vickery, eds. (East Lansing, Mich.: Michigan State College Press, 1951), pp. 217-243. Reprinted by permission of Michigan State University Press.*

Sutpen's story, the dramatic center of this novel. Indeed,
in *Absalom, Absalom!* Quentin is nearly allowed to appropriate
the position of the author.

But this is not to say, as many have, that Quentin or
some other character is Faulkner's spokesman. Faulkner is
extremely careful to prevent his novels from ever being controlled by the "efficient confessionals" which Kenneth Burke
claims to find in them.[3] The form in both *The Sound and the
Fury* and *Absalom, Absalom!* prevents any one of the narrators
from seducing the reader to a restricted, wholly individual
point of view. It is quite clear that the author sympathizes
in the earlier book with Benjy and Quentin. But if we are
looking for Faulkner to express himself, we shall find that
he does so impersonally in the structure of the work itself.
Benjy, Quentin, and Jason tend, in different degrees, to
neutralize one another. It is the structure of *The Sound
and the Fury* which emphasizes the wholeness of Dilsey's point
of view and which affirms the presence, if only as a choral
effect, of a traditional and moral context in which we can
place the whole novel.

The adaptation of this method to a new set of circumstances
constitutes the most significant connection between *The Sound
and the Fury* and *Absalom, Absalom!* In the formal arrangement
of this later novel, for example, we see Faulkner's sense of
history played off against the social irresponsibility of
Rosa Coldfield, the most consciously incantatory of all his
narrators. We see Thomas Sutpen try to make history begin in
his own image and, when the damage is done, Quentin Compson
attempts to discover the meaning of his historical background
with Sutpen as the central figure. The attempt to create
history is both the story of Sutpen and, with a difference,
the conscious effort of Quentin as a narrator of that story.
Faulkner has joined the two themes so that the persisting
disruptions caused by Sutpen almost fatally affect Quentin's
attempt to discover the meaning of his heritage.

Because Quentin, if he is to define himself, must confront
these persisting disruptions, it is little wonder that Faulkner
is so obviously fond of him. The preoccupations and the difficulties of the two are not dissimilar. Within the chaotic
nature of Sutpen's history and Rosa's "demonizing," Quentin
tries to find some human value adhering to what is apparently
a representative anecdote of his homeland. In doing so, he
must somehow overcome a problem such as confronts the contemporary writer. As T.S. Eliot defines it, it is the problem
of overcoming "the damage of a lifetime and of having been
born into an unsettled society."[4] And Quentin is "older at
twenty," he tells Shreve, "than a lot of people who have died"
(p. 377).[5]

In Quentin's mind, the career of Thomas Sutpen is the most
persistently disturbing element in the history of his native
region, and one in which all of his family have been involved.
Indeed, his preoccupation with the meaning of the story is so
distressing that he can see no respite from it even in the
future: "Nevermore of peace. Nevermore of peace. Nevermore
Nevermore Nevermore" (p. 373). The reader who is acquainted
with *The Sound and the Fury* may understandably wish to view
Quentin's problem here in terms of his experience in the
earlier novel. Quentin cannot, for example, hear Rosa continue the story past her recounting of the murder of Charles
Bon. He may see in this incident a distorted image of his
own failure in *The Sound and the Fury* to defend the honor of
his sister, Caddy, and of the incest which he claims to have
committed. At different times Quentin associates himself
both with Bon, who feels compelled to threaten incest, and
with Henry, Judith's brother, who must kill his friend to
prevent it and the accompanying evil of miscegenation.
Quentin, who could neither dignify Caddy's immorality by
the damning sin of incest nor properly defend his sister's
honor, discovers something of himself in history by recreating
the circumstances which led to Bon's murder. But it is well
to remember that Quentin's interest in Sutpen's story transcends any reference he finds in it for such personal problems,
which, after all, we are acquainted with only from observing
his activity outside the context of *Absalom, Absalom!* Had
Quentin assumed the luxury of treating the Sutpen story
merely as an objectification of some personal obsession,
the total effect of the novel would have partaken of the overindulgent and romantic self-dramatization of Rosa's soliloquy.

Quentin tries to place Sutpen in a social and historical
context. By doing so he can perhaps discover his own tradition
and the reasons for its collapse. His father tells him that
in Sutpen's day, in Quentin's past, the circumstances in which
people operated at least simplified what Mr. Robert Penn
Warren refers to as the risks of being human:[6]

> of that day and time, of a dead time; people too as we
> are, and victims too as we are, but victims of a dif-
> ferent circumstance, simpler and therefore, integer for
> integer, larger, more heroic ... not dwarfed and in-
> volved but distinct, uncomplex who had the gift of living
> once or dying once instead of being diffused and scat-
> tered creatures.... (p. 89)

Quentin will discover that the times were not so "simple" as
his father imagines. But he is still painfully aware of the
deprivation his father defines, a deprivation which Shreve,
who lays no claim either on the past or to a tradition, cannot

fully understand. Perhaps Malcolm Cowley is right and the
Sutpen story represents for Quentin the essence of the Deep
South.[7] But *Absalom, Absalom!* is not primarily about the
South or about a doomed family as a symbol of the South. It
is a novel about the meaning of history for Quentin Compson.
The story of Sutpen simply represents that part of the past
which Quentin must understand if he is to understand himself.
In this respect, Quentin's dilemma is very similar to that of
Stephen Dedalus in *Ulysses*. Whether the scene is Ireland or
the South, the problem of extracting value from a cultural
heritage remains about the same. Indeed, Quentin has his own
Buck Mulligan in his roommate, Shreve McCannon. When Shreve
and other students at Harvard ask Quentin about the South,
they really demand that he justify his own existence: *Tell
about the South. What's it like there. What do they do there.
Why do they live there. Why do they live at all ...* (p. 174).
The painful consequence of Quentin's reply--which is the
story of Sutpen--is that all of the questions remain for
Shreve unanswered. Part of the history which Quentin recon-
structs is a record of violence and evil. But Quentin hopes,
when he begins, that in the world in which Sutpen lived, unlike his own world in *The Sound and the Fury*, violence was of
some moral consequence and evil was at least a violation of
a corruptible but not wholly devitalized moral code.

Regardless of what Sutpen might represent in Quentin's
mind, it is soon made obvious to the reader, though the point
is often missed, that he is above all a special case. In the
context of the novel he is not even a typical Southern planter.
It is emphasized that at least three of the other characters,
Wash Jones, Charles Bon, and Mr. Coldfield, were at one time
confronted respectively with the very things which injured
Sutpen: the same social antagonism, nearly the same act of
repudiation, and an almost identical opportunity to exploit
the evils of the economic system. Sutpen alone seems able to
pursue his ambition, what he calls his "design," not only in
defiance of an outraged community but in ignorance of its
codes and customs and with a complete insensitivity to human
character.

Like the violence of Joe Christmas in *Light in August*,
Sutpen's "design" is directed as much against a terrifying
sense of his own insufficiency as against a society which
apparently standardizes that insufficiency by caste or class
systems. When his family moves from the primitively communal
society of their mountain home to settle in the Tidewater,
young Sutpen finds everything in the new environment phenomenal: the Negroes, the social customs, the differences in
living standards among the white men employed, like his
father, on the plantation. The boy cannot understand how

or why this place should differ from the mountain settlement
where "the land belonged to anybody and everybody" (p. 221).
He is naturally humiliated and confused when, carrying a
message to the plantation owner, he is ordered away from the
front door by a Negro in livery. Because he has been brought
up in a society outside the one in which he now lives, he
cannot fit the action of the "monkey nigger" into any acknowleged
social pattern. It can be seen by young Sutpen only as a wholly
personal affront. At the door, he finds himself "looking out
from within the balloon face" of the Negro (p. 234), and at
himself. Having no past, no background of his own by which
he could appreciate the social complexity of the incident, he
prejudicially assumes the position of his insulter, or the
agent of his insulter, and both pities and degrades himself.
At first he considers immediate revenge: he will shoot the
Negro and the owner of the house. But he finally decides that
the best thing he can do is to become as rich and powerful as
the man from whose door he has been turned. This ambition
develops into what he later calls his "design."

When Sutpen tells Quentin's grandfather about this incident, he claims that he felt then that "he would have to do
something about it in order to live with himself for the rest
of his life" (p. 234). Years later he explains to General
Compson that the "design" was "not what he wanted to do but
what he just had to do, had to do it whether he wanted to or
not" (p. 220). He justifies himself by an appeal not to any
moral code which might have been violated at the plantation
door, but to some inexplicable compulsion over which he apparently can exert no discipline. It might be argued that
Sutpen makes the worst of what someone like Wash Jones would
have assimilated into the accepted order of things. In any
case, the rest of his life is dedicated to a vindication of
that little boy at the door, what he himself calls "the boy
symbol" (p. 261).

The "boy symbol" motif persists throughout the novel and
becomes connected with Sutpen's desire for a son. Indeed,
the whole "design" is a calculated bid for a kind of immortality. His son and the rest of his descendants shall have
all Sutpen lacked: wealth, power, untainted respectability.
To that end, he first goes to Haiti to make a fortune only to
abandon it and to repudiate his first wife and son, Charles
Bon, when he discovers that she has a trace of Negro blood.
The hundred-square-mile plantation called Sutpen's Hundred
which he later builds in Mississippi is really a second and,
it seems, unassailable foundation of the power and wealth that
his heir, Henry Sutpen, shall perpetuate. And for respectability he chooses, much to the town's indignation, Ellen
Coldfield, daughter not of the richest but of the most primly

respectable and most religious family in Jefferson. It is
characteristic of Sutpen that in selecting his wife he chooses,
in place of the aristocratic connection he wishes to make, a
marriage into a family which is merely priggishly proud.
Without any sense of knowledge of the past, Sutpen, through
his son, would belong only to the future. Quentin imagines
that Bon recognized Henry as his brother by seeing in his
face the image of *"the man who shaped us both out of that
blind chancy darkness which we call the future"* (p. 317).
As a reflection of the vindicated boy symbol, Henry becomes
for his father a means of disowning the past.

When Sutpen arrived in Jefferson to upset the town first
by his unorthodox and dishonest methods and then by apparently
corrupting the Coldfields, he was, Rosa says, "a man who so
far as anyone ... knew, either had no past or did not dare
reveal it--a man who rode into town out of nowhere" (p. 16).
It is significant that Sutpen gives a very poor account of
his own experiences and that he treats his activity prior to
Jefferson with boredom, almost with disinterest. Quentin's
grandfather, who is really the one person in town who befriends
Sutpen, manages to induce him to recount some of his past life.
When Sutpen does so, it is as if he were just

> ... telling a story about something a man named Thomas
> Sutpen had experienced, which would still have been the
> same story if the man had had no name at all, if it had
> been told about any man or no man over whiskey at night.
> (p. 247)

He shows no regard whatever for cause and effect and, General
Compson explains, little for logical sequence. Such an inability to tell his own story is indicative of Sutpen's refusal to believe that anyone could have any interest in his
past activity. He can ignore the details of his past because,
as far as he is concerned, they hold no portent of his future.
In terms of his "design," he has achieved a self-identification
beyond anything that has been done or can be done to him.

But ironically enough, that part of his past which he
outlines for General Compson will later indicate to Quentin
the source and the reasons for the retribution which overtakes
him. The General himself is aware of the perilous quality of
this man's calculated activity when he hears Sutpen bombas-
tically explain the disposition of his first wife. He has
dared treat her as an abstract, expendable counter to be used
by him with "fairness" but with complete impersonality:

> I found that she was not and could never be, through no
> fault of her own, adjunctive or incremental to the de-
> sign which I had in mind, so I provided for her and put
> her aside. (p. 240)

According to Quentin, "Sutpen's trouble was 'innocence'":

> ... that innocence which believed that the ingredients
> of morality were like the ingredients of pie or cake
> and once you had measured them and balanced them and
> mixed them and put them into the oven it was all finished
> and nothing but pie or cake could come out. (p. 263)

Part of that "innocence" is, of course, the belief that any
woman will accept money as a final recompense for desertion.
Bon's sudden and ironically unintentional appearance with
Henry at Sutpen's Hundred makes that expression of Sutpen's
"innocence" seem purblind indeed. Sutpen, who at least gave
Bon the name he bears, is the only one in the family who is
aware of the guest's real identity. But all he can do for the
present is to remain silent. To acknowledge that Charles Bon
is his son would be to infuse humanity into the "ingredients"
of his "design." He is simply incapable of doing it. He fails
to realize that Bon is demanding only the same sort of recognition denied him as a boy at the plantation door. And he
can forget human need so completely that he cannot understand
how or why his plans could be so affected by what he calls "a
maelstrom of unpredictable and unreasoning human beings" (p.
275).

Sutpen's story might well be about his opportunities for
becoming human. There are countless opportunities, like the
appearance of Bon, which he has ignored. Potentially there
were others during his childhood experience on the plantation
which, for someone with his particular background, the social
order simply did not make available. But Sutpen, as we have
seen, comes totally to express the very inhumanity and in-
justice which he would have us believe compelled the "design"
in the first place. When Judith's life is ruined as a consequence of the complications which lead to the murder of Bon,
she complains to Quentin's grandmother that the fulfillment
of her life was frustrated by forces over which she had no
control.

> Because you make so little impression, you see. You
> get born and you try this and don't know why only you
> keep on trying it and you are born at the same time
> with a lot of other people, all mixed up with them,
> like trying to, having to, move your arms and legs
> with strings only the same strings are hitched to all
> the other arms and legs and the others all trying and
> they don't know why either except that the strings are
> all in one another's way like five or six people all
> trying to make a rug on the same loom only each one
> wants to weave his own pattern into the rug.... (p. 127)

Actually, it is her father's "innocence" of anything but his
own compulsion which disorders her life and the lives of "a
lot of other people." Quentin, only with much pain, finally
discovers in the career of Thomas Sutpen not the essence of his
past so much as a force which disrupts all that was possibly
coherent, orderly, and humane in the past.

Both in *Go Down, Moses* and in this novel, Faulkner clearly
recognizes the evil tendencies of the plantation system. But
Sutpen acts as a wholly "modern" element in that system. He
unknowingly abstracts those evil tendencies from the controlling
fiber of the community and its traditions, simply exploiting
them without discipline for the purposes of his own ambition.
It is no wonder that Mr. Compson feels able to observe that
perhaps the Civil War was "instigated by that family fatality"
(p. 118) for which Sutpen is largely responsible. We are
told that Rosa's father, who actually equated the force of
the Civil War with the exploitations of his son-in-law, firmly
believed that in both of these the South "was now paying the
price for having erected its economic edifice not on the rock
of stern morality but on the shifting sands of opportunism and
moral brigandage" (p. 260). Faulkner, in these and other remarks made in *Absalom, Absalom!*, gives full notice to the
opinion that the true nature of the plantation system and
of Sutpen's "design" was revealed negatively at the moment
and in the act of breakdown.

But the novel itself does not allow us to be so categorical.
We have already seen how factitious is so close an identification between the character of Sutpen and that of the social
system he exploits. As Faulkner sees it, the system was
corrupt enough not to be able to control its Thomas Sutpens.
And we may even view the Civil War as a consequence of such
a further corruption of existing order as that which was
carried on by Sutpen. It is well to remember, however, that
a civil war was lost by Jefferson, Mississippi, when Sutpen
finished his home and married Ellen Coldfield in 1838. The
terrible result of both his "design" and the war between the
states was fratricide. Faulkner's metaphorical use of the
Sutpen story does not go much further than that; it is never
extended into allegory. Sutpen is not what is called the Old
South, but rather a force in it which was so corrupting that
possibly, as Quentin thinks Rosa believes, *"only through the
blood of our men and the tears of our women could He stay
this demon and efface his name and lineage from the earth"*
(p. 11). But such a statement, in itself, is merely a re-
phrasing of Quentin's problem and of the theme of the novel.
Quentin is trying to find in the issues of the conflicts
within the Sutpen family and within the community of Jefferson
some expression of a sense of human and moral value.

The structure of *Absalom, Absalom!* is a reflection of
both the nature and the method of Quentin's search, in a confusion of historical fact, for value. Consideration of that
structure might begin simply by dividing the novel into two
parts of four chapters each, leaving Rosa's monologue, which
separates them by exclusively occupying all of Chapter V, for
special consideration. The first four chapters, in which the
whole of Sutpen's story is continually repeated with changing
emphases, are really a dramatization of Quentin's activity at
the sources of his information. In the last four chapters,
during which he is at Harvard College, Quentin, with the help
of his rommmate, Shreve, pieces together all of the facts
and opinions about the story held by Rosa, his father, and
his grandfather, along with a good deal of information which
is apparently a part of his heritage. All of the data, as it
comes to him in the early chapters, is confused, contradictory, and phenomenal in character. It is like the letter
which Judith had given to his grandmother and which is now
a document in his attempt to order the story coherently:

> the writing faded, almost indecipherable, yet meaning-
> ful, familiar in shape and sense, the name and presence
> of volatile and sentient forces; you bring them together
> in the proportions called for, but nothing happens; you
> re-read, tedious and intent, poring, making sure that
> you have forgotten nothing, made no miscalculation; you
> bring them together again and again nothing happens:
> just the words, the symbols, the shapes themselves,
> shadowy inscrutable and serene, against that turgid
> background of a horrible and bloody mischancing of human
> affairs. (p. 101)

The events of the Sutpen narrative are neither so contemporary nor, except for Rosa, so personally consequential to
the speakers here as are those in *The Sound and the Fury*.
Yet neither Rosa nor Mr. Compson, both of whom first tell
the story to Quentin in the early chapters, are wholly trust-
worthy narrators. In the first chapter, Quentin becomes
directly involved in the story, parts of which he has heard
throughout his childhood, when he visits Rosa Coldfield in com-
pliance with a note she has sent him. Before revealing the
task she has planned, Rosa, by way of justifying herself,
begins to tell her version of Sutpen's character and activity.
As he listens, Quentin does not yet realize that, like her
handwriting, Rosa's "demonizing" of Sutpen is indicative of
a character which is "cold, implacable, and even ruthless"
(p. 10).
     Her description of Sutpen's first years in Jefferson is
wild and incredible. Sutpen becomes *"an ogre, some beast out of*

tales to frighten children with" (p. 158). But the distortions resulting from her nightmarish sensibility are continually being revealed to the reader by the contradictory nature of Rosa's own testimony. At other times, her version of an incident may remain consistent throughout her conversation, only to be invalidated by some other narrator who is either more informed or at least less prejudiced. Her "outraged recapitulation" evokes for Quentin a vision of Sutpen's arrival in Jefferson--"Out of quiet thunderclap he would abrupt (man-horse-demon) ... with grouped behind him his band of wild niggers like beasts" (p. 8). We are given quite a different picture, however, in the next chapter. Mr. Compson describes Sutpen's first appearance in Jefferson as it was viewed by Quentin's grandfather. We see in place of Rosa's "demon," a man "gaunt now almost to emaciation" (p. 32) trying to reach his property before dark so that he can find food for his Negroes, who, though wild, sit quietly in the wagon. The point is not that Rosa is unfair to Sutpen. He is a "demon" to be sure. But, as I hope to show presently, her reasons for calling him one are as ambiguous and questionable as her version of the event just discussed.

The detailing of incidents by Quentin's father, in Chapters II, III, and IV, if not as distorted as Rosa's, is no less riddled with faulty information. On the basis of what he knows, Mr. Compson believes, for example, that Sutpen forbade Judith's marriage merely because her fiancé, Charles Bon, kept an octoroon mistress in New Orleans. Considering the final consequences of the father's refusal, Mr. Compson understandably remarks: "It's just incredible. It just does not explain" (p. 100). But Quentin, after his trip to Sutpen's Hundred with Rosa, comes into possession of more information. In the process of retelling the story in Chapter VII, he corrects his father's error in Chapter II. We learn what only Sutpen knew at the time: the real identity of Charles Bon. Judith's betrothal to him was forbidden by Sutpen because it would have resulted not only in incest, but in miscegenation. This new information not only partially invalidates Mr. Compson's analysis, but also reflects adversely on the already questionable account of the story given by Rosa. In the first chapter she tells Quentin that she "saw Judith's marriage forbidden without rhyme or reason or shadow of excuse" (p. 18). It is this belief, based on ignorance of the facts, which partly explains the peculiar quality of her hatred of Sutpen. Rosa's bitterness and frustration at being the last child of cold and unloving parents finds total expression in the collapse of the romantic life she had lived vicariously in that of her niece, Judith.

In the light of the new facts uncovered by Quentin, the reader must now re-evaluate Rosa's emotional state which has its reference in the incredibility for her of Sutpen's prohibition of the marriage. By doing so the reader sees that the attitude of Rosa, or it might be of any other narrator, is understandable not in terms of what actually has happened but because of either her lack of information or her inability to change her mind when new information is made available. To Quentin's already prodigious task of finally ordering the story is added the responsibility of reinterpreting all that Rosa has told him and, at the same time, of giving an understandable context to her "incredulous and unbearable amazement" (p. 14). Quentin's version of the Judith-Bon affair causes a reorientation of the whole Sutpen story. Sutpen's attitude toward the marriage becomes a coherent element in his "design," and Bon's insistence on returning to marry his half-sister becomes a dramatically powerful gesture activated by his need for paternal recognition.

This correction of Mr. Compson's statement in Chapter IV (p. 100) by Quentin in Chapter VII (p. 266) is superficially indicative of the form of the novel. But as I have pointed out, the dramatization in the early chapters of Quentin's attempt to assemble all the facts is separated from his painful effort in the later chapters meaningfully to order this material by the long soliloquy of Rosa Coldfield. The novel seems to turn upon her chapter. Indeed, before Quentin begins to piece the whole story together in his room at Harvard, the opposition to Sutpen seems most strenuously represented by her.

Before dealing with Rosa Coldfield in greater detail, I want to suggest once again that the emphasis here is primarily upon Quentin, that neither Rosa nor Sutpen can serve as the dramatic center of this novel. Quentin's acts of remembrance actually determine the form of the novel. Rosa's soliloquy is apparently a product of her mind. But it is presented as if it were being recalled in Quentin's even as he sits listening to her. Before he and Shreve begin the job of historical recreation, Quentin can see in Rosa's approach to the Sutpen story the great difficulty which will beset him in his effort to discover the human content of his heritage. From her involvement in the "design," Rosa seems to conclude that history fulfills itself not through the efforts or aspirations of human beings, but wholly in an impersonal, antagonistic universe, through abstract "designs" or by the action of Fate. If that is the case, Quentin's tradition is devoid of human value. Eventually, his attempt to discover a meaningful tradition depends for its success upon his discovery of a participant in the conflict with Sutpen with whom he can share

an active sense of association. Whoever that individual is,
he must be able, as Rosa is not, to acknowledge the world
outside himself; he must surrender some of his individuality
in order actively to participate in society. Rosa simply
compounds for Quentin the already frightening phenomena of
Sutpen. She is no more aware than her "demon" of any necessary
relationship between her aspirations and the moral codes and
social disciplines of the community.

Considering the possibility that Sutpen's "design" has
denied to Rosa any hope for the future, it is a not-unimportant
irony, for its effect on the total meaning of the novel, that
Rosa's association with Sutpen is actually only intermittent
and largely vicarious. Even before seeing him for the first
time, Rosa is conditioned by her guardian, a spinster aunt,
to think of Sutpen as an "ogre," a "demon." Her only direct
involvement with him, other than the yearly visits discontinued
at her father's death, occurs when Miss Rosa is Judith's com-
panion and Sutpen suddenly proposes to her. But the most in-
jurious contact exists without Sutpen's knowledge and operates
in Miss Rosa's dream state as part of her romantic illusions
about Charles Bon.

Although she has never seen him, Rosa has fallen deeply
in love with her vision of the man who she never learns is
Sutpen's unrecognized son. She has heard him discussed by
Ellen, whose plans for an engagement between him and Judith,
also made in ignorance of Bon's identity, come to objectify
Rosa's own romantic longings. Her dream of Bon is a dream of
a future, a "living fairy tale" (p. 76). Like Sutpen's dream
of the future, it is a "fairy tale" which is foolishly isolated
from the world of other human beings in which it must, if at
all, exist. Rosa's dream was concocted in the hallways of
her darkened house. Only there could she remain *"shod with
the very damp and velvet silence of the womb"* (p. 145), un-
apprehended by what she calls *"some cold head-nuzzling forceps
of the savage time"* (p. 144).

When Wash Jones shouts beneath her window that Henry has
"kilt" Charles Bon "dead as a beef" (p. 133), she leaves this
"hallway" and rushes out to Sutpen's Hundred. She does not
go, as she claims, to rescue Judith from the curse which seems
to be on the house. Rather, she is trying desperately to save
some of the enchantment of Judith's proposed wedding, her own
"vicarious bridal" (p. 77). But when she rushes into the hall
calling for Judith, her *"shadow-realm of make-believe"* (p. 147)
comes into direct conflict with Sutpen's *"factual scheme"* (p.
143). This is embodied for Rosa in Clytie, Sutpen's daughter
by a Negro slave and, Rosa claims, *"his own image the cold
Cerberus of his private hell"* (p. 136). Clytie has blocked
Rosa's path, which leads to Judith's room, to Bon's body, which

has been placed there. The moment of conflict has finally
been achieved. But even Rosa knows that her involvement in
the Sutpen tragedy is indirect: *"we seemed to glare at one
another not as two faces but as two abstract contradictions
which we actually were"* (p. 138).

At this point the narrative stops. Attention is focused
by Rosa upon the significance of Clytie's grip on her arm.
She cries out, not at Clytie but at what she calls the *"cumu-
lative over-reach of despair itself"* (p. 140). In attempting
to define its elements, Rosa expands this single moment,
which is in a sense out of time, into her whole experience
of life. Her immediate response becomes enlarged into the
total response of an individual who has encountered the dis-
abling grip of damaging past as she tries to realize her
dream of the future. But even as she stands there, Rosa
persists in believing that there *"is a might-have-been which
is more true than truth"* (p. 143). Only when she is released
by Clytie are her illusions completely shattered. She finds
that though Bon is dead, she still is denied by Judith the
chance to look at him, that Judith, left nearly a widow,
refuses to grieve for him. Rosa at last faces what Sutpen
optimistically refused to face: *"that sickness somewhere at
the prime foundation of this factual scheme"* (p. 143). That
"sickness," one might say, is primarily an ignorance of context. The pattern of events which Rosa had chosen to recognize
was only a dream. One action, which to a narrator like Quentin
might fit naturally into the sequence of events, can suddenly
thrust a *"maelstrom of unbearable reality"* (p. 150) into her
dream life.

The collapse of Rosa's illusions is roughly equivalent to
Sutpen's sudden discovery, also due to Bon's activity, that
in pursuit of his "design" he seems to have arrived "at a
result absolutely and forever incredible" (p. 263). Sutpen
still believes that it is merely a matter of miscalculation
and that "whether it was a good or a bad design is beside the
point" (p. 263). But he feels compelled to go to General
Compson in order to "review the facts for an impartial ...
mind to examine and find and point out to him" his mistake
(p. 267). Similarly, Rosa must reassess her whole experience
in relation to her fatal excursion into the "factual scheme"
of things. And she tells the story of her life to Quentin
after she has experienced the effects of having been awakened
out of the dream state. The shock and revulsion resulting from
the stair episode is imposed back upon situations from which
the necessity of Rosa's emotions would not seem naturally to
have arisen. Rosa can acknowledge the past only through the
retroactive distortions of her own rage and frustration.
Her version of the story is infinitely more complex than

Sutpen's. But it cannot assist Quentin in his task even as
much as that superficial outline of his experience which is
all Sutpen could give to General Compson.

The poverty of Sutpen's imagination and the neurotic
richness of Rosa's place the two figures at poles. Yet in
their different ways, both express a wholly nonsocial, dan-
gerously individualistic point of view. This polar equality
between Sutpen and Rosa is similar in kind to the thematic
relationship existing in *Light in August* between Hightower
and Joe Christmas, neither of whom even meet until the climax
of that novel. Hightower's hysterical suggestion that he and
Joe Christmas had spent the evening of the murder in an il-
licit relationship is only factually implausible. Rosa and
Sutpen were, as pathetically, made for each other. That is
the ironic appropriateness of Sutpen's proposal. What Rosa
confesses to Quentin, and to us, is the story of a woman who,
confronting a world as furiously antagonistic as Sutpen's,
feels that she can come to life only as a man:

> But it was no summer of a virgin's itching discontent;
> no summer's caesarean lack which should have torn me,
> dead flesh or even embryo, from the living: or else,
> by friction's ravishing of the male-furrowed meat, also
> weaponed and panoplied as a man instead of hollow woman.
> (p. 145).

It is sufficient to say that Sutpen represents all that she
would but cannot be. In her soliloquy he is given alternately
the face of an ogre and the *"shape of a hero"* (p. 167). She
recalls that her life *"was at last worth something"* (p. 162)
when she helped care for him after the war. His proposal is
accepted simply because he is a man and, she thinks then, a
heroic one: she *"lost all the shibboleth erupting of cannot,
will not, never will in one red instant's fierce obliteration"*
(p. 163). The breaking of the engagement occurs only when he
intimates that she is merely the means to provide him with
another son to carry on the "design." In a rage, she returns
to her "womb-like corridor" (p. 112) to live on the charity
of the town and to continue her "demonizing" of Sutpen, a
role which her aunt "seems to have invested her with at birth
along with the swaddling clothes" (p. 61).

But the very attitudes implicated in her final revulsion
and hatred of Sutpen further the ironic similarities already
suggested as existing between Sutpen and Rosa Coldfield. Both
of them try desperately to disown the past. Rosa has her own
design, one by which she was obsessed with a future even more
impossible of achievement than Sutpen's. Sutpen's scapegoat
is the "monkey nigger"; Rosa's is Sutpen. She uses him, as
Sutpen used his experience at the plantation door, to objectify

an exclusively egocentric and romantic view of life which has
been wrenched apart by forces and events for which she holds
this remarkably childish man too exclusively responsible.
She never sees in the very nature of her illusions--nor does
he in his--the source of their destruction.

Faulkner's own literary position is powerfully suggested
by the dramatic function in the novel of Rosa's self-negating
soliloquy. Chapter V is comparable, in this respect, to
Yeats's poem *Meditations in Time of Civil War*. If I read
that poem correctly, it dramatizes the dilemma of a literary
artist attempting to find his metaphors in an unsettled
society, a society bent on disvaluation. Recognizing this
feature in *Absalom, Absalom!*, one is almost obliged to
associate the problems of the author with the problems of
Quentin Compson. In Rosa Coldfield's soliloquy, Faulkner
has dramatically fused literary with social disorders. These
very disorders are in large part what T.S. Eliot is concerned
with in *After Strange Gods*. Both Rosa's point of view and
the career of Thomas Sutpen, which concerns her, are illus-
trative of the heretical sensibility on the loose, of the
danger, which Eliot defines for us, of overindulgent individualism: "when morals cease to be a matter of tradition
and orthodoxy ... and when each man is to elaborate his own,
then *personality* becomes a thing of alarming importance."[8]
This sort of "elaboration" is clearly dramatized by Rosa's
obliviousness to anything but her own needs and compulsions.
But its literary applications are made most evident by the
stylistic quality of her version of the Sutpen story. Through
the style of Rosa's soliloquy, we are made aware that Sutpen
is not alone in his pursuit of "strange Gods." A rather
peculiar Eros intrudes upon Agape despite Rosa's incantations
to an avenging God. Perhaps because of this, her soliloquy
is reminiscent of the Gerty McDowell sequence in Joyce's
Ulysses. Such a parallel is particularly noticeable in those
passages in which Rosa's poetic sensibility seems to function
in the soul of a pathetic, antebellum "bobby-soxer." She
remarks of Bon's picture:

> *And I know this: if I were God I would invent out of*
> *this seething turmoil we call progress something (a*
> *machine perhaps) which would adorn the barren mirror*
> *altars of every plain girl who breathes with such as*
> *this--which is so little since we want so little--this*
> *pictured face. It would not even need a skull behind*
> *it; almost anonymous, it would only need vague inference*
> *of some walking flesh and blood desired by someone else*
> *even if only in some shadow-realm of make-believe.*
> (p. 147)

Such tortuous, verbalized relieving of emotion, and there are
more obvious examples throughout this soliloquy, is a consequence of Rosa's neurotic self-absorption. She is bringing
herself to life through emotional paroxysms. Eliot observes
much the same thing happening, but not with Faulkner's ironic
purpose, in the novels of Hardy. Indeed, Eliot's definition
of the kind of "heresy" Hardy is supposed to have committed
in his novels applies exactly to those qualities of Rosa's
soliloquy which I am anxious to point out. Eliot observes

> ... an interesting example of a powerful personality
> uncurbed ... by submission to any objective beliefs;
> unhampered by any ideas, or even by what sometimes acts
> as a partial restraint ... the desire to please a large
> public. [Hardy] ... seems to me to have written as
> nearly for the sake of self-expression as a man well
> can....[9]

The point I should like to make is that Eliot's remarks
can apply to Rosa but cannot in any sense be applied to
Faulkner. This is precisely the mistake made by those critics
who have accused Faulkner of being irresponsibly romantic.
Mr. Alfred Kazin, for example, asserts that Faulkner represents
"a tormented individualism in the contemporary novel, a self-
centered romanticism."[10] If this were true, we might use
Rosa Coldfield's soliloquy to direct irony against the author
himself. Obviously, the novel does not allow us to do this.
The context in which Faulkner places her soliloquy prevents
it from having any persuasively incantatory effect upon the
reader. Rosa's romantic verbalization is consistent with
her avocation as a poet but reflects only in a most negative
way Faulkner's sense of his own vocation. When Quentin
visits Rosa, he remarks that even in his father's youth she
had composed over one thousand poems to the soldiers of the
Confederacy,

> ... had already established herself as the town's and
> county's poetess laureate by issuing to the stern and
> meager subscription list of the county newspaper poems,
> ode, eulogy and epitaph, out of some bitter and im-
> placable reserve of undefeat. (p. 11)

The "undefeat" of what? Certainly not the war, since Rosa
pretends on several occasions to subscribe to the moral
necessity of the South's defeat. Rosa's indiscriminate outrage has a primarily personal and an ambiguously sexual content. Quentin, even before he begins his re-creation of the
story, listens to Rosa as the last and most vociferous op-
ponent of Sutpen. But the reader will be disappointed who
tries to discover in Rosa's soliloquy the moral basis for her

hatred of Sutpen. All that she can reveal to Quentin is the
"undefeat" not of moral rigor but of an essentially unregen-
erate personality.

When Rosa is finished, Sutpen remains where Quentin
found him, bewilderingly inexplicable. The explanation for
this is part of the logic of Faulkner's method, which is really
the method of historical research and re-creation. But the
historical method has to this point proved, so far as Quentin
is concerned, tragically unsuccessful. Rosa's inability to
place events in their human and historical context, an inability
which she shares with Sutpen, results quite naturally in the
treatment of both individuals and complex social action as
phenomena. The "phenomenon" for Sutpen was the "monkey nigger." It compelled the "design." Rosa's inability to give
human proportions to Sutpen, "the demon," results eventually
in her romantic and pessimistic view of history. The implications are obvious. Both Rosa and Sutpen are really ignorant
of what is going on about them. Knowledge is the basis of
historical perspective, and knowledge is essentially an act
of remembrance, an awareness of tradition.[11]

The form of *The Sound and the Fury*, of *Absalom, Absalom!*,
and of most of Faulkner's major works is determined by this
conception. The reader is witness to a conscious stockpiling
of information by the characters as the story is repeated
over and over again with a different focus upon the material,
a persistent encirclement of alien facts and enigmatic personalities by all the accumulated knowledge of an individual,
a family, or an entire community. In *Knight's Gambit*, this
form is used to allow a gathering of anecdotes by the attorney
Gavin Stevens from the whole countryside. Eventually, the
form of each of Gavin's stories is the same as the process
of community justice in the solution of the crime and in the
judging of the criminal.

Quentin's persistent acts of remembrance in the last four
chapters finally are successful in placing Sutpen in a comprehensible human context. Quentin and his roommate, Shreve
McCannon, bring both a fairly complete knowledge of the facts
and an inventive curiosity to the job of historical re-creation.
Sutpen himself ceases to be a phenomenon in Quentin's past.

In their final ordering of the story, Quentin and Shreve
are primarily concerned with the activity of Charles Bon and
Henry Sutpen. Quentin's perceptive awareness of the meaning
of that activity infuses a wholly human content into what has
been the mechanical abstract nature of those past experiences
which seem to constitute his heritage. It is specifically
this human content, we have seen, which Sutpen tacitly ejected
from his "design" by his refusal ever to recognize Bon as his
son. And it is ironic, in view of Quentin's presentation of

Bon, that in Rosa's soliloquy, as well as in Mr. Compson's
version of the story, Sutpen is never more inhuman. Rosa
herself never seems more fantastic than in [her version of]
their relationships to Charles Bon.

The account of the Bon story which finally emerges from
the conversations of Quentin and Shreve may be viewed as an
attempted rejection by Quentin of both his father's and Rosa's
points of view. The effect, in terms of the novel, is a rejection of naturalism. The activity of Bon and Henry, as
it is seen by Quentin, simply does not sustain a conception
of history either as an impersonal mechanism or in which "blind
Fate" slowly and solemnly triumphs. Faulkner quite admirably
makes his own job extremely difficult. He endows Bon's career
with all the material which should by its very nature keep
Rosa's "current of retribution and fatality" (p. 269) moving
on unaffected by Bon's own feelings and desires. Bon's
childhood, according to Shreve, was almost a ritual in which
his mother prepared him as an agent of her revenge on her
husband. And, as we have already seen, Bon's experience at
Sutpen's Hundred is made equivalent to that of Sutpen as a
child standing before the plantation door.

Actually, however, Bon gives Sutpen numerous opportunities
to correct his "mistake." Rather than revenge for his mother,
all he is seeking is his father *out of the shadow of whose
absence my spirit's posthumeity has never escaped"* (p. 317).
If Sutpen had for one moment equally transcended the effects
of his childhood and of his repudiation, if he had once perceived Bon's human motive, then the latter would, he claims,
have sacrificed the love of Henry and whatever claim he might
have to the love of Judith:

> *Yes. Yes. I will renounce her; I will renounce love
> and all; that will be cheap, cheap, even though he say
> to me "never look upon my face again; take my love and
> my acknowledgment in secret, and go" I will do that;
> I will not even demand to know of him what it was my
> mother did that justified his action toward her and me.*
> (p. 327)

But he at last falls victim, as Sutpen himself is a victim, to the ravages of this abstract "design." Incest with
Judith or death at the hands of his brother become the only
ways in which Bon can identify himself as Sutpen's son. Henry,
after four years of painful indecision, kills his friend and
brother at the gates of Sutpen's Hundred. For Bon, this was
the ultimate recognition of his sonship. For Henry, it was a
terribly difficult moral act. It had to be carried out in a
world which his father, like Quentin's mother in *The Sound
and the Fury*, has almost wholly corrupted. Henry acts not in

obedience to his father, but to an inherent sense of a moral
code which is stronger than his love for Bon. The act, though
Sutpen insisted upon it, is really a transcendence by Henry
of the dehumanized quality of his father's "design." This
part of the story is proof for Quentin, if he needed proof,
that life in the past was not as easily heroic as his father
once imagined, the circumstances neither so "simple" nor the
people so "distinct, uncomplex." What is important is that
Quentin can see in the activity of Charles and Henry an active
expression, however confused and frustrated, of human value
responding to the inhumanity of Sutpen.

Shreve is genuinely moved by the account he and Quentin
are able to make of Bon's and Henry's dilemmas. By the time
that element of the story is finished, he has ceased both his
self-conscious demonizing of Rosa and the picayune, witty
interjections at which Quentin is silently but visibly annoyed.
At one point, both he and Quentin become so engrossed in their
own efforts fully to re-create the story that "it did not
matter to either of them which one did the talking" (p. 316).
As the story develops, it becomes profoundly human, profoundly
noumenal in content. So much so that for the first time the
two boys at Harvard find themselves understandably situated
within the destinies of the "shades" they create:

> They were both in Carolina and the time was forty-six
> years ago, and it was not even four now but compounded
> still further since now both of them were Henry Sutpen
> and both of them were Bon. (p. 351)

But the conversations of Quentin and Shreve do not end
with the killing of Bon, with a personal action carried out
in painful recognition of a moral code. As they continue
with the Sutpen story, its natural sequence is significantly
disrupted. Chronologically, though all of the details are
made available to us in earlier chapters, the death of Bon
should be followed by Wash Jones's murder of Thomas Sutpen
and by the violent escapades of Bon's son, Valery Bon, who
has been brought by Clytie and Judith to Sutpen's Hundred.
Structurally, however, the next incident with which Quentin
and Shreve concern themselves is the final catastrophe of
the Sutpen family, a catastrophe which seems to affirm the
workings of a grotesquely deterministic universe. Such a
focus on the material as a chronological ordering of the Wash
Jones and Valery Bon stories would have allowed might have
permitted Quentin a more substantial mitigation of the meaning
which Shreve desperately assigns in the end to the idiot who
alone survives at Sutpen's Hundred.

The actions of Wash Jones and of Valery Bon suggest as
clearly as the final actions of Bon and Henry a distorted but

eloquent sense of moral revulsion at the corruption and inhumanity of Sutpen's "design." When there seems no hope of
reinstituting that "design," Sutpen perhaps consciously provokes Wash into killing him. In Wash's hearing, he crudely
repudiates Milly, Wash's granddaughter, when she fails to bear
him a son. But we can as easily view the murder less as a
credit to Sutpen's scheming than as an assertion by Wash of
human pride. In order to reaffirm his manhood and his dignity, he must destroy the man who has been his hero. His
conduct partakes of the same traditional morality which justifies, in the short story "Tomorrow," the murder of Buck
Thorpe by an outraged father. The murder in both instances
can be viewed as punishment for a gross violation of primitive
social mores.

Like Milly and Wash, Valery Bon discovers that he, too,
is a part of the rejected residue of his grandfather's career.
His subsequent conduct is a comment upon the consequences of
Sutpen's invalidation of the habits and customs of the community which, taken together, constitute a kind of moral or social
discipline. Having no family of his own, his real identity
hidden from the town, Valery Bon seeks literally to make a
name for himself by violent and extraordinary action. Though
he could pass for a white man, he marries a woman who is an
extremely dark Negress, and insists on being recognized as a
Negro himself. Considering the social consequences, this is
really a conscious form of self-degradation similar in its
motivation to that of Joe Christmas in *Light in August*. Valery
Bon's violence, like Joe's unkindness to Mrs. McEachern, is
directed against the feminizing pity of those about him.
They are aware of their own incompleteness; and symbolically
this may be viewed as a dimly Christian awareness of the possible glory of being human. Joe and Valery Bon can define
themselves only horribly. In Sutpen's world, all Valery Bon
can do is to assert negatively his potential dignity as a man.

But the structure of the final episodes dramatically ex-
cludes from the immediate attention of Quentin and Shreve
the moral affirmations, however deformed, of Wash and Valery
Bon. Instead, we have in the sharpest possible juxtaposition,
the circumstances of Bon's death and the almost theatrical
horror of the burning of Sutpen's Hundred. Valery Bon's son,
the heir to the estate and a Negro idiot, is left to "lurk
around those ashes and howl" (p. 376). The howling of Jim
Bond is totally devoid of the kind of value which was tragically
dramatized by Henry's murder of his friend. Quentin actually
trembles in his bed as he remembers it.

The structure insists on the persistent quality of
Quentin's problem. The Negro idiot seems powerfully to re-
introduce the apparently inhuman and mechanistic nature of

Sutpen's history and of Quentin's heritage. Shreve is moved
almost as much as Quentin by the ambiguous quality of the
story they have finally pieced together, by the insoluble
tension between the human needs and passions inherent in the
tale and the impersonally deterministic form it seems to take.
But he rather pathetically disguises his feelings and doubts.
He grasps what is for him the easiest solution, what is for
Quentin an emotionally impossible solution--the cliché of the
idiot as symbol of predestined doom. The final catastrophe,
he tells Quentin, "clears the whole ledger, you can tear all
the pages out and burn them, except for one thing" (p. 378).
That one thing, Shreve facetiously concludes, is the mechanism
itself by which "the Jim Bonds are going to conquer the
western hemisphere":

> So it took Charles Bon and his mother to get rid of old
> Tom, and Charles Bon and the octoroon to get rid of
> Judith, and Charles Bon and Clytie to get rid of Henry;
> and Charles Bon's mother and Charles Bon's grandmother
> got rid of Charles Bon. So it takes two niggers to get
> rid of one Sutpen, dont it? (pp. 377-378)

Shreve ends his remarks, to which Quentin has listened silently
and unwillingly, with a final question: "Why do you hate the
South?" What he assumes is that Quentin can afford to hate
not simply the South, but his past, his paternity, and himself
as a product of all three.

Quentin gives the only possible answer with a terrifying
urgency:

> "I dont hate it," Quentin said, quickly, at once, im-
> mediately: "I dont hate it," he said. *I dont hate it*
> he thought, panting in the cold air, the iron New
> England dark; *I dont. I dont! I dont hate it! I dont
> hate it!* (p. 378)

His only other possible answer would be a telling of the whole
story of Sutpen over again. But Quentin speaks to himself as
much as to his friend. Annoying to Quentin as Shreve's easy
and terrible solution might seem, the possibility exists for
him even at the end of the novel that man and his history
are mutually hostile and alien; that he is merely the reflex
of some impersonal and abstract historical process. But it
is a possibility to which he refuses wholly to succumb. Inherent in the tragically suggestive ambiguity of the conclusion is the justification for the structure of *Absalom, Absalom!* The form of the novel itself insists that the act of
placing Sutpen in the understandable context of human society
and history is a continually necessary act, a never-ending
responsibility and an act of humanistic faith.

NOTES

1. *The Sewanee Review*, 53 (Summer, 1945), 343–361.

2. *The Sound and the Fury* (New York: Random House, 1946), p. 123.

3. Kenneth Burke, *The Philosohpy of Literary Form* (Baton Rouge, 1941), p. 117.

4. *After Strange Gods* (London, 1934), p. 54.

5. Page references to *Absalom, Absalom!* are to the Random House edition, 1936.

6. "Cowley's Faulkner," *The New Republic*, 115 (August 12, 1946), 177.

7. Cowley, 344.

8. P. 54.

9. *Ibid.*

10. *On Native Grounds* (New York, 1942), p. 466. See also J. Donald Adams, *The Shape of Books to Come* (New York, 1944), p. 131; Elizabeth Hardwick, "Faulkner and the South Today," *Partisan Review*, October, 1948, pp. 1130–1135; Granville Hicks, *The Great Tradition* (New York, 1935), p. 291; Wyndham Lewis, *Men Without Art* (London, 1934), pp. 44–48; Edmund Wilson, "William Faulkner's Reply to the Civil Rights Program," *The New Yorker*, October 23, 1948, p. 106.

11. I am remembering some observations by Nicholas Berdyaev on the general problem of value in history. Nicholas Berdyaev, *The Meaning of History* (London, 1936).

THE MYRIAD PERSPECTIVES
OF *ABSALOM, ABSALOM!*

Arthur L. Scott

The acclaim which has greeted William Faulkner since he won
the Nobel Prize for literature in 1950 has directed renewed
attention to the problem of his obscurity. "There is a kind
of sullen Puritanic strain in Faulkner," writes Herbert Poster,
"which compels him to view clarity, charm and easy persuasive-
ness with suspicion and hostility."[1] Nowhere is this sullen
strain more pronounced than in *Absalom, Absalom!* (1936), now
recognized as the key book in the great Yoknapatawpha series
and sometimes called "the greatest of Faulkner's novels."[2]
And yet it is possible to demonstrate that the apparent chaos
of this unique novel may spring from the use of techniques
more often encountered in arts other than fiction.

Absalom, Absalom! describes the fierce attempt of Thomas
Sutpen to establish a respectable white dynasty in Mississippi
during the middle of the last century. All goes well, until
suddenly a mysterious young man named Charles Bon arrives to
court his daughter. Sutpen now, for some reason, quarrels
with his only son, Henry, and is repudiated by the boy. Henry
rides off with Charles Bon, but several years later murders
him and becomes a fugitive from justice. Again desperate for
a white heir, Sutpen seduces a poor-white girl named Milly.
When the offspring turns out to be a girl, Sutpen so reviles
Milly that her outraged grandfather kills him. Forty years
later the crumbling Sutpen mansion burns to the ground, destroying Henry who has returned there to hide. Sutpen's ill-starred
"dynasty" thus descends to his sole heir—a moaning Negro idiot.

This is the story of Thomas Sutpen, stripped of its
savagery and complications, and with no hint of its implications in terms of myth, tragedy, or allegory. Regardless of
its meaning, *Absalom, Absalom!* is one of the most extraordinary

From American Quarterly, 6 (Fall 1954), pp. 210-220, copyright
1954, Trustees of the University of Pennsylvania. Reprinted
by permission of the publisher.

psychological mysteries of all time, because its method is
frankly experimental. To inspect this method, we must begin
with the point of view, for, as Percy Lubbock has shown, "The
whole intricate question of method, in the craft of fiction,
... [is] governed by the question of the point of view--the
question of the relation in which the narrator stands to the
story."[3]

The four narrators of the Sutpen tragedy are Quentin Compson (a Harvard freshman), Shreve McCannon (his Canadian roommate), Quentin's father (son of Sutpen's best friend), and
Rosa Coldfield (Sutpen's sister-in-law). Between September
1909 and January 1910 these four people tell and retell one
another divers aspects of the Sutpen story. A rough breakdown
shows them commanding in turn the following pages of the novel:

> Rosa . . . . 7-30; 134-173.
> Mr. Compson . . . . . . 43-134.
> Quentin . . . . 174-292; 358-378.
> Shreve . . . . 293-345.
> Omniscient author . . . 31-43; 346-358.[4]

Such an outline is an absurd simplification, because the novel
is not divided into neatly specified books or chapters in the
fashion of *The Sound and the Fury* (1929) or *As I Lay Dying*
(1930). In mid-sentence the viewpoint may shift from the
spoken dialogue of Shreve to the interior monologue of Quentin
or to objective reality. The clue for the shift--and there is
usually *something*--may be a parenthesis, italics, double or
single quotation marks, a dash, or any combination of these
things. The shift may be for three words or for three pages.
Faulkner makes his own rules of rhetoric to suit his immediate
whims. Often the words "he said" are within quotes (or in
parentheses or italics), while the dialogue is not. There are
parentheses within parentheses, quotes within quotes within
quotes, and dashes employed to mean almost anything. The
reader, furiously intent upon piecing together the facts about
Sutpen, is only subconsciously puzzled regarding the narrator,
until he suddenly realizes that the speech or thought of 1910
has subtly merged with the reality of 1833. "Half the time we
are swimming under water," says Joseph Warren Beach, "holding
our breath and straining our eyes to read off the meaning of
submarine phenomena.... We are forever on the point of giving
up, throwing ourselves upon some reef and letting the ocean
thunder by."[5]

Since there are at least five simpler ways of telling this
story, Faulkner must have some reason for his complex machinery,
even though he once protested that he had "never given the subject of form a single thought."[6] At the outset two important
facts must be recognized: 1) Faulkner seldom confuses the reader

unintentionally, and 2) *Absalom, Absalom!* is *not* incoherent.
The whole plan of the novel is one of calculated confusion and
yet, in the long view, the book is wonderfully cohesive. Save
in rare instances, Faulkner knows what he is doing.

> Those oft are stratagems which errors seem,
> Nor is it Homer nods but we that dream.

The book is far from being the uncharted chaos that it first
appears. It is tightly plotted. A comment by Quentin describes
perfectly the basic confusion inherent in the presentation.
Quentin is referring to the night when his grandfather listened
to Sutpen narrate his life-story, while slaves with torches
were hunting down the runaway French architect:

> ... [Sutpen] getting himself and Grandfather both into
> that besieged Haitian room as simply as he got himself
> to the West Indies by saying that he decided to go to
> the West Indies and so he went there. This anecdote was
> no deliberate continuation of the other one but was merely
> called to his mind by the picture of the niggers and
> torches in front of them.... And I reckon Grandfather
> was saying "Wait, wait for God's sake wait" about like
> you are, until he finally did stop and back up and start
> over again with at least some regard for cause and effect
> even if none for logical sequence and continuity. (pp.
> 246-247)

Like old Mr. Compson and Shreve, the reader often cries, "Wait,
for God's sake wait." But the plea falls upon deaf ears.
Faulkner persists in his apparent disregard for cause and effect,
as well as for logical sequence and continuity.

This indifference to conventional story-telling methods is,
of course, forced upon the four narrators or "reflectors" (to
use Henry James's term). The question at once arises, why does
Faulkner bother with these narrators in the first place? In
reply, it has been argued that they help establish *the moral
atmosphere* of the book[7] and also rescue the novel from nihilism
and sensationalism.[8] Despite Faulkner's eloquent championing
of idealism in his Nobel Prize acceptance speech, however, his
experiments with shifting viewpoints are surely rooted, not in
moral earnestness, but in aesthetics.

Aesthetically, the most obvious aim of *Absalom, Absalom!*
is suspense. The rapid shifts in viewpoint, the baroque sentence structure, the cavalier indifference to time sequence
are all part of an elaborate scheme of tantalization. The
novel is a masterpiece of progressive revelation, accomplished
by means of a system of hints and obstacles, of ambiguous in-
terpolations and postponements. It is a genuine *tour de force*
of withheld meaning and it "pants intricately with suspense."[9]

Recognizing, perhaps, that mere suspense is a cheap device by
means of which even the worst trash can hold us basely en-
thralled, Faulkner refines the suspense by reversing his depiction of cause and effect. Deeds, therefore, are described
before their motives—a distortion of reality which makes
Absalom, Absalom! truly a puzzle of causality.

In this connection, let us examine for a moment the chief
mystery of the novel. We learn on page 18 that Henry murders
his sister's sweetheart, be we are not told the reason. On
page 90 we find that Charles Bon (the murdered sweetheart)
already has a wife and child—colored ones (p. 92). Is this
the murder motive? Much later (p. 265) we discover that Charles
Bon is really Sutpen's own son by a previous marriage. A-ha!
we think; not bigamy but incest is Henry's main dread! The
real motive for the killing, however, is withheld until page
355: Charles Bon has Negro blood in his veins. Henry's repug-
nance for bigamy and incest pales beside his southern horror
of miscegenation.

The spasmodic, delayed clarification of this mystery has
been called "one of the most extraordinary tricks of narrative
skill in the history of fiction. And all the more so because
it is not a mere trick in plotting."[10] True, the reader's
pattern of discovery does parallel that of the murderer; and
yet the whole method of gradual disclosure *is* merely a trick
in presentation. Structurally, the novel is a series of monologues about a man long dead. The four monologuists, for no
apparent reason, however, seldom mention until the last moment
crucial facts which they have known from the start. Cleanth
Brooks believes that the two roommates are making an "imaginative reconstruction" of the past,[11] while searching for the
meaning of Sutpen's failure, but the *actual* reconstruction must
have preceded their present colloquy. Obviously the boys have
covered this ground before and the horrific events no longer
shock them. For instance, nothing but Faulkner's whim keeps
them from mentioning Charles Bon's Negro blood. Until the last
moment they refer to it always by some mysterious circumlocution
such as "[Sutpen's] last trump card" (pp. 244-247). Other cases
of this same sort of authorial caprice prove that the novel's
multiple viewpoints are far from ideal for the mere purpose of
holding back information. In general, the viewpoint of Henry
the murderer, for *this* purpose would serve most authors perfectly (cf. *The Ambassadors* and *Rebecca*).

Might it not be, then, that Faulkner has other aesthetic
purposes besides progressive revelation and suspense? A certain variety is achieved by means of the contrasted attitudes
expressed by the narrators towards Sutpen, but this variety is
minimized by the fact that all four express themselves in the
same ponderous, involute, unearthly Faulknerese.[12] Nor is the

arbitrary pattern of *Absalom, Absalom!* justifiable by virtue
of the dramatic unity which the employment of these narrators
lends to the Yoknapatawpha series in general, where they appear
in other novels.[13] The end would not justify the means. Why
did Faulkner append to the novel the brief Genealogy and
Chronology, which together summarize the plot? Did he wish
these tables referred to during the reading of the book, or
did he want them read last for clarification--or should they
be read first, as Bernard DeVoto suggests?[14] DeVoto's suggestion is not flippant. Advance knowledge of the main events
and relationships will destroy the suspense, of course, but at
the same time it will uncover riches that otherwise remain hidden until a second or third reading.

These new riches are not easy to describe, yet they may
possibly explain Faulkner's true reason for narrating Sutpen's
story in a circular manner from varying points of view. In a
very special way, *Absalom, Absalom!* is a fictional experiment
in time and space, although it is by no means a science-fiction
story. The clearest way to describe this experiment is in
terms of other art forms.

It has become fashionable to compare the fiction of William
Faulkner to music, stressing its fugue-like qualities and its
contrapuntal method.[15] As yet no one has fully explored the
similarities between his narrative technique and such contrapuntal devices as imitation, canon, inversion, cancrizans, and
inverted cancrizans. Music, however, progressing through
measurable time, is not the best analogy to this particular
novel, because Faulkner's chief concern here is to *escape* from
this very sense of progression. (This would seem to refute
Walter Pater's famous dictum that "all art constantly aspires
towards the condition of music.")

I suggest that what *Absalom, Absalom!* attempts in words is
more closely allied to certain experiments with line and color.
At least one critic has noted the apparent kinship of Faulkner's
work with Surrealism "in its direct appeal to the Unconscious."[16]
With its apotheosis of the irrational, however, and its denial
of the rôle of the intelligence and will in human existence,
Surrealism is simply spontaneity uninhibited by reason, logic,
or technique. Critics hostile to Faulkner--and they have become scarce since 1942[17]--may complain that his novels do evidence what Dali calls the "paranoic vision" of Surrealism. It
is hardly necessary today, however, to demonstrate that the
Surrealist emphasis upon chaotic dream-images has little in
common with the calculated complexity of Faulkner's novels.

On the other hand, *Absalom, Absalom!* does bear a marked
resemblance to two earlier art movements: Cubism and Futurism.
About 1909 Picasso painted his first Cubist picture and a new
movement was born. Seeking a better way of viewing things,

Picasso presented, not whole objects, but parts of objects in
new and generally dislocated relations. "In my case," he
said, "a picture is a sum of destructions." For example, he
split a head into sections and then shuffled the sections together again so as to bring into a single focus aspects observed from several points of view. Or, as his followers put
it, "Moving round an object, he seized several successive appearances which, when fused into a single image, reconstituted
it in time."[18] Is this not also the method of *Absalom, Absalom!*? "The fundamental idea of Cubism is, I think," explains
Sheldon Cheney, "that it is possible to dissociate the planes
of an object seen, and to rearrange them in a picture, so organized that they will give a truer emotional or structural
sense than the original 'appearance.' One sees an object from
one side; it is an incomplete vision. A complete vision would
show it not only as synthesized visually from all sides and
aspects, but as it is from within."[19] Guillaume Apollinaire
termed this kind of complete vision "the fourth dimension."
"It represents," he said, "the immensity of space eternalizing
itself in all directions at any given moment."[20]

The Cubist's interest in multiple viewpoints merged at
times with the Italian Futurist's desire to introduce motion
into painting. Futurism regarded itself as a species of plas-
tic dynamics. Debased though both movements did become in a
few years, they both contained a pregnant idea behind their
principle of Simultaneity. This is the principle of looking,
with the mind's eye, at all the outward aspects of an object
at once, thus getting a sort of composite or synthetic view of
it. Such a view can lead to that sort of emotional intensifi-
cation which is the first aim of modernism in nearly all the
arts. In Futurism this principle evoked such a cinematographic
painting as Balla's "Moving Dog in Leash," whose blurred outlines give the picture the appearance of a photograph snapped
too slowly to arrest the action. More significant is Marcel
Duchamp's famous "Nude Descending a Staircase," which shocked
the art world in 1912. Spectators were nonplussed by the wilder-
ness of lines seemingly without plan or meaning. Cubism and
Futurism meet in this painting. Divers shapes--presented from
all angles--are juxtaposed and subtly overlapped, as Duchamp
explained, in order "to capture the entire movement as well as
the entire form of the figure." The motion-picture camera
encircles a figure--shooting it from all angles. The Cubist
tries to combine all these viewpoints in a single canvas. Not
only that. He often ignores size and perspective, making a
banana as big as a barn in a painting which is depthless. He
is experimenting, then, in the medium of time-space. In a
single instant in a single painting--which may appear tortured
and formless--the Cubist strives to capture an *entire form*,

sometimes together with its *movement*.

This is an ambitious enterprise which seldom results in popular art. The public's attitude towards *Absalom, Absalom!*, by the same token, is partly due to what might be termed the Futuristic Cubism of the novel. Both time and space are also treated in a most unconventional manner by William Faulkner. As Conrad Aiken observes, there is no real beginning or end to the novel and therefore no logical point of entrance: "... we must just submit, and follow the circling of the author's interest, which turns a light inward towards the center, but every moment from a new angle, a new point of view."[21] The truly impressive experiment in the novel, therefore, is not its search for a new type of variety or suspense, but rather its bold adaptation to fiction of new concepts regarding time and space. Consider, for example, this important pronouncement of the Futurists, and observe its curious applicability to the complex method of *Absalom, Absalom!*:

> The simultaneousness of states of mind in the work of art: that is the intoxicating aim of our art.... In painting a person on a balcony, seen from inside the room, we do not limit the scene to what the square frame of the window renders visible; but we try to render the sum total of visual sensations which the person on the balcony has experienced; the sun-bathed throng in the street, the double row of houses which stretch to right and left, the beflowered balconies, etc. This implies the simultaneousness of the ambient, and, therefore, the dislocation and dismemberment of objects, the scattering and fusion of details, freed from accepted logic, and independent from one another. In order to make the spectator live in the center of the picture, as we express it in our manifesto, the picture must be the synthesis of *what one remembers* and of *what one sees*.[22]

Moreover, whether he knows it or not, Faulkner is acclaimed by the French partly because of his own treatment of what is called the Existential Mode of Time. This theory maintains that the past acts upon us precisely as an existent object does. C.S. Pierce uses a simple illustration to prove that the mode of the Past is that of Actuality: "For instance, when a Nova Stella bursts out in the heavens, it acts upon one's eye just as a light struck in the dark by one's own hand would; and yet it is an event which happened before the Pyramids were built."[23] For several decades now the meaning of Simultaneity has been a central problem in connection with time. And surely one aesthetic aim of *Absalom, Absalom!* is to portray the interaction of past and present, to demonstrate the powerful effect of the old upon the new (especially upon Quentin),[24]

and to prove that the Sutpen tragedy is still charged with
spiritual dynamite, even though its great protagonist has
mouldered to dust.

Time and again within the novel Faulkner makes this aim
clear. He even likens his own method to "the mask in Greek
tragedy, interchangeable not only from scene to scene, but from
actor to actor and behind which the events and occasions took
place without chronology or sequence" (p. 62). And Quentin
formulates the Existential Mode of Time thus:

> Maybe we are both Father. Maybe nothing ever happens
> once and is finished. Maybe happen is never once but
> like ripples maybe on water after the pebble sinks, the
> ripples moving on, spreading, the pool attached by a
> narrow umbilical water-cord to the next pool which the
> first pool feeds, has fed, did feed.... Yes, we are both
> Father. Or maybe Father and I are both Shreve, maybe
> it took Father and me both to make Shreve or Shreve and
> me both to make father or maybe Thomas Sutpen to make all
> of us. (pp. 261-262)

In the light of these concepts, consider the scene at Harvard where the two boys rehearse the past. "It was Shreve
speaking, though ... it might have been either of them and
was in a sense both: both thinking as one ..." (p. 303). From
this simple union of minds it is but a step back into history
for the boys to become imaginatively absorbed by the characters
they are examining: "So that now it was not two but four of
them riding the two horses through the dark over the frozen December ruts of that Christmas Eve ..." (p. 334). And eventually:
"They were both in Carolina and the time was forty-six years
ago, and it was not even four now but compounded still further,
since now both of them were Henry Sutpen and both of them were
Bon, compounded each of both yet either neither ..." (p. 351).

Quentin and Shreve in their "tomblike room" are practically
in a state of trance--which helps explain the absence of the
temporal factor. The objective physical time of immediate experience and the subjective psychological time of mediate conception[25] become coextensive in this long scene. The Existential concept permits Faulkner to develop several planes of
action simultaneously, somewhat in the manner of the Cubists.[26]
In fact, he is so preoccupied with presenting the past from
the viewpoint of the present that a clever critic might argue
that *Absalom, Absalom!* is actually not a novel, but a "recital."
"The novel is the representation of events which take place in
time," says Ramon Fernandez, "a representation submitted to the
conditions of apparition and development of these events. The
recital is the presentation of events which have taken place,
and of which the reproduction is regulated by the narrator in

conformity with the laws of exposition and persuasion."[27] Certainly *Absalom, Absalom!* does conform to the laws of persuasion more closely than to the conditions of development, and yet we cannot ignore its underlying purpose of *fusing* past and present --of making passage from one time to another as fluid and undetectable as in life itself. "Time in fact is 'before' and 'after' in one;" says F.H. Bradley, "and without this diversity it is not time. 'Before in relation to after' is the character of time."[28] Indeed, the concept of time in this novel is not very different from Henri Bergson's "durée," which is described as "pure continuity, and is neither measurable nor divisible without destroying its character."[29]

Supporting this sense of continuity and simultaneousness is Faulkner's fantastic style, which has been called "perhaps the most elaborate, intermittently incoherent and ungrammatical, thunderous, polyphonic rhetoric in all American writing."[30] Faulkner is a true verbal voluptuary whose love for language amounts practically to a lust. By reason of their very obscurity, however, his sprawling, labyrinthine sentences give him uncommon freedom and lend to his time-scheme a great deal of the fluidity he desires. As Conrad Aiken points out, they parallel in a curious way the whole elaborate plan of partial and delayed disclosure.[31] Their most tantalizing device is the frequent allusion to events as yet undescribed, as well as to known happenings. This, of course, enhances the methodical mystification, while also fusing past, present, and future in a single moment.

The inevitable question arises: do these innovations prevent *Absalom, Absalom!* from "making sense" as form--as all art must? No, they do not, regardless of popular opinion. Cubism erroneously made design an end and not a means, but William Faulkner has never agreed with the Cubists that all human attributes are irrelevant to art. Only the casual reader of *Absalom, Absalom!* complains that its method completely vitiates its content. And this novel, more than others, should have no casual readers. Faulkner is an aristocrat of letters, an aesthetic thoroughbred whose novels demand of the reader an effort commensurate with the author's. "Pleasure results from many degrees of perception," explains Herbert Read, "and the purest pleasure is ... intellectual as well as (at the same time) sensuous. This most refined degree of pleasure is only given in response to disciplined effort."[32]

In other words, half the difficulty which readers find in appreciating *Absalom, Absalom!* comes from insufficient effort towards comprehending the way the work is put together. This is true of all the modern arts. The discerning and disciplined reader understands that this novel is no aesthetic humbug, but truly contains *la grande ligne*,[33] which gives it a sense of

flow--a sense of continuity from the first word to the last.
Like Joyce in *Ulysses*, Faulkner even achieves a kind of continuum in *Absalom, Absalom!* He achieves it at some expense,
however. Although employing Cubist perspectives and Existential
time modes, he still demands the element of mystery--which depends upon a carefully limited perspective, if not always upon
an orderly time sequence. Because the story-teller is not
willing to sacrifice suspense, therefore, the experimenter is
sometimes obliged to violate his chosen viewpoints. And these
violations create artificial stases in that otherwise "fluid
cradle of events (time)" (p. 66).

These stases--organic flaws in the novel--are obscured by
the convolutions of language and deliberate disorder of the
narrative presentation. They are still flaws, however, and as
such they do take some of the bloom from Faulkner's ingenious
experiment. Perhaps it was, from the start, a synesthetic
fallacy to attempt to combine in a single art form--whether
Faulkner was aware of the combination or not--the varied techniques of the Cubist, the Existentialist, and the mystery
writer. Should we say that the experiment is a failure?

>Great wits sometimes may gloriously offend,
>And rise to faults true Critics dare not mend.

The tragedy of Thomas Sutpen is almost Euripidean in power.
It is Euripidean, however, *in spite of* its grotesque style
and its prismatic form which refract light from many sources
at the same time. Not by virtue of its innovations and
novelty, but rather by virtue of its power and gusto and rich
meaning, *Absalom, Absalom!* will remain a major contribution
to American letters.

NOTES

1. "Faulkner's Folly," *American Mercury*, 73 (December,
1951), 111.

2. Cleanth Brooks, "*Absalom, Absalom!*: The Definition of
Innocence," *Sewanee Review*, 59 (Autumn 1951), 543.

3. *The Craft of Fiction* (London: Jonathan Cape, 1921), p.
251.

4. The text referred to throughout is the Modern Library
Edition (New York: Random House, 1951).

5. *American Fiction 1920-1940* (New York: Macmillan Co.,
1941), p. 160.

6. Anthony Buttitta, "William Faulkner: That Writin' Man
of Oxford," *Saturday Review of Literature*, 18 (May 21, 1938), 7.

7. Delmore Schwartz, "The Fiction of William Faulkner," *Southern Review*, 7 (1941), 150.

8. Warren Beck, "Faulkner's Point of View," *College English*, 2 (May 1941), 741.

9. Maxwell Geismar, *Writers in Crisis* (Boston: Houghton Mifflin Co., 1942), p. 172.

10. Beach, *American Fiction 1920-1940*, pp. 167-168.

11. *Op. cit.*, p. 554.

12. It is true, however, that the shifting "reflectors" do lend the novel something of the effect achieved in music by four-voiced polyphony, which bears repeated hearings better than music of homophonic texture. As Aaron Copland points out, "Homophonic music ... generally has more immediate appeal for the listener than polyphonic music. But polyphonic music brings with it a greater intellectual participation." *What to Listen for in Music* (New York: McGraw-Hill Book Co., 1939), pp. 110-111.

13. This is one explanation advanced by Harry M. Campbell, "Structural Devices in the Works of Faulkner," *Perspective*, 3 (Autumn 1950), 209-226.

14. "Witchcraft in Mississippi," *Saturday Review of Literature*, 15 (October 31, 1936), 3.

15. Conrad Aiken, "William Faulkner: The Novel as Form," *Atlantic Monthly*, 64 (November, 1939), 653. James W. Linn and Houghton W. Taylor, *A Foreword to Fiction* (New York: D. Appleton-Century Co., 1935), p. 144. Warren Beck, "A Note on Faulkner's Style," *Rocky Mountain Review*, 6, nos. 3-4 (Spring-Summer 1942), 5-6.

16. Vincent F. Hopper, "Faulkner's Paradise Lost," *Virginia Quarterly Review*, 23 (Summer 1947), 418.

17. See John L. Longley, Jr., and Robert Daniel, "Faulkner's Critics: A Selective Bibliography," *Perspective*, 3 (Autumn 1950), 202-208.

18. Quoted from Thomas Craven, *Men of Art* (New York: Simon and Schuster, 1936), p. 498.

19. *A Primer of Modern Art* (New York: Boni and Liveright 1942), p. 101.

20. *The Cubist Painters* [1913], translated from French by Lionel Abel (New York: Wittenborn and Co., 1944), p. 12.

21. "William Faulkner: The Novel as Form," pp. 653-654.

22. Quoted from Sheldon Cheney, *The Story of Modern Art* (New York: Viking Press, 1945), pp. 468-469.

23. *Collected Papers* (Harvard University Press, 1934), 5, 311.

24. Not in the romantic fashion of *The House of the Seven Gables*, but in the philosophic sense suggested by Ivy Mackenzie: "No animal is to be compared with man in the extent to which, through organic time, the experience of the past is represented in the present." "The Biological Basis of the Sense of Time," in *Aristotelian Society Supplement*, V (London: Williams and Norgate, 1925), 74.

25. The two modes of times recognized by the theory of relativity.

26. W.M. Frohock believes that Faulkner's people move in *three* merging time planes--"their constant apprehension over what is imminent constituting what amounts to a third temporal dimension." "William Faulkner: The Private versus the Public Vision," *Southwest Review*, 34 (Summer 1949), 290.

27. Quoted by Edwin Muir, *The Structure of the Novel* (London: L. & V. Woolf, 1928), pp. 119-120.

28. *Appearance and Reality* (London: Swan Sonnenschein, 1893), p. 39.

29. Louise R. Heath, *The Concept of Time* (University of Chicago Press, 1936), p. 181.

30. Alfred Kazin, *On Native Grounds* (New York: Reynal and Hitchcock, 1942), p. 462. For detailed analysis see my "The Faulknerian Sentence," *Prairie Schooner*, 27 (Spring 1953), 91-98.

31. "William Faulkner: The Novel as Form," p. 652.

32. *The Philosophy of Modern Art* (New York: Horizon Press, 1953), pp. 232-233.

33. I adapt this phrase from its musical application by Aaron Copland, *What to Listen for in Music*, p. 32.

THE EPIC DESIGN OF *ABSALOM, ABSALOM!*

James H. Justus

When Cleanth Brooks in 1951 declared that Faulkner's *Absalom, Absalom!* is "more than a bottle of Gothic sauce to be used to spice up our own pre-conceptions about the history of American society,"[1] he was attempting to reverse the simplifying tendencies of previous critics who read the novel minimally-- as sociological allegory or Gothic myth. He insisted that this novel is Faulkner's greatest and buttressed this opinion (at that time clearly a minority view) by reading it as tragedy. Seeing the novel as an attempt to wrest something cosmic out of a local legend that is itself part of a larger myth, Brooks stressed Faulkner's creation of a character of heroic dimensions, whose key condition is isolation, whose definition is made in terms of his innocence, and whose downfall is invested with something akin to tragic dignity. Only in the last five years, when Faulkner criticism has been stripped of its earlier sociological bases, have Brooks' efforts been rewarded by more extensive interpretations of *Absalom* as tragedy.[2]

If we look at *Absalom* as a tragedy, however, a structural difficulty arises. What is essentially a carefully unified plot becomes a series of climaxes with a dubious perspective. If Sutpen is the tragic hero, a disproportionate attention is directed to the Judith-Bon-Henry plot--too much so to be explained as an underplot or a thematically sanctioned epilogue about the sins of a father. The story of the young Sutpens constitutes an impressive unity, though certainly not a detachable kind that would make it superfluous to old Sutpen's story.[3]

The difficulty of reading the novel as tragedy is further complicated when we identify the hero not as Sutpen but as the first-born, Bon, sometimes argued because he is the focus of the affirmation part of the plot, because he is a sacrificial

From Texas Studies in Literature and Language, *4 (Summer 1962), pp. 157-176. Published by the University of Texas Press; reprinted by permission of the publisher.*

victim to the "villainy" of his father, and because he helps
to release the values that Quentin and Shreve seek in the
legend. But this view surely wrenches the structure in the
other direction. Quentin becomes more involved in the fate of
the second generation, but it is of the source of their fate
he must first ask *why*? The meaning of the Judith-Bon-Henry
story is inherent in Sutpen, which is of course the reason
Faulkner is careful to devote so much time in defining Sutpen's
legend, not Bon's. In this tale of shades and ghosts, Bon remains the most shadowy figure, who is refleshed according to
the now-primed creative imaginations of Quentin and Shreve.
In their youthful empathy they may identify Bon as their tragic
hero, but that does not make him so for the novel or the legend
that lies behind it. It is also important to note that the
divided and "human" Bon comes only in their re-creation; according to the other (admittedly biased) points of view, he is
passive, world-weary, tolerantly bemused—a fatalist who is
willing if necessary to duplicate his father's repudiation and
desertion. So to insist on either old Sutpen or Bon as a fun-
damentally tragic protagonist is to throw the structure of the
novel off-balance, to refocus what is already in focus. And
yet the grandeur of tragedy remains. The impressive character
of Sutpen remains. The sense of heightened purpose and accomplishment evident in the evoking of a legend remains. All
these imply certainly something no less than tragedy, and if
not tragedy, what?

I would suggest that *Absalom, Absalom!* be read as epic.
It is the one genre that equals and even surpasses tragedy in
dignity and grandeur. It is no less artistic than tragedy in
its selection of incident, though that selection is determined
by different impulses. For Aristotle it comprised the same
elements (notably the same *fable*) as tragedy; but it was narrated rather than acted, its meter was different, and it required a larger dimension for the telling of its story. The
first two differences are resolved historically in the rise
of prose fiction, which not only absorbed the elements of
tragedy and comedy but also, as Professor Tillyard has described,
increasingly assumed the responsibilities and characteristics
that had been earlier embodied in verse narrative. Tillyard
has formulated the epic impulse into four distinguishing prin-
ciples by which the product may be identified in whatever
form: high seriousness (or gravity of subject), amplitude (or
breadth and inclusiveness necessarily absent from drama), a
control equal to the material (or powerful predetermination of
purpose), and a choric quality (or an expression of the feelings
of a large group of people living in or near the writer's own
time).[4]

For my own use, I would modify Tillyard's position only
to the extent of insisting that the term *epic* be applied to
narrative fiction whether in prose or verse. It would exclude
clear-cut pieces of drama and would retain all the other associations: characters of high position engaged in a series
of adventures, organic narrative revolving about a central
figure of heroic proportions, action important to a nation or
a race at a specific point in its development, and a style
that is dignified, majestic, and elevated. Such is the minimum
boundary within which the term operates; in addition, certain
secondary characteristics emerge as common and proper to epic.

There is much to indicate that *Absalom* occupies a rather
special position in the Yoknapatawpha saga. There is the
general observation that Faulkner has never ceased to experiment with his material; even in his so-called declining years,
he has demonstrated a remarkable vigor in approach and form--
Requiem for a Nun and *A Fable* are examples. All of the novels
in the 1929-1932 period differ radically in technique. And in
Absalom, coming as it does after a cooling-off process, in
1936, Faulkner is obviously doing something more than adding
another strand to the tangled cluster of legends that abound
in the county; even "recapitulation" seems inadequate for it.
The close-knit dissection of the fall of the House of Compson
in *The Sound and the Fury*, though it achieves a larger significance, is primarily directed to the disintegration of a
single family. The fall of the House of Sutpen is accompanied
by a fully conscious analysis of the evil effects of that family
on its own members and on the immediate community, on the
South, and by extension on the nation and the world at large.
The technical virtuosity of *The Sound and the Fury* should not
obscure the fact that *Absalom, Absalom!* is the more ambitious
work.[5]

Faulkner lavishes on Sutpen the most detailed and the most
careful filling-in of any of his characters; it is as if he
alone of all the Faulkner characters were meant to be full-
scale, to possess in full what Quentin, Bayard Sartoris, Jewel
Bundren, Joe Christmas, and a half-dozen others possess in part.
In no other novel is there so much energy devoted to the
characterization of one man; no single point of view (not
even the one direct-three refracted techniques of *The Sound
and the Fury*) can possibly explain Sutpen: his very substance
depends on a pooling of impressions by three and sometimes
four or five different people. And when all this is done, he
remains mythic, as if even the legend that he generates in the
county cannot wholly apprehend him. In no other novel is
Faulkner so consciously aware of history as history, of not
only recounting the facts and quasi facts of history but also
of attempting to order them, to understand them, to ask *why*?

And in no other novel is there so unambiguous an answer. Because of the monumental task, the process of getting to the
answer results in an agony of style far more heightened than
that in his other novels. I am reading *Absalom, Absalom!* as
epic, then, because no other reading can so fully explain its
height and breadth.

W.P. Ker saw the epic as grand not only because it was of
heroic nature but also because it was capable of absorbing so
many other types--romance, history, tragedy, idyll, panegyric,
lament.[6] Any discussion of epic must assume the controlling
importance of (a) its material (character or characters of considerable stature whose adventures, however disparate, are related to and reflect the nation or race at a specific stage
in its history), (b) its method (this story told by a consciously present narrator), and (c) its manner (a profoundly
ordered control of this story, however various its versions
become, in a formalized and elevated style). Whatever other
traits contribute to the impressive edifice, and they are
numerous, it is this scaffolding that determines its shape and
function.

I

The heroic stature of Thomas Sutpen is measured in terms
of his compulsion, an obsessive plan for founding a dynasty
at whatever cost. The cost is heavy, and the dynasty comes
to nothing; but between the wrenching of Sutpen's Hundred out
of the swamps and the escape of his great-grandson, the idiot
Jim Bond, the acts of Sutpen are impressive. That these acts
are demonic is not to be denied, but it is a misplaced dependence
upon Rosa Coldfield's narration to conclude that Sutpen is in
fact a "demon" or that he is wholly a "villain."

The demonic element in Sutpen is inherent in his compulsion, and the term can in varying degrees apply to the entire
range of characters who are repeatedly, from all points of
view, called "ghosts." Some are doomed and some are damned;
all are "invoked" and the entire legend is "recapitulation
evoked." It is not accidental that the frame scenes are
drenched with atmosphere common to the invoking ritual--the
overall frame itself is a cold, tomblike sitting room at
Harvard in late evening, and the subframes are a "dim hot
airless room" in the "long still hot weary dead September afternoon"; a front gallery quiet and hushed in the wistaria twilight; a buggy at night leading to a house inhabited by ghosts
both dead and alive; a swamp campsite guarded by naked, wild
Negroes. And the ghosts so invoked do attain a kind of permanence, at least long enough to play out their legend again
for meaning-seeking Quentin. Rosa's "this demon" becomes

itself "enclosed by its effluvium of hell, its aura of unre-
generation," and "ogre-shape" and "djinn," and "the evil's
source and head" outlasting most of its victims. But in her
railing, self-pitying moments, Rosa momentarily forgets the
"ogre" as the forty-three-year-old object of her pure hate,
and even allows herself respect for Sutpen, his energy, and
stern self-consistency. There is that moment when the three
women sit at the mansion waiting for him to return from the
war:

> *"We talked of him ... of what he would do: how begin
> the Herculean task which we knew he would set himself,
> into which ... he would undoubtedly sweep us with the
> old ruthlessness whether we would or no."*[7]

And to this respect is added, in small measure, a touch of
pity that she can pass on to someone other than herself. This
strange mixture of respect and pity is most obvious when she
is describing the "old man's solitary fury" as he dismisses
the Ku Klux Klan delegation, the symbol of the "changed new
time" which Sutpen fights "as though he were trying to dam a
river with his bare hands and a shingle." Even in Rosa's
version Sutpen attains something out of the mythic mold, of
man's struggle to order his world, even when it is crumbling
and even when most of its collapse is attributable to his own
pride.
     The "demon" Sutpen is even more modified by Mr. Compson's
(and his father's) version of the story. Here the key is the
more human one of "ambition." The phrases that come to charac-
terize Sutpen in these versions are "gaunt and tireless driving,
that conviction for haste and of fleeing time," "grim and un-
flagging fury," "watchfulness" that only sporadically turns to
"braggadocio or belligerence"--he becomes, in short, "the slave
of his secret and furious impatience." He is the spiritual
solitary who, frustrated in his first attempts to build his
design in an alien land, without bitterness but with honed
haste makes his second attempt in an equally alien land. The
power he wields comes not in fact from an alliance with the
underworld (though certainly with the permissive detachment
of providence and the natural world), but from an attenuated
faith in himself. Mr. Compson remembers his father's impression: "Given the occasion and the need, this man can and
will do anything." Sutpen says that during his brief sojourn
in the West Indies he learned that any man could get rich if
he could boast cleverness and courage: "the latter of which I
believed that I possessed, the former of which I believed that
... I should learn." And his Mississippi venture, Mr. Compson
surmises, he takes seriously, watchfully, with

> "that unsleeping care which must have known that it
> could permit itself but one mistake; that alertness for

> measuring and weighing event against eventuality, circum-
> stance against human nature, his own fallible judgment
> and mortal clay against not only human but natural
> forces, choosing and discarding, compromising with his
> dream and his ambition." (p. 53)

The emphasis here is clear: Sutpen is mortal, he is fallible,
he is a compromiser. Whatever element of superhumanity is
generated by his legend, it comes from Sutpen's own knowledge
of his needs and methods for accomplishing them. He becomes
the self-made man in its apotheosis.

Here lies Faulkner's version of the epic hero—perhaps the
only version a modern American writer could bring to life.
It is only as the pieces of the legend are fitted together
that Sutpen's weaknesses as self-made hero are allowed to enter
the story. Our first vision of him, without the later undercutting, is at least one continuing strand of the legend—the
communal attitude of Jefferson:

> Immobile, bearded and hand palm-lifted the horseman sat;
> behind him the wild blacks and the captive architect
> huddled quietly, carrying in bloodless paradox the
> shovels and picks and axes of peaceful conquest. Then
> in the long unamaze Quentin seemed to watch them overrun
> suddenly the hundred square miles of tranquil and as-
> tonished earth and drag house and formal gardens violently
> out of the soundless Nothing and clap them down like cards
> upon a table beneath the up-palm immobile and pontific,
> creating the Sutpen's Hundred, the *Be Sutpen's Hundred*
> like the oldentime *Be Light*. (pp. 8-9)

He is a composite Achilles-Aeneas-Agamemnon—and more: he is
God Himself.[8] This incredible picture, in terms of a painting,
an etching, or a frieze, is a powerful stimulant for the community; it is only with the most severe diminution—much later—
that the picture is blurred. And we may be sure that for many
in Jefferson the picture is never really blurred.

Still another Sutpen emerges from the imaginary reconstruction by Quentin and Shreve; with partial understanding Shreve
whimsically echoes Rosa's "demon" Sutpen, but in an obvious
attempt to clarify this view, the two students call forth an
entire cluster of epithets and metaphors that will come closer
to striking the truth of Sutpen: "this Faustus, this demon,
this Beelzebub" escaping his harried Creditor, hoping with
"outrageous bravado" to fool the Creditor by the illusion that
"time had not elapsed." They even imagine Sutpen more an
"ancient stiff-jointed Pyramus" than a "widowed Agamemnon," a
"mad impotent old man" seeing himself as the "old wornout can-
non which realizes that it can deliver just one more fierce

shot and crumble to dust in its own furious blast and re-
coil."

The perplexed images of Sutpen reach their height in Chapter VI, where these youthful minds sit through all the stories
looking for a complete image. Appropriately, this is the only
version which asks questions of itself. The other views, while
partial, are products of long-consolidated musing: whether
outraged, bemused, or comprehending, they each offer the fragmented Sutpen to Quentin and Shreve with an assurance that ex-
cludes the necessity for further questions.

But Sutpen's own story, transmitted through Quentin's
grandfather, not only gives the legendary figure a history; it
also opens up an important area of his nature--his justness--
which proves to be the most elusive of his qualities and the
one most violently rejected by the narrators. Sutpen's original repudiation, the sin that is to reverberate all the way
through the stark mansion halls to 1910, is in his terms not so
much a consciously immoral act as a satisfactory legal arrangement. It is his innocence, of course, that can see such a
momentous act in those terms; and, though our realization of
this does not neutralize the wrong act, it does almost eliminate
the much touted demonic, consciously villainous side of his
nature.

After this, his own version, he stands as an unfortunate
creature without self-knowledge, without even knowing he needs
self-knowledge. Apparently there is no advance in moral mastery of himself from the night of the architect-hunt (when he
related the first part of his story to Quentin's grandfather)
to the time in General Compson's office thirty years later
(when he tells the second part). There is only a puzzled calm,
as if he "had long since given up any hope of understanding"
what went wrong with his design. There is no evidence in this
section that the repudiation of a wife and child cursed Sutpen's conscience; his innocence, his trust in his own brand
of rationality, told him what old General Compson had to admit
was "a good and valid claim"--that because he entered into a
marriage "in good faith, with no reservations as to his obscure
origin and material equipment," he could dissolve that marriage
when he discovered in his wife "not only reservation but actual misrepresentation."

The act of taking only twenty Negroes from all that he
might have taken--when he voluntarily relinquished the first
design in Haiti--had both "legal and moral sanction even if not
the delicate one of conscience." When judgment is injected
into this account, it comes not from the grandfather (at least
not directly), but from Quentin, who with no little tone of
exasperation, defines that special kind of Sutpenism: "that
innocence which believed that the ingredients of morality were

like the ingredients of pie or cake and once you had measured
them and balanced them and mixed them and put them into the
oven it was all finished and nothing but pie or cake could
come out." But to Sutpen, his own behavior is just:

> "I made no attempt to keep not only that which I might
> consider myself to have earned at the risk of my life
> but which had been given to me by signed testimonials,
> but on the contrary I declined and resigned all right
> and claim to this in order that I might repair whatever
> injustice I might be considered to have done by so pro-
> viding for the two persons whom I might be considered
> to have deprived of anything I might later possess: and
> this was agreed to, mind; agreed to between the two
> parties." (p. 264)

This legalistic morality does not take away the recognition
that a deeper morality is needed, but it does take away the
"monstrousness" of the act. And it is further alleviated when
(according to Shreve and Quentin) the cast-off wife enters into
a vicious and revengeful "design" of her own to destroy Sutpen's. Further, the very quality of Sutpen's speech is as
indicative of his strengths as of his radical weaknesses. Our
distaste for the self-conscious, florid bombast derived from
books and the swaggering painfully learned is considerably
lessened as it filters through this perpetual and clinging
innocence. (This brilliant suspension of characteristics is
not unlike Fitzgerald's Jay Gatsby, whose own innocence and
perplexity go far in neutralizing his vulgar commitment to
success.)

There is nothing of regret or even frustration when Sutpen
rides off to war; rather, it is another gesture apparently
confirming himself in his belief that he possessed something
that caused "destiny to shape itself to him like his clothes
did," a destiny that "fitted itself to him, to his innocence,
his pristine aptitude for platform drama and childlike heroic
simplicity." And it is in this particular role that he
achieves full heroic stature in the eyes of Wash Jones, who
sees him as a "fine proud man." He speculates that if "God
Himself was to come down and ride the natural earth, that's
what He would aim to look like." And just before his final
and only disillusionment, Wash indulges himself in a sincere
panegyric:

> "He is bigger than all them Yankees that killed us and
> ourn, that killed his wife and widowed his daughter
> and druv his son from home, that stole his niggers and
> ruined his land; bigger than this whole county that he
> fit for and in payment for which has brung him to keeping

> a little country store for his bread and meat; bigger
> than the scorn and denial which hit helt to his lips
> like the bitter cup in the Book. And how could I have
> lived nigh to him for twenty years without being touched
> and changed by him? Maybe I am not as big as he is and
> maybe I did not do any of the galloping. But at least
> I was drug along where he went. And me and him can still
> do hit and will ever so, if so be he will show me what
> he aims for me to do." (p. 287)

There is no evidence to support Quentin and Shreve's idea that
Wash saw through the shabby pretensions of the country store-
keeper or that he saw him as a "furious lecherous wreck." As
he has faith in the heroic figure who once galloped about on a
black thoroughbred, so he has faith that that hero's association with his granddaughter will turn out honorably. Mr. Compson explains the reason for such a faith when he says that
Wash's morality was "a good deal like Sutpen's, that told him
he was right in the face of all fact and usage and everything
else." Certainly Wash's attitude toward Sutpen, coming as it
does in Sutpen's inglorious years, cannot be ignored. The
glory of both his character and his accomplishments trails
horizontally all the way from the battlefields to the crossroads store and vertically all through the layers of acceptance
and faith up to the very moment of murder and suicide.

Sutpen's refusal to recognize Bon is again a failure in
morality; it is not, however, a question of hate, either personal (for Bon as "avenging" son) or impersonal (for Bon as
the vessel of mingled blood). It is not a question of love,
for there is little evidence to suppose Sutpen felt love for
any of his children or either of his wives. It is a question
of his amoral rationality--that cool assessment of what would
and what would not be "adjunctive or incremental" to his design. In a very real sense, then, there is strength as well
as weakness in Sutpen's consistency and singlemindedness.
He is wrong, but he is impressive. His isolation carries with
it an imperious air throughout all his relationships with
others--his solitary fact-finding trip to New Orleans, his
arch wedding ceremony with Ellen, and aloof hospitality to
the community in the half-finished mansion, his curt dismissal
of the Klan delegation. Even his most impious acts have an
air of stolid impersonality; his very obduracy is removed from
the brunt of human passions and elevated to a peak of dis-
interested immunity.

Because of the nature of the narrators, it is easy to forget the admirable qualities of Sutpen: his refusal to accept
neighborly favors when he cannot return them, his practical
demonstrations of superiority over his slaves by sportsmanlike

contests, his steadfast though puzzled search for personal
fault rather than the easier act of blaming fate. Sutpen's
fall is the death and dismemberment of the demigod, and if he
cannot command his own reassembling and resurrection, there
are plenty of ordinary mortals who gladly confer immortality
on him by rising to sing of his glory. But, however strenuously
invoked, his summoning remains partial; though he is declared
in "this shadowy attenuation of time" to be "possessing now
heroic proportions," he still hovers "shadowy, inscrutable and
serene"--a satisfactory state for Mr. Compson, who as a sentimental, bemused cynic is more comfortable with these figures
as ghosts. Mr. Compson recognizes that the indulgent pleasure
he gets in invoking these shades can never be equaled by a
complete comprehension of the legend. He takes refuge in
contrasting the unheroic present with the heroic past with
all its legendary attributes: "not dwarfed and involved but
distinct, uncomplex" people who had "the gift of living once
or dying once instead of being diffused and scattered creatures."
     Mr. Compson contributes not a little to the wormy tone of
this story. Defeated himself, he revels in the principle of
Fate, which he characterizes as the grim equalizer of all ambition and assertion of human will. From no other narrator
do we get so much romanticized glorification of Fate. It is
not surprising that he salutes the Sutpens as heroic. As long
as their defeat is so luxuriantly sung, the futile effort for
victory itself is worth a chorus or two. Both are of a single
piece: if seeing Fate, doom, and a general curse as an answer
for the Sutpen fall is easy, seeing the grand resistance to
those inexorables is even easier. What is to Faulkner's credit
is that something of heroic dimensions is visible when we cut
through the Compson personality. Perhaps the undercutting by
an easy cynicism strengthens the heroic image of Sutpen, for
what does remain is earned (just as in Rosa's account) and,
with all views assimilated, remarkably substantial for a ghost
in a legend.

II

     Another of the controlling elements of epic is its narra-
tion. The story is told rather than acted, and the telling
process is a conscious one, which means that the point of view
is clearly something other than sophisticated omniscience.
The felt presence of the storyteller is never far away from
the events he is relating. C.S. Lewis has commented at length
on the calculated, formalized quality of epic narration, the
frank absence of subtle, soothing, and skillful devices to
advance the pretense that a fiction is not really taking place,
that it is "real" and that the listener is in a semiconscious

state of empathic rapport.[9] A distinguishing mark of epic narration is the ritual of storytelling itself; participation in
a ritual demands a full knowledge of content and procedure.
Spontaneity is not the yardstick by which the success of the
narrative is measured, though surprise and modification can
often contribute to the narrative. Instead of spontaneity,
the key is solemnity. The mythic proportions of the story
require that the storyteller give the impression from the outset
that his tale will be impressive and extraordinary, and this
impression must be transmitted to the listener, who absorbs
the sense that something special is being done.

Harvey Breit may be correct when he says that of all Faulkner's novels, *Absalom* "appears to be the most personal."[10] But
in one sense it is the most impersonal. The bard-audience participation by the reader is at once removed and capable of
further participation. Several times we are made aware of the
fact that the Sutpen legend is not such a "painfully secret
history" except for Rosa, that the various gaps in the legend
are no more than the necessary lacunae in any legend of such
proportions. Quentin's obsessive search for the links that
connect the strands of the legend is his own private torturing,
and the *I-don't-hate-it* speech comes only at the end of the
recounting. For much of the book we (and even his roommate)
follow the legend on its own terms without connecting it to
the narrator's private anxieties. (The fact that Quentin commits suicide over issues similar to those that troubled Henry
Sutpen is secondary, and even allusions to this anxiety Faulkner
omits as inorganic to this specific work.) The gaps in the
legend are important to Quentin the synthesizer, but many of
these are nothing more than familiar or inferred material
viewed suddenly from a different perspective. Faulkner does
not tell us, and it is not especially important, exactly how
much of the story is common knowledge; but it is reasonable to
expect Jefferson, on whom the arrival, career, and death of
Sutpen created such an impact, to hold the bulk of the legend
in perpetuity almost in the manner of a single consciousness.
Part of Mr. Compson's narration, in fact, is the point of view
of the town. Only the first few lines of the story are necessary to trigger Quentin's conscious-unconscious repository:

> It was a part of his twenty years' heritage of breathing
> the same air and hearing his father talk about the man
> Sutpen; a part of the town's--Jefferson's--eighty years'
> heritage of the same air which the man himself had
> breathed.... Quentin had grown up with that; the mere
> names were interchangeable and almost myriad ... he was
> not a being, an entity, he was a commonwealth. (pp. 11-
> 12).

The communal ubiquity of the story is further impersonalized by the complex *in medias res* and narration-within-narration. The frame (Quentin the narrator and Shreve the audience) which controls and orders each of the secondary narrations is not perceptible until after the first evocation, which recounts in miniature in less than a half-page the Sutpen legend through the building of the mansion. From the beginning, the story, whose major substance is gathered about the axis of powerful personalities, is related at two removes from its participants; at one point it is related at four removes (Sutpen-to-General Compson-to-Mr. Compson-to-Quentin-to-Shreve). This narrative distance provides a kind of protective cushion that mutes the confused and commingled cries sparked by intense, personal dilemmas.

The ghost imagery, besides its primary thematic function, has a structural purpose also, in that the horrible and incredible seem less so if performed by ghosts ("the long silence of notpeople, in notlanguage"). The insistence that the legendary cast of characters is ghostly runs like a leitmotif throughout the novel. The setting itself is of a piece with its characters: Shreve sees it as "the deep South dead since 1865 and peopled with garrulous outraged baffled ghosts, listening, having to listen, to one of the ghosts which had refused to lie still even longer than most had, telling him about ghost-times." Likewise, Quentin sees himself as "a barracks filled with stubborn back-looking ghosts." And in a moment of ironic whimsy, Mr. Compson reminds Quentin of the historical reason why Rosa wants to tell him the story: "Years ago we in the South made our women into ladies. Then the War came and made the ladies into ghosts. So what else can we do, being gentlemen, but listen to them being ghosts?"

Shreve's perplexity at the conclusion of the story has led many readers to conclude that the Fall of the House of Sutpen, while certainly mythic and legendary, is so firmly a product of its environment that it is merely another rehashing of the story of the ruined Southern homeland. Certainly the identification of the Sutpen legend to the overall Southern myth (whatever that may be) is necessary, just as it is necessary to insist that Quentin is a Southerner telling a Southern story to a Canadian. The point of view of the central, ordering narrator is important in *Absalom* in a way that it is not with such a similar narrator as Conrad's Marlow. Quentin, steeped in the particular myth, has a kind of commitment (however ambivalent) that widens and deepens the meaning of the story. He can accept the incredulity of it because he is part of it. If for us any larger meaning emerges from the recital of the legend, it depends considerably upon Quentin, who submits his involvement, however ill-understood, to the refining fires of

.a perspective and an awareness. Like the traditional epic
narrator, he expresses the feelings of the people of his region. Though his intellectualizing goes beyond the bardic
role, he yet reflects the group-consciousness of his own time
and country. To push back the limiting local significance of
his story is not necessary for him, since he is still a narrator, or for Shreve, since he is still the audience and perhaps like any audience only half understands the import of the
story. To the reader is left this act of seizing the local
crisis and expanding its moral import, adding value that comes
with our expanding realization until (to use Morton Zabel's
comments on Conrad) the crisis "comes to include not only the
personal fate of the character but the fate of the society,
world, or moral universe he inhabits."[11]

The remarkable achievement in *Absalom* is that the frontier
of this added dimension is reached by both Quentin and Shreve.
And the choice of Shreve, as one utterly alien to the consciousness of both the narrator and the hero he sings about, is
necessary to prevent the legend from degenerating into a personal soul-searching quest. His presence is felt strongly
even before his own contribution to the legend--such quiet
insertions as his expletives that lace the storytelling, the
detail of snow on his overcoat sleeve, and the real stimulus
for the story long after the beginning: *"Tell about the South."*
Quentin responds to that invitation but not without Shreve's
interruptions, exclamations of disbelief, modifications of
previous statements, and occasional recapitulations. They
are reminders that the narrative has never been removed from
the basic physical situation of epic: the ritual of the storyteller and his audience. By this conscious referral to the
overall frame, Faulkner is assuring its continuing relevance,
and whatever emphatic identification the reader comes to make
with the story must be made in terms of that primary frame.

Even the frames for the subnarrations are cast in this
formal shape. Both Rosa's and Mr. Compson's sessions with
Quentin are not casual either in their inception or execution:
their stories are told with an air that makes even the act of
telling something memorable. This is made clear not only by
the atmosphere and the teller's consciously heightened rhetoric
but also by the respectful response of the listener (as in
Quentin's "Yessum" and occasional questions for clarification).
One of the subnarrations (Sutpen's story to General Compson)
goes so far as to duplicate the frame of the primitive epic
origins--the bard sitting by an open fire reciting his version
of a story to a semicircle of listeners. These subordinate
narrations--they can almost be called cycles of a tale--at once
reinforce the overall frame and are restrained by it. A subtle
dissolution of the overall frame, once it had secured the

reader's attention, would have made the entire work one of
some brand of "historical novel," and obviously *Absalom* is
concerned with a story in which that category is practically
meaningless. Past and present coexist in a kind of permanent
but ever-modifying continuum. The identification of Quentin
and Shreve with Bon and Henry near the end of the story is
done legitimately within terms of the storyteller-audience
situation and as such is a kind of objectification that fore-
stalls a bogus and effortless identification by the larger
audience. For the reader the process is emanative rather than
self-absorptive, ritualistic rather than psycho-dramatic.

That Quentin is intended to be elevated from private status
to Hierophant is not only revealed by the structure that scaf-
folds the story but also reinforced by the grandeur of the style
itself. Edgar Whan has seen this depersonalized speech the vehicle for carrying the "quasi-religious, mythic tone," a tone that
derives "from the feeling that some force from another world
or some mystic experience has intruded itself upon the characters and they, like the tribal shaman, can articulate this
experience most nearly by ritual language."[12] Even the conventional chapter divisions suggest the "pausing for breath" between lays.

III

That Faulkner's prose style in *Absalom* is stately, even to
the point of "torturousness," has been noted all too frequently.
The reason for the torturousness lies, of course, in the subject.

Without flirting with the fallacy of imitative form, we
should still insist on an organic relationship between matter
and manner. Certainly Faulkner achieves that relationship in
Absalom. We know, for instance, that he makes the choric
quality of the novel rest squarely on the ruined homeland
theme; but once we agree that Sutpen's destruction is a paradigm of the homeland's fate, we are not compelled to stop there.
Neither should we lightly seize upon "disorders of the age" and
"social collapse" and "decay of traditional morality" as the
theme of the expanded paradigm, for such phrases smack of the
grab-bag comprehensiveness that can include James T. Farrell,
Graham Greene, Jack Kerouac, and most of the pot-boiling pro-
testers as well as Faulkner.

The Sutpen legend posits an anatomy of love: (a) its absence, (b) its disguises (as duty, commitment, honor), (c) its
dangers. The necessity for love, even with its elusiveness,
is a perpetual concern of both Shreve and Quentin, which we
can see in their tortured, tentative attempts to define love,
the rejection of those as inadequate, and the haunting non-
resolution at the end. But the legend plays out the theme
despite the lack of its adequate formulation by the characters.

   The absence of love in Sutpen is demonstrated by his inability to see anyone or anything as more than object; his
design is to be furthered by an accumulation of objects--a respectable wife, slaves, an architect, children, even the re-
spected tradition of the land and its people. The disguises
of love are revealed in the suffering and expiation of the
children, which for Henry begins with the flight to New Orleans
and which for Judith begins with Bon's death at the gate; in
Rosa's outraged departure from Sutpen's Hundred and in Wash's
murder of Sutpen, which repudiates Sutpen's concept of humanity
as object; in Clytie's mission to assume physical responsibility
of Bon's son and in her caretaking years at the disintegrating
mansion. The dangers of love are demonstrated in the complex
spectrum of the Judith-Bon-Henry relationship.

   Not only is the Sutpen legend structurally initiated *in
medias res*, but the dominant pattern of feeling, of attitude,
toward the legend is also established in the beginning sentence,
which in its highly conscious use of sonorous, mood-making
words enriched by open vowels and liquids is not unlike Poe:

>   From a little after two oclock until almost sundown
>   of the long still hot weary dead September afternoon
>   they sat in what Miss Coldfield still called the office
>   because her father had called it that--a dim hot airless
>   room with the blinds all closed and fastened for forty-
>   three summers because when she was a girl someone had
>   believed that light and moving air carried heat and that
>   dark was always cooler, and which (as the sun shone
>   fuller and fuller on that side of the house) became
>   latticed with yellow slashes full of dust motes which
>   Quentin thought of as being flecks of the dead old dried
>   paint itself blown inward from the scaling blinds as
>   wind might have blown them. (p. 7)

The compulsion for the furious rushing of the narration that
dominates the later chapters is already suggested here in a
setting appropriate to the calling up of ghosts that will be
the chief activity throughout. It foreshadows the syntactical
complexity that will soon emerge--the alteration and over-
lapping of time, the delayed modification to take in not only
more than one time but also more than one narrator, the suspension of description for including peripheral material or
meanings. This opening sentence also begins the dominant
technique in *Absalom*, a contrivance whereby phrases and sentences enter the reader's consciousness in a lump rather than
sequentially, and the sequential rearranging is done unconsciously as the narration progresses with other masses of
material. The reader accepts description both impressionistic
("dim coffin-smelling gloom sweet and oversweet with the twice-

bloomed wistaria") and objectified ("the wan haggard face
watched him above the faint triangle of lace at wrists and
throat from the too tall chair in which she resembled a crucified child") almost simultaneously. Both bardic technique and
style are refined to the most ambitious limits of language.

The ways in which separate episodes thread in and out of
the conscious strands of the narration to meet as a single,
unified tale reflect another characteristic common to epic
poetry. The traditional epic hero, unlike a purely tragic
protagonist, is rarely seen as a complex personality at any
given moment; at times he may appear to be a creature of one
dimension, or worse, a creature whose single dimension is
undercut by apparent inconsistencies. The bardic poet, concentrating on the immediate episode, neglecting chronology and
obvious coherence, even concludes by introducing still another
prospect that suggests future action. In *Absalom* the coda in
which we learn that Henry, now old and mad, has returned to the
ruined mansion, is prepared for long before before we know there
is even to be such a coda. In Chapter V Quentin is caught up
out of his trancelike depression with Rosa's roundabout explanation for the night ride to Sutpen's Hundred:

> "There's something in that house."
> "In that house? It's Clytie. Dont she--"
> "No. Something living in it. Hidden in it. It has
> been there for four years, living hidden in that house."
> (p. 172)

This closes the chapter and the matter is suspended rather than
resolved while in Chapter VI the entire story up to that point
is recapitulated by Shreve, and we get the expansion of earlier
details. Shreve presses Quentin on what he found at the mansion
but interrupts himself with "For God's sake wait." This waiting
covers Chapters VII and VIII, which introduce General Compson's story of Sutpen and advance the Judith-Bon-Henry dilemma.
Appropriately, this major item of suspense is resolved only in
Chapter IX, near the end of the novel. This same principle
is used for other important points in the story.

One of the most brilliant modifications of an epic device
which Faulkner applies to *Absalom* is his treatment of the
classical improvisational formulae, those sets of descriptive
words and epithets that were used normally with little change
whenever standard situations occurred or, more practically,
when the poet felt the need to fill in with familiar phrases
while remembering what came next. Faulkner uses these formulae as key verbal units to (1) help particularize the sub-
narrator in character and speech, and (2) unify the particular
narrative segment by rhetorical variation of repetitive phrases.

In Chapter II, where the central advance in the Sutpen
narrative revolves about his marriage to Ellen, the wedding is

described partly in terms of Ellen's tears. The first phrase
Mr. Compson uses is "Ellen seems to have entered the church
that night out of weeping as though out of rain"; a few pages
later it recurs as "For a time Ellen walked out of the weeping,
the tears, and so into the church," and "she was weeping again
now; it did, indeed, rain on that marriage." This pattern is
reinforced by numerous brief insertions--"to see her weep,"
"where the tears stopped," "the tears won," "the tears again,
the same tears even, the same rain." In Chapter III, Ellen's
wedded life is described in terms of butterfly imagery, where
the central metaphor occupies almost an entire page. But this
metaphor is formularized also in rhetorical rhythm: "the woman
who had quitted home and kin on a flood of tears and ... produced two children and then rose like the swamp-hatched butterfly." This is continued with "Ellen the butterfly, from beneath whom without warning the very sunbuoyed air had been with-
drawn," "the butterfly, the moth caught in a gale and blown
against a wall and clinging there beating feebly," "the clinging
moth, even alive, would have been incapable now of feeling any-
more."

     In Chapter IV, much of the story concerns Henry's flight
with Bon--in Mr. Compson's formulae: "Because Henry loved Bon.
He repudiated blood birthright and material security for his
sake, for the sake of this man who was at least an intending
bigamist even if not an out and out blackguard." This is
varied and expanded with "Because he loved Bon," "Because he
loved Judith," "Henry's violent repudiation of his father and
his birthright," "Yes, he loved Bon, who seduced him as surely
as he seduced Judith," "still loving Bon, the man to whom he
gave four years of probation," "Henry had formally abjured his
home and birthright," "the youth and the man, the youth deprived
twice now of his birthright," "the mentor, the man for whom he
had repudiated not only blood and kin but food and shelter and
clothing too." The pattern in these cases is the same: it reflects the narrator's mind and speech; Mr. Compson's gentle,
nostalgic rhetoric reveals an indulgence in words, pauses, and
repetitions as much as in the wistaria, the twilight, and the
cigar smoke.

     The same use of formulae by Rosa results in a different
kind of rhetoric. In the lengthy apologia her recurrent phrases
often consist of "I, self-mesmered fool" and "I, the dreamer"
in the earlier part when she tells how Clytie stopped her on
the stairs. When she comes to tell of her sexless puberty,
the phrases are "a pervading everywhere of wistaria (I was fourteen then)" and "a vintage year of wistaria" and "fourteen in
years if they could have been called years." When she tells
of her abbreviated and brutal courtship with Sutpen, the phrases
are "Oh, I hold no brief for myself," "I claim no brief, no
pity, who did not answer 'I will' not because I was not asked,"

and "No, I hold no brief, ask no pity." The stage-by-stage process is marked by a different set of dominant repetitive phrases, each one demonstrating a different aspect of her personality.

To cite one other example, the second half of Shreve and Quentin's reconstruction of the Judith-Bon-Henry plot is marked by a series of *tableau-vivants* which are unified by the phrase "think of" preceding each one: "And Jesus, think of him, Bon," and "Jesus, think how Henry must have talked," and "Think of the two of them." These are missing from the first half, where the manufactured narration is identified as imaginary with the more leisurely "maybe." With the growing creativeness, the narrative begins to make imaginative leaps, and the frequent "think of" phrase reflects the growing incantatory nature of the chapter, until its climax with Shreve's chanting, romanticized explanation for Bon's photograph of his wife and child when Henry kills him.

Such minor points of epic as the precisely treated arrivals and departures are reflected in Faulkner's reiterated and varied stress on the coming of Sutpen (mentioned or described four times in Chapter I and expanded by Mr. Compson at the beginning of Chapter II) and the repudiation ride of Henry and Bon to New Orleans. The close attention the bardic poet devotes to the hero's weapons, dress, and horse has its counterpart in Sutpen's arrival ("the strong spent horse ... and a small saddlebag ... and the two pistols ... with the butts worn smooth as pickhandles and which he used with the precision of knitting needles"). We later see Sutpen in full Confederate uniform and even more closely associated with his horses. The familiar feasts and entertainments of the epic, with their grandiose descriptions of eating and drinking and their illustration of the prince's generosity in his splendid house make ironic appearances in *Absalom*. Parties of townsmen gather in the unfinished rooms of the mansion for drinking, card-playing, and hunting meets; the Coldfields visit after Ellen's marriage to Sutpen; and Sutpen and Wash meet regularly under the scuppernong arbor for ritualized drinking sessions.

A reading of *Absalom, Absalom!* as epic, then, does not necessitate a rigid categorization, for certainly many traditional aspects of epic as a specialized genre will not be found in Faulkner's novel. Nor should they be. If Faulkner's novel were an epic in this sense, it would be so as recognizable form just as we recognize *The Iliad* and *Paradise Lost* as epics. Indeed, the purpose in reading *Absalom* as epic is to avoid such a tidy reduction of the novel to a narrower classification. To force the novel peremptorily into the category as epic, however stamped with grandeur it may be, is to follow the pattern of those who commandeer it into the ranks of "social

allegory" or "Gothic myth." All such efforts suggest an annoy-
ance if not contempt for Faulkner as an independent artist who
is as eclectic in methods of execution as he is in materials
and themes.

Of all the major works *Absalom* is the only one (until *A
Fable*, the title of which suggests directions for reading it)
where the customary humor is sharply curtailed. The occasional
whimsy in Mr. Compson and Shreve's impatience are so low-keyed
that their function as comic relief is questionable. This
novel comes four years after the first great outpouring of the
Yoknapatawpha myth. This suggests that Faulkner had made a
thoughtful reconsideration of the myth, which made possible yet
a more effective version. The prose style in *Absalom* marks the
high point in a manner carefully wrought, consciously weighted,
and tonally controlled. This style (which has more inner
variation than has been generally granted) has been accused
of being "echoes of a master ventriloquist rather than [con-
sisting of] individual voices attuned to Jamesian distinctions,"[13]
and though this is true, it is not a vice. A Jamesian distinction between narrators in *Absalom* would be so out of place as
to wreck the entire balance of the structure and distort the
massive centrality of the legend. It is necessary for Faulkner
to keep all modulations of the various contributors under the
control of a master style. *The Sound and the Fury* is Faulkner's
accomplishment in clear-cut stylistic differences (there is no
reason why even *they* should be Jamesian). But in *Absalom* he
is doing something else.

The story is narrated, and the narrator is both a public
voice as well as Quentin Compson, the morbid, too-sensitive
suicide-to-be. No other major novel in the series posits an
action, a theme, on so high an eminence and on so broad an ex-
panse. Nor does any other of the Yoknapatawpha novels attempt
a full-scale characterization of such scope with all the atten-
dant legendary attributes of a mythic hero dominating that
action or illustrating that theme. For these reasons it seems
mandatory that we reject any attempt to read *Absalom, Absalom!*
minimally; its "category" must be sufficiently flexible and inclusive so that it will not only incorporate minimal readings
but also consolidate and transmute them under its governing design. The design that comes closest to achieving this is the
epic.

NOTES

    1. "*Absalom, Absalom!*: The Definition of Innocence,"
Sewanee Review, 59 (Autumn 1951), 544.

2. See particularly Ilse Dusoir Lind's excellent essay, "The Design and Meaning of *Absalom, Absalom!*," *PMLA*, 70 (December, 1955), 887-912.

3. Though she does not explore the issue from a structural standpoint, Ilse Dusoir Lind says that the analogies of characters suggest that "the Oedipus trilogy might have served as a general guide in the drafting" of the Sutpen story. But she adds—rightly—that impressive analogies also exist between these characters and "epic Biblical figures" who suffer "the visitations of Divine justice upon third and fourth generations." ("The Design and Meaning of *Absalom, Absalom!*, 889-890.)

4. *The English Epic and Its Background* (New York, 1954), pp. 530-531.

5. Although Olga W. Vickery discusses with penetration both theme and structure in the novel, she rarely sees these elements working as an artistic whole, and *Absalom* becomes merely "an extension" of *The Sound and the Fury* in technique (multiple narrators) and theme (the ambiguity of truth). See *The Novels of William Faulkner: A Critical Interpretation* (Baton Rouge, 1959), p. 102. Hyatt H. Waggoner is more nearly correct when he says that *Absalom* "has no close precedent, even in Faulkner's own works." See *William Faulkner: From Jefferson to the World* (Lexington, 1959), p. 148.

6. *Epic and Romance: Essays on Medieval Literature*, 2nd ed. (New York, 1908), p. 16.

7. William Faulkner, *Absalom, Absalom!* (New York, 1951), p. 157. All subsequent references are to this Modern Library edition.

8. Sutpen also possesses the godlike function of naming. As Mr. Compson observes, "He named Clytie as he named them all, the one before Clytie and Henry and Judith even, with that same robust and sardonic temerity, naming with his own mouth his own ironic fecundity of dragon's teeth." Mr. Compson states that Sutpen intended Clytie to be Cassandra, but inadequate schooling confused the names.

9. *A Preface to Paradise Lost* (London, 1942), Chapters VI-VII.

10. Introduction, Modern Library edition, p. ix.

11. Morton D. Zabel, *Craft and Character: Text, Method, and Vocation in Modern Fiction* (New York, 1957), p. 219.

12. Edgar W. Whan, "*Absalom, Absalom!* as Gothic Myth," *Perspective*, 3 (Autumn 1950), 200.

13. Robert H. Zoellner, "Faulkner's Prose Style in *Absalom, Absalom!*," *American Literature*, 30 (January, 1959), 491.

WHAT HAPPENS IN *ABSALOM, ABSALOM!*?

Floyd C. Watkins

Factual accuracy and consistency in a work of literature
are not generally regarded as major criteria of the success
of the author. *King Lear*, perhaps Shakespeare's greatest
tragedy, contains many minor errors and inconsistencies. The
mistaken identity of the discoverer of the Pacific in Keats's
"On First Looking into Chapman's Homer" is not of great poetic
significance. Many inconsistencies often slip by the reader
unnoticed. I had read Hawthorne's "The Minister's Black Veil"
several times before a friend pointed out a striking discrepancy. The Reverend Hooper visits his "plighted wife" in
her home. After the visit has ended, she leaves! The story,
of course, is not damaged irreparably, but the smile at the
first recognition of this unintentional comedy may ruin for a
moment the unity of tone.

Deliberate error and planned inconsistency have become
significant in some modern fiction. The detective story or
the mystery relies heavily on accurate and detailed information.
Such a work attempts to mislead a reader as much as possible
until the denouement and then to explain the inexplicable and
to reconcile with great ease all the facts which have seemed
almost impossibly unreconcilable. The pattern of this puzzling
kind of fiction always was attractive to William Faulkner,
especially in such works as *Intruder in the Dust*, *Knight's
Gambit*, and *Absalom, Absalom!*. In other ways, also, Faulkner
has been intrigued by fact and detail. No construction of
interrelated works in modern fiction is so elaborate as the
short stories and novels about Yoknapatawpha County. Faulkner
seems to have carried about in his head the whole history,
folklore, and gossip for a century and a half of his invented
private domain. Small episodes in the early fiction become
dominant plots in the later works. In the last few years

From Modern Fiction Studies, *13 (Spring 1967), pp. 79-87. Reprinted by permission of* Modern Fiction Studies, © *1967 by
Purdue Research Foundation, West Lafayette, Indiana 47907.*

numerous scholarly genealogies, glossaries, and character in-
dexes have been compiled for the reader interested in the in-
terrelationships between different works. Each story and each
novel may be read as separate and independent or as part of an
elaborate construction of a complex society. The reader may
wonder at the marvelous tangles of facts and people, or he may
be struck by Faulkner's careless forgettings, changes, and inconsistencies.

In many respects *Absalom, Absalom!* is unique in modern fiction. More than any other work of fiction I know, it is filled
with errors and inconsistencies which the author intends to
remain uncorrected and unresolved. It is almost as if Faulkner
were asking the reader to take the few facts and the many conjectures and to tell his own story. Several narrators in the
novel attempt to reconstruct the events in the life of a family
over a period of nearly a century; even when deeds are known,
the narrators must hunt for the motives; no narrator is reliable (Faulkner has said, indeed, that the facts are unreliable
and that he only hopes that the reader can arrive at the truth
never expressed in the novel); a major narrator of *Absalom,
Absalom!* (Quentin Compson) is also a central figure in *The
Sound and the Fury*, and it is obvious that there are inexplicable relationships between his own life and problems and
the events which he conjectures about the people in *Absalom,
Absalom!*.

Any attempted summary of the plot of *Absalom* is therefore
necessarily impossible. Numerous plots need to be summarized
and guessed at. If no condensation can do the novel justice,
unfortunately it is difficult to write about it without giving
some kind of view of the events as a means of exposition.
Quentin Compson, his father, Miss Rosa Coldfield, and the
Canadian Shreve McCannon tell a story about the family of
Thomas Sutpen. A poor white in Virginia, Sutpen was turned
away from the front door of a plantation; this affront made
him determined to build his own plantation and to found a dynasty; he married a woman who bore him a son; then he discovered
that she had Negro blood and put her aside; he married a woman
from a respectable but poor family, and she bore him a son and
a daughter; the son by the first marriage wooed the daughter
by the second; after years of debate and waiting, the second
son killed the first to stop the marriage and then became a
fugitive; left without a male heir, Sutpen proposed to the
sister of his deceased second wife, then impulsively asked her
to breed with him and promised marriage if there was a son; he
did breed with the granddaughter of a poor white on his plantation, but refused to marry her when the offspring was a daughter;
the poor white killed him. At the end of the novel the only
living descendant of Thomas Sutpen is a mulatto idiot, the
grandson of Sutpen's son by his first wife.

Always the novel returns to one basic question: did Thomas
Sutpen's second son kill the first because he had a quadroon
mistress, or because the marriage to his sister would be incestuous, or because of the miscegenation? Although the reader
cannot arrive at absolute certainty, the critic can hardly deal
with the novel without facing and attempting to answer this
question of motive. It is central. But the conjectures of
the narrators in the novel about this point merely establish
a pattern of conflicting facts and motives. And the inconsistencies in the main point extend as a principle into small
details and events in the novel, even into minutiae. Most of
the discrepancies have been overlooked and ignored. Their
kind and number, however, are amazing.

Many of the inconsistencies and conflicting stories may be
plants by the author to suggest the unreliability of his narrators, who have little real information and who wish to probe
the Sutpen family for the smallest facts and the deepest motives.
A narrator's error of fact may suggest that he also makes errors of interpretation and opinion. Mr. Compson, whose account
seems at first as accurate as such hearsay could be, makes
many errors. Details of his narrative directly conflict with
facts reported by Miss Rosa Coldfield. His conjectures, indeed, sometimes contradict Miss Rosa's memory of her own experience. Her aunt, who lived with the Coldfields after the
death of the mother, eloped four years before Charles Bon's
summer visit to the Sutpen plantation, Mr. Compson says (p. 70);
according to Miss Rosa's report (and she ought to know) the
elopement came during the same year as Bon's visit (p. 145).[1]
The timing of Miss Rosa's going to live with her niece, Judith
Sutpen, and the mulatto Clytie is also in dispute. Mr. Compson
first implies that Rosa went to Sutpen's soon after her father
died in 1864 (p. 59); twenty-eight pages later in the same conversation with Quentin he says that she "didn't go out there
at once" (p. 87). Miss Rosa herself says that she stayed for
food and shelter after she went to Sutpen's on the night when
Henry killed Charles Bon in 1865 (p. 153). In ignorance or
carelessness, Mr. Compson states that Rosa saw Bon's body (p.
104); later Miss Rosa tells Quentin, *"I never saw him. I never
even saw him dead"* (p. 146). Acting as a sort of pallbearer, she
*"tried to take the full weight of the coffin to prove ... that
he was really in it."* She *"could not tell"* (pp. 150-151). At
any rate, Miss Rosa at some time came to stay at Sutpen's.
When Sutpen returned from the Civil War and saw Miss Rosa,
his sister-in-law, she recalled that he had to be told who she
was because he did not remember her (p. 159). But when Quentin
remembers his father's account of the return, Sutpen immediately
recognizes Miss Rosa and greets her and Clytie in the same
breath (p. 277).

These errors, in direct conflict with Miss Rosa's memory
of what she experienced, prove the extent of Mr. Compson's
conjecturings, and they reveal his imagination. At different
times he also tells differing versions of the same story.
Once, for example, he says that Colonel Sutpen brought his
wife's tombstone "in the regimental forage wagon from Charles-
ton, South Carolina ..." (p. 126). . Later, he says, Sutpen
bought tombstones for his wife and himself while he was in
Virginia, "ordered them from Italy," carried them around with
his regiment for a year, hauled them to Gettysburg, "then
through the Cumberland Gap and down through the Tennessee
mountains ..., and into Mississippi ..." (pp. 188-190). The
second and more elaborate account treats with more exaggeration
Sutpen's foolhardy persistence, and it may indicate how a
story grows as Mr. Compson turns it over in his mind. At
another point either Mr. Compson's arithmetic falls far short
of his imagination, or his carelessness becomes extreme, or
Faulkner himself nods. "After Mr Coldfield died in '64, Miss
Rosa moved out to Sutpen's Hundred to live with Judith. She
was twenty then ..." (p. 59). Four lines later, in the next
sentence, "She (Miss Rosa) was born in 1845...." If the year
of her birth is correct, she was at most only nineteen in
1864, possibly only eighteen. Why should both Mr. Compson
and Faulkner be so aware of age and years and yet lapse immediately into egregious error? Is this subtle characterization, a point to plant doubts about Mr. Compson's narration,
or some sort of slip by the author?

Shreve's flippancy, his insensitivity at times, his modern-
ity, and his remoteness from the South and from the life he
talks about are all reflected in his errors, which are more
serious than Mr. Compson's. That he should tell part of the
story of Sutpen, know the details of Sutpen's rejection of
Wash Jones's granddaughter, Milly, after she bore him a child,
and know about the death of Sutpen and Jones—all these
without recognizing that the problem was Sutpen's disappointment and callousness when he learned the child was a girl—
that he should still have to be told by Quentin that the child
was not a son is an indication of his inability to comprehend
Sutpen's motive, Quentin's feelings, and the myth he is helping
to reconstruct. Shreve's error about the sex of the child is
one of the most conspicuous errors by a narrator in the novel.
Yet until Quentin says "It was a girl" the reader is also misled
while Faulkner dribbles out information and then closes a chapter with a fact of startling import.

Shreve also makes other mistakes. Sutpen, Quentin says,
did not tell Grandfather Compson "whether the voyage was hard
or not" (p. 244). A little later Shreve disregards this statement, or greatly distorts it, and says that Sutpen "didn't

remember how he got to Haiti" (p. 255). He also makes a
doubtful conjecture about the finding of Sutpen's body after
Wash killed him. Quentin says that Judith sent a "half-grown
boy" to look for Sutpen, and he found the body in "mid-
afternoon" (p. 285); Shreve had surmised that "they" found him
"that night" (p. 185). Twice Quentin and Shreve report that
Bon was wounded in the War, but later they surmise that Henry
was actually the one wounded. They have little evidence, they
never know, and the reader's guess as to which was wounded is
possibly as good as Shreve's or Quentin's or perhaps even
Faulkner's. Here again the novel may aim to make the close
reader puzzle out his own plot.

Of the four main narrators of the novel, only Miss Rosa
has known the central characters. Her testimony, therefore,
should be the most accurate, but she too is unreliable. When
Sutpen proposed that they breed and then marry only if the
child was a son, she says, "*he had not thought of it until
that moment* ..." (p. 168). Three pages later she completely
contradicts this surmise: when she heard the proposition,
"*she realized like thunderclap that it must have been in his
mind for a day, a week, even a month maybe* ..." (p. 171). She
does not indicate here a change in what she had thought. Both
views may have lived in contradiction in Miss Rosa's outraged
mind for more than four decades. What she reports, however,
often is the only standard by which to judge the facts in the
narrations of Quentin, Mr. Compson, and Shreve. Even when her
memory and her facts are right, her interpretations of the
characters, of human nature, and of motivations may be clues
to her own character instead of explanations of others'.

Some conjectures about crucial facts in the lives of the
Sutpen family remain enigmatic. Single details which might
clearly reveal the very depths of the older characters are
known only through the interpretation of a modern narrator,
who may create the fact in accordance with his own view of
life. In turn, the reader's guess at the fact may reflect his
own outlook. When Charles Bon is killed, for example, he has
on his person a picture in a metal case which Judith had given
him. Miss Rosa sees Judith's "*lax and negligent hand*" holding
"*the photograph, the picture of herself in its metal case
which she had given him.* ..." But Miss Rosa may have seen
only the case and just assumed that it contained Judith's picture (p. 142). Mr. Compson's more cynical account contends
that this "intending bigamist even if not an out and out
blackguard" had removed Judith's picture and substituted that
of his octoroon mistress and child (p. 90). A romanticizer,
Shreve believes that Mr. Compson is right in the fact but wrong
in the meaning. Bon changed the picture, Shreve says, because,
if Henry did kill him, then the photograph of the mistress

would nobly and selflessly say, *"I was no good; do not grieve
for me"* (pp. 358-359). But the possible motives do not end
with the conjectures of the narrators, who might all be wrong.
Ilse Dusoir Lind accepts the fact as reported by Mr. Compson,
but proposes a different motive. Bon to her seems to be no
blackguard; his changing the picture is an understandable
"defiance and counter-retaliation."[2] Cleanth Brooks distrusts
the idea of retaliation and suggests that Bon's "inept" gesture
may have puzzled Judith but it did not shake her love for him,
"if we are to judge from Judith's kindness to Bon's mistress
and her care for his child...."[3] Ultimately, the reader cannot
know what picture was in the case or *why* it was there. Anyone
can conjecture, but any conjecture may be wrong.

Many other problems also involve the character of the members of the Sutpen family, the nature of the mind of the narrator, and the opinion of the reader, Charles Bon, Mr. Compson
believes, "maybe" showed Henry the letter which he wrote to
Judith during the War, "and maybe he did not ..." (p. 132).
Quentin, on the other hand, assumes a closer relationship,
more frankness between Bon and Henry; therefore he believes
that Henry either had read the letter or knew a great deal
about it (p. 353). Until this letter from Charles saying *"We
have waited long enough"* (p. 131), Judith received no letters
from him. Mr. Compson believes that Henry in his indecision
refused to allow Bon to write; Shreve argues that Bon, more
interested in recognition from Sutpen than in marriage to
Judith, did not write because he did not care (p. 343).
Similarly, Mr. Compson says that Bon wrote letters to Judith
in the summer of 1860 (p. 105); Shreve surmises that he did
not write Judith then (p. 336). Bon, according to Mr. Compson,
knew of Sutpen's visit to New Orleans to confirm his identity
(p. 92); Shreve, however, speculates that Bon never learned
of the visit. Mr. Compson, Miss Rosa, and the epitaph on
Judith's tomb disagree in the difference between the ages of
Rosa and Judith (pp. 23, 25, 26, 59, 211). If Mr. Compson
"can not even imagine" Bon and Judith "alone together" (p. 97),
Quentin and Shreve spend eight lines thinking about Henry's
view of "the sister and the lover in the garden" (pp. 294-295)
and eight more lines about Bon's and Judith's first kiss,
"maybe" (p. 330). Shreve reports in the first account of the
death of Sutpen that the old Negro woman who overheard the
murder scene did not hear the scythe *"since always that ...
which evokes the last silence occurs in silence"* (p. 185).
In the next account, Quentin emphasizes the Negro's fear
rather than truth. She hears "the whip on Wash's face but
she didn't know if she heard the scythe or not because now
she found out that she could move, get up, run out of the cabin
and into the weeds, running ..." (p. 286). Miss Rosa thinks

Sutpen was such a demon that he brought his French architect
to Yoknapatwapha County a "manacled" prisoner (p. 8); Mr.
Compson, who has more regard for Sutpen, believes that the
architect came of his own volition "on Sutpen's bare promise"
(p. 35).

If the modern narrators have considerable difficulty in
understanding the story which they are telling and in comprehending the motives of the older characters, several inconsistencies indicate that the Sutpens also could not accurately
interpret each other. Bon was born in Haiti, but his tombstone,
purchased by Judith, indicates that New Orleans is his birthplace. The careful reader should realize, as Cleanth Brooks
says, that "Judith's knowledge of her fiancé is so slight that
she does not know his age and birthplace."[4] Similarly, Wash
Jones never knows Sutpen for what he is. Wash admires him
excessively until he rejects Milly; then he kills him. He
never knows that when Sutpen got up early on the day of his
death he was anxious to learn whether Milly had borne him a
son. Ignorant of the cause of the rejection, he dies believing
that Sutpen rose to see about the birth of a foal rather than
of his own child. Inhumane as Sutpen is, poor Wash understandably cannot give him credit for the little humanity he
has.

Precise historical facts are also obscure in the novel
because of the tendency of these narrators, like most tellers
of stories, to exaggerate or to use round numbers. Generally,
the reports agree that Miss Rosa lived in hate of Sutpen for
forty-three years, but at least twice the figure is rounded
off to forty-five. Sutpen told Grandfather Compson "that he
did not know within a year on either side just how old he was"
(p. 227), but often in the novel he is given an exact age: he
is 14 (p. 224), and 25 (p. 17), and 59 (p. 160). After his
mansion is built, he brings four wagonloads of furnishings to
his house, Mr. Compson says (p. 44); but Shreve exaggerates
the number to six wagons (p. 178). Again, Mr. Compson makes
a similar mistake. He reports that Bon spent "a week or so
of the summer vacation" at Sutpen's (p. 70); Miss Rosa remembers
the length of the visit as two days (p. 145). When Henry Sutpen
returned to his home after decades as a fugitive, Miss Rosa
went to see him and took Quentin with her. She had been gone
from Sutpen's Hundred, Quentin says, for "almost fifty years."
Two lines later he rounds the number off to "after fifty
years" (p. 362). And Shreve once says that it was sixty
years between the last days of the Civil War in Virginia
(1865) and Miss Rosa's trip to Sutpen's in 1909 (p. 294).
Faulkner himself seldom narrates in his own person in the
novel, but when he does, he is guilty of exaggeration like
that of the other narrators. After Henry kills Bon, he and

Judith speak "to one another in short brief staccato sentences
like slaps":

> *Now you cant marry him.*
> *Why cant I marry him?*
> *Because he's dead.*
> *Dead?*
> *Yes. I killed him.* (p. 172)

Brief as the conversation is, what they say is still repetitious. They use only eighteen words and only twelve different
ones. Two pages later, Faulkner exaggerates the terseness
of his own characters when he describes them as "slashing at
one another with twelve or fourteen words and most of these
the same words repeated two or three times so that when you
boiled it down they did it with eight or ten" (p. 174).

Over and over again the narrators repeat dialogues between
characters who speak harshly to each other at moments of
terrible confrontations and conflict, moments of murder and
death. Twice, for example, they tell the story of the deaths
of Sutpen and Wash; three times they recount how Sutpen returned from the War to greet Rosa, Clytie, Judith, and Wash
and to learn of the death of Bon and the flight of Henry. In
every instance, the reported conversations are similar, but
they are seldom identical. The later versions change a few
words and add a few. The variations suggest the kinds of errors made by the folk when they retell a story, the impossi-
bility of knowing history and the past fully and accurately,
and perhaps even the method of development of myth.

Finally, a few inconsistencies remain puzzling and inexplicable. Only a careless and unintentional mistake or some
kind of incredible subtlety, it seems, could explain Quentin's
memory of how he heard "*Mrs* Coldfield's feet ... approaching
along the upper hall" as she returned from seeing the sick
Henry Sutpen at the end of the novel (p. 370). The *Mrs* is
the more amazing because of Miss Rosa's old-maidish lifetime
of hate and virginity.

These, then, are some of the inconsistencies in *Absalom,
Absalom!*. Probably many are still undiscovered. Some, no
doubt, are careless and unintentional. Whether working by a
sort of folk memory of his own fictional country or charting
the elaborate details in some fashion or making entries on
three-by-five filing cards, no authorial mind could hope to
be altogether consistent in such a complicated work. Fortunately, in the design of the novel, there is more purpose for
inconsistency than for consistency. It is a reflection of
the art of the novel that the minor differences are mirrors
of the important ones. Together, all the inconsistencies in
narration reflect the technique, the meanings, the aims, and

the artistic accomplishments of the novel. In summary, the
discrepancies prove the narrators and their memories and their
interpretations interesting but in many ways unreliable; they
confirm misunderstandings which existed between the characters
about whom the main actions revolve; they allow every reader
room to puzzle out the mysteries of the actions and the natures
of these people for himself.

Many years after Faulkner completed *Absalom, Absalom!* he
still summed up well its difficulties, its technique, and its
meaning:

> I think that no one individual can look at truth. It
> blinds you. You look at it and you see one phase of it.
> Someone else looks at it and sees a slightly awry phase
> of it. But taken all together, the truth is in what they
> saw though nobody saw the truth intact. So these are
> true as far as Miss Rosa and as Quentin saw it. Quentin's
> father saw what he believed was truth, that was all he
> saw. But the old man was himself a little too big for
> people no greater in stature than Quentin and Miss Rosa
> and Mr. Compson to see all at once. It would have taken
> perhaps a wiser or more tolerant or more sensitive or
> more thoughtful person to see him as he was. It was ...
> thirteen ways of looking at a blackbird. But the truth,
> I would like to think, comes out, that when the reader
> has read all these thirteen different ways of looking at
> the blackbird, the reader has his own fourteenth image
> of that blackbird which I would like to think is the
> truth.[5]

Surely, however, no reader's "fourteenth image" can be "the
truth" about the past and the Sutpens. Indeed, the uniqueness
of *Absalom, Absalom!* is that the search for fact and the
speculation about meaning can never arrive at the truth. Possibly after many years Faulkner had forgotten that too positive
certainty about fact and even meaning might destroy the effect.
The most meaningful reading of the novel may conclude that the
reader, like the characters, is not supposed to break through
to the clear fact and the simple motive in the hard light of
day. The only possible "fourteenth image" is that thirteen
ways of looking have not produced the true blackbird. Part of
the magnificence of *Absalom, Absalom!* is that the reader keeps
looking in wonder and mild surmise.

NOTES

1. All page numbers refer to the Modern Library edition of
Absalom, Absalom!. In the spring of 1964 I asked each student

in my undergraduate class in Southern literature to find and list ten factual discrepancies in the novel. They found all the inconsistencies which I had known about and added a good many new ones to my list.

2. Ilse Dusoir Lind, "The Design and Meaning of *Absalom, Absalom!*," *PMLA*, 70 (December, 1955), 904.

3. Cleanth Brooks, *William Faulkner: The Yoknapatawpha Country* (New Haven and London, 1963), pp. 442-443.

4. Brooks, p. 425.

5. Frederick L. Gwynn and Joseph L. Blotner, eds., *Faulkner in the University* (Charlottesville, 1959), pp. 273-274.

ABSALOM, ABSALOM!: THE EXTENDED SIMILE

James Guetti

Absalom, Absalom! at first seems to be merely a puzzle.
If, as is likely, we assume that novels are usually coherent
and consistent, then the incapacities of the narrators who
present the first and second accounts of Thomas Sutpen will
appear to be temporary difficulties that will at last be solved.
The confusing introduction to the story of Sutpen through Mr.
Compson and Rosa Coldfield will be followed, we might suppose,
by a more able narrator and by relative clarity and comprehension. We find, however, that the third of the principal narrators of the book, Quentin Compson, provides no simplification
of the complexities we have encountered. Some of the supposed
"facts" have been changed, to be sure, and Sutpen's experiences
now appear to make better sense as a sequence of cause and effect. But the circumstances in which this last story is told,
Quentin's drastically ambivalent attitude toward the value of
his own remarks and perceptions, his relation to his account
as it is described by the anonymous narrator, and the implications of that account all suggest that the inability of the
narrators to understand the experience surrounding Sutpen may
be an expression of a consistent theme: that human experience
cannot be understood, that order cannot be created.

The view of the story presented by Quentin's father depends
both upon a lack of information--or what a reader assumes, at
this point, to be information--and upon the apparent demands
of Mr. Compson's own sensibility. In his hands the story becomes not what happened but what, in the absence of certainty
as to the facts, he would like to think happened. His narrative is constantly shown to be his own hypothesis as to what
"must have been" and is always explicitly bounded by what he
is able to imagine and what he prefers to believe.

Mr. Compson's remarks express a great many motives and actions that he cannot explain. And what he cannot explain he
characteristically redefines as what cannot be explained and
then as evidence of something he calls "chance." In attempting
to understand Sutpen's investigation of Bon, he remarks, "You
would almost believe that Sutpen's trip to New Orleans was just
sheer chance, just a little more of the illogical machinations
of a fatality."[1] As may be noted here, "chance" and "fatality"
are closely associated, perhaps synonymous, in Mr. Compson's
mind and in his story. The movement toward an insistence upon
the operation of this chance-fatality is clearly exemplified
in the following passage:

> ... we see dimly people ... possessing now heroic propor-
> tions, performing their acts of simple passion and simple
> violence, impervious to time and inexplicable--Yes,
> Judith, Bon, Henry, Sutpen: all of them. They are there,
> yet something is missing; they are like a chemical formula
> exhumed along with the letters from that forgotten chest
> ... you bring them together in the proportions called
> for, but nothing happens; you re-read, tedious and in-
> tent, poring, making sure that you have forgotten nothing,
> made no miscalculation; you bring them together again and
> again nothing happens: just the words, the symbols, the
> shapes themselves, shadowy inscrutable and serene, against
> that turgid background of a horrible and bloody mischancing
> of human affairs. (p. 101)

All of Mr. Compson's important attitudes are present here: his
inability to understand the story or even to appreciate the
reality of the characters; his concomitant sense of the story
as "mischancing"; and an assumption that seems to underlie it
all--that these characters possessed "heroic proportions." It
appears that Mr. Compson's insistence upon the presence of the
inexplicable in his narrative has a partial source in his
desire to view the Sutpens as heroes, that by presenting them
in conflict with a "fatality" he is able to lend them great
stature. In this way, what he cannot explain becomes sacred
to him, and "they dont explain" becomes "we are not supposed
to know" (p. 100). It is as if he is aware that his view of
the story as heroic tragedy depends upon its remaining unexplained and that he is therefore reluctant to pursue his in-
quiries.

Mr. Compson's heroic view, in fact, is unquestionably self-
conscious: "Fate," he suggests, is the "stage manager" (p. 73),
and the history of the Sutpens is like a "Greek tragedy" (p.
62). On the one hand, this explicit labeling of his perspective
draws our attention to the inadequacy of the view itself, but
on the other hand it is evidence of Mr. Compson's own awareness

that his understanding of the story arises from a stock meta-
phor--the world as heroic stage--founded upon what he cannot
explain. It may be, in short, that Mr. Compson himself, as
well as a reader, is aware that his heroic past is as fictional
as Greek tragedy itself. His assertion of such a past will
thus seem the result not of a private compulsion but of a more
balanced attempt to deal with a circumstantial lack of knowledge
and vision.

Because of these limitations that are perhaps psychological
and certainly circumstantial, a reader is acutely conscious of
the artificiality of Mr. Compson's narrative. This same artificiality, however, seems evidence of a reality to come; Mr.
Compson's failure, we suppose, is simply preparation for a
speaker of greater imaginative flexibility and fuller knowledge.
We imagine that a story about Thomas Sutpen will be told--some
yet unrevealed story for which Mr. Compson's narrative is a
momentary disguise and substitute.

But this more capable speaker is not Rosa Coldfield, for
she, like her predecessor, may be seen to transform an inadequacy
into a suspect virtue. Rosa continually reveals her feelings
of amazement and her inability to make any sense whatever of
the story, but at the same time she exhibits a fanatical certainty about it. As in the case of Mr. Compson, the certainty
depends upon the inability, for by viewing Sutpen's story as
inexplicable in terms of what she judges to be predictable
human activity, she is able to insist that the man is super-
human. Sutpen becomes a "demon" who appears out of nowhere
to enact an evil fatality:

> I saw Judith's marriage forbidden without rhyme or reason
> or shadow of excuse; I saw Ellen die with only me, a
> child, to turn to and ask to protect her remaining child;
> I saw Henry repudiate his home and birthright and then
> return and practically fling the bloody corpse of his
> sister's sweetheart at the hem of her wedding gown; I
> saw that man return--the evil's source and head which
> had outlasted all its victims--who had created two
> children not only to destroy one another and his own
> line, but my line as well, yet I agreed to marry him.
> (p. 18)

Throughout her narrative Rosa insists that she was a passive
observer and the victim of an outrageous fatality beyond her
understanding. In the intensity of her failure to understand
she declares that the story cannot be understood; she insists
further that what is incomprehensible to her must be supernatural.

Rosa's understanding of the story, in other words, is inseparable from her feeling of outrage. She occasionally asserts

that Sutpen's goal was "respectability" (p. 16), and at
another moment, she is sure that he is driven by "ruthless
pride" and a "lust for vain magnificence" (p. 162). These
characterizations of Sutpen may be seen to depend upon Rosa's
more personal concerns, upon her response to what may have
been a proposal of a trial copulation. They depend upon her
view of herself as the image of that respectability which Sutpen, in her terms, constantly offended and finally outraged.

It now becomes possible, once again, to see Rosa's narrative as we have seen Mr. Compson's: the narrative problem appears to be a defined psychological problem. But also like
Mr. Compson, Rosa Coldfield's supposed psychological difficulties are questioned by her own awareness of the way in which
they work; she insists, in fact, upon the fallibility of her
perspective: *"there is no such thing as memory: the brain recalls just what the muscles grope for: no more, no less: and
its resultant sum is usually incorrect and false and worthy
only of the name of dream"* (p. 143). If we say that she sees
what she wants to see, we must also admit that she knows that
she is doing so.

The problem of perception, however, extends beyond the
matter of memory, for Rosa often declares that the very past
in which she lived and of which she speaks did not exist for her
at the time. This feeling reaches its culmination when she
describes Charles Bon, who is to her the most important figure
of that past. She loved Bon, she says, with a love founded
upon contradiction and paradox, *"beyond the compass of glib
books: that love which gives up what it never had"* (p. 149).
She loved, as she remarks, a man who may not have ever existed
at all except as her own imagined creation, a man she never saw
alive or dead: *"That was all. Or rather, not all, since there
is no all, no finish.... You see, I never saw him. I never
even saw him dead. I heard an echo, but not the shot; I saw
a closed door but did not enter it"* (p. 150). What for her is
the climax of the story that began with Thomas Sutpen's arrival
in Jefferson is exactly that which is most anticlimactic, and
what is most important to her is least real. And this was because, she tells us elsewhere, she was then *"living in that
womb-like corridor where the world came not even as living
echo but as dead incomprehensible shadow"* (p. 162). Bon was
unreal to her simply because he was somewhere outside that
"corridor," beyond which even the commonplace might have been
unreal.

Again as with Quentin's father, Rosa's self-awareness
tends to modify a reader's conception of her limitations. If
these limitations themselves make us aware of the fictional
quality of her narrative, her confession of them suggests that
her problem is not largely "psychological" nor even definitely

emotional. This feeling is corroborated later when we learn
that her sense of outrage and amazement has a more significant
source than the insulting of her virginal and respectable
self-conception; *"for almost fifty years"* Rosa has asked of
Sutpen's second proposal, *"Why? Why? and Why?"* (p. 167).
Whereas before her inability to comprehend the experience of
which she tells seemed to be the product of a lesser, simply
old-maidish outrage, at this point her failure appears the
result of a genuine, even desperate attempt to understand.

In both the case of Mr. Compson and that of Rosa, then,
internal, psychological difficulties seem less important than
the sheer external facts of their situations. Rosa's awareness
of her failure deflects the emphasis from a supposed neurosis
within her to something acting upon her from without--a "corridor," a set of limitations which she somehow cannot escape.
The emphasis upon circumstances in her case, it appears, is
even greater than for Mr. Compson.

A reader may assume even now, however, that *Absalom, Absalom!* is a novel like other novels, that a story exists and
will be told. No matter how circumstantial the narrative insufficiencies of Quentin's father and Rosa Coldfield may seem,
as insufficiencies they are inseparable from the characters
themselves, and we continue to expect a better speaker; the
narrative difficulties, we suppose, are still difficulties
that the last character-narrator of the novel--Quentin Compson--
will not have.

Both Rosa and Mr. Compson are present in the story that
Quentin tells. While the long, frequently interrupted dialogue
with Shreve in a room at Harvard is always subject to his modification and approval, the narrative that it comprises is an
amalgamation of the narratives of many: General Compson, Mr.
Compson, Rosa, Shreve, and of course Quentin himself.[2] This
section of the novel, that is, contains narrative matter and
techniques that we recognize, and both Shreve and Quentin are
aware, more specifically, that they sound like "father."

One aspect of Quentin's own particular method, however,
is immediately apparent. In the narratives of Rosa and his
father it is the limitations of these speakers that are initially most striking and most revealing, but Quentin's story
is different. For the first time in the novel a reader is
presented with a powerfully imagined narrative that--no matter
how much it may be questioned ultimately nor how puzzling its
arrangement--is in general consistent and reasonable within
itself.

Quentin's relation to the story he tells is often characterized as that of direct perception: "It seemed to Quentin
that he could actually see" (p. 132). This remark is on occasions simply repeated verbatim, on others slightly modified.

And at times it serves to introduce a narrative of startling imaginative intensity, as, for example, when Henry Sutpen and Bon confront each other on an approach to Sutpen's Hundred, one brother about to destroy the other. Considering that Quentin is frequently described as a seer, that he has moments of clarity that other narrators do not have, and that the story he tells seems to work as a story, he appears to be the narrator we have been awaiting, who will endow the story with meaning and imaginative reality.

It is necessary to notice, however, that it only *seems* to Quentin that he can see. The limitation that begins here in the word "seems" grows larger when we consider that Quentin is often described as exhibiting a quality that is generally antithetical to his supposed imaginative vitality. He is said to speak in a "flat, curiously dead voice" (p. 258), or in an "almost sullen flat tone" (p. 255); he displays a "brooding bemusement" in a room that is "tomb-like." Quentin also reveals explicitly his feeling of tiredness, of repetition, and of deadness, and what is most interesting about these revelations is their contrast with his imaginative powers. This paradox, of course, has a literary precedent; it might simply be the stock schizophrenia of the seer, the man whose powers of vision are extraordinary but who is exhausted by them because he, at last, is only mortal. In Quentin's case, however, the paradox stems not from an emphasis upon his imaginative activity, but from an insistence upon his passivity: *"Yes,"* he thinks, *"I have heard too much, I have been told too much; I have had to listen to too much"* (p. 207). This paradox of vitality and deadness, of Quentin as active seer and passive sounding board for all the voices he has ever heard, is pervasive in his narrative, and, considering our optimistic view of his perspective, this paradox is crucial.

Quentin's exhausted despair is most often associated with the voice of his father, and it is suggested in this way that Quentin's problem may be, as in the possible views of previous narrators, psychological. But this obsessive concern with his father is only significant and, perhaps, only exists for him in terms of the telling of the story:

> *Am I going to have to have to hear it all again* he thought *I am going to have to hear it all over again I am already hearing it all over again I am listening to it all over again I shall have to never listen to anything else but this again forever so apparently not only a man never outlives his father but not even his friends and acquaintances do.* (p. 277)

This paradox of imaginative vitality as opposed to exhaustion and deadness is aligned with another, which comes to our

attention when Quentin tells Shreve that it was he, Quentin,
who told his father the rest of the story on the basis of what
he discovered out at Sutpen's mansion, and when he admits that
at the mansion, even though he saw Clytie and Henry Sutpen,
he was told nothing. Shreve says: "... it just came out of
the terror and the fear after she turned you loose ... and she
looked at you and you saw it was not rage but terror ... and
she didn't tell you in the actual words because even in the
terror she kept the secret; nevertheless she told you, or at
least all of a sudden you knew--" (pp. 350-351). The case for
Quentin's clairvoyance that Shreve presents here may be seen
to be a substantiation of the vitality I have mentioned, and a
reader may feel that Quentin really can know without being told,
and see without knowing. In view of the narrators that have
preceded him, however, and of our awareness of his own sense
of frustration and futility, the fact that Quentin's vision
springs from what is apparently nothing becomes a problem. In
his discovery of Henry Sutpen at the mansion we may see an
enactment of this polarity of vision and nothingness, and this
dramatic moment itself, I think, takes the form of a negation
of vision and of imaginative vitality. The impact of the supposed dialogue between Quentin and Henry is great, but this
impact depends upon the fact that nothing is said:

> *And you are--?*
> *Henry Sutpen.*
> *And you have been here--?*
> *Four years.*
> *And you came home--?*
> *To die. Yes.*
> *To die?*
> *Yes. To die.*
> *And you have been here--?*
> *Four years.*
> *And you are--?*
> *Henry Sutpen.* (p. 373)

This dialogue is a kind of play within a play; it is a
crystallization of the sources of Quentin's vision and of the
vision itself: nothing happens and nothing is said, but Quentin
sees and knows. The qualities of this moment, of course, are
anything but persuasive as to the reality or relevance of
Quentin's imaginative perceptions. If his vision arises out
of clairvoyance, this very clairvoyance has the tone of despair: in Quentin the moment of supposed perception is dramatized
as a moment of hypnotic and futile circularity. This dialogue
serves, rather than to demonstrate Quentin's powers as a seer,
to reassert the elements of the paradox I have noted: it
possesses imaginative intensity and the suggestion of meaning

as opposed to its circularity and deadness, and I suggest that
the sense of torturous repetition here is the same as that
which Quentin feels in his despair at hearing and telling the
story again and again. Here, however, we realize that this
hypnotic futility lies at the foundation of Quentin's imaginative vitality; his vitality arises from deadness.

There is nothing but the talking, it seems, and the talking
is dead, futile, circular. Quentin's narrative is significant
not as the resolution that a reader has expected but only as
the summation of all the speculation and misguided intensity
that has preceded it. The anonymous narrator—whom we may
associate with Faulkner—defines the Quentin-Shreve dialogue in
these terms: "... the two of them creating between them, out of
the rag-tag and bob-ends of old tales and talking, people who
perhaps had never existed at all anywhere" (p. 303). Henry
Sutpen, we know, "existed," but he existed only as part of a
dialogue that is for Quentin the reminder of his failure to
understand what the story means, the reminder that each attempt to understand, each vision, arises out of a moment of
failure. Quentin's very assertion that he "knows" is inseparable
from his conviction that he cannot know—a conviction displayed
in his sense of futile repetition, in his implied awareness that
his ability to "see" is based upon this same futility, and in
a simple, literal admission to Shreve. "Do you understand it?"
Shreve asks, and the exchange continues:

> "I dont know," Quentin said. "Yes, of course I
> understand it." They breathed in the darkness. After
> a moment Quentin said" "I dont know."
> "Yes. You dont know. You dont even know about the
> old dame, the Aunt Rosa."
> "Miss Rosa," Quentin said.
> "All right. You dont even know about her.... Do
> you?"
> "No," Quentin said peacefully. He could taste the
> dust. (p. 362)

Quentin resembles his father and Rosa Coldfield in that
his story is founded upon what he cannot know, but he is distinguished from them by the persistence and intensity of his
attempt to make the story meaningful. There is a distinct
progression in *Absalom, Absalom!* from the placid and remote
speculation of Mr. Compson through the narrow but more immediate
incapacity of Rosa to Quentin's attempt, and this final attempt
is both more ambitious and more seriously frustrated than
those of previous narrators. It is no longer a question of
Mr. Compson's errors or Rosa's ignorance: there can be no errors
or ignorance in a narrative world where we are concerned with

what cannot be meaningful or what may not exist as comprehensible experience at all.

Instead of an answer to what we had assumed was a puzzle, we encounter in Quentin's narrative the indication that the puzzle itself may not be real, that the gap between experience and meaning in this novel must remain unbridgable, and that the narrative is only, after all, words, only a product of "old tales and talking." The paradox of Quentin's narrative is that he forms this "talking" into a vital, articulated vision while demonstrating--and of this he is aware--that its basis is only dead speculation upon a dead past.

The tension between imagined reality and empty words that we find sustained in Quentin's narrative is never resolved in *Absalom, Absalom!* It may be said to be explained, however, if we consider its relation to the unreal story it creates, to the conception and progress of Thomas Sutpen's "design."

"Sutpen's trouble was innocence," we are told as Quentin begins his account. "All of a sudden he discovered, not what he wanted to do but what he just had to do, had to do it whether he wanted to or not" (p. 220). Sutpen has been sent with a message to the mansion of a white planter whom he has repeatedly watched lounging in a barrel-stave hammock; he is thinking of the house and "thinking how at last he was going to see the inside of it, see what else a man was bound to own who could have a special nigger to hand him his liquor" (p. 229). A "monkey nigger" meets him at the door, and even while he is talking, telling Sutpen never to come to the front door again, Sutpen has flashes of memory concerning his previous experience with Negroes:

> You knew that you could hit them, he told Grandfather,
> and they would not hit back or even resist. But you
> did not want to, because they (the niggers) were not it,
> not what you wanted to hit; that you knew when you hit
> them you would just be hitting a child's toy balloon
> with a face painted on it, a face slick and smooth and
> distended and about to burst into laughing, and so you
> did not dare strike it because it would merely burst
> and you would rather let it walk on out of your sight
> than to have stood there in the loud laughing. (p. 230)

"The niggers" somehow prevent one's assaulting whatever it is that is important; their faces are the faces of balloons that-- if one takes action against them--burst into laughter, "the roaring waves of mellow laughter meaningless and terrifying and loud" (p. 232). Sutpen characterizes the barrier that prevents him from entering the house as something so artificial and empty as to be unassailable, a barrier that can only serve to reassert the futility of his situation.

The parallels between Sutpen and Ahab here are so striking as to be worth detailed comment. The significance of the "monkey nigger" for Sutpen is that of an artificial barrier that prevents him from penetrating to what he has assumed is a reality. Ahab would call it a "pasteboard mask"; for Sutpen it is a "balloon face." Ahab, on the one hand, is conscious of many such masks in the visual and verbal universe; they are all the suggestions, omens, and half-meanings that torture him in their uncertainty and multiplicity. Sutpen's particular problem at the moment, on the other hand, is less sophisticated and more simply a matter of deprivation. It is a social, not a natural, artificiality with which he is concerned, and this single absence of meaning—the fact that he cannot enter the house—becomes for him, as I shall try to show later, a universal negation. The color significance works almost too well here: Ahab's tortured uncertainty is incarnated in the "colorless all-color" of whiteness, whereas Sutpen's sense of complete futility and negation is symbolized in the blackness of the "monkey nigger." Both colors are generally significant as the expressions of a nothingness.

Sutpen is not yet, however, explicitly conscious of such a nothingness. He runs into the woods and attempts to understand what has happened. It was not the "nigger" that was important, he later tells General Compson:

> The nigger was just another balloon face slick and distended ... during that instant in which, before he knew it, something in him had escaped and—he unable to close the eyes of it—was looking out from within the balloon face just as the man who did not even have to wear the shoes he owned, whom the laughter which the balloon held barricaded and protected from such as he, looked out from whatever invisible place he (the man) happened to be at the moment, at the boy outside the barred door in his patched garments and splayed bare feet, looking through and beyond the boy, he himself seeing his own father and sisters and brothers as the owner, the rich man (not the nigger) must have been seeing them all the time—as cattle, creatures heavy and without grace, brutely evacuated into a world without hope or purpose for them, who would in turn spawn with brutish and vicious prolixity, populate, double treble and compound ... with for sole heritage that expression on a balloon face bursting with laughter which had looked out at some unremembered and nameless progenitor who had knocked at a door when he was a little boy and had been told by a nigger to go around to the back. (pp. 234-235)

What Sutpen himself appears to mean by the discovery of his "innocence" is the birth of a kind of self-consciousness;

"something in him had escaped," and as the white owner has
done before and does now Sutpen looks out upon himself. In
terms of this view Sutpen and his descendants become purpose-
less animals, participants in a brutish chaos whose heritage
is the balloon face and the laughter.

The boy's feelings of senselessness and futility are defined in terms of the plantation owner's position inside the
big white house. He reflects that he can do nothing to reach
the man, that if the house were on fire he would be unable to
warn its owner:

> ... *there aint any good or harm either in the living
> world that I can do to him.* It was like that, he said,
> like an explosion—a bright glare that vanished and left
> nothing, no ashes nor refuse; just a limitless flat plain
> with the severe shape of his intact innocence rising from
> it like a monument; that innocence instructing him as
> calm as the others had ever spoken, using his own rifle
> analogy to do it with, and when it said *them* in place of
> *he* or *him*, it meant more than all the human puny mortals
> under the sun that might lie in hammocks all afternoon
> with their shoes off: He thought 'If you were fixing to
> combat them that had the fine rifles, the first thing you
> would do would be to get yourself the nearest thing to a
> fine rifle you could borrow or steal or make, wouldn't
> it?' and he said Yes. (p. 238)

Sutpen feels a complete impotence; his significance is totally
negative. The awareness of negation, which was previously
suggested in blackness, now takes a spatial form. He conceives
an image of himself rising from a "plain" that is flat and
without limits, and his "innocence" is defined both as this
image in the midst of nothingness and that which instructs
him how to overcome the nothingness. He must combat "them,"
and "them" means more, we are told, than a group of socially
defined mortals; it is not simply the class, perhaps, but the
rules by which the class is established. He will combat these
rules by means of the possessions that express the rules, by
means of the signs and tokens of the social system, "land and
niggers and a fine house" (p. 238).

Sutpen's design is thus social in form; he is attempting
to make use of the social system to overcome that system.
Like Ahab, he attacks the artificial quality of his experience
—which separates him from what he assumes will be a reality—
and like Ahab Sutpen employs as a means of progress the artificial itself, the social structure that prevents him from
entering the house. By entering the house, Sutpen will be
enabled to transform himself and his descendants. They are to
be "riven forever free from brutehood" and to have—like Sutpen
himself—a meaningful identity (p. 261).

This identity is finally based on the acquiring of possessions, which in accordance with the social structure will express the meaning that Sutpen desires. In Ahab's case a multiple artifice is to be penetrated and reduced to a single revelation by one final thrust of a harpoon; for Sutpen the void of his life is to be filled with possessions and descendants, which in turn must be expressive of a completely controlled and defined design. What the meaning of the design is, exactly, has not been defined as yet; Sutpen, in fact, does not seem to know what it is, but he is convinced that it will be meaning, an alleviation of his vision of chaos and impotence.

A reader's conception of the nature of Sutpen's design takes its form at the outset from what seems antithetical to the design--hollowness, arbitrariness, unreality, impotence-- and this continues to be so as he proceeds through the story of Sutpen. For example, Sutpen's first wife, as we learn from the speculations of Quentin and Shreve, was part Negro; it is this that Sutpen appears to be talking about when he declares that a certain aspect of his wife and child would have made his work toward the design an "ironic delusion," and he later enlarges upon this as follows: "I was faced with condoning a fact which had been foisted upon me without my knowledge during the process of building toward my design, which meant the absolute and irrevocable negation of the design; or in holding to my original plan for the design in pursuit of which I had incurred this negation" (p. 273).[3] This passage is characteristic of those by which Sutpen and the narrators express the design; in it there is defined a particular negation of the design, a specific and temporary failure, and the design is given shape in terms of what it is not.

It is the Negro blood in his wife and son, we may suppose, to which Sutpen objects and that constitutes this particular "negation," and it seems clear that the design is intensely social in its method. It is just the fanatical intensity of Sutpen's supposedly social aspirations, in fact, that is most problematic. Quentin remarks that Sutpen need not have rejected his wife and child, that he might have bluffed the matter out somehow, but that he was apparently forced to reject them by his "conscience" (p. 266). The quality of this "conscience" may be illuminated if we consider Sutpen's later refusal to recognize the same child, now Charles Bon, as his son--the refusal that ultimately results in the collapse of the entire design.

Bon's visits to the plantation, as Mr. Compson suggests to Quentin, are a metaphorical re-enactment of Sutpen's childhood experience: "... he stood there at his own door, just as he had imagined, planned, designed, and sure enough after fifty years the forlorn nameless and homeless lost child came to

knock at it and no monkey-dressed nigger anywhere under the
sun to come to the door and order the child away" (p. 267).
No "monkey-dressed nigger," perhaps, because now the boy himself, Bon, contains in his Negro blood the means of his own
prohibition; in this way Sutpen need not order him away; at
any rate, he does not. He simply does nothing. He refuses to
take the only action that would alleviate the problem and enable him to continue with his design; he refuses to recognize
Bon on any terms. It is as if his childhood imaginings have
come true: a boy comes to tell a man that his house is on fire
and cannot be heard.[4]

Sutpen has declared to General Compson, we are told, that
he felt he had made a mistake somewhere and that his inaction
toward Bon--"the fact that for a time he did nothing and so
perhaps helped to bring about the very situation which he
dreaded"--was "not the result of any failing of courage or
shrewdness or ruthlessness, but ... the result of his conviction that it had all come from a mistake and until he discovered
what that mistake had been he did not intend to risk making
another one" (p. 268). The language of this passage is mild
considering the duration and the intensity of Sutpen's paralysis; his refusal to recognize Bon in any way seems insane, out
of all proportion to what we suppose are the facts, and out of
proportion even to the sustained bemusement that Sutpen is
said to have admitted. The "choice" that he felt he had to
make, as we learn later, was no choice at all; either way his
design would have been destroyed. But in his choice he made
no provision for direct action toward Bon, but only for either
playing his "last trump card"--telling Henry that Bon is part
Negro--or doing nothing.

What is truly inexplicable here is that Bon seems to pose
no literal threat whatever to the design; if exposed as a frac-
tionally Negro son he could not participate in the design or
even oppose it, and Sutpen might have known this as well as
Bon. If the only important consideration were social, also,
Sutpen could have either accepted Bon and concealed his Negro
blood or refused to accept him and proclaimed it. In either
case a merely social design would have been unimpaired. Because
Bon is surely not an insurmountable obstacle to the design in
social terms, the failure to recognize him becomes significant
evidence that Sutpen's demands are more than social, that if
he is making use of the particular ingredients of the social
system to accomplish his design, the design itself is to be
defined not in terms of that system but of something more. It
is more, in short, than the sum of its apparent parts.

Sutpen's frantic inaction toward Bon reveals the two important qualities of his design: that it is both an attempt
to dominate the arbitrariness that Sutpen perceives in his

universe and an attempt to make real the artificial significances that this arbitrariness creates. Sutpen, perhaps, sees Bon as an incarnation of both the arbitrary and the artificial, as the reincarnation, in fact, of the "monkey nigger" of his childhood and all that that figure represented. We must remember, in this connection, that before his experience at the door of the plantation house Sutpen did not question the chaos of "luck" in which he lived; it was only after that experience that this chaos became significant in terms of the meaning, or lack of meaning, of his life. In that moment at the door, Sutpen begins to demand meaning of his experience; he begins to view his world metaphorically. It is just this metaphorical vision, as I have suggested, that is most apparent when he confronts Charles Bon: Bon's Negro blood is literally insignificant, but for Sutpen it implies a crucial lack of control over past and present; in his metaphorical view it represents the total negation that he experienced at the door of the plantation house, where he first became conscious of a possible world of meaning that was beyond him. The characteristic irony of Sutpen's situation is that his demands for meaning, his fierce attempts to create a metaphor from the arbitrariness of his experience, are frustrated even in their conception; when viewed metaphorically this experience yields only what a reader may see as images that imply the unreality of metaphor--a limitless plain, a blackness, a paralysis.

The relentlessness of Sutpen's insistence upon clarity and control in his experience is constantly revealed in his treatment of what a reader might have assumed to be only literal details. He is not content with merely owning slaves for which the social system provides, but must on numerous occasions strip to the waist and engage a Negro in savage, hand-to-hand combat, fighting until the Negro can fight no longer. This apparently insane desire to dominate his slaves again dramatizes the connection in Sutpen's mind between literal control over the elements of the system he employs and the metaphorical vision of blackness--of unreal significance and negation of self--that he possesses. By defeating the Negro, Sutpen is not only destroying a social artificiality in the relation of the parts of his design to himself but also destroying what he sees metaphorically to be the continued existence of that negation which his design was to overcome.

His will to dominate, of course, is not always displayed in such direct association to the specific metaphor of blackness, but it is always an indication of his desire for unambiguous meaning. We may consider, for example, his treatment of the French architect who designs his plantation house. He does not simply employ the architect, but possesses him completely until the house is finished. The set of conventions

which the architect represents are thus redefined as Sutpen's
own conventions--not arbitrary significances from a world outside Sutpen, but a part of his very being.

It should be apparent, then, that to Sutpen's mind the
complete possession and control of the previously uncontrolled
details of experience must inevitably result in the creation
of a meaningful identity, that the clarity which is to follow
from this control will be an alleviation of disorder and
meaninglessness. The physical and literal order of his design
are in this way an imaginative order, and his entire progress
toward a moment when all the details will fall into place is
an uncompromising imaginative act.

Throughout his life the desire for unambiguous order
dominates Sutpen's imagination; at every crucial moment in his
progress toward failure he views the details of his world as
the ingredients of a metaphorical structure that he believes
he can and must create. In a conversation with General Compson,
he reveals the most important elements of such a metaphor; he
reduces his design to what are for him its most important
terms: "You see, all I wanted was just a son. Which seems to
me, when I look at my contemporary scene, no exorbitant gift
from nature or circumstance to demand--" (p. 292). The very
simplicity of this statement renders it incomprehensible as a
literal remark, for Sutpen had two sons--two sons whose literal
destruction was brought about by his demands for control and
meaning, by his metaphorical view in which Charles Bon was the
negation of such control.

Sutpen's conception of fatherhood, as his conception of
the entire world, is founded upon the conviction that the begetting of a son is not a physical or a literal act, but an
imaginative and metaphorical achievement; fatherhood is the
creation of the essential element in a design, in a structure
that will endure. His only desire in the years of his decline
is to beget the evidence of his significance, and by doing so
to complete the arrangement that he feels is not yet right;
the result is the proposal that outrages Rosa Coldfield and
which Quentin's father calls another "failing" of Sutpen's
shrewdness. A reader, however, may wonder what else at this
point Sutpen could have done, given his assumption that his
mistake must lie in the arrangement and details of his design.
He was a master of detail, but his mastery only resulted in
failure. The futile circularity of his course is crystallized
in his attempt to father a son upon Milly Jones, whose situation is reminiscent of Sutpen's own childhood, and whose
grandfather bears the same relation to the balloon faces and
the laughter of Negroes as did Sutpen himself as a child, but
who endures it by means of the delusion that he is Sutpen.
To Wash Jones "this world where he walked always in mocking

and jeering echoes of nigger laughter, was just a dream and an
illusion and ... the actual world was the one where his own
lonely apotheosis (Father said) galloped on the black thoroughbred" (p. 282). Sutpen's desire for a son, in this way,
brings him back to his origins, back to the brutish senselessness and lack of significance that the laughter first made apparent and that were to become the motivation of his design.
Wash Jones views Sutpen as his (Jones's) apotheosis and later
destroys him and it, just as Sutpen himself--in his final
equivalence to Wash--has returned to his sources and thereby
destroyed the apotheosis of himself that was half-created but
could not endure: that apotheosis by which he was both the
creator of meaning and the product of his creation, the meaning
itself, all opposed to the senseless and absurd condition where
at last he ends as he began.

General Compson's remarks often support the view of the
"apotheosis" that I am suggesting. He declares that Sutpen's
failure must be defined in terms of a tension between sense
and senselessness, between a "code" and a "maelstrom of unpredictable and unreasoning human beings" (p. 275). And at
moments he indicates that it is a matter of even greater proportions, as in Quentin's secondhand account of Sutpen's over-
seeing of the West Indian plantation:

> And he overseeing it, riding peacefully about on his
> horse while he learned the language (that meager and
> fragile thread, Grandfather said, by which the little
> surface corners and edges of men's secret and solitary
> lives may be joined for an instant now and then before
> sinking back into the darkness where the spirit cried
> for the first time and was not heard and will cry for
> the last time and will not be heard then either), not
> knowing that what he rode upon was a volcano, hearing
> the air tremble and throb at night with the drums and
> the chanting and not knowing that it was the heart of
> the earth itself he heard, who believed (Grandfather
> said) that earth was kind and gentle and that darkness
> was merely something you saw, or could not see in....
> (p. 251)

Here General Compson has constructed a metaphor by which the
incomprehensibilities and confusions of human experience are
not particular or momentary difficulties to be resolved by
better language, but the expressions of a failure that is absolute and inevitable. The metaphor is that of a "darkness,"
a darkness that is not "merely something you saw, or could not
see in."

But while Quentin's grandfather appears to suggest that
the only metaphor that can be created is a vague expression

of unavoidable defeat, Sutpen's glimpses of the supposed
nothingness only goad him to more violent attempts to overcome
it. He cannot understand the perpetuation of his impotence;
he assumes again and again that he has made a mistake in the
details of his design. We are told that Sutpen never loses his
innocence, and this innocence may be finally defined as his
conviction that the world consists of potential metaphor that
need only be accumulated and arranged in order to be real.

And yet the essential quality and paradox of Sutpen's
metaphorical vision of the world, again, is that by means of
this vision he perceives nothing but the contradictions of it.
His determination to establish order, as I have suggested,
springs not only from a perception of disorder but also from
a vision in which disorder becomes a void, a nothingness.
His imagination, in this way, is constantly at war with itself; his attempt to overcome a lack of control, to accumulate
and arrange the details of his design, is always at odds with
his feeling that this lack of control is evidence of a complete
absence of identity, an absolute negation of the "self" that
he is striving to create. Sutpen may thus be seen both to
deny and to accept General Compson's awareness of a universal
"darkness." In Charles Bon, for example, he sees both a simple,
literal "mistake" that might be rectified and an absolute,
metaphorical contradiction of his ability to create a meaning
that, while he cannot admit it as a complete negation of his
efforts, paralyzes him, prevents him from acting upon the "mistake." When we consider General Compson's attitude, we may
understand why Sutpen's innocence was associated with nothingness in the very conseption of his design, for this innocence
is what persuades Sutpen throughout his career that meaning
can and must be created from disorder even while he appears
to view this same disorder as the evidence of absolute negation.

The course of his design is not simply circular; it is no
course at all. His conviction that the world consists of
potential metaphor that only needs arranging--the conviction
that is the guiding principle of this design and of all design--
is inseparable from his sense of perfect futility. His maniacal
desire to dominate his world is thus explained, for even a
momentary failure becomes the metaphorical expression of the
void in which he somehow believes and yet which he cannot accept. His attempt to make his world a metaphor succeeds only
in reasserting that the only possible metaphor is that of
"darkness."

Sutpen's design thus contains its own destruction, and
his course of action and vision is inevitably a series of
failures. The particular failures of Sutpen, however, may
seem unsatisfactory to a reader as evidence for a more general
failure. It is possible to reject General Compson's conviction

that all is darkness, in terms of which, as I have tried to
show, the interdependence in Sutpen's design between the desire for meaning and the feeling of ultimate failure is revealed.

The question that arises is whether such a connection between not only order and disorder but also meaning and darkness
is necessary throughout the world of this novel, for in Sutpen's case it seems suspect in two ways. The vision of meaninglessness from which the design arises and which it implies
throughout in the manner of its failures may be questioned if
we consider Sutpen's naïveté--the naïveté of a boy born in the
mountains of West Virginia and possessing perhaps the simplest
code of logic and morality. If, when this code is destroyed,
he becomes aware of the complete absence of meaning, it is
possible to say that this awareness is simply a product of the
narrowness of his mind. In the same manner, both the intensity
and the failure of the man's struggle toward his design, de-
pending as they do upon the initial vision, may be seen as a
mania arising from the outrage of a peculiarly rigid imagination. In short, the childhood vision was just what half of
Sutpen's mind thought it was: only a temporary confusion that
could be, with the right method, alleviated. The second objection, then, is that Sutpen does not use the right method,
that there is something wrong with the particular metaphor
that he is trying to create. Because the implements of his
design are those of the social structure of the South, and
because he wields these implements with even more ruthless
energy than they permit in the first place, we might conclude
that Sutpen is simply an immoral man in a moral book, and that
therefore he must fail.

It may be noted here that Sutpen is again the counterpart
of Ahab, for we have seen that the latter figure can be viewed
in just these terms: as a monomaniac whose limitations are
those of insanity and folly or as a being of heroic stature
who may be termed insane only because he attempts to move
beyond the fatal limits of his world. And to view Sutpen as
immoral or even insane, of course, is to reduce his significance
drastically. In its relation to the narrative method of Quentin,
however, and to the paradox of vitality and deadness that I have
mentioned, the history of Sutpen's design becomes meaningful,
as I shall now show more clearly, as one expression of the
fallibility of all order and all imagination in *Absalom, Absalom!* If Sutpen's problem may be termed a kind of imaginative
schizophrenia, his particular insanity is general throughout
the entire novel.

I have previously dwelt at length upon Quentin's failure
to understand the story he articulates, but it is necessary at

this point to examine a few details of this failure in order
to show that it correlates with Sutpen's history so as to illuminate the structural theme of the novel. When Quentin admits his lack of comprehension to Shreve, for example, he does
so "peacefully," and at that moment he can taste the "dust."
The "dust" is the dust rising around the buggy as he and Rosa
Coldfield make their nocturnal journey to Sutpen's Hundred:

> ... the dust cloud moving on, enclosing them with not
> threat exactly but maybe warning, bland, almost friendly,
> warning, as if to say, *Come on if you like. But I will
> get there first; accumulating ahead of you I will arrive
> first, lifting, sloping gently upward under hooves and
> wheels so that you will find no destination but will
> merely abrupt gently onto a plateau and a panorama of
> harmless and inscrutable night and there will be nothing
> for you to do but return.* (p. 175)

The dust is suggestive not only of mortality but also of
chaos; it is the precursor of a "plateau" that resembles the
flat plain of meaninglessness in Sutpen's childhood vision;
it implies that when Quentin arrives he will discover *"nothing."*[5]
And although Henry Sutpen is there at the mansion, Quentin
learns nothing from him. His supposed actual conversation
with Henry demonstrates that there is indeed nothing to do but
return. In this way the flashes of perception that Quentin
displays are implied to be parallel to Sutpen's design in that
both arise from a precognition of meaninglessness and from a
subsequent, anticlimactic awareness of a flat and barren
nothingness.

Another parallel to Sutpen arises when the anonymous narrator describes the room at Harvard as "this snug monastic
coign, this dreamy and heatless alcove of what we call the best
of thought." The room is the point of most advantage, where
the history of the Sutpens will certainly be understood if it
can be. The narrator continues by remarking that Mr. Compson's
letter has filled the room with "unratiocinative djinns and
demons" (p. 258). The room is filled, perhaps, with the
ghostly presences of the Sutpens, who are "unratiocinative"
in some supposed lack of systematic thought. Somewhat later
the matter becomes clearer: "in the cold room ... dedicated
to that best of ratiocination which after all was a good deal
like Sutpen's morality and Miss Coldfield's demonizing ..."
(p. 280). An explicit equivalence is drawn here between the
logic of Sutpen that failed and the logic of Quentin and Shreve
as they attempt to comprehend the failure; they indulge in the
"best of thought" and are able only to demonstrate their own
similarity to Sutpen and to the narrators that have preceded
them.

Earlier Quentin visualizes the death of Thomas Sutpen in
a way that further supports the schematic organization for the
novel that I am proposing: "... *she heard the whip too though
not the scythe, no whistling air, no blow, nothing since always
that which merely consummates punishment evokes a cry while
that which evokes the last silence occurs in silence*" (p. 185).
Sutpen's death evokes "the last silence," and that silence is
the entire narrative of *Absalom, Absalom!* All of the particular uncertainties, inadequacies, and cruxes of this narrative,
although they may appear to be of only temporary significance
initially, are shown to have a larger relevance; they are all
part of a general and absolute inability to render experience
meaningful—an inability that the supposed story of Sutpen itself implies.

Sutpen's problem, then, becomes part of a larger, thematic
problem. And it must be added here that unlike Quentin's
father and Rosa, whose information is incomplete, Sutpen is a
master of detail; he accumulates all the literal facts necessary
to his design. In his own terms, of course, he is sure that
he has made a mistake in detail, but, again, his mistake is
shown to be of greater dimensions than this—a mistake of
vision itself, that "innocent" vision which dictates that the
world is metaphor and must mean something, and in terms of
which a disorder becomes a "darkness."

This is the vision to which every narrator in the novel
holds in his account of Sutpen. Mr. Compson's attitude that
the story does not explain is understandable considering his
lack of "information"; his mistake lies in the fact that he
sees this inexplicability as a metaphor. The inconsistency
of details, for him, is an expression of a great meaning that
has to do with fate. Rosa, too, possesses a view of the world
as metaphor. Her inability to understand Sutpen and the events
surrounding him is significant to her as an expression of
Sutpen's demonhood. She seems superior to Quentin's father,
however, in the intensity with which she asserts the unreality
of the experience upon which the story is founded and in the
apparently greater cost of her frustrated attempts to give it
meaning. She may be said to question her own metaphors more
thoroughly.

In Quentin's case the matter of the story appears to become more consistent; of the narrators of the book he is most
analogous to Sutpen in that he too is capable in the accumulation of details, details that should comprise a pattern that
will be controlled and significant. Nonetheless, he cannot
understand, cannot achieve the meaning that both he and Shreve
think exists. His inability is partly expressed, again, in
his sources, in the approximations that he inherits from Rosa
and from his father and grandfather as well as in his perceptions

that seem to arise from nothing. His most crucial moment of
vision takes place in the dialogue, which is so hypnotically
repetitive, with Henry Sutpen. This dialogue indicates that
what I have called "approximations" and "nothing" are really
in Quentin's case the same thing and the same source. We have
been prepared for it as a climactic moment of understanding
and as such it is a failure. And it is a failure that repeats
itself, the repetition suggesting that it means something,
that it is a metaphor, and the same repetition denying that
the metaphor can be realized. In this way it is equivalent
to all the stories that Quentin has heard since he was old
enough to listen, stories repeated over and over, whose un-
fulfilled reiteration both asserts their metaphorical nature
and denies it.

It is this tension between the meaningful and the meaningless that Quentin has inherited in the approximations of his
father, and it is understandable that he feels he must escape
from his father and hence from the unrealized story itself.
His only moment of peace in the novel comes when for a moment
he dissolves the tension, relinquishes the need for meaning
that was bequeathed to him as a history of uncertainties, and
admits to Shreve "peacefully" that he does not understand.[6]

In a remark that is relevant to the idea of the "last
silence," the anonymous narrator speaks of Sutpen as "Quentin's
Mississippi shade who in life had acted and reacted to the
minimum of logic and morality, who dying had escaped it completely, who dead remained not only indifferent but impervious
to it, somehow a thousand times more potent and alive" (p.
280). Sutpen is more "alive" because he is impervious to attempts to understand him. The meanings that surround him lend
him a vitality that arises out of their impotence and deadness.
The analogy with the supposed story of Sutpen himself is clear,
for in that story his presence and power depended upon impotence not simply in the motivation but in the definition of
the design, for the design as an attempted metaphorical vision
is articulated in what it cannot do, in the intensity and
scope of its failures. Thomas Sutpen's power is inseparable
from his impotence, and it is in understanding this paradox
that we may better understand the tension of vitality and
deadness in Quentin and all the narrative uncertainties of
the "last silence."

Quentin's vision, like Sutpen's, is composed of an intense
desire to perceive and the conviction that his perception must
fail. His situation is as tortured as Sutpen's because his inheritance is a body of approximations that possess contradictory implications: first, that they are evidence of the progress
toward meaning; second, that the very fact that there are only
approximations, repeated and sustained, denies the possibility
of achieving a meaning.

The mode of expression to which Quentin is heir is incredibly powerful; a reader feels that something is always.
just about to be defined, the heart of the problem revealed.
The story which Quentin tells, furthermore, possesses all the
more imaginative vitality *because* it is never composed; it is
surrounded with countless possible significances; the multiple
suggestions by which the story becomes so powerful continue
to exist precisely because no single meaning is ever achieved.
The vitality of the entire narrative of *Absalom, Absalom!* depends upon the inability to create a single, dominant metaphor; the multiple significances arise out of a permanent
stalemate, a failure, a deadness. It is in this way that
Thomas Sutpen is most alive because he is dead and that the
language of the entire novel is most suggestive of meaning
because it constitutes the refutation of a dominant meaning.

As I have attempted to show, it is impossible for Quentin
to move beyond a language that is approximate. In his very
moments of perception the significances he remarks seem to
spring from a denial of meaning and to be given their sugges-
tiveness by the denial, whether it takes the form of the multiple, qualified speculations of all the narrators who have
preceded him or that of a hypnotically repeated dialogue that
never comes to issue. Quentin's, and a reader's, position
regarding the story he tells is always one of uncertainty,
where a meaning seems to exist and not to exist. It is ultimately characterized in the relation that Quentin imagines
between the men who have come to take Henry Sutpen and Jim
Bond, the part Negro idiot who is the last element of the
Sutpen story: "They could hear him; he didn't seem to ever get
any further away but they couldn't get any nearer and maybe
in time they could not even locate the direction any more of
the howling" (p. 376). Bond represents the entire story: he
is potential meaning, always just out of reach, but asserting
in his idiot howling the negation of meaning. The suggestive-
ness of his presence is denied by the very quality that
establishes it, his incomprehensibility. Shreve, with characteristic callousness, reminds Quentin: "... you've got him
there still. You still hear him at night sometimes. Don't
you?" (p. 378). But a reader is aware that no reminder is
necessary, that Bond represents the constant tension that
haunts Quentin, the story that must be meaningful and cannot
be. For Sutpen, Bond would have been the final symbol of
nothingness, the last failure, and he thus embodies the defeat
of both narrator and character. He is General Compson's
"spirit" crying in the "darkness," and he is a refutation of
all that "design," for both Quentin and Sutpen, ever meant.

In my discussions of *Moby-Dick* and "Heart of Darkness," I
have frequently remarked Ishmael's and Marlow's reliance upon

approximate language of various kinds, from obviously limited
special and artificial vocabularies to intensely qualified and
just as intensely rendered allusions, reports, and figures.
It should be clear now that Quentin Compson, like Marlow, is
Ishmael's counterpart in his use of verbal approximations--
specifically both in his use of narrative matter taken or inherited from sources outside himself and in his own characteristic imaginative tensions of the artificial and the real,
deadness and vitality. It should be clear also that the "last
silence" of *Absalom, Absalom!* is equivalent to the "dumb blank-
ness, full of meaning" of *Moby-Dick*. In each case profundity
is expressed by the fact that the attempt to achieve profundity
must always be qualified, that all the suggestive voices must
always be "silent." I have characterized this use of language
generally as "simile," in its opposition to the potentially
metaphorical visions of Ahab, Kurtz, and Sutpen, and I shall
now summarize particularly how the narrative of *Absalom, Absalom!* exhibits its quality as extended simile.

Although the quality of this narrative as simile is most
obvious when it is laced with words and phrases like "as
though," "perhaps," "I think," and "I would like to believe,"
and most emphatic when Quentin demonstrates the suggestive
failure that all these tags imply, this quality is shown to
be a constant property of the entire narrative in that Quentin
is the sum of all the narrators and in that the anonymous nar-
rator--in a striking extension of Ishmael's unwillingness to
commit himself--refuses to sanction the entire narrative as
anything more than hypothesis. The story thus becomes one
great "as though" based upon a supposed body of literal details
like those of the "Chronology" and "Genealogy" and the attempt
to make these details meaningful. All of the narrators attempt
to compose these details into a story by which they will become
significant both to narrator and listener, and the result is
always a suspect relation between literal and metaphorical
represented in the approximated story--an extended simile whose
assertion of potential meaning insists that such meaning must
only be potential. In this way the inability of the imagination to proceed beyond approximation is reflected in both the
theme and the method of *Absalom, Absalom!*, and this phenomenon
constitutes, I think, the success and the failure of this
novel.

In Sutpen's conviction that order lies just beyond his
reach and in the constant frustration of his attempts to grasp
it, he is himself--like Ahab at the last--a kind of living
simile. He represents a distinct kind of language that in his
failure is shown to be inadequate. And in his case the simile
into which he is transformed is demonstrated to be both the
beginning and the end of metaphor, both a step forward to and
backward from metaphor. We feel justified in describing him

in this way because, as I have suggested previously, both a
meaning that he desires and his own sense of its negation are
observable in the source and progress of his design. Sutpen's
particular negation, furthermore, may be seen to partake of
the "darkness" that General Compson holds to be universal and
inevitable.

For the narrators of the novel, however, "darkness" is
apparent only by reference to the hypothetical story of Sutpen.
We are unable, for this reason, to say just why it is that
Quentin fails to make the story more than hypothesis. In the
case of Sutpen, again, we are presented with a defined and
dramatic polarity: "design" and "darkness." His history and
his ultimate defeat may be understood in terms of a conflict
between these elements. For Quentin there is no such conflict,
but only what might be the result of one; the particular
vitality-deadness paradox exhibited in his perceptions may
well be simply an inherited quality of imagination. Even
though his attempt to understand the story is unquestionably
genuine, and even though his failure often seems generally
persuasive, he may be said to be restricted by his inheritance
from previous speakers of both an unresolved story and the
conviction that it must remain unresolved. And if we return
to these speakers, we find that even here there is no conclusive or even dramatic conflict which decides that the imagination must inevitably fail. The failures of Rosa Coldfield,
Quentin's father, and thus of Quentin himself seem at worst a
matter of psychology and at best a matter of circumstance,
of limitations acting upon them from without and for which they
seem not responsible, limitations imposed, of course, by
Faulkner. In either case their defeat appears unconvincing
as an instance of a defeat to which all men are liable, or as
evidence of a "darkness."

The ambiguous problem that the narrators reveal may become generally meaningful, again, in relation to the conflict
in Sutpen, but this conflict is not only open to various
specific qualifications but also is itself the general product
of the narrators' speculations, and we have come full circle.
If the inconclusiveness of the narrative is the result of a
conflict like the hypothetical struggle of Thomas Sutpen, that
conflict does not appear in the narrative except as a creation
of and an example of the inconclusiveness itself. The "darkness" itself is only a possibility, and the presentation of
imaginative failure as a theme has its ultimate source not in
a real tension that is brought to issue in the novel but in
the anonymous narrator's declaration that the story may not
exist at all. The failure to define a story and to create a
metaphor, in other words, seems assumed and lacks force as
evidence of the necessity of failure.

For Faulkner, then, the use of extended simile and the defeat it implies becomes the total narrative method: not a dramatized struggle with whatever may lie beyond imagination, and not simply a structural theme that he assumes, but a manner of proceeding that implies that as a theme it is unstable. The fact that the supposed conflict between design and darkness is itself unrealizable may be seen to be an extension of this theme when we consider that Faulkner postulates the failure of *all* metaphor.

This failure was exhibited at the outset in the narratives of Quentin's father and Rosa Coldfield, for the fallibility of both these speakers was expressed in their attempt to transform kinds of disorder, their own inabilities to understand, into metaphor. For Mr. Compson this disorder meant "Fate"; for Rosa it meant Sutpen's "demonhood." In either version the characters of the Sutpen story were shown in futile conflict with something supernatural--in Mr. Compson's case a supernatural force and in Rosa's a supernatural entity. The distinction between these narrators and General Compson, of course, rests in the fact that Quentin's grandfather will postulate only the metaphor of "darkness," but this distinction is not so meaningful as one might suppose, for the "darkness" too suggests the presence of supernatural powers who cannot be defeated. The imaginative failure here thus becomes a metaphor itself, an assertion of the order of the universe, in terms of which Sutpen's defeat is explainable and significant.

This matter may be clarified if we remember that in *Moby-Dick* the ineffable is supposed to have, at least until Ahab finally fails, a metaphorical existence in the white whale and that Melville suggests, in this manner, the reality of a conflict between mind and the ineffable. In "Heart of Darkness," too, we are still dealing--because of Marlow's persistent moral concern--with the "powers of darkness," even though such powers lose significance throughout and the polarity between mind and darkness is, I think, finally destroyed. In both cases the attempts at order are suggested to be meaningful--again, in different degrees--in terms of their conflict with the nature of the universe, with the ineffable.

In *Absalom, Absalom!* the darkness itself--and the metaphorical struggle--is hypothetical. We are thus allowed to question Sutpen's vision of design and nothingness--the vision that causes his failure--and we may even see it as an example of a kind of schizophrenia. In the case of Quentin Compson, where "darkness" is not even directly suggested, the temptation to use the language of psychopathology is even greater, and we cannot understand why he appears to be the most sympathetically treated narrator. The paradox here is that Quentin

seems most psychologically deranged precisely because in terms
of the theme of the novel he is most sane: he does not worship
the fictions of fate or darkness, but simply, and desperately,
confesses that he does not understand. Faulkner suggests in
this way that the failure here is just that; it cannot be
alleviated or explained by any metaphor, even a metaphor of
inevitable failure. In other words, this failure can be displayed conscientiously and realistically only by exhibiting a
flat absence of imaginative control and the terrible cost of
that absence.

It is for this reason, I think, that Faulkner deliberately
places the story beyond his narrators; the essential imaginative problem, he appears to suggest, can be consistently
demonstrated only in the failure to create any story at all.
No dramatic tensions or conflicts may exist unequivocally in
this novel, and we are left with the sheer verbal disorder
that reflects the inability to create a fictional world. But
the failure to compose a story is the failure to compose a
novel, and we have only Faulkner's word that the failure was
the unavoidable result of his most conscientious perception,
his word for the necessity of defeat.

The last paradox of *Absalom, Absalom!*, then, is the complete interdependence of success with failure in the novel,
and this paradox cannot be resolved. That the imagination must
fail is not really demonstrated in the novel, and the lack of
imaginative control in the novel is, on the one hand, Faulkner's insufficiency. On the other hand, the novel suggests
that such a failure could not be demonstrated; it suggests
that to resolve the matter by creating a "darkness" is to
falsify. This novel is the most thorough-going of those
works of fiction that call into question the possibilities of
language and meaning; as an immense display of fallen language
and as a revelation of the nature of this language, it seems
unparalleled. In it Faulkner insists that, as Sutpen's active
force and Quentin's imaginative vitality arise from and are
exhibited in their failure, the greatest success of language
itself is to create a potential of meaning that must remain
unrealized, a tension between order and disorder that cannot
be resolved but only repeated, and repeated. Language may be
defined in this way, however, only because no meaning is ever
achieved, because no metaphor is ever constructed.

It is not simply that *Absalom, Absalom!* is possibly one
kind of novel or another but that it is possibly no novel at
all. Faulkner's insistence that the imagination must fail
completely can never be evaluated because it can only remain
an insistence. The supposed struggle that it implies could
only be revealed metaphorically and thus cannot be revealed--
given the insistence--at all. Faulkner's position is super-

ficially equivalent to that of Rosa Coldfield herself, when
Rosa questions the metaphors she employs; his assertion that
the function of language can only be to create a hypothetical
and insoluble potential is *"that true wisdom which can compre-*
hend that there is a might-have-been which is more true than
truth" (p. 143). It may be that Faulkner's inability to
dramatize this wisdom, as he suggests, is indicative of a
general and inevitable failure of the human mind to order and
of his imaginative balance in dealing with this failure; it
may be also that, like Rosa, he is not balanced at all, that
he is simply unable to allow this wisdom to be tested. There
is no way of knowing.

NOTES

   1. William Faulkner, *Absalom, Absalom!* (New York: Random
House, Inc., 1951), p. 102. All subsequent references to
Absalom, Absalom! are to this edition.

   2. Because this "dialogue" is always subject to Quentin's
approval, we may for the sake of economy of reference consider
it as a unified section of the narrative. In my discussion,
also, I rely much more upon Quentin's remarks than upon
Shreve's, for the latter may be the only unquestionable
psychopathological case in the novel—in his capacity for
sadism, the emphatic vicariousness of his pleasures, and so
on.

   3. This sentence may be best understood if we observe a
grammatical parallelism that Faulkner has neglected to establish: read "or *with* holding" for "or *in* holding."

   4. The phenomenon of impotence is thus dramatized also in
the hypothetical account of Bon, a search for design in itself. Richard Poirier has remarked that "incest with Judith
or death at the hands of his brother become the only ways in
which Bon can identify himself as Sutpen's son." "Strange
Gods in Jefferson, Mississippi," in *William Faulkner: Two*
Decades of Criticism, ed. Frederick J. Hoffman and Olga W.
Vickery, (East Lansing: Michigan State College Press, 1951),
p. 239. For explicit images, in Shreve's account, of Bon's
failure to "penetrate" and his encounters with "nothingness,"
see in *Absalom, Absalom!*, for example, pp. 320, 327, 348.

   5. The connection between mortality and disorder in the
imagination of Quentin and Faulkner himself becomes most
obvious in *The Sound and the Fury*.

   6. Our knowledge, from *The Sound and the Fury*, that Quentin

commits suicide in the spring of this year is surely relevant here, and would suggest a final relinquishment and "dissolution of the tension."

THE PUZZLING DESIGN
OF *ABSALOM, ABSALOM!*

Duncan Aswell

It is now generally recognized that *Absalom, Absalom!* consists of several interrelated attempts to make sense out of
the past, that none of these attempts is definitive, and that
the contorted, jungle-like style so offensive to Clifton
Fadiman is an essential counterpart to the search for meaning
and certainty undertaken by the characters. Yet, none of the
interpretations of the novel thus far offered pursues the implications of these statements. If none of the narrators
reports reliably, we cannot use their analyses of events as
clues to Faulkner's own attitude toward the past and the
South. Each successive insight provides us with crucial information about the narrator who is offering it, but every
addition to our knowledge of the Sutpen legend only gives
further proof that it is impossible to interpret human experience
objectively, to draw conclusions from it that will be valid for
anyone but the speaker and interpreter of the moment.

Faulkner dramatizes on every page the futility of imposing
any kind of order or pattern upon human life, while at the same
time revealing with the utmost compassion, and making us feel
with the greatest poignancy, that the yearning to make logical
sense out of events is a compulsive, inescapable need, one of
the defining characteristics of the human soul. More than
this, while he takes great pains to remind us that the narrators' interpretations are unreliable and wholly subjective,
and while a close study of his text will lead the reader to
total skepticism, Faulkner has constructed the novel with such
extraordinary skill that our disbelief is almost wholly suspended as we read it for the first time. His daring and
brilliant strategy in *Absalom, Absalom!* is to divide us against
ourselves, our emotional against our intellectual responses, by
providing us with continually more irresistible and subtle

From The Kenyon Review, *30 (1968), pp. 67-84. Copyright 1968
by Kenyon College. Reprinted by permission of Kenyon College.*

rhetorical arguments until we forget what we have been asked
to take on faith and what we can safely accept as known and
proven. Faulkner plays upon precisely those needs and desires
in us that he shows operating in his characters, and demonstrates the truth of his fable by making us equally blind and
hopeful participants in the search for illumination. He knows
which springs to touch in us at which moment; we respond with
increasing eagerness to the successive accounts of his characters because each new interpretation appeals more to our innate trust that human experience not only can be understood
but will be found to accord with the laws and precepts of
logic and morality that we like to believe govern our lives,
though we might have trouble actually demonstrating their
prominence. Yet, a dispassionate, analytical review of the
novel's structure should demonstrate that, far from clarifying
the original subjects of concern and uncertainty, the different
revelations actually obscure the *facts* of Sutpen's life and
hinder the reader from evaluating their significance.

One distinctive feature of *Absalom, Absalom!* is the number
and importance of the uncertainties about the central events
voiced by each of the narrators of the legend. Every attempt
to discover the causes and origins of behavior is marked by
breaks in the narrative introduced by some variation on the
central refrain: "Nobody ever knew," "He didn't remember,"
"He didn't say," "He didn't know," and so on. Some of the
missing items in the material reliably reported at first hand
and so presumably true are the following: the birthplace and
birth date of Thomas Sutpen; his manner of reaching the West
Indies; how he spent his time there; how he subdued the natives;
what was wrong with his first wife; how he reached Jefferson;
how he made his money; the nature of the deal with Coldfield;
the activities and feelings of all the principals before the
wedding with Ellen; what Sutpen told Henry at Christmas 1860,
and, again, in the Confederate camp just before the end of
the war; what Sutpen meant when he told Quentin's grandfather
he had to make a choice; why Rosa agreed to marry Sutpen and
why Sutpen insulted Rosa; the identity of the boy adopted by
Judith and Clytie after the war; what Quentin learned when he
went to Sutpen's Hundred with Miss Rosa; and, most importantly,
whether Bon was the son of Sutpen and whether he was a Negro.
Some information that we know to be true--if, after reading
the novel, we can ever again use the words "know" and "true"
without embarrassment--is that Thomas Sutpen arrived in Jefferson in 1833, determined to complete a "design" undertaken because of certain specified childhood experiences; that he
married Ellen Coldfield; that his son Henry killed his daughter
Judith's fiancé; that he insulted his sister-in-law Rosa after
proposing marriage to her; that he fathered a daughter upon

Milly Jones, whose grandfather killed him; that his son Henry
and daughter Clytemnestra perished in a fire that consumed
Sutpen's great house. These are the basic materials of the
Sutpen legend; the rest is pure conjecture.

   All of this is not to say that the conjectures are necessarily false; there is excellent reason to believe, for instance,
that Bon was Sutpen's son by a woman with Negro blood. But it
must be recognized that such a statement is a supposition,
since there is no objective evidence upon which to support
such a belief. Faulkner has shown what a splendid story can
be constructed upon such an assumption, but he takes elaborate
precautions to prevent his readers from being able to prove its
veracity. Neither Quentin's grandfather nor his father knew
that Sutpen had fathered Bon; the "fact" is first revealed to
us by Shreve in an imaginative leap based upon the way Quentin
has told him about Sutpen's early life. Shreve matter-of-
factly tosses out this startling conclusion, which Quentin
and his father had already arrived at independently and used
as the basis for a whole new theory of Sutpen's life. Only
later does Shreve ask Quentin where he got the additional information for a new version of the legend and intuits that it
came from Quentin's visit to Sutpen's Hundred with Miss Rosa.
Much later, when that visit is actually described, the reader
can find no substantiating detail that shows how Quentin
learned the "truth" about Bon. Instead, Faulkner provides
us with several unsatisfying possible explanations.

   For instance, Quentin might have found out about Bon by
seeing Clytie at Sutpen's Hundred. Earlier, Shreve had said,
"... you wouldn't have known what anybody was talking about if
you hadn't been out there and seen Clytie. Is that right?"
And Quentin answers, "Yes." Shreve's emphasis on the importance
of seeing Clytie is repeated in his imaginative reconstruction
of Quentin's meeting with her: "... and she didn't tell you
in the actual words because even in the terror she kept the
secret; nevertheless she told you, or at least all of a sudden
you knew--." One possible source for Quentin's certainty,
then, is simply the sight of this one part-Negro child of
Thomas Sutpen, whose presence suggests the possibility that
another such child was born and caused all the mysterious difficulty. Such a tenuous connection between stimulus and response is characteristic of the operations of the human mind
in its search for valid meaning that Faulkner depicts in this
novel.

   There is no certainty, however, that Quentin's insight
comes from Clytie. When he recalls the visit himself at the
end of the novel, he attributes no particular significance to
the meeting with Sutpen's daughter. Instead, he suggests a
wholly different line of reasoning that might have led to the

new theory. When he catches sight of Jim Bond in the hall,
"He remembered how he thought, 'The scion, the heir, and apparent (though not obvious).'" "Apparent" and "not obvious"
serve more than a punning function to imply the operations
of Quentin's own mind and perceptions. Since, at this point
in chronological time, Quentin knows nothing of Bon's parent-
hood, his insight suggests a real revelation. It is cast into
relief a moment later when Rosa orders Jim Bond to help her
up, saying, "You aint any Sutpen!" Again, though, Quentin
does not dramatize the moment as an illumination; the whole
episode is written to emphasize the confrontation with Henry
as climactic. And yet, that confrontation is masterfully
reported in as inconclusive and frustrating a form as possible.
The nearly perfect chiastic structure of the dialogue in this
scene--with the first question-and-answer pairing repeated as
the final pairing, the second repeated as the next-to-last,
the third almost exactly repeated as the fourth--precisely
captures the quality of Quentin's mind as it is revealed
throughout the novel, endlessly circling round and round an
experience without ever coming to grips with it. The dialogue is somewhat like the ripples Quentin visualizes on a
pond when he realizes he is doomed to retrace his father's
steps. Thus, Quentin's comment on the impact of his dialogue
with Henry is poignantly characteristic: "... waking or sleep-
ing it was the same and would be the same forever as long as
he lived." The form of the dialogue and everything we know
about Quentin strongly suggests that nothing conclusive or
objectively verifiable took place at Sutpen's Hundred. The
scene functions as another tantalizing enigma which Faulkner
leaves for us to solve. He teases us with numerous possibilities, none of them wholly satisfying. Like his characters,
we cannot connect a cause with its effect. We know that
Quentin decided Bon was Sutpen's Negro son; we know that his
trip to the great mansion brought about this decision; but we
know no more. No one ever knows.

Faulkner taunts and challenges his readers in similar ways
throughout the novel, carefully leading up to a revelation
that will illuminate the obscure corners of the legend and
then leaving us in darkness. His central theme is the mystery
of human conduct and man's futile but compulsive efforts to
control, limit, define, explain, and conquer that mystery.
Every one of the characters--both the narrators and those
narrated about--is seeking not only an answer to the mystery
of his own and others' experience, but, as an essential corol-
lary to this search for motive, justification, and understanding, each also hunts for some kind of affirmation that his
existence is endowed with *permanent* significance, some assurance
that his finite being can transcend the limits of time and space
and reach infinitude.

Sutpen's obsession with his "design" is the most important search of this kind, since it serves as the model for all the others; and it is also the compelling reason why his onlookers must return to his story over and over again. When he first outlines it to Quentin's grandfather, he speaks merely of competing with and outdoing the rich landowners he envied as a boy, and he describes his decision to go to the West Indies by saying, "I realized that to accomplish my design I should need first of all and above all things money in considerable quantities and in the quite immediate future...." Faulkner intentionally obscures the nature of this original, limited design by having Quentin interpose between the telling of Sutpen's decision and of his arrival in the West Indies the much later conversation between Sutpen and Quentin's grandfather during which Sutpen says about his first wife, "I found that she was not and could never be, through no fault of her own, adjunctive or incremental to the design which I had in mind, so I provided for her and put her aside." Faulkner's strategy here, as throughout the novel, is to telescope time so as to suggest that an original action contains within it all the later consequences to which it will lead, making potentialities into actualities. Yet, by emphasizing the limits of Sutpen's initial design, we can trace the tragic course of his obsession more clearly, observing the stages by which his energies become riveted upon the single goal of bearing a son, even when there is nothing much for that son to inherit and nothing left of the impulse behind the original design. Sutpen's attention thus shifts from a project he can achieve in his own lifetime to a defiant gesture toward the future, the age-old compulsion to insure immortality in the only imperfect manner nature will allow. Viewed in this light, his tragedy follows the arc not of Faustus, which Shreve jokingly suggests, but of Tamburlaine.

While *Absalom, Absalom!* pivots around Sutpen's lust for permanence, his story is framed at beginning and end by Rosa Coldfield's pathetic and muted quest for some sort of lasting gesture of her own. Before she has really begun her version of the Sutpen legend, Faulkner sets down her reason for summoning Quentin as the hope that "some day you will remember this and write about it." Yet, her wish for remembrance is the most hopeless of all, doomed in the reader's mind as soon as articulated. For Faulkner has already written the story of Quentin Compson with its tragic ending, so that all of Rosa's theorizing about his marriage and wife and house seems cruelly ironic. Nevertheless, after Sutpen's story is told—as much of it as can be reconstructed—Rosa's hope is given voice once again, this time by Quentin's father in the letter that has lain open in the cold Cambridge room all through the wintry hours of recitation and fantasizing: "*Surely it can harm no one to believe that perhaps she has escaped not at all the privilege of being outraged and amazed and of not forgiving but on the contrary has herself gained that place or bourne where the objects of the outrage and of the commiseration also are no longer ghosts but are actual people to be actual recipients of the hatred and the pity.*" Rosa's death had been announced in the beginning of the letter over 200 pages earlier, at the central point of the novel when the locale changes from Mississippi to Massachusetts. Faulkner thus carefully constructs the novel around Rosa's hopes, using her as one of the minor variations on his central theme. Her position all through the work--as a fixed and frozen figure who, as Quentin says, "died young of outrage in 1866 one summer"--emphasizes her timelessness in the present and her need for some kind of memorial that will outlast her own life span. Mr. Compson's vision of her after death, frozen forevermore into the same attitudes and passions that possessed her in life, is the final reduction of all human pretensions to a meaningful immortality, any hopes for betterment and growth. As such, it picks up and reinforces Quentin's desperate cry just before he recalls the letter--"Nevermore of peace. Nevermore of peace. Nevermore Nevermore Nevermore"--and serves as a fitting counterpart to Shreve's cynical speech immediately following, which reduces the whole Sutpen legend to a series of arithmetical equations, and concludes: "... it clears the whole ledger, you can tear all the pages out and burn them...." Rosa's changeless, static existence finds its last reflection in, and is partly responsible for, the hopeless cry of Quentin that concludes the book and that implies allegiance to the values and commitments that have governed all the characters' lives.

The yearning for permanence may also be observed in the activity of Wash Jones, whom Quentin envisions in an afterlife similar to the one Mr. Compson constructs for Rosa. Quentin imagines Wash and Sutpen in "the same place" after death talking together amicably, perhaps drinking as they had in life, with only the faintest recollection that something important had happened between them, and neither of them remembering what it was. "Then the shadow would fade, the wind die away until at last Jones would say, serene, not even triumphant: 'They mought have kilt us, but they aint whupped us yit, air they?'" The theme of *not knowing, not remembering*, not being able to take intellectual possession of one's own experience continues after death here. This is, of course, Quentin's vision and chiefly reveals the state of his mind, yet this depiction of business as usual on the other side of the grave serves as an ironic backdrop to the subsequent interpretations

of Wash's life offered by Quentin and his father. Mr. Compson
believed that for Wash the real world was "just a dream and an
illusion" and the actual world was the one where Sutpen rode
his great horse, looking to Wash like God Himself. Like God,
Sutpen is "forever and forever immortal" to Wash, but this
revelation comes just before Sutpen insults Wash's granddaughter and is cut down forever. Quentin then visualizes
Wash immediately after the murder stripped of his illusions,
as he waits fatalistically for the sheriff and his men to come,
knowing "that if he ran he would be fleeing merely one set of
bragging and evil shadows for another, since they (men) were
all of a kind throughout all of earth which he knew...." There
are no more distinctions to be made between men now; human
life is a stretch of meaningless time, a tale told by an idiot
signifying nothing: "the murmuring of tomorrow and tomorrow
and tomorrow beyond the immediate fury."

Of course, Wash's story comes to us filtered through the
consciousness of Quentin and Mr. Compson, and it is their
struggles for meaning and permanence, together with Sutpen's,
which occupy the center of *Absalom, Absalom!* The most important
gesture toward eternity that the novel records is the act of
storytelling itself, already glimpsed in Rosa's futile yearning, further reflected in Judith's handing on of Bon's letter
to Quentin's grandmother, and fully dramatized in Sutpen and
in three generations of Compsons. Yet, it is far from Faulkner's
purpose to glorify the act of fictionalizing, to say that life
gains significance through being analyzed, ordered, reconstituted for dramatic or historical purposes. The act of interpreting experience is possibly the highest of which man is
capable, but it is simply another of his futile efforts to
transcend finite limits, important only because of the struggle
and ambition it involves and reveals, not because of its
achievement. Storytelling is of necessity falsification,
not a method of getting at the facts but a means of satisfying
the innate human desire for logic and coherence. In the middle
of Sutpen's recital of his early life to Quentin's grandfather,
Quentin records his ancestor's dissatisfaction with a narrative
that showed no "regard for cause and effect" and his insistence
that Sutpen start over again. Even when Sutpen does begin
again, however, Quentin goes on, "it was not absolutely clear--
the how and the why he was there and what he was--since he was
not talking about himself. He was telling a story. He was not
bragging about something he had done; he was just telling a
story about something a man named Thomas Sutpen had experienced,
which would still have been the same story if the man had had
no name at all, if it had been told about any man or no man
over whiskey at night." What is this "same story" that would
have applied to "any man or no man"? Is it not the very search

for and failure to find some lasting significance in life that
every character in the novel is engaged in and that the telling
of the story--from Sutpen to Quentin's grandfather to Mr. Compson to Quentin to Shreve--itself reflects? We never learn the
how and the why and the what; Quentin says of Sutpen, "So he
knew neither where he had come from nor where he was nor why,"
and the statement applies to everyone else in the novel. It
is in this sense that "that best of ratiocination" undertaken
by Quentin and Shreve is "after all ... a good deal like
Sutpen's morality and Miss Coldfield's demonizing." Each man
searches for logic, for cause and effect, for meaning, and
none is successful.

The fact remains that as we read through the book for the
first time, desperately looking for "answers," we feel that we
keep getting nearer and nearer the truth. But this feeling
actually depends upon the emotional convictions of the successive narrators, not on any objectively verifiable information. The account of the first narrator, Rosa, is full of
admissions that nothing makes sense, that the motives of all
the actors in her drama, including her own, are indecipherable,
irretrievably lost. Because of this and because of her hysterical demonizing, the reader forgets that she is the only
interpreter whose story is based upon firsthand observation
and that her old-fashioned, theological view of the events
is as plausible as any of the other attempts to order and explain them.

Mr. Compson seems to us at first more reliable than Rosa
because he makes up for his personal distance from the legend
by theorizing and philosophizing about it, and he compels our
temporary credence by the passion and carefulness of his rendi-
tion. Although he admits that his explanation of Henry's
reasons for leaving Sutpen's Hundred is unsatisfactory, he is
as committed to the art of storytelling as are Quentin and
Shreve later. His narrative of Henry and Bon in New Orleans
is elaborately circumstantial and detailed and based upon the
kind of psychological explanation of motives that we look for
and believe in when we read conventional fiction. We are
perfectly content to accept Mr. Compson's interpretation until
Shreve and Quentin fabricate an even more compelling version.

When we hear from Quentin's grandfather, we feel we have
moved even nearer to verifiable fact because his knowledge
comes straight from the horse's mouth. We tend to forget that
this is Sutpen's "story," not his biography, and to overlook
all the reminders of its arbitrariness and subjectivity. The
narrative is riddled with unremembered details, unknown facts,
and withheld information. It is only when we come to Shreve's
and Quentin's account, which is nothing but fantasy, that we
have left ambiguities and uncertainties behind altogether. As

if to answer all those who did not know or did not remember,
the young men insist on full awareness of all motives and
circumstances by all the actors in their story. Compare, for
instance, Mr. Compson's version of the ride away from Sutpen's
Hundred in 1860--"Bon was riding beside [Henry], trying to
find out from him what had happened"--with Shreve's and Quentin's reconstruction of the meeting of Henry and his father
in the Confederate camp: *"To [Henry] it is logical and natural
that their father should know of his and Bon's decision: that
rapport of blood which should bring Bon to decide to write,
himself to agree to it and their father to know of it at the
same identical instant, after a period of four years, out of
all time."* *Absalom, Absalom!* demonstrates the paradoxical
truth that only when the imagination is totally freed from
the tyranny of known facts, from the chaotic puzzle of lived
experience, is it able to create a picture of reality that is
totally consistent, plausible, and convincing. The reckless
bravado and assurance of Shreve's dramatization dare us to
question any of its particulars. The young men draw us step
by step into their imaginary world, until we actually enter
their vision of the Civil War completely, with no narrative
voice between us and the events chronicled. Have we not
finally reached and recovered the past here?

    The answer is *no*. We are still observing the anguished
attempts of the living to explain the activities of the dead.
Faulkner is careful to warn us at the beginning of the young
men's fantasy that we are not to look for facts and objective
truth from them. They start by imagining Bon and Judith pacing
in the garden among the luxuriating and exotic blooms of the
South, and Faulkner comments: "It would not matter here in
Cambridge that the time had been winter in that garden too,
and hence no bloom nor leaf.... But that did not matter because it had been so long ago ... and that not mattering
either: what faces and what names they called themselves and
were called by so long as the blood coursed...." What matters
is the present, not the past, and what the boys record is the
behavior they imagine they themselves would have performed had
they been Bon and Henry. Shreve's whimsical insistence upon
calling Rosa Coldfield "Aunt Rosa"--a label Quentin finally
stops objecting to--not only suggests her mediate position
between the Sutpens and Compsons and her close similarity to
Quentin, but identifies Quentin with Henry Sutpen, whose aunt
really was Rosa Coldfield. In several other ways Shreve's
reconstruction of the Henry-Judith-Bon triangle recalls the
Quentin-Caddy-Ames tangle described in *The Sound and the Fury*,
which was perhaps already familiar to Shreve. Faulkner insists
on reminding us that it is Shreve and Quentin who ride through
the Mississippi countryside, and, thus, when the italicized

passages of direct depiction occur, he makes sure that we know
these are continuations of the boys' "game," not literal events.
During the unforgettable scene of Henry's meeting with his
father, Sutpen is made to say, "*You were hit at Shiloh, Colonel
Willow tells me*," thus picking up Shreve's conjecture that it
was Henry, not Bon, who was wounded at Shiloh. This was one
of Shreve's frankly fabricated notions, offered because it
simply "had to be," given the premises of his theory. As such,
it fits beautifully into the total scheme, and we are bludgeoned
into accepting the scene of the father-son confrontation by the
boys' insistence upon Henry's complete and conscious mental
grasp of the experience: "*Nor did Henry ever say that he did
not remember leaving the tent. He remembers all of it. He
remembers....*" The verb "*remembers*" keeps echoing throughout
the passage. This compulsive stress upon the act of recalling
is picked up again in the scene where Henry's counterpart,
Quentin, goes to Sutpen's Hundred. Yet, even with these
assurances of intellectual possession and after all their
fanciful literary reconstructions of the past and their extraordinary investment and commitment of imagination, Quentin is
forced to admit to Shreve that he is hopelessly confused. To
Shreve's question whether he understands the South, Quentin
answers, "I don't know.... Yes, of course I understand it....
I don't know." Their theory about the Sutpen legend is most
ingenious and attractive, but it doesn't answer any of the
really important questions raised by the known facts. If there
is such a simple, neat, "logical" explanation for the Sutpen
mysteries, what is to be learned from the legend? Why is
Quentin still so vexed and dissatisfied in the last section
of the novel? Why is there no sense of exultation and achievement at having "cracked" the mystery? Shreve's comment, at
the end of his exhausting recital, is, "Let's get out of this
refrigerator and go to bed." What has been accomplished by
all the ratiocination and the passion?

Once again, Faulkner stresses that it is the struggle, not
the achievement, that is memorable. No single human act,
however profound or significant, can hold the attention for
very long. Having amused himself with the foibles of these
queer Southerners for a while, Shreve, at least, is ready to
move on to something new. Quentin's position is more complicated. He seems doomed to keep haunting the places where his
honor died, but his final assertion that he doesn't hate the
South suggests that he is not yet ready to throw himself into
the Charles. However, *Absalom, Absalom!* has provided sufficient
material to explain the inevitability of that final act.
Quentin has not only observed and articulated the failure of
all the attempts to assert a more than momentary significance,
but he too is engaged in the same hopeless task through an

imaginative projection of his own obsessions upon the historical personalities he is trying to recreate. In response
to Quentin's desire to see *love* exemplified in the Bon-Henry-
Judith story, Shreve imagines Bon to be interested in Judith
in language nearly identical to that Quentin used to express
his passion for his sister Caddy in *The Sound and the Fury*:
"And who to say if it wasn't maybe the possibility of incest,
because who ... has been in love and not discovered the vain
evanescence of the fleshly encounter ... but maybe if there
were sin too maybe you would not be permitted to escape, un-
couple, return.--Aint that right?" To this Quentin, after a
long silence, replies, "I don't know." Then Henry, in one of
the italicized passages of direct dramatization, is imagined
by both boys to be grateful for Bon's decision to marry Judith
*not for the incest of course but because at last they were
going to do something, at last he could be something even
though that something was the irrevocable repudiation of the
old heredity and training and the acceptance of eternal damna-
tion.*" Even in the world of his imagination, where everything
is possible, Quentin cannot so contradict the facts of human
experience as to give Henry that eternal achievement. Indeed,
one reason why he is so devastated by the meeting with Henry
at Sutpen's Hundred is the revelation of the literal, squalid
reality to which Henry and his own romantic fantasy have been
reduced. Once again, the limits of significant and heroic action and meaningful choice have shrunk to nothing. Quentin and
Henry, like all those who have gone before them and all those
who will come after, are committed irrevocably to this world of
adventitiousness, impermanence, chance, and change. Quentin
can imagine making gestures to defy time, but he cannot actually perform them, much less conquer time itself.

The text of *Absalom, Absalom!* ends with Quentin's recognition of his hopeless impasse, but Faulkner has not finished
demonstrating the futility of our quest for objectively
verifiable truth and certainty. He has additional jokes to
play upon our lust for logic or for what he calls, with respect
to Sutpen's motivating drive, some "formula and recipe of fact
and deduction." All printings of the novel, beginning with
the original Random House edition of 1936, provide a "Chronology" and "Genealogy" after the text. This material is not
like the "Appendix" Faulkner wrote many years later for *The
Sound and the Fury*, but an integral part of the experience of
reading *Absalom, Absalom!* Indeed, Bernard De Voto, one of the
original reviewers of the novel, felt that the ordering provided by the chronology and genealogy was an essential aid to
the reader, and that this material should be studied first so
as to facilitate understanding of the Sutpen legend. This
facetious notion stems not only from a misconception of the

novel's purpose but from a careless reading of the two lists.
Far from helping to unscramble the confused events of the narrative, these appendices add to our uncertainty because of
the numerous discrepancies between their details and the text.
Faulkner must have been aware of these inconsistencies, and
have intentionally included them in order to develop his theme
still further at the expense of the reader's expectations.
The chronology, in particular, reads like the lucubrations
of some crazy and drunken Kinbote wilfully misinterpreting
his Southern Shade. Not only are the birth and death dates
of Ellen Coldfield and the birth date of Charles Bon different
from those in the text, but Charles Etienne Saint-Valery Bon's
name is spelled here St. Velery and barbarized in the genealogy
as Charles Etienne de Saint Velery. All of these details could
have been easily squared with the text by a quick check of the
passages describing the tombstones in the Sutpen graveyard.
The dates labeled 1910 in the chronology should be corrected
to read 1909. The misdating is precisely the sort of mistake
a careless reader would make, but it is hardly likely that
Faulkner did so unintentionally, since he correctly records
in the genealogy that Quentin died in 1910.

The most interesting errors have to do with Sutpen's early
life. The birth date, for instance, is given as 1807, though
Shreve estimates it to have been 1808. Since he is figuring
backward twenty-five years from 1833, and since we don't know
the month of birth, 1807 is as plausible a suggestion as 1808,
though one wonders on what authority it was chosen. When we
recall that Sutpen himself "did not know within a year on
either side just how old he was," the date begins to seem
completely arbitrary. Our suspicions are confirmed upon
reading in the chronology under 1820: "Sutpen ran away from
home. Fourteen years old." Not only does this contradict the
text, which says he went to sea in 1823, but it cannot possibly
be squared with the time scheme of the chronology itself.
There was no reason for Faulkner to call attention to such a
discrepancy by inserting "Fourteen years old"--a kind of dating
used nowhere else in the chronology--if he wanted the material
to seem authentic.

The fact is, of course, that a reliable and objective time-
schedule would run counter to all the intentions of the novel.
It would suggest that some kind of logical, rigid pattern that
makes absolute sense can be imposed upon human experience and
that an ordering of events in the form of a timetable will
actually tell us something about the lives whose dates it
records. The odd chronology Faulkner provides is the product
of more-than-usually fallible human ingenuity working upon the
hints and conjectures contained within the text. One can
imagine the fun Faulkner had compiling this idiotic chart, the

sort of fun he has throughout the novel mocking our attempts
to find logical connections between events (and there is considerably more wry humor in *Absalom, Absalom!* than is generally
recognized). Not only does the chronology contradict the text
and itself, but it contains a great deal of whimsically irrelevant information that contributes nothing to our understanding of the saga and simply adds to the burden of meaningless and unassimilated "facts" of which we have far too many
already. The chronology, in fact, should make us question
whether we have any of the facts straight about the Sutpen
legend. Who knows how Charles Bon's son's name should be
spelled, or even if the child taken in by Clytie and Judith
was Bon's son, since the boy himself doesn't know? Who knows
if Bon was born in Haiti, since Judith, who ought to know
better than Shreve or Quentin, put on his tombstone that he
was born in New Orleans? One thing is clear: the list can
obviously not be used to corroborate any of the suppositions
provided by the narrators since they are so wilfully confused
themselves.

Faulkner pursues his Nabokovian game to delightful ends in
the "Genealogy," where he continues to pretend at times that
he is a literal and not very bright reader, while he plays at
being God at other times. By filling us in on the activities
of Shreve after the novel closes and on his present whereabouts,
for instance, he reminds us that our knowledge is hopelessly
limited and that he has not allowed us to share more than a
tiny portion of the vast and wonderful material he has at hand.
The technique of the whole novel and the attitude of each of
the narrators suggest that the different interpretations are
drawn from a great reservoir of material which is all known
beforehand and which needs only the proper ordering and perspective for its full significance to be revealed. Of course,
that perfect insight is never provided, but Faulkner undercuts
even the possibility of such a solution by suggesting through
his chaotic appended details that there is no rounded and complete whole within which the meaning of his novel can be contained. The effect of his genealogy is to evoke the capricious-
ness of human experience and the arbitrariness of structuring
it in ordered works of art. This was the effect Gide aimed at
in *The Counterfeiters* and stressed by including an "Appendix"
of factual material upon which his story was based, though
Faulkner's purpose is not so specifically spelled out nor so
schematically pursued.

In all the ways examined in this study, *Absalom, Absalom!*
represents a radical questioning of the ability of the human
mind to deal adequately with its own experience. The very title
suggests that none of the attempts to explain the Sutpen story
is accurate or at least complete. The Biblical story of David,

Absalom, and Amnon stresses quite different relationships and
aspects of the legend from any given prominence in the novel.
Out of the chaos of conflicting opinions and fotgotten facts
that form the subject of the work, however, one idea continues
to be articulated and to resonate in harmony with the structure
and central theme. This is the idea that the mind, for all its
arrogance and self-regard, is merely an instrument altogether
inferior in strength, accuracy, and refinement to the body and
the physical senses. Bon expresses this notion in his letter
to Judith about the hardship and privation of the war to which,
he says, man never becomes really inured: "... *it is only the
mind, the gross omnivorous carrion-heavy soul which becomes
inured; the body itself, thank God, never reconciled from the
old soft feel of soap and clean linen and something between
the sole of the foot and the earth to distinguish it from the
foot of a beast.*" Rosa echoes him in her fierce recital of
the meeting with Clytie after she has learned of Bon's death.
She speaks of the "*touch of flesh with flesh*" that reaches to
"*the citadel of the central I-Am's private own: not spirit,
soul; the liquorish and ungirdled mind is anyone's to take in
any darkened hallway of this earthly tenement. But let flesh
touch with flesh, and watch the fall of all the eggshell
shibboleth of caste and color too.*" Shortly afterward she
describes in a very moving passage the end result of all her
disillusionment about Judith's grief for Bon, the end of the
agonizing process by which the mind--her own mind--confronts
and comes to terms with its own fantasies. What is left is
not the mind at all, nor anything to do with it, but some
residue of physical sensations: "*That is the substance of re-
membering--sense, sight, smell: the muscles with which we see
and hear and feel--not mind, not thought: there is no such
thing as memory: the brain recalls just what the muscles grope
for: no more, no less: and its resultant sum is usually incorrect and false and worthy only of the name of dream....
Ay, grief goes, fades; we know that--but ask the tear ducts
if they have forgotten how to weep.*" These beautiful words
may serve as an epigraph for the entire novel, and they should
be set beside the speech Quentin and Shreve attribute to Bon
as the Civil War is drawing to its close: "... *if you haven't
got honor and pride, then nothing matters. Only there is
something in you that doesn't care about honor and pride yet
that lives ... that probably even when this is over and there
is not even defeat left, will still decline to sit still in
the sun and die, but will be out of the woods, moving and
seeking where just will and endurance could not move it,
grubbing for roots and such--the old mindless sentient undreaming meat that doesn't even know any difference between
despair and victory....*" This, tentative as it may be, repre-

sents the affirmation of the novel, the idea summed up in the word that is repeated over and over throughout the text, "un-defeat." The restless struggle and dissatisfaction, the re-fusal to acknowledge defeat, exemplified by all the characters, is a form of that permanence for which they all seek, yet, ironically, the form none of them is willing to accept. Any other achievement satisfactory to the restless intellect the novel proves to be a dream and a delusion. *Absalom, Absalom!*, like *The Sound and the Fury*, asserts that the old, mindless, sentient, undreaming meat endures. Yet, both novels are com-posed of and dedicated to the *mind's* search for purpose, meaning, and truth; how, then, one may ask, is the *body's* endurance relevant to that search?

FAULKNER'S "MYTHOLOGY"

Walter Brylowski

[Editor's note: In the introductory chapter of his book,
Faulkner's Olympian Laugh: Myth in the Novels, *Professor Bry-*
lowski begins by identifying four levels of myth in Faulkner's
work: (1) allusion and analogy, (2) mythos or myth as plot,
(3) the mythic mode of thought, and (4) the "myth of the
South." Having briefly defined these four uses of myth, Bry-
lowski proposes to illustrate them with reference to Absalom,
Absalom!*]*

On the first level of myth, that of allusion and analogy,
Absalom, Absalom! is particularly rich. The title, not reinforced by any allusion in the text itself, establishes the
analogy between Henry and Absalom and Charles Bon and Amman
and is used thematically in the incest motif and the fratricide.
Ilse Dusoir Lind in her study, "The Design and Meaning of
Absalom, Absalom!" suggests further parallels between these
characters and classical and biblical mythology:

> If the characters in the Sutpen story remind us of Greek
> actors and epic Biblical figures, so does the action
> itself recall the events of an ancient tragic myth. A
> synopsis of the Sutpen legend would read like one of the
> summaries of Greek myths conveniently placed as prologue
> to modern translations of Greek plays. The continuing
> (though loose) analogies which exist between Sutpen and
> Oedipus, Sutpen's sons and Eteocles and Polyneices,
> Judith and Antigone, suggest that the Oedipus trilogy
> might have served as a general guide in the drafting of
> the plot. At the same time, Sutpen's fall and the ob-
> literation of his house bring to mind the great myth of
> man's original fall from innocence and the visitations

of Divine justice upon third and fourth generations.
Old Testament violence evoking God's wrath is recaptured
here in a legend of father turning against son, son
against father, and brother against brother.[1]

In the passage (pp. 355-356) where Henry returns to the camp-
fire and the waiting Bon, she finds the language and allusions
by which this "Cain-Abel conflict" are rendered "appropriately
Biblical."

There are further biblical analogies in Mr. Compson's
structuring of the account of Sutpen's early life. Born in
the Edenic mountain life of what was to become West Virginia,

> he didn't listen to the vague and cloudy tales of Tide-
> water splendor that penetrated even his mountains because
> then he could not understand what the people who told
> him about it meant ... and when he got to be a youth and
> curiosity itself exhumed the tales which he did not know
> he had heard and speculated on, he was interested and
> would have liked to see the places once, but without
> envy or regret. (p. 222)

Then, after the death of the mother who had been responsible
for the family's push into the mountains, "They fell into it,
the whole family, returned to the coast from which the first
Sutpen had come ..., tumbled head over heels back to Tidewater
by sheer altitude, elevation and gravity, as if whatever
slight hold the family had had on the mountain had broken"
(pp. 222-223). Unlike the biblical fall, however, Sutpen's
takes place after the departure from "Eden" and is not a
manifestation of the will, but imposed upon him by society.
Lind points out that with the loss of innocence before the
door of the plantation house where he had been sent upon an
errand, Sutpen felt, "like Adam in Paradise, the shameful inadequacy of his natural garb ('his patched overalls and no
shoes')."[2] The fall leads to the godlike formulation of Sutpen's design, "creating the Sutpen's Hundred, the *Be Sutpen's
Hundred* like the oldentime *Be Light*" (p. 9).

Returned from the war, his "design" fallen in ruins, Sutpen becomes in Shreve's words an Abraham:

> "the old Abraham full of years and weak and incapable
> now of further harm, caught at last and the captains and
> collectors saying, 'Old man, we dont want you' and
> Abraham would say, 'Praise the Lord, I have raised about
> me sons to bear the burden of mine iniquities and perse-
> cutions' ... the same old Abraham who was so old and weak
> now nobody would want him in the flesh on any debt."
> (pp. 325-326)

The Cadmus myth is invoked three times to suggest the
nature of the strife bred between Sutpen's "get." Mr. Compson
naming over the children first uses the image: "Yes. He
named Clytie as he named them all, the one before Clytie and
Henry and Judith even, with that same robust and sardonic
temerity, naming with his own mouth his own ironic fecundity
of dragon's teeth" (p. 62). This is repeated in one of Quentin's silent musings (p. 182) and finally repeated aloud to
Shreve (p. 266).

Sutpen might also be associated with the fisher king of
myth through the wounds received in the Haitian uprising, "'one
of which, Grandfather said, came pretty near leaving him that
virgin for the rest of his life too'" (p. 254). In terms of
theme, this might relate the color-line flaw of Sutpen's (and
allegorically, the South's) "design" to the social-political
sterility of the South, a flaw that could be eliminated (and,
in terms of the myth, with resultant "fertility") upon the
recognition of Charles Bon as his son. But the recognition
does not occur; Henry, who inherits the flaw, kills Bon and
the decay increases in tempo.

All of these analogies serve in a general explication of
one of the two major themes of the novel, the theme of the
myth, or plot, tracing the life of Thomas Sutpen. There are
other allusions to myths which are either very minor or which,
although used repetitiously, do not reflect this close unity
with theme. The constant use of the Agamemnon myth would, if
attributable to Faulkner as narrator, constitute grounds for
the charge that he had not outgrown the habit of liberally
sprinkling his writing with the casual allusions which is
evidenced in the early novels. However, in this novel, these
allusions, sometimes inadequate in their application, are
found in the voices of the characters and their limited value
serves to reflect and to heighten these characterizations.

Faulkner, in the person of narrator, first describes Miss
Rosa as having "an air Cassandralike and humorless and profoundly and sternly prophetic out of all proportion to the
actual years even of a child who had never been young" (p. 22).
Later Mr. Compson picks up the image: "In a grim mausoleum air
of Puritan righteousness and outraged female vindictiveness
Miss Rosa's childhood was passed, that aged and ancient and
timeless absence of youth which consisted of a Cassandralike
listening beyond closed doors ..." (p. 60). But Mr. Compson
seems to love the sense of doom aroused by the name and a few
pages later is applying it to Clytie. "I have always liked
to believe that he intended to name Clytie, Cassandra, prompted
by some pure dramatic economy not only to beget but to desig-
nate the presiding augur of his own disaster ..." (p. 62).
Shreve echoes the image and expands it in several directions:

> "... and she was right about the brother-in-law because
> if he hadn't been a demon and his children wouldn't have
> needed protection from him and she wouldn't have had to
> go out there and be betrayed by the old meat and find
> instead of a widowed Agamemnon to her Cassandra an an-
> cient stiff-jointed Pyramus to her eager though untried
> Thisbe who could approach her in this unbidden April's
> compounded demonry and suggest that they breed together
> for test and sample and if it was a boy they would
> marry." (p. 177)

Shreve's ranging for allusions to fit the story taking shape
makes of the scythe that killed Sutpen "'that scythe, symbolic
laurel of a caesar's triumph,'" and then Sutpen becomes "'this
Faustus, this demon, this Beelzebub'" (pp. 177-178). The tone
of these images found in these various perspectives will be
discussed in terms of the second and third levels of myth as
they relate to the characters involved.

It remains only to note some decorative allusions in Mr.
Compson's narration and two in Rosa's. Mr. Compson describes
Ellen, Sutpen's wife, as "this Niobe without tears who had
conceived to the demon in a kind of nightmare" (p. 13), "the
woman who had quitted home and kin on a flood of tears and in
a shadowy miasmic region something like the bitter purlieus of
Styx had produced two children" (p. 69). Charles Bon appeared
on the scene as "almost phoenix-like" (p. 74), "'a man a little
older than his actual years and enclosed and surrounded by a
sort of Scythian glitter'" (p. 93). The young men leaving for
war provide a moving spectacle, "'far more so than the spectacle of so many virgins going to be sacrificed to some
heathen Principle, some Priapus'" (p. 122), and Bon's son
becomes a "'delicate and perverse spirit-symbol, immortal page
of the ancient immortal Lilith'" (p. 196). Miss Rosa is given
a short flight of allusiveness in her long monologue when
Clytie becomes "*the cold Cerberus of his* [Sutpen's] *private
hell*" who had watched her approach to the house with a sense
of "*that justice whose Moloch's palate-paunch makes no distinction between gristle bone and tender flesh*" (pp. 136-137).

So much, then, for the first level of myth. From the time
of his first novel, Faulkner made much use of such allusions,
but in no novel besides *Absalom, Absalom!* is this level so rich
and so completely controlled.

The second level of myth in *Absalom, Absalom!* is that of
the action and theme. This theme, the rise and fall of Thomas
Sutpen in terms of his "design" and, on a larger, allegorical
level, the flaw in the design of the antebellum South, includes
not only the subject of the narrative, but the narrators as
well insofar as they are included in the cycle of history

under examination and are, by their drives to tell the story,
still attempting to find the flaw in the grand design and
thereby to understand their own lives as well as the life of
Thomas Sutpen. The flaw is quite apparent: the mortal failure
of Negro-white relations.

When the young Sutpen was sent to the planter's mansion
and turned away from the door by the Negro servant, like Huck
Finn he went to the woods to think. The design he conceives
to cope with the world is based on simple acceptance of the
terms of that world: wealth equals social acceptance and power.
But the design is also dynastic and calls for progeny--at least
one male child of pure blood. It is the undeviating commitment to his design and the inevitable consequences of this
commitment that makes Sutpen the tragic figure he is. Like
Lord Jim, Sutpen will attempt to live his life in terms of an
idea established by society's propaganda, an attempt that can
only be accounted for by his innocence, while the rest of
society, protected by an ironic sense against too complete
acceptance of the very words they mouth, look on puzzled and
try to understand this fanaticism. This view of Sutpen is, of
course, ironic and emerges only at the end of the novel and in
the reader's mind as he puts together the total meaning of the
various narratives.

These narratives offer four major viewpoints of Sutpen's
life, which can, I think, be best classified by Northrop Frye's
theory of modes to illustrate the richness of depth Faulkner
has achieved in this novel. Frye, proceeding from Aristotle's
Poetics, establishes five modes of fiction:

> In literary fiction, the plot consists of somebody doing
> something. The somebody, if an individual, is the hero,
> and the something he does or fails to do is what he can
> do, or could have done, on the level of the postulations
> made about him by the author and the consequent expecta-
> tions of the audience. Fictions, therefore, may be
> classified, not morally, but by the hero's power of ac-
> tion, which may be greater than ours, less, or roughly
> the same.[3]

Of the modes thus posited, the first involves a hero "superior
in *kind* both to other men and to the environment of other men,"
a divine being, "and the story about him will be a *myth* in the
common sense of a story about a god." The second mode posits
a hero "superior in *degree* to other men and to his environment
... whose actions are marvellous but who is himself identified
as a human being." This is the hero of romance who "moves in
a world in which the ordinary laws of nature are slightly suspended: prodigies of courage and endurance, unnatural to us,
are natural to him." The third mode posits a hero "superior

in degree to other men but not to his natural environment....
He has authority, passions, and powers of expression far greater than ours, but what he does is subject both to social criticism and to the order of nature. This is the hero of the *high
mimetic* mode." The hero of the fourth mode is "superior neither
to other men nor to his environment," but is one of us. This
is the hero of the low mimetic mode. And the hero of the
fifth, or ironic, mode is "inferior in power or intelligence
to ourselves, so that we have the sense of looking down on a
scene of bondage, frustration, or absurdity."[4]

Much of the complexity of the narrative structure of the
novel can be explained by examining the perspective each narrator has toward Sutpen. He is obviously not the god of the
mythic mode, but in Miss Rosa's demonizing of him, he assumes
some of the stature of the hero of the romantic mode with overtones of myth lingering on. As Quentin sits with Miss Rosa in
the opening pages of the book, the author establishes the tone
of her vision of Sutpen:

> Meanwhile, as though in inverse ratio to the vanishing
> voice, the invoked ghost of the man whom she could neither
> forgive nor revenge herself upon began to assume the
> quality almost of solidity, permanence. Itself circum-
> ambient and enclosed by its effluvium of hell, its aura
> of unregeneration, it mused (mused, thought, seemed to
> possess sentience, as if, though dispossessed of the
> peace--who was impervious anyhow to fatigue--which she
> declined to give it, was still irrevocably outside the
> scope of her hurt or harm) with that quality peaceful
> and now harmless and not even very attentive--the ogre-
> shape which, as Miss Coldfield's voice went on, resolved
> out of itself before Quentin's eyes the two half-ogre
> children, the three of them forming a shadowy background
> for the fourth one. (p. 13)

As the narrative moves into Miss Rosa's own voice, Sutpen becomes a "'fiend, blackguard and devil, in Virginia fighting,
where the chances of the earth's being rid of him were the
best anywhere under the sun, yet Ellen and I both knowing that
he would return, that every man in our armies would have to
fall before bullet or ball found him'" (p. 15). Her imagery
evoking the supernatural qualities of Sutpen incorporates the
mythic allusions already noted: Clytie is *"the cold Cerberus
of his private hell*," and Sutpen returns from the War to under-
take his "Herculean task," while at table *"talking that which
sounded like the bombast of a madman who creates within his
very coffin walls his fabulous immeasurable Camelots and Car-
cassonnes"* (p. 160). As her narrative reaches the point of
Sutpen's proposition to breed for test, her hysterical note

calls forth repeatedly the designations of "demon" and "ogre" that will be picked up in Shreve's ironic part of the narration.

Mr. Compson picks up the narrative in the low mimetic mode. To him, Sutpen partakes of nothing of the supernatural, nor, since he was of the same planter class does he envision him as superior to himself in the high mimetic status of leader. There is a slight tendency for him to regard Sutpen in the ironic mode when he conceives of him as a player in some kind of cosmic drama with "behind him Fate, destiny, retribution, irony--the stage manager, call him what you will--" calling the tune. But his limited knowledge of the facts of the story as finally pieced together by Shreve and Quentin keeps his narration largely on the low mimetic plane, especially since what we know of Mr. Compson as a character indicates that he too regards himself as a kind of player in a controlled drama.

It is when Mr. Compson communicates the vision of Sutpen held by Wash that we see Sutpen in the high mimetic role of leader, a man superior to other men. Mr. Compson imagines Wash watching Sutpen galloping on the black thoroughbred, "'thinking maybe, ... *If God Himself was to come down and ride the natural earth, that's what He would aim to look like'*" (p. 282). And when Wash is faced with the idea of Sutpen's seduction of his fifteen-year-old granddaughter, unaware that it is merely breeding "for test," he is able to reconcile himself to it because Sutpen is "different." This attitude persists right up to the moment of the ultimate insult which forces Wash to accept his own dignity as a human being and to kill Sutpen with the scythe. On the morning when the granddaughter is delivered of child, his view is still that

> "*he is bigger than all them Yankees that killed us and ourn, that killed his wife and widowed his daughter and druv his son from home, that stole his niggers and ruined his land; bigger than this whole country that he fit for and in payment for which has brung him to keeping a little country store for his bread and meat; bigger than the scorn and denial which hit helt to his lips like the bitter cup in the Book.*" (p. 287)

Quentin's perspective of Sutpen is not so simple. Based as it is on derivative views, it partakes somewhat of each view. Yet it remains toward the center of Frye's spectrum of modes, not following Miss Rosa's hysterical demonizing toward myth and resisting Shreve's use of the same imagery in the ironic mode which, Frye observes, "moves steadily toward myth, ... dim outlines of sacrificial rituals and dying gods" beginning to reappear in it.[5] Although Shreve's ironic view is at first pronounced, Faulkner insists on a

modification of this as he is taken up by and becomes emotionally involved with the story: "This was not flippancy either.
It too was just that protective coloring of levity behind
which the youthful shame of being moved hid itself" (p. 280),
"that incorrigible unsentimental sentimentality of the young
which takes the form of hard and often crass levity" (p. 275).
The burden of the final ironic view is transferred to the reader.

The narrative thus moves back and forth through the spectrum of modes as different views of Sutpen are presented.
For Miss Rosa he partakes of something of the supernatural,
his evil something like Faustus' covenant with the devil,
immune to death on the battlefield, spared that his pattern
of evil may fulfill itself. For Wash and for Quentin's
moments of longing for romantic ideals he partakes of the
high mimetic mode with its elevation of the hero to a position
superior to other men. At the same time, Quentin recognizes
him with his father as a man no different than other men and,
with Shreve, witnessing the frustration, bondage, and absurdity
of his quest, partakes somewhat of the ironic vision of the
man. With all the facts of the story as given him, it is
finally the reader, however, who is filled with "the sense of
looking down on a scene of bondage, frustration, or absurdity,"
not only for Sutpen but for the narrators of the story.

Whatever overtones of myth surround Sutpen in this final
ironic vision of the novel, he does not take on the garb of
the *pharmakos* unless we force him into the position of a figure
sacrificed to the design of the South. Yet, his full and active acceptance of this design and his commitment to it
throughout the action, albeit a result of the "innocence"
stressed by General Compson, makes of him the tragic actor,
the agent of his own destruction. The role of *pharmakos* is
filled by his unacknowledged progeny, especially Charles Bon,
the innocent victim of a fraction of Negro blood in his veins.
When Sutpen takes over the design of the planter class of the
South as his own to protect that boy knocking at the front
door of the mansion and commits himself to it irrevocably, he
becomes in a sense the priest of that cult, capable of sac-
rificing his first born son. As Frye says of the *pharmakos*,
"He is innocent in the sense that what happens to him is far
greater than anything he has done provokes ... He is guilty
in the sense that he is a member of a guilty society, or
living in a world where such injustices are an inescapable
part of existence."[6] Bon partakes of some of the guilt of
this society in taking an octoroon wife whom he is willing to
set aside. He is passive until the moment he writes to Judith,
"We have waited long enough," and sets in motion the inevitability of his own sacrifice. Henry, who is willing to tolerate
the idea of a morganatic marriage and even incest, cannot brook

the idea of miscegenation and kills his brother. The sequence
of choices offered Henry magnifies the moral quality of the
one thing the cult will not allow, the one thing that can
bring him to fratricide. Bon's death, "Aged 33 years and 5
months," merely repeats Faulkner's device of identifying the
scapegoat with the archetypal Christian pattern of the *pharmakos*, not with the person of Christ.

After Charles Bon, the sufferings for the sins of the
father are carried unto the fourth generation as the grandson,
Charles Etienne Saint-Valery Bon, strikes out in his confusion
at a society that is willing to let him pass as white if he
will remove himself from the scene. Like Joe Christmas, he
forces himself into a series of situations that will bring
him violence, flouting his coal black wife at those who would
let him pass, "'treading the thorny and flint-paved path toward
the Gethsemane which he had decreed and created for himself,
where he had crucified himself and come down from his cross
for a moment and now returned to it'" (p. 209). Charles
Etienne's son, the "bright-colored" Negro idiot who now passes
by the name of Jim Bond, completes the biblical pattern of the
four generations.

Viewed in its overall pattern, *Absalom, Absalom!* illustrates Faulkner's habit of probing the moral situation of the
South and projecting it against a screen of mythic references
where the actions find their analogues. This technique of
extending the meaning of a work into the realm of myth is
further supplemented by employing as points of view characters
whose modes of thought might be termed mythic. As Faulkner
sought to construct a fictional world embracing the sum total
of his vision, both the rational-empiric and the intuitive, he
discovered the necessity of creating characters whose perceptions could communicate these intuitions, for Faulkner's work
in this period stands as a demonstration of Croce's axiom that
"intuitive activity possesses intuitions to the extent that it
expresses them." This brings us to the third level of myth
in his work.

Criticism has devoted much of its time to translating, or
to an attempt at translating, the reality of some of Faulkner's
characters into a scientific-empiric order of reality which
will easily communicate the "facts" of that experience to the
reader. As an end in itself, the "facts" so translated become
dead and the characters, labeled neurotic or moronic, are sent
off to join Benjy and Darl at Jackson. As Faulkner began
writing the novels of the great middle period, beginning with
The Sound and the Fury, two of his great discoveries in technique were the use of a narrator disoriented from the scientific-
empiric mode of perception and the destruction of empiric time,
usually through the mind of the disoriented perceiver. The

narrations of Faulkner's neurotics and idiots bear out many of
the qualities of the mythic consciousness as outlined by
Cassirer in the second volume of *The Philosophy of Symbolic
Forms*.

Miss Rosa's narrative, dominated by a passionate reaction
to an insult received forty-three years before, presents the
story of Sutpen in the immediacy of the fury felt then, a fury
that has prevented her from the analysis and abstraction necessary to arrive at an understanding of the events in terms of
a scientific epistemology. Instead, the entire life of Sutpen
has become equated with a mythic pattern of evil haunted by
demons and ogres. It is, indeed, a version of reality which
in Cassirer's terms of analysis is a product of the mythical
consciousness. "For the mythical consciousness," says Cassirer,
"the impression is not merely relative but absolute":

> It manifests and confirms itself by the simple intensity
> of its presence, by the irresistible force with which it
> impresses itself upon consciousness. Whereas scientific
> thought takes an attitude of inquiry and doubt toward
> the "object" with its claim to objectivity and necessity,
> myth knows no such opposition. It "has" the object
> only insofar as it is overpowered by it.... It has no
> will to understand the object by encompassing it logically
> and articulating it with a complex of causes and effects;
> it is simply overpowered by the object.[7]

Miss Rosa lives not in a world of "'things' and their 'attributes' but of mythical potencies and powers, of demons and
gods." Sutpen's story is inextricably mixed with the fate of
the South in her mind, a part of the whole, and therefore,
in the mythic consciousness, equal to the whole. The Coldfield
family is but another part in which the workings of the whole
are evident and which becomes an identity of the whole:

> "... as though there were a fatality and curse on our
> family and God Himself were seeing to it that it was
> performed and discharged to the last drop and dreg.
> Yes, fatality and curse on the South and on our family
> as though because some ancestor of ours had elected to
> establish his descent in a land primed for fatality and
> already cursed with it, even if it had not rather been
> our family, our father's progenitors, who had incurred
> the curse long years before and had been coerced by
> Heaven into establishing itself in the land and the
> time already cursed." (p. 21).

For Miss Rosa Coldfield, this constitutes the entire meaning
of Sutpen's story and with the completion of the "curse," the
burning of Sutpen's house and what she believes to be the last

of his line, the curse will have fulfilled itself and it is fitting that she dies soon after, evidently with the belief that
her death completes the spiritual reality with which she has
lived so long.

That her narrative is incomplete and filled with errors
indicates that her reality does not call for the cause and effect rationale of empiric thought, the pattern that will only
be constructed as Quentin and Shreve piece out the story in
their rooms. For Miss Rosa it is enough that there is a central
"curse" which unifies her reality; beyond that she does not
seek. It is for her pure form of myth. This mode of thought
is understood as different by the Compsons, father and son,
but is analyzed in terms of a kind of male chauvinism and is
tolerated in terms of a kind of chivalry:

> "Ah," Mr. Compson said. "Years ago we in the South made
> our women into ladies. Then the War came and made the
> ladies into ghosts. So what else can we do, being gentle-
> men, but listen to them being ghosts?" (p. 12)

> "Yes. They lead beautiful lives--women. Lives not only
> divorced from, but irrevocably excommunicated from, all
> reality." (p. 191)

Which in Quentin's elaboration becomes:

> *Beautiful lives women live--women do. In very breathing*
> *they draw meat and drink from some beautiful attenuation*
> *of unreality in which the shades and shapes of facts--of*
> *birth and bereavement, of suffering and bewilderment and*
> *despair--move with the substanceless decorum of lawn*
> *party charades, perfect in gesture and without sig-*
> *nificance or any ability to hurt.* (p. 211)

Mr. Compson creates for Quentin an image of the young Rosa
sitting at Sutpen's table

> with still and curious and profound intensity as though
> she actually had some intimation gained from that rapport
> with the fluid cradle of events (time) which she had
> acquired or cultivated by listening beyond closed doors
> not to what she heard there, but by becoming supine and
> receptive, incapable of either discrimination or opinion
> or incredulity, listening to the prefever's temperature
> of disaster, which makes soothsayers and sometimes makes
> them right. (p. 66)

"To seek a 'form' of mythical consciousness," says Cassirer,
"is solely to seek the unity of the spiritual *principle* by which
all its particular configurations, with all their vast empirical
diversity, appear to be governed."[8] The principle which governs

Miss Rosa's reality unifying her sensory impressions of an empirical diversity embracing her strange childhood, the War, the suffering of the South, and her forty-three year fury is a complex of the sacredness of the South in terms of its mythic status engendered by the War and the biblical idea of an evil rooted out over the generations. Add to this a feminine mystique of love and we have the core of her thought.

As independent agent of action, her first gestures are to offer her housekeeping knowledge to Judith upon her betrothal and next, upon being rejected in this, to steal cloth from her father's store to sew articles for Judith's trousseau. When the War begins and her father boards himself up in the attic of their house, it is on that night she begins the composition of the odes and elegies on the Confederates which will reach more than a thousand in number. Her ambivalence toward Sutpen who was the "ogre" of her youth but becomes the accepted suitor after the War, partakes also of the sacredness of the cause which he has come to represent through his courageous action in the field:

> ... there was a shape which rode away beneath a flag
> and (demon or no) courageously suffered--and I did more
> than just forgive: I slew it [the image of the ogre],
> because the body, the blood, the memory which that ogre
> had dwelt in returned five years later and held out its
> hand and said 'Come' as you might say to a dog, and I
> came. (p. 167)

Then after the insult, she seeks to find an image to express his nature in the typical mythic opposition of light to darkness:

> Because he was not articulated in this world. He was
> a walking shadow. He was the light-blinded bat-like
> image of his own torment cast by the fierce demoniac
> lantern up from beneath the earth's crust and hence in
> retrograde, reverse; from abysmal and chaotic dark to
> eternal and abysmal dark completing his descending (do
> you mark the gradation?) ellipsis, clinging, trying to
> cling with vain unsubstantial hands· to what he hoped
> would help him, save him, arrest him-- (p. 176)

Her romantic evocation of Bon which calls forth that bit of incredible rhetoric, "*I became all polymath love's androgynous advocate*," is punctuated by the refrain, "*I never saw him.*" Of Bon, Mr. Compson admits,

> "He is the curious one to me.... He seems to hover,
> shadowy, almost substanceless, a little behind and above
> all the other straightforward and logical, even though

(to him) incomprehensible, ultimatums and affirmations
and defiances and challenges and repudiations, with an
air of sardonic and indolent detachment.... with that
sardonic and surprised distaste which seems to have been
the ordinary manifestation of the impenetrable and
shadowy character. Yes, shadowy: a myth, a phantom:
something which they engendered and created whole themselves; some effluvium of Sutpen blood and character,
as though as a man he did not exist at all." (pp. 93,
104)

Mr. Compson can identify the product of her configuration,
but it is Miss Rosa herself who must attempt to communicate
something of the mode of that configuration to Quentin:

*There are some things which happen to us which the in-
telligence and the senses refuse just as the stomach
sometimes refuses what the palate has accepted but which
digestion cannot compass--occurrences which stop us dead
as though by some impalpable intervention, like a sheet
of glass through which we watch all subsequent events
transpire as though in a soundless vacuum, and fade,
vanish; are gone, leaving us immobile, impotent, help-
less; fixed, until we can die.* (pp. 151-152)

*That is the substance of remembering--sense, sight,
smell: the muscles with which we see and hear and feel--
not mind, not thought: there is no such thing as memory:
the brain recalls just what the muscles grope for: no
more, no less: and its resultant sum is usually incorrect and false and worthy only of the name of dream.*
(p. 143)

Or, one might suggest, worthy of the name of myth.
     Faulkner relies upon the mythic mode of perception mani-
fested by Miss Rosa to fill out that part of expression and
meaning which has always eluded words used in a theoretical-
empirical manner, a failure of language behind the many com-
plaints Faulkner voices about words throughout his works.
Mr. Compson, Quentin, and Shreve as narrators remain largely
within this latter mode of thought, and, restricted to their
narratives, we would miss much of the moral pattern which Miss
Rosa's narrative supplies. Their mode of thought governs the
search for the "facts" of Sutpen's story, but it is Miss Rosa
who posits and makes explicit the concept of an evil rising
beyond the lives of the actors into a symbolic and allegorical
level of meaning embracing the history of the South. In this
sense, she is adequately called the Cassandra figure in that
her frenzied half-knowledge fixes upon a larger moral order,
the "curse," and enables her to explain cryptically the moral
truth of the action.

As it is illuminating in an analysis of Miss Rosa's forms
of reality to counterpoint quotations from Faulkner's text
with quotations from Cassirer's study of mythic thought, so
it is helpful to note other aspects of this symbolic mode
functioning in Sutpen's vision of the world. Sutpen's actions
are those of a figure operating within the magical world view.
His struggles against social traditions, nature, and time may
be seen as a struggle to achieve a concept of the I or the
soul. It is a feature of myth, Cassirer tells us, that it
does not start from a finished concept of the I or the soul,
but achieves this concept, forms this picture, out of itself.[9]
Sutpen's grand scheme admits of no external force that he
cannot conquer through his will and desire. It is this *desire*
which Cassirer calls the first energy by which man achieves
an independent being in opposition to things; he is no longer
content to accept the world and the reality of things, but,
in terms of this desire, gives a new form to reality, a form
to which everything else must submit. In this magical world
view, the I has almost unlimited power over reality and
"through the magical omnipotence of the will ... seeks to
seize upon all things and bend them to its purpose."[10]

> The soul itself appears as a demonic power which acts
> upon man's body from outside and possesses it--and hence
> possesses the man himself with all his vital functions.
> Thus precisely the increased intensity of the I-feeling
> and the resulting hypertrophy of action produce a mere
> illusion of activity.[11]

However, it is precisely at this point in the evolution of
his soul concept that Sutpen falters. As empirical reality
forces more and more upon him the distinction between the
object of his desire and the I, as these two spheres gain independent reality, he gives up and walks out to meet Wash and
his death. It is in the fullest Aristotelian sense that we
may look upon Sutpen as a tragic character, his action charting
a quest for a concept of self which he cannot cope with when
he faces it.

Although Quentin's mind is dominated by the scientific-
empiric mode of thought and must pursue the story of Sutpen
with an objective logic, there is one aspect of his participation in the story that is primarily mythic in mode: the disintegration of empiric time. "For myth," Cassirer tells us,

> there is no time "as such," no perpetual duration and
> no regular recurrence or succession; there are only con-
> figurations of particular content which in turn reveal a
> certain temporal *gestalt*, a coming and going, a rhythmical
> being and becoming.[12]

> The stages of time--past, present, future--do not
> remain distinct; over and over again the mythical con-
> sciousness succumbs to the tendency and temptation to
> level the differences and ultimately transform them into
> pure identity.... The magical "now" is by no means a
> *mere* now, a simple, differentiated present, but is ...
> laden with the past and pregnant with the future.[13]

Faulkner as narrator sets out at once to establish the timelessness of the tale in Quentin's mind and to pose one of the
theoretical problems of his technique:

> It (the talking, the telling) seemed (to him, to Quen-
> tin) to partake of that logic- and reason-flouting
> quality of a dream which the sleeper knows must have
> occurred, stillborn and complete, in a second, yet the
> very quality upon which it must depend to move the
> dreamer (verisimilitude) to credulity--horror or pleasure
> or amazement--depends as completely upon a formal recog-
> nition of and acceptance of elapsed and yet-elapsing
> time as music or a printed tale. (p. 22)

When Quentin is challenged in the course of his narrative by
Shreve's "'Dont say it's just me that sounds like your old
man,'" his musing on time that follows is primarily in terms
of biological rhythms, a feature belonging to the earliest
configurations of the mythic consciousness:

> *Maybe we are both Father. Maybe nothing ever happens*
> *once and is finished. Maybe happen is never once but*
> *like ripples maybe on water after the pebble sinks, the*
> *ripples moving on, spreading, the pool attached by a*
> *narrow umbilical water-cord to the next pool which the*
> *first pool feeds, has fed, did feed, let this second*
> *pool contain a different temperature of water, a dif-*
> *ferent molecularity of having seen, felt, remembered,*
> *reflect in a different tone the infinite unchanging sky,*
> *it doesn't matter: that pebble's watery echo whose fall*
> *it did not even see moves across its surface too at the*
> *original ripple-space, to the old ineradicable rhythm*
> *thinking Yes, we are both Father. Or maybe Father and*
> *I are both Shreve, maybe it took Father and me both to*
> *make Shreve or Shreve and me both to make Father or*
> *maybe Thomas Sutpen to make all of us.* (pp. 261-262)

And finally as the rhythm of the story reaches its crescendo,
the emotional quality of timeless identity is fully achieved
in the minds of both Quentin and Shreve:

> So that now it was not two but four of them riding the
> two horses through the dark over the frozen December

ruts of that Christmas Eve: four of them and then just
two--Charles-Shreve and Quentin-Henry. (p. 334)

Four of them there, in that room in New Orleans in 1860,
just as in a sense there were four of them here in this
tomb-like room in Massachusetts in 1910. (p. 336)

Miss Rosa's vision of Sutpen is completely mythic in orien-
tation. We have seen that her vision "begins with the intuition of purposive action" common to myth--the "curse" already
upon the land to which her ancestors came like actors to a
stage to play the roles directed by Mr. Compson's cosmic stage
manager. It is her vision that reaches back through layers of
time to find the definite beginning, positing a genesis of
forces that later find their definite forms in the persons of
the story, forms which are elevated to the sphere of the sacred
(not necessarily morally "good") with the stature of demons,
romantic gods, or Jobs suffering under an enormous evil. In
her mythic sense of time the past has no "why"--it *is* the why
of things. Her consciousness singles out only those things
in time that have the sacred quality of being a part and
therefore equivalent to the whole of the mythic pattern of
evil seeking its end through the sufferings of its chosen
actors; all else is relegated to the sphere of the profane
and elided from her consciousness. It is her vision that
primarily lends to the novel its mythic tone.

But this tone could not be sustained without some rein-
forcement in the other narratives. Miss Rosa's monologue is
rather short and cannot bear the burden for the entire novel.
We have already seen that mythic allusions in the other narratives help to sustain this tone as does the disintegration
of time for Quentin and Shreve. Mr. Compson, although primarily given to the rational-empiric mode, contributes, besides
his many classical allusions, images and ideas that strike a
mythic chord. Ellen's change of character in the middle life
is a "metamorphosis, emerging into her next lustrum with the
finality of actual rebirth" (p. 64); the octoroon mistress-
wife of Bon dies a death that is but another such metamorphosis
removed from the empiric understanding of death (p. 196); Bon
is a shadowy creation belonging to the realm of myth; and the
entire tale is "'just incredible. It just does not explain.
Or perhaps that's it: they dont explain and we are not supposed to know'" (p. 100).

There is no evidence to support the idea that Faulkner was
conscious of a mythic mode as such. There is, I believe,
enough evidence in the works that Faulkner by this time had
penetrated to the true force of mythic thought underlying the
residual fictions with which he was so familiar. His intuitive
readings in classical and Christian mythology provided him with

a knowledge necessary to reconcile poles of a vision of life,
poles essentially incompatible on the level of theoretical-
empirical thought: the pervasiveness of evil and suffering,
and the optimistic faith in man's ability to prevail over this
fact of his existence. Throughout his writings, this basic
opposition resists synthesis. In the middle period, to which
Absalom, Absalom! belongs, Faulkner gains the presence of
these two poles on his scene by comic contrast or by structural juxtaposition; in the later novels there is some attempt
to deal with this problem through the initiation of a character into the experience of a society that embraces him in a
kind of equilibrium; then, after the heroic attempt at transcendence represented by *A Fable*, there is an attempt to demonstrate
the general impotence of evil.

    Absalom, Absalom! offers us neither the comic contrast of
As I Lay Dying nor the structural juxtaposition of his two
views as found in *Light in August*. Instead we have the ambiguous and highly dramatic close of the novel, Shreve's question:

> "Now I want you to tell me just one thing more. Why do
> you hate the South?"
>   "I dont hate it," Quentin said, quickly, at once,
> immediately; "I dont hate it," he said. *I dont hate it*
> he thought, panting in the cold air, the iron New
> England dark; *I dont. I dont! I dont hate it! I dont
> hate it!* (p. 378)

This acceptance by negation is as close as we come to Faulkner's optimism in this novel. In the sense that this acceptance
is almost entirely without empiric justification, we might label
it irrational and dismiss the whole question by attributing it
completely to the character of Quentin. But if we hear Faulkner in this, the problem remains. Among the critics, Hoffman,
Slatoff, and Waggoner have attempted to come to grips with
Faulkner's pronouncements about the endurance of man and his
faith that man will prevail. Their approach has been in terms
of "What do the words *exactly* mean?" and their conclusions are
generally frustration. I believe that instead of labeling
these pronouncements irrational with all of that word's de-
rogatory connotations we might better accept them as a statement of a mythic configuration of man's condition, something
of the same sort that we might find in the better of those be-
liefs we accept with that irrational quality, "faith."

    On the fourth level of myth, that equated with a quasi-
historical saga, our examination must work in two directions:
toward the historical "reality" which the saga reflects and toward the explanation of that history which Faulkner seeks to
make in his works. The idea evoked by the cliché "the myth
of the South" is strictly a fabulous projection a short way

back in time to a golden age, an age when peace and manners
reigned, when romances flourished in jasmine-scented gardens,
and every woman was a lady and every man a gentleman committed
to the highest standards of chivalry. All well and good, but
rather inadequate to counterpoint a study of Faulkner's use of
the southern history in his works. Even a cursory reading of
Faulkner will establish the fact that this cliché of fiction
does not occupy his attention.

The golden age does have a position in Faulkner's work,
but it is there as part of a larger mythic reading of history.
It presupposes and focuses upon an actual presence which is
understood to be decadent and inadequate by comparison with
that time in the past which is termed golden; it accepts the
suffering and apparent chaos of the present and places upon it
a moral evaluation in terms of some mythic "fall" which occurred
in a definite historical moment. The golden age serves primarily as a norm against which the present is to be judged,
but it is the *present* which is the focal point of attention.

This reading of a cyclical theory of history in terms of
myth has been studied by Mircea Eliade who contrasts the empiric
view of history with that held by "archaic man"--man operating
in terms of the mythic consciousness:

> Archaic man ... tends to set himself in opposition, by
> every means in his power, to history, regarded as a suc-
> cession of events that are irreversible, unforeseeable,
> possessed of autonomous value. He refuses to accept it
> and to grant it value as such, as *history*--without, how-
> ever, always being able to exorcise it; for example, he
> is powerless against cosmic catastrophes, military dis-
> asters, social injustices bound up with the very struc-
> ture of society, personal misfortunes, and so forth.[14]

Archaic man opposes the empiric-scientific view of history
through ritual action which "guarantees" the cyclical rejuvena-
tion of life in harmony with the rhythms of nature. As the
sufferings of the dead season are contrasted with the memory
of the ease of the fertile period of the year, so the social
catastrophes of the present are contrasted with the order of
the golden past. And as ritual action secures the return of
the fecundity of the earth, so ritual action can restore cosmos
to the chaos of the present. The key to this theory in Eliade's
view is the acceptance on the part of archaic man of the "nor-
mality of suffering" and the insistence upon a moral reading
of history:

> What could suffering and pain signify? Certainly
> not a meaningless experience that man can only "tolerate"
> insofar as it is inevitable, as, for example, he tolerates

the rigors of climate. Whatever its nature and whatever
its apparent cause, his suffering had a meaning; it cor-
responded, if not always to a prototype, at least to an
order whose value was not contested.

If it was possible to tolerate such sufferings, it
is precisely because they seemed neither gratuitous nor
arbitrary.... The archaic mind cannot conceive of an
unprovoked suffering; it arises from a personal fault
... or from his neighbor's malevolence ...; but there
is always a fault at the bottom of it, or at the very
least a cause, recognized in the will of the forgotten
Supreme God, to whom man is finally forced to address
himself. In each case the suffering becomes intelligible
and hence tolerable.[15]

It is this reading of history that is found in many of
Faulkner's characters and which, I believe, informs Faulkner's
own understanding of the history of the South. The moral
guilt is equated with the exploitation of the land and of the
Negro. The apparent cosmos of the antebellum period, the
golden age, was wiped out in the chaos of the War and the suffering compounded by the Reconstruction. The suffering persists into Faulkner's historical present and the moral searching for culpability remains. This is not a complex, intellectual reading of the history of the South, but Faulkner is
not an intellectual writer. It is an emotional and mythic
reading of history, not unlike that offered by the southern
agrarians in their manifesto *I'll Take My Stand* where the in-
ertia and decay of the South is posited against an assumed
golden age which can be restored if only the scapegoat of in-
dustrialism can be driven out of the land.

Throughout Faulkner's work we find the attempt to deal
with the immediacy of suffering, the desire to annul time,
and the pressing need to understand the cause of chaos, of
suffering. In *Absalom, Absalom!* this necessity of understanding the suffering of the South as it is embodied in the tale
of Sutpen provides the structural framework. Through the
minds of the various narrators a tale is eventually constructed that in part reflects what is termed the myth of the Old
South: the taking of the virgin land, the construction of the
great plantation, and by deft touches, the period of social
grandeur with its Wedgwood, crystal, gowns and balls—the
period of cosmos. But how little this is the object of Faulkner's tale can be seen by the economy with which he presents
it. Cosmos became chaos in the War. It is through the narrators' examinations of the prototype Sutpen that the moral
flaw which brought down this chaos will become apparent.

Upon being summoned by Miss Rosa, Quentin,

> the Quentin Compson preparing for Harvard in the South,
> the deep South dead since 1865 and peopled with garru-
> lous outraged baffled ghosts, listening, having to listen,
> to one of the ghosts which had refused to lie still even
> longer than most had, telling him about old ghost-times
> (p. 9),

thinks at first,

> *It's because she wants it told ... so that people whom*
> *she will never see and whose names she will never hear*
> *and who have never heard her name nor seen her face will*
> *read it and know at last why God let us lose the War:*
> *that only through the blood of our men and the tears of*
> *our women could He stay this demon and efface his name*
> *and lineage from the earth.* (p. 11)

Within Quentin's heritage, a South filled with "garrulous outraged baffled ghosts" each with a moral solution to the problem
of the South's history, this is the normal initial reaction to
a summons from such a "ghost" of the past.

The suffering of the South in the War is pervasive. Bon's
letter to Judith, preserved by the Compsons, tells of the
ironic capture of the Union stove polish by the starving soldiers. The scarcity of food and clothing is like a refrain
throughout both Miss Rosa's narration and the other parts concerned with her history. Although accustomed to a life of
penury, she makes much of the weed gathering and the remaking
of handed-down clothing. Judith's wedding gown is made of
"'scraps--perhaps scraps intended for, which should have gone
for, lint and did not'" (p. 132). In this respect, Sutpen's
mansion becomes a central symbol of the ravages of war and
continuing decay after the War. Once the showpiece of the
county, at War's end it is

> "the huge house where a young girl waited in a wedding
> dress made from stolen scraps, the house partaking too
> of that air of scaling desolation, not having suffered
> from invasion but a shell marooned and forgotten in a
> backwater of catastrophe--a skeleton giving of itself
> in slow driblets of furniture and carpet, linen and
> silver, to help to die torn and anguished men who knew,
> even while dying, that for months now the sacrifice and
> the anguish were in vain." (pp. 132-133)

The house waits to play its final role in the cycle of the
myth, the final and ultimate catastrophe, the conflagration
that should mark an end to Sutpen's world. But Faulkner's
vision is not the limited vision of Miss Rosa. Sutpen's idiot

great grandson haunts the scene at the close and the moral guilt remains, not wiped out by the gothic flames.

Faulkner's reading of the "myth of the South" does not dwell on an antebellum golden age but posits a deeper historical view. The golden age can be defined only morally and that in relation to the land. In *Go Down, Moses*, Ike postulates the end of that golden age as the moment the Indian assumed the illusory sense of ownership for the purposes of trade. The guilt which the white man brought, slavery, merely compounded a fallen state. There is no immediate solution to this problem. With Ike of *Go Down, Moses*, Shreve posits a period of years in the thousands before the problem can be solved:

> "I think that in time the Jim Bonds are going to conquer the Western hemisphere. Of course it won't quite be in our time and of course as they spread toward the poles they will bleach out again like the rabbits and the birds do, so they won't show up so sharp against the snow. But it will still be Jim Bond; and so in a few thousand years, I who regard you will also have sprung from the loins of African kings." (p. 378)

Within the context of the body of works built up around Yoknapatawpha County, *Absalom, Absalom!* presents yet another vision of this search for a moral reading of history.

NOTES

1. *William Faulkner: Three Decades of Criticism*, ed. Frederick Hoffman and Olga Vickery (East Lansing, 1960), p. 281.

2. Lind, p. 297.

3. *Anatomy of Criticism* (Princeton, 1957), p. 33.

4. *Ibid.*, pp. 33-34.

5. *Ibid.*, p. 42.

6. *Ibid.*, p. 41.

7. Ernst Cassirer, *The Philosophy of Symbolic Forms*, vol. II. *Mythical Thought*, trans. Ralph Manheim (New Haven, 1955), pp. 73-74.

8. *Ibid.*, pp. 11-12.

9. *Ibid.*, p. 156.

10. *Ibid.*, pp. 157-158.

11. *Ibid.*, p. 158.

12. *Ibid.*, p. 108.

13. *Ibid.*, p. 111.

14. *Cosmos and History: The Myth of the Eternal Return*, trans. Willard Trask (New York, 1959), p. 95.

15. *Ibid.*, pp. 96-98.

THE BIBLICAL BACKGROUND
OF FAULKNER'S *ABSALOM, ABSALOM!*

John V. Hagopian

As Faulkner himself indicated, the title of his greatest
novel comes from David's lament, "O my son Absalom, O Absalom,
my son, my son!" (II Samuel, 19:4). But Faulkner's comment
that "the story in that book was of a man who wanted a son
and lost that son"[1] is not really very illuminating. And it
is curious that, although the novel is full of Biblical allusions, there is not a single reference to David or to Absalom,
and it is likely that without the cue of the title no reader
would think of the story in II Samuel. In fact, when Shreve
feels driven to compare Sutpen with one of the patriarchs,
he thinks of Abraham:

> now that the old man was bankrupt with the incompetence
> of age, who should do the paying if not his sons, his
> get, because wasn't it done that way in the old days?
> the old Abraham full of years and weak and incapable
> now of further harm, caught at last and the captains
> and the collectors saying, 'Old man, we dont want you'
> and Abraham would say, 'Praise the Lord, I have raised
> about me sons to bear the burden of mine iniquities and
> persecutions; yea, perhaps even to restore my flocks
> and herds from the hand of the ravisher: that I might
> rest mine eyes upon my goods and chattels, upon the
> generations of them and of my descendants increased an
> hundred fold as my soul goeth out of me.'[2]

Shreve obviously has a faulty knowledge of the Bible, for he
cites Abraham as having many sons and quotes a passage that
does not exist.

Nor have the critics been any more helpful in exploring
the significance of Faulkner's title. Edmond L. Volpe goes

Reprinted from The CEA Critic, *36 (January, 1974), pp. 22-24,
by permission of the publisher. Copyright by The College
English Association, Inc., 1974.*

131

about as far as anyone when he observes that

> like King David in the Biblical story ..., Thomas Sutpen
> rises through his own power to high station among men,
> breaks the moral law and brings suffering upon his
> children. In both the house of David and the house of
> Sutpen, retribution takes the form of violent crimes by
> the children--revolt, incest, fratricide. The parallels
> in the stories are not extensive, but sufficient to in-
> dicate a continuity in the human condition through
> centuries of time.[3]

These are rather vague generalizations. Volpe does structure the parallels between the Biblical narrative and the novel
and is totally unaware of the rich extent of the complex ironic
involutions of those parallels.

The story of revolt, incest and fratricide in II Samuel:
13-19 might be summarized as follows. Among his many children,
David had a son Absalom and a daughter Tamar by one wife, and
a son Amnon by another wife. Amnon "fell sick for his sister,"
and Tamar was willing to seek her father's permission to be
mated with him. Upon the advice of his cousin Jonadab, Amnon
tricked Tamar into coming to his bedside where he raped her.
Immediately his love for her turned to hatred and he had her
removed from his house. When he learned of these events, David
was angry, but did not seek retribution. Absalom, however,
nursed his wrath for two years; then, during a sheep-shearing
festival at which all the king's sons were present, he commanded
his servants to slay Amnon. Absalom then fled to Geshur for
three years, returning only after the king's councilor Joab
interceded with David on his behalf. Three sons and a daughter
(also named Tamar) were born to Absalom, but David would not
see him. When Joab refused to arrange a meeting between the
king and his son, the angry Absalom set fire to Joab's crops.
Upon being summoned by David to account for this, Absalom
bowed down in a gesture of submission and David embraced him.
Restored to his father's favor, Absalom became ambitious. As
judge and intercessor with David for all who had any suit,
he built a powerful following among the people and developed
a network of spies. When the time was ripe, Absalom led a
successful revolt against David, and the king, accompanied by
loyal followers, fled to Jerusalem. Absalom then rejected
the advice of Achitophel to seek a reconciliation with David's
followers and heeded instead the advice of Hushai to pursue the
fleeing King and his retinue and crush them all. But Hushai
was secretly loyal to David and sent him warning of the plans.
Although David commanded that in the forthcoming battle Absalom
be spared, Joab slew Absalom when he found him hanging from a

tree in which his hair had been caught. Despite victory in a
battle in which 20,000 men were killed, David so lamented the
death of Absalom that he had no interest in ruling his restored kingdom. Only after Joab chided him and warned of
further strife in the land did David agree to return to Jerusalem and resume his authority.

The parallels between the Biblical narrative and *Absalom,
Absalom!* may be diagrammed as follows:

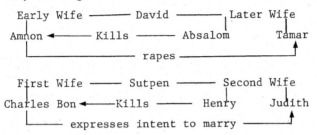

The story in II Samuel and Faulkner's novel do indeed seem to
be remarkably alike. In both, the eldest son of a vital and
forceful patriarch seeks an incestuous relationship with his
half-sister and is killed by his half-brother. But when the
actions and especially the motives and emotional attitudes
involved in both narratives are closely examined, the similarities appear rather specious: (1) Tamar knows that Amnon
is her half-brother, but welcomes his attentions and believes
that they can be legitimized with David's sanction: Judith
never learns that Bon is her half-brother. (2) Amnon, an
acknowledged son of David, merely lusts for Tamar, does not
seek marriage with her, and feels revulsion for her after he
rapes her; Bon (in Shreve's final version of the Sutpen legend)
loves and respects Judith to the end, but values even more
highly Sutpen's acknowledgment of his paternity. In his
despair at failing to receive that acknowledgment, Bon deliberately provokes Henry into murdering him. (3) Absalom waits
two years after the rape of Tamar to seek retribution, and
his murder of Amnon appears to be motivated more by rivalry
for the inheritance of his father's power and status than by
incestuous jealousy or revenge; Henry welcomed and even abetted
the relationship between Bon and Judith even after he became
aware that it was incestuous. He is prompted to murder only
by his obsessive bigotry against miscegenation. (4) David remains unaware of Amnon's lust for Tamar until after the rape,
and even then maintains his love for his oldest son, making
no gesture of punishment; Sutpen tries desperately to prevent
the union of Judith and Bon (without acknowledging that Bon
is his son) and finally goads Henry into acting as his instrument of doom by revealing to Henry that Bon is a Negro.

Many other differences can be noted, but these appear to
be the crucial ones and they suggest that if *Absalom, Absalom!*
is indeed related to the Old Testament, it is by ironic inversion. For, unlike David, Sutpen neither triumphs nor survives his younger son and he does not lament his disappearance.
There is no cry of "O my son Henry, O Henry, my son, my son!"
because Sutpen is simply incapable of that degree of love and
compassion. That, in fact, would seem to be the main point
of the Sutpen story.

NOTES

1. Frederick L. Gwynn and Joseph Blotner, eds., *Faulkner
in the University* (New York: Vintage Books, 1965), p. 143.

2. William Faulkner, *Absalom, Absalom!* (New York: Modern
Library, 1951), p. 325.

3. *A Reader's Guide to William Faulkner* (London: Thames &
Hudson, 1964), p. 205.

CHILDREN OF THE IDEA:
HEROES AND FAMILY ROMANCES
IN *ABSALOM, ABSALOM!*

T.H. Adamowski

"To be more than a man, in a world of men,
To escape man's fate...."

Gisors, in Malraux's *Man's Fate*

It is not unusual, when reading the criticism of Faulkner's
Absalom, Absalom!, to find the prevailing demons of our culture
associated with the character of Thomas Sutpen. F. Garvin
Davenport, Jr. places Sutpen in the context of the "American
dream of success," and of "exploitation of the crass worship
of material goods."[1] Sutpen is placed in more refined, though
still evil, company in Hyatt Waggoner's account of him as a
"rationalist and positivist." Waggoner thinks that Sutpen
would believe in the inevitable progress of humanity if men
would only be as willing to use the power of reason on their
special experiences as the scientist is.[2] And Cleanth Brooks
fuses the notion of Sutpen as a vulgar materialist with that
of Sutpen, the positivist and simple-minded scientist. Brooks
claims that Sutpen "would seize upon 'the tradition' as a pure
abstraction" and that Thorstein Veblen would have known him
for what he was: "Sutpen is on all fours with the robber baron
of the Gilded Age building a fake Renaissance palace on the
banks of the Hudson."[3] Brooks even sees in Sutpen Faulkner's
indictment of liberal "planners."[4] One thinks of Rexford
Tugwell with slaves.

These claims about Sutpen are not, of course, entirely
misplaced. They call attention to his rage for order, his
apparent disregard for human values, and his obsessive concern
with his own vision (the "design"). They respond to our

This article originally appeared in MOSAIC; A Journal for the
Comparative Study of Literature and Ideas, *published by the
University of Manitoba, Volume 10, No. 1 (Fall 1976), pp. 115-
131, to whom acknowledgment is herewith made.*

awareness of the frightening solitude of Sutpen's life, but
they are, nevertheless, shrill on the matter of rationalism,
positivism, and materialism. They risk losing sight of Sutpen's concrete experience by placing it in the generality of
our cultural battles (humanism vs. positivism, tradition vs.
abstraction, and the like). What I should like to do is to
reconsider Sutpen's experience and put aside questions about
its relation to our ideological disputes. I agree that he is
rationalistic, a planner (but not a "liberal" one), a seeker
of goods, and a solitary. I agree that these traits suggest
a desire for autonomy. But rather than evaluate these qualities by placing Sutpen in implicit coincidence with the Tweed
Ring, the New Deal, or logical positivism, I would like to
consider why he possesses them, and how his solitude is
shaped by the text.

We have, in Sutpen, an example of what Walter J. Slatoff
has called "the quest for failure." Slatoff points out the
tension in Faulkner's writing that comes from

> the persistent placement of entities of all sorts into
> highly tense relationships with one another, relation-
> ships which to varying degrees resemble the relationships
> between the terms of an oxymoron.[5]

Slatoff's is primarily a study of the language of Faulkner,
but I want to consider this tension at the level of character.
And where Slatoff finds in Bergson a philosopher who offers a
"valid and illuminating way" to look at Faulkner's work,[6] I
would like to rely on another French philosopher, Sartre,
who, in *Being and Nothingness*, outlines another quest for
failure, the *passion inutile* of man to be in-itself-for-itself.
In addition, I will be relying on certain notions put forward
long ago by Freud and Otto Rank that bear on Sutpen's quest in
another way. Essentially I will argue that Sutpen is seeking,
through his Design, to be autonomous, "more than a man in a
world of men," and that this quest is aptly conveyed by a narrative structure that bears comparison to a fantasy that is
itself a quest for autonomy.

Sutpen is one of those who would like to make appointments
with himself. For him this desire takes the form of the
design he tries to give his life. It is apt that Faulkner
compares Sutpen to the Jehovah of the Old Testament:

> Like the Creation itself, Sutpen's Hundred is formed
> 'violently out of the soundless Nothing,' as if with no
> greater effort than the Lord saying let there be light:
> 'the *Be Sutpen's Hundred* like the oldentime *Be Light*.'
> This apparently conscious allusion to the creation is
> continued in the amount of time necessary to complete

> the foundation of his design: six years (1833-1839) to
> build a house, and in the sixth year to create man, to
> beget a son, Jehovah-like, Sutpen 'was not liked (which
> he evidently did not want, anyway) but feared, which
> seemed to amuse, if not actually please him'; and
> Creator-like, 'he named them all, the one before Clytie
> and Henry and Judith even....'[7]

The novel records the ultimate failure of this passion to be
a life in control of itself. It is Sutpen's desire for autonomy, for the power to mold his life to a certain shape, that
makes of him a man who "struggled to hold clear and free above
a maelstrom of unpredictable and unreasoning human beings"
(p. 275).[8] To find the birth of that struggle one must turn
to the account he gives to Quentin Compson's grandfather,
General Compson, of the crisis of his childhood, when he
learned who he was and who he wished to be.

> In effect, the literary work dreams a dream for us. It
> embodies and wakes in us a central fantasy by devices
> that, were they in a mind, we would call defenses, but,
> being on a page, we call 'form.'[9]

So writes Norman H. Holland, in *The Dynamics of Literary Response*, and, although my own discussion of *Absalom, Absalom!*
will not be congruent with the kind of approach Holland might
take to the novel, I would like to adopt his idea of a central
fantasy. The desire of Sutpen is to make himself over in such
a way as to guarantee himself autonomy. If I understand
Holland's argument, this is not what he would call the central
fantasy of the novel but rather a displacement of a more fundamental desire suggested by the "form" of the narrative. What
I am proposing is that Sutpen's desire is structured in such
a way by the narrative that it is reminiscent of a fantasy
common in childhood, a fantasy which may reappear in the life
of the neurotic, and which seems to underlie a number of myths
of the births and careers of heroes. It is this fantasy,
called by Freud the "family romance," that is central to *Absalom, Absalom!* and it may account for much of the power of
the book. The family romance is dialectically suited to Sutpen's quest for autonomy, for it is a fantasy that comes from
the child's over-valuation of the power of thought; and it
leads him to recreate his origins and to define his prospects.

The family romance occurs because of "one of the most
painful results brought about by the course of [a person's]
development," his liberation, "as he grows up, from the
authority of his parents."[10] This "liberation" is never
easy to effect, and it is attended by the child's effort to
adjust to this new world of freedom in the shadow of anxiety

by recourse to the age of gold, of carefree dependency, which
he must leave behind. Sutpen's design takes its departure
from the well-known scene of rejection at the door to Pettibone's mansion. The design is an effort to make up for the
loss of an initial state of equilibrium in his life, a loss
occasioned by the shock administered by the slave at the door.
I do not mean to suggest that Sutpen "has" a family romance
fantasy, but only that the novel seems to include as a vehicle
for Sutpen's design a narrative structure resembling the
structure of the fantasy. The latter is transformed into the
"meaning" of Sutpen's life:

> It is this transformational process, this management of
> fantasy, that we take into ourselves, feeling it as
> though it were our own mental activity which, indeed,
> it in part is. Further, we not only contribute meaning,
> we analogize, enriching the central fantasy with our
> own associations and experiences that relate to it.[11]

At the level of conscious response, Sutpen has appeared to
readers as a rationalist, a "planner," a failed God, and a
tragic hero. It is my contention that such associations are
understandable responses to a man whose career is presented
in a way that is reminiscent of a childhood fantasy which is
itself an attempt to play God.

First it is necessary to rehearse the important elements
in the romance. As a child grows up there is a painful detachment from his parents. They begin to demand of him things
they never demanded in the age of gold. Acquaintance with
other adults may lead him to draw unfavorable comparisons with
his parents, and the child may conclude that he would be better
off with a new mother and father. Rank claims, for instance,
that a child will use accidental occurrences, such as "meetings
with the lord of the manor or the proprietor of the estate,"
to flesh out his wish for new parents. My parents, the
romancer concludes, are not these poor people; my parents
are great and wealthy, and one day they will reclaim me.[12]

Coupled with discontent and envy is the growing sexual
curiosity of the child: how was he born? where did he come
from? what goes on between mother and father in that bedroom?
Soon, says Freud, he learns that "'*pater semper incertus est*,'
while the mother is '*certissima*.'"[13] Since descent from mother
cannot be altered (an Oedipal wish helps to father this
thought), the child is forced to content himself with raising
the status of father and, thereby, of himself. Erotic and
ambitious wishes coincide here. Both Freud and Rank agree
that the debased father forms part of the picture of the ennobled father, since the newly desired father of the romance
is given qualities recalled by the child from the golden time.

What we learn of Sutpen's childhood is that an initial harmony with the world is disturbed by a certain encounter—— "with the lord of the manor or the proprietor of the estate." Sutpen had barely heard of a world of privilege, says Quentin, "until he fell into it" (p. 222). One day his wretchedly poor family left their mountain home for the Tidewater. This episode is replete with evidence of their abject poverty, but Sutpen does not yet perceive this as an intolerable situation (p. 221). His mother, "a fine wearying woman" (p. 223), has recently died, and we are told time and again of his father's besotted condition, "oblivious among the quilts and lanterns and well-buckets and bundles of clothing and children, snoring with alcohol" (p. 224). On one occasion, a "huge bull of a nigger" emerges from a saloon "with the old man over his shoulder like a sack of meal" (p. 225). And yet we hear of no shame for his father in the account the adult Sutpen gives of that time, nor of any discomfort at being one of a "passel" of semi-abandoned siblings. In Holland's terms, this aspect of the boy's life, the part that is passed over in silence, is being taken into ourselves. It is interesting to note, however, that Sutpen does recall, when the family reaches the flatlands, "the taverns where the old man was not even allowed to come in by the front door and. from which his mountain drinking manners got him ejected before he would have time to get drunk good ..." (p. 225). To the calm surface of what we might have expected to be a horrifying memory, floats a memory that has its parallel in Sutpen's own experience of rejection at a front door.

Eventually he begins to see that there are differences "not only between white men and black ones" but also "between white men and white men" (p. 226). But his perception registers no discontent, for he is apparently egalitarian and assumes that the successful will feel tender towards the "unlucky." It is only after they reach the shack that is their new home that discontent enters the boy, at a time when the father has become a more or less sober provider (p. 227). There is suddenly a new curiosity in the boy about the man

> who owned all the land and the niggers and apparently
> the white men who superintended the work, and who lived
> in the biggest house he had ever seen.... (p. 227)

He tells General Compson of "how he would creep up among the tangled shrubbery of the lawn and lie hidden and watch the man" (p. 228). It is strange behavior for an egalitarian child, and reveals one of the paradoxes that define Sutpen's life.

The novel insists on his "innocence" at this point, and Quentin believes that he "no more envied the man than he would

have envied a mountain man who happened to own a fine rifle"
(p. 228). When, on an errand from his father, he walks up to
the door of the great house, it is with confidence that Pettibone would be "as pleased to show him the balance of his things
as the mountain man would have been to show the powder horn
and bullet mold that went with the rifle" (p. 229). All the
same, I suspect that the structure of the narrator forces a
feeling of discontent and envy on us because of the contrast
of Sutpen's father's degradation with the leisurely swinging
of Pettibone in his hammock, a slave at his side who does
"nothing else but fan him and bring him drink" (p. 228). Sutpen's claim to egalitarian innocence is already denied by that
image of the boy who creeps in the bushes to watch a man whose
like he has never seen.

What he finds at Pettibone's door is not open admission
but the censorious "monkey-nigger" who puts an end to Sutpen's
childhood by ordering him to go to the back door. As I have
said, I do not mean to suggest that Sutpen is in the midst of
a family romance fantasy at this point, but only that his move
from the almost "Lockean state of nature where the sanctity
of the individual was absolute, [and] where nature was held
in common by all man,"[14] is not far from the structure of the
romance fantasy. C.L. Barber has said that the drama "controls
magic by reunderstanding it as imagination."[15] *Absalom, Absalom!* controls fantasy by reunderstanding it imaginatively,
making of it the structure within which a character's experience
takes place, just as the career of Macbeth may be given order
by its association with the career of the winter king. Sutpen
does not first turn on his father to idealize Pettibone, but
the narrative makes us sensitive to the inferiority of the
father and the idealization of the new "father," who employs
Mr. Sutpen, and who has, mistakenly, been given the sanctity
of the mountain man's egalitarian ethic. In a sense, the
romance comes all at once: childhood harmony, discontent, the
move to a new father who is ennobled with the old father's
virtues, and the flight from both fathers in order to create
a third with traces of both, Sutpen himself. The last step,
the desire to father oneself, is the secret meaning of the
romancer's fantasy.

When he is turned away from the door, the boy suddenly
realizes the lowly status of his family. He transposes to
the reflective plane the contrast that has already been suggested by the description of both houses. He takes as his
model for the future not his real father but the man who turned
him away and who is not his parent. This is what psychoanalysts
call an "identification with the aggressor." The history of
his solitude and of the anguish of his future family come from
this choice.

He leaves Pettibone's door with a sharp sense of himself as an object in the world, among other objects, seeing suddenly the brutal condition in which he has been brought up:

> ... he himself seeing his own father and sisters and brothers *as the owner, the rich man* (not the nigger) must have been seeing them all the time--as cattle, brutely evacuated into a world without hope or purpose for them.... (p. 235 [my italics])

Suddenly Sutpen sees himself, and through the gaze of another person his stability comes to an end in shame: "Shame is by nature *recognition*. I recognize that I *am* as the Other sees me."[16] The boy's world has been taken from him by a look, for he "never even remembered what the nigger said" (p. 232). He is overcome by a glance that reveals to him other points of reference than his own:

> And now he stood there before that white door with the monkey-nigger barring it and looking down at him in his patched made-over jeans clothes.... (p. 232)

Too much emphasis on Sutpen's "materialism" can cause us to overlook the "radical metamorphosis" that comes with his sudden degradation.[17] He now recalls the meaning of another episode, when he and his sister were nearly run down by the carriage belonging to the plantation family. He remembers the "two faces beneath the parasols glaring at his sister" (p. 231). His being-seen constitutes him "as a defenceless being for a freedom which is not [his] freedom."[18] Sutpen does not fall from innocent egalitarianism into class consciousness because he is poor but because he "apprehends his condition and that of other members of [his] collectivity as looked-at and thought about by a consciousness that ascapes him":[19]

> The 'master,' the 'feudal lord,' the 'bourgeois,' the 'capitalist,' all appear not only as powerful people who command but in addition and above all as *Thirds*; that is, as those who are outside the oppressed community and *for whom* this community exists. It is therefore *for* them and *in their freedom* that the reality of the oppressed class is going to exist. They cause it to be learned by their look.[20]

Sartre points out that the person who falls into a class (an "Us-object") can only reclaim his "selfness" in the face of the man who *sees* him, by "[looking] at him in turn."[21] What Sutpen needs to effect is a counter-glance, so to speak, some way of recovering his object-status, that "outside" of himself the existence of which, during his egalitarian period, he seemed never to suspect. His identification with the

aggressor occurs at the very instant of objectification: "he
himself seeing his own father and sisters and brothers as the
owner, the rich man (not the nigger) must have been seeing
them." It is through this appropriation of the look of the
other that Sutpen comes to his choice of action. That he
must recover himself is clear from his feeling that when the
master's eyes, in the person of the slave, had seen him "something in him had escaped and was looking out from within the
balloon face [of the slave]" (p. 234). To regain his lost
subjectivity, the feeling that he is a point of organization
in the world, requires that he become one of "them." He
concludes that

> to combat them you have got to have what they have that
> made them do what the man did. You got to have land and
> niggers and a fine house to combat them with. (p. 238)

"My original fall is the existence of the Other," Sartre
claims, and it is true for Sutpen. He falls from the familial
world into a world in which he is an outsider who is always
trying to "catch up." A psychoanalytical disciple of Sartre
has described this fall in another context:

> Now the peculiar thing about Them is that They are crea-
> ted only by each one of us repudiating his own identity.
> When we have installed Them in our hearts, we are only
> a plurality of solitudes in which what each person has
> in common is his allocation to the other of the necessity
> for his own actions.[22]

It is less interesting to know that Sutpen has embarked on the
"American Dream of success" than it is to see precisely what
is happening to him. He plunges into a paradoxical solitude
in this moment of relationship to another:

> Thus myself-as-object is neither knowledge nor a unity
> of knowledge but an uneasiness, a lived wrenching away
> from the ecstatic unity of the for-itself, a limit which
> I can not reach and which yet I am. The Other through
> whom this Me comes to me is neither knowledge nor category
> but the fact of the presence of a strange freedom. In fact
> my wrenching away from myself and the upsurge of the Other's
> freedom are one; I can feel them and live them only as
> an ensemble: I cannot even try to conceive of one without
> the other.[23]

The freedom of Pettibone (symbolized by the leisurely swaying
of a hammock) forces the boy out of his unity with all men
(a false unity) into the life-long uneasiness of the Design.
At the heart of his quest to recover his life and to create a
barrier against future degradations by "them" is a dependence
on others. The family romance is well suited to serve as a

psychological vehicle for this ontological journey, for the
fantasy of the romancer is a paradoxical attempt to father
himself by choosing a father from the adults of the world.
Others are the limits to his freedom of invention.

That Sutpen seeks to father himself is clear from the
analysis he offers to General Compson of the meaning for him
of what he calls the "boy-symbol," the boy at the door of a
great house. His design is meant to enable him, one day, to
open his door to an "amazed and desperate" child,[24] so that
the latter might in turn "shut the door himself forever behind him on all that he had ever known" (p. 261). But this
feeling is offered to a shadow of himself, for when an actual
boy does come to him, Sutpen does not allow Charles Bon to escape his past, but, according to Quentin, inflicts it on him.
Sutpen's projection of himself (the boy he would *like* to see
at his door) would be able to look to a future in which his
descendants

> who might not even hear his (the boy's) name, wanted to
> be born without even having to know that they had once
> been riven forever free from brutehood just as his own
> (Sutpen's) children were.... (p. 261)

The boy is a double of Sutpen. He is to "shut the door himself" on his past, as Sutpen's design suggests he would like
to do for himself; and he is to turn this willed amnesia into
an asset for his descendants. Unlike the boy, however, Sutpen
cannot spare his children his past because of the actual boy
whom he does not allow into the house and whose revenge im-
perils the design.

Sutpen's little allegory attests to his failure to leave
his own past behind, for to be always at work on the design
attests to the continued power of that objectifying glance.
His attempt to recover his original harmony consists in this
desire to receive, somehow, the child at the door, to usher
him in, and to close the door. It is a project reminiscent
of that of the "worldless spirit" described by Max Stirner:

> Yet as it has only moved away from the world and made
> of itself a being *free from the world*, without being
> able really to annihilate the world, this remains to
> it a stumbling block that cannot be cleared away....[25]

Sutpen's boy-symbol suggests his desire to be free from the
world by "spiritualizing" the world, that is, by taking the
brutal fact of existence (poor boys and rich men) and infusing
them with an aim, a meaning. The self-made man is here someone who must be understood to have embarked on a project of
fathering himself, of spiritualizing paternity.

One reason for considering it inaccurate to call Sutpen
merely an arrogant rationalist is that this pride is founded
on the original upsurge of shame. Before the shame he was
one of the "same," a unity of egalitarians. But after the
fall his arrogant solitude, his claim to the body of Rosa
Coldfield, his French architect are only signs of his failed
subjectivity. He now plays at being one of "them." By ap-
propriating their gestures he further objectifies himself.
Sutpen is solitary because he cannot leave his objectivity
behind him:

> We are therefore dealing with a primary reaction to
> shame, and it is already a flight and of bad faith; for
> without ceasing to hold the Other as a subject, I try
> to apprehend myself as affecting the Other by my object-
> state.[26]

This is not the "authentic" mode of arrogance that Sartre
then goes on to describe, although Sutpen seems to treat
others only as objects. He is, however, no de Sade, despite
Rosa's hair-raising account of him. He is too committed to
the adoption of the gestures of the original Other, Pettibone
("land and niggers and a fine house"). His effort to father
himself and to become autonomous is too deeply haunted by
"them" to make Sutpen simply the arrogant rationalist before
the facts of history. He is aching for the "tradition."

As he tells his story to General Compson, it is clear that
flawlessness (no brute objectivity) must be part of the design;
there must be nothing they or he (for he sees with *their* eyes)
can see. A Sutpen family must be able to defuse looks. His
trip across the water, when he flees Pettibone and his father,
brings him to another plantation, another planter's house, and,
I submit, we see a new spiral in the family romance. The romance sometimes includes, says Freud, the "phantasy of rescuing
his father from danger and saving his life; in this way he puts
his account square with him. This phantasy is commonly enough
displaced on to the emperor, king or some other great man;
after being thus distorted it becomes admissible to consciousness, and may even be made use of by creative writers."[27]
Sutpen wrenches himself away from the land of his fathers,
goes to Haiti, where, like his father on the continent, he
works for a planter and rescues the latter from danger. If
one is prepared to stretch the role of Eulalia, the fractional
Negro who gives to her planter father some of the objectivity
of Sutpen's own family (he slept with a black woman!), to include the role of a mother-surrogate, then we find another
aspect of the romance. It also includes the desire to rescue
the mother, a phantasy which contains the wish "to have by his
mother a son who is like himself." Latent in such a fantasy

is, of course, identification with the very father the day-
dreamer wishes to supersede.

In Haiti Sutpen rescues the planter and his daughter, in
a literally fantastic manner, from a slave-revolt:

> That was how he told it: he went out and subdued them,
> and when he returned he and the girl became engaged to
> marry.... (p. 254)

We never learn how he performed this miracle, but it seems he

> put the musket down ... and walked out in the darkness
> and subdued them, maybe by yelling louder, maybe by
> standing, bearing more than they believed any bones and
> flesh could or should.... (p. 254)

To marry the boss's daughter after saving both of them is a
fine adaptation of the rescue fantasy, but Eulalia and her
father are specious Pettibones. Her blackness objectifies
her, and in the son she gives him Sutpen sires only his own
objectivity--again he is the fool of a black. He tries then
to make himself independent of this family, returning the
dowry, and taking as his fair share (appropriately) the wild
slaves who are both the sign of his error and his degradation,
just as was the slave at the door. Brooks notes the seeming
absence of "personal feeling" in Sutpen's adoption of the
color bar;[28] Sutpen even seems to violate it by keeping Clytie
in the house. It makes sense, this lack of personal feeling,
for to Sutpen the Negro is a sign of objectivity that he must
subdue (as in his wrestling matches with the slaves). He only
uses "mere" Southern racism to further his design. His is not
the racism of those who would lynch Lucas Beauchamp in *Intruder
in the Dust*.

After he leaves Haiti he searches for a "real" wife. She
must be good, not too far above him (no planter's daughter
with all-seeing eyes to look down at him from beneath her
parasol). So he marries Ellen Coldfield. Here too he proves
himself superior to a father, and once more it is not clear
how. This time Sutpen uses Mr. Coldfield's credit to make a
good deal of money for them. The old Methodist, however, is
shocked into refusing his share (pp. 259-260). Another mother-
surrogate, less sexual (cold field) is rescued from another
father. He carries her off to Sutpen's Hundred where she gives
him another image of himself. Henry Sutpen is, presumably, to
be one of the children who will never know of a brutal past.
Sutpen is a paradoxical solitary, with doubles of himself and
his past in every direction.

With the return of the repressed, Charles Bon, Sutpen's
design is suddenly imperiled, and, as we shall see, Bon also

acts out an aspect of the family romance. What I have been
suggesting is that in *Absalom, Absalom!* the quest for autonomy
is conveyed in a way that is analogous to the fantasy of controlling one's own parentage, and that it serves as a vehicle
for an ontological quest (to be the seen-seeing) which is the
real meaning of Sutpen's design. Ideally, for Sutpen, the
creation of offspring should be subject to the necessities of
the design, but to carry out the design requires a dependence
on others, thereby immediately placing Sutpen's autonomy in
jeopardy. He seeks to live by necessity and meets only con-
tingency.

When Bon arrives the romance spirals up again, and this
time Sutpen is the lord of the manor whom Bon accidentally
meets, while for Henry, the son who apes the exotic Bon, Sutpen
becomes a father-to-be-replaced. The account offered by Shreve
and Quentin of the family reunion begins to suggest romances
within romances.

At the time of Bon's arrival, Sutpen seems to have attained
his goal and to have become a Pettibone. More precisely, he
is, as is suitable in a family romance, a *nouveau riche*; with
a mean past and a present success, he is a hillbilly patrician.
The trappings of his design suggest how he has topped his
ideal, and also how anxious he remains about it:

> The design.--Getting richer and richer. It must have
> looked fine and clear ahead for him now: house furnished
> and even bigger and whiter than the one he had gone to
> the door of that day; ... and he with his own brand of
> niggers even, which the man who lay in the hammock with
> his shoes off didn't have.... (p. 260)

Sutpen achieves grandeur, and it is no wonder that, as critics
have pointed out, the novel is full of allusions to heroes of
the Classical and Biblical traditions. When Bon arrives he
finds a Great Man, the Lord of Sutpen's Hundred, a father to
himself.[29]

But Bon has affinities of his own with the hero. The return of the repressed repeats the family romance by way of
the birth of the hero. In Rank's view the hero is generally
the son of distinguished parents, and his birth is often preceded by difficulties for his progenitors such as, for example, continence or barrenness. During or before the preg-
nancy of his mother, ominous portents (dreams, oracles) advise
against his birth, usually threatening danger from him to his
father. The neonate is then abandoned by his father and saved
by lowly people, but upon reaching maturity he finds his first
parents, takes revenge on his father, is acknowledged, and
achieves rank and honors.[30] The family romance, which Rank
claims is transformed into the various hero myths, is reversed

in that the real parents are the "higher" parents. In the
myth the lowly parents are kind, and the hero may ennoble them
when he achieves his birthright. The son's hostility towards
the father is also reversed, and we find, instead, that fathers
are first hostile towards their sons, whom they fear. Thus
the son's victory over his father is justified by its status
as an act of vengeance. Rank argues that the incest motive
is present in those myths wherein the father seeks to keep his
daughter from the hero,[31] or those in which the hero is abandoned along with his mother (for example, those of Perseus
and of Telephus).[32]

I think it not at all farfetched to say that Rank's mythic
pattern is present, to some degree, in Faulkner's novel.
First, Sutpen himself reminds us of the Rankian hero. He is
fascinating to others because of his "decisiveness of thought,
... strength of will, [and] energy of action," qualities that
Freud saw in the heroic Moses.[33] His "design," the influence
of which is still felt forty years after his death, bears
comparison to the "idea which [the great man] puts forward,"
according to Freud. These qualities of the hero, Freud says,
form "part of the picture of a father." In addition, Sutpen
has the essential quality of the "great man," "autonomy and
independence, ... his divine unconcern which may grow into
ruthlessness."[34] Sutpen is surrounded by sons, not only
Henry and Bon, but also the two Harvard students whom Faulkner
repeatedly identifies with Bon and Henry, and also, I submit,
by Wash Jones, who exceeds even the boy Sutpen in his idealization of a planter:

> ... and so [Wash] would look at Sutpen and think A fine
> proud man. If God himself was to come down and ride
> the natural earth, that's what he would aim to look
> like. (p. 282)

Sutpen names his children, disposes of wives, ruins his
daughter's life, proposes a breeding experiment to Rosa, and
carries one out on Milly Jones. He is the primal father of
Totem and Taboo reappeared in Yoknapatawpha County, Miss.
The heroic myth has taken an odd turn, however. We see the
original romance acted out by Sutpen, and we remember that
Freud's hero is "someone who has had the courage to rebel
against his father and has in the end victoriously overcome
him."[35] But because we know the origin of Sutpen's "rebellion,"
we know that he is engaged in the dialectical dance of the son
before the father, overcoming him by becoming him. The heroic
birth, that is the mythic birth, the one whose compromising
details are lost in the generality of its status as a trans-
formation of a collective fantasy, is more that of Charles
Bon. Bon is *one* part of Sutpen only, the denied objective

side, which returns to cause torment to the whole man. But
Bon, too, is an abortive hero.

Much has been written on what is fact and what is conjecture in *Absalom, Absalom!* For example, the statement that I
attribute to Wash Jones is, in fact, a fancy of Quentin. Is
it true that Bon knew he was Sutpen's son and that he was also
partly Negro? These, and other questions, are very important,
and critics have been wise to attend to them. It seems to me,
however, that we might also consider the conjectures of Quentin
and Shreve in the light of the family romance and its relationship to the heroic myth. Their struggle with the Sutpen story
is a form of mythmaking. They fill in factual gaps with con-
nective narratives, and their mythologizing recalls Rank's
claim that the hero is a creation of the others, a kind of
collective ego: "This extraordinary childhood of the hero ...
is constructed by the individual myth-makers ... from the consciousness of their own infancy."[36] Now Quentin and Shreve
really have no infancy--they are, I realize, no more than their
appearances in the text. But Quentin does become fascinated
with the "other family," and throughout the whole book he
thinks about it, this incest-obsessed character from *The Sound
and the Fury*, whose relation to that book is inevitably evoked
by the appendix to *Absalom, Absalom!*, with its ironic: "Died,
Cambridge, Mass., 1910." Even in his childhood, Quentin and
his playmates were intrigued by the old Sutpen house, and they
would dare each other to approach it. Rank says that the folk
"identify themselves with [the hero],"[37] and Faulkner's many
references to Shreve and Quentin as being, "both of them," Henry
and Bon, must inevitably suggest identification. They are like
the ancient myth-makers, "creating between them, out of the
rag-tag and bob-ends of old tales and talking, people who
perhaps had never existed at all anywhere" (p. 303). Quentin's
own heroic adventure, his decision to climb the old Sutpen
staircase and look into the bedroom, in which he finds Henry
Sutpen, allows him to overthrow his own father, or at least
to reject Mr. Compson's interpretation of the Sutpen disaster.[38]

As with Sutpen, the parallels between Bon and the Rankian
hero are not exact. Nevertheless, what similarities (and differences) there are are suggestive. Bon's first family is the
aristocratic one, since it includes the man, Sutpen. Bon's
"low" father might well be the shifty, hypothetical lawyer of
Shreve, a man who is not ennobled in this myth. Difficulties
precede Bon's birth. Sutpen speaks of how he maintained his
virginity prior to his marriage to Eulalia (p. 248), and we
know of the trial-by-combat preceding his marriage. No oracles
or dreams precede Bon's birth and presage danger to his father,
unless it be that this motif is displaced onto Eulalia's blackness, of which Sutpen learns after his son's birth. It is this

objectifying blackness which threatens Sutpen's design and
accounts for the father's hostility towards his son, and
finally leads him to abandon mother and child together. The
rediscovery of the father is achieved in the "highly versatile"
fashion of Rank in the long effort of the lawyer to reunite
son with father (pp. 300-301). Their reunion includes, in
Quentin's myth, the element of recognition, and it evokes
Sutpen's own visual trauma at Pettibone's door. Bon seeks
repeatedly for the "sign in the eyes" that would indicate
Sutpen's recognition of him. He watches those eyes; but there
is "no flicker in them." Sutpen invites him in, but not as
his son (p. 268). One also detects, in this scene, the old
motif of the father who must keep his daughter from the
questing hero:

> ... he [Sutpen] stood there at his own door just as he
> had imagined, planned, designed, and sure enough and
> after fifty years the forlorn nameless and homeless lost
> child came to knock at it and no monkey-dressed nigger
> anywhere under the sun to come to the door and order
> the child away; and Father said that even then, even
> though he knew that Bon and Judith had never laid eyes
> on one another, he must have felt and heard the design--
> house, position, posterity and all--come down....
> (p. 267)

This is not the child of Sutpen's allegory. That child, as
befitted a symbol, could be paradoxical, that is, both pure
(non-objective) and like himself *as he was* at Pettibone's
door (objective). Instead, he must fight off a being mediated
by blackness, as he was mediated by the "monkey-nigger," to
preserve the purity of his daughter. A circle is being closed,
but not the one he intended to close himself.

This civil war of the divided self, forming as it does the
skeletal structure of the pattern of relationships in Sutpen's
life, accounts for a difference in Bon's relation to the
heroic myth. He does not seem to "rebel against the father
and ... overcome him." Instead, the old rescue fantasy re-
appears now in the speculations of the students who deal with
the life of Lord Sutpen. Bon seems strangely eager to spare
his father the difficulties of public recognition of him:

> 'He need not even acknowledge me: I will let him under-
> stand just as quickly that he need not do that, that I
> do not expect that, will not be hurt by that, just as
> he will let me know quickly that I am his son....'
> (p. 319)

He also wishes to be as certain of paternity as he is of
maternity: "'I am my mother's son, at least ...'" (p. 319).

Bon's case illustrates the dependence on fathers that is discerned in many arrogant claims in the family romance. But
this primal father does not care to be rescued by a son who
is a shadow of himself, and the confirmatory glance is not
forthcoming:

> Then for the second time he looked at the expressionless
> and rocklike face [of Sutpen], at the pale boring eyes
> in which there was no flicker, nothing, the face in
> which he saw his own features, in which he saw recognition,
> and that was all. (p. 348)

In this version of the myth of the hero, Sutpen reveals the
flaw in Bon, his negritude, and destroys his sons who, in their
love for each other, threaten to ruin him. No black son could
ever be admitted by Sutpen. Even if the secret could be kept
from the "others," Sutpen would see himself in Bon, would see
the poor yokel who thought a Negro woman in Haiti was really
a Spaniard.

Sutpen's original fall has, it seems, peopled the novel
with transformations of the kernel family romance situation
which was the vehicle of his own crisis. His sons are "splits"
of himself: the object-Negro, Bon, and the heir apparent to
subjective purity, Henry. If women, in the romance, suggest
the Oedipal drama, the mother-wife in this novel takes two
forms: the degraded Eulalia ("the old Sabine") and the genteel,
de-sexualized Ellen. His white daughter, Sutpen "locks up in
some inaccessible place, so as to safeguard her virginity"--
or, to qualify this formula of Rank's interpretation, Sutpen
effectively does so by killing Bon through Henry's agency. As
I suggested above, Henry's aping of Bon is itself a variant
of the romance:

> A bucolic heir apparent who had probably never spent a
> dozen nights outside of his paternal house ... until he
> came to school, whom [Bon] watched aping his clothing
> carriage speech and all.... (p. 315)

Like Sutpen, Bon has two love-objects, the woman who parallels
his mother in debasement, the octoroon, and the good girl,
Judith, who remains true to his memory. And Henry, Bon's
sibling rival, as it were, preserves Judith's goodness by
murdering their brother. Later Henry is himself cared for by
a degraded woman, the black Clytemnestra, his sister, who
destroys them both in her final incendiary act. The punishment for the sins of the father continues into the next generation as well. Etienne, Bon's son by the octoroon, is forced,
after his mother's death, to come to the door of a white
family's house. He moves up, caught now in a family romance

that is running amok. But by learning of his race, Etienne moves down from his privileged ignorance into the dense objectivity of his caste. He accepts, more authentically than Sutpen, his object status, and he flaunts his "coal black" idiot wife at the white Others. Yet, like his grandfather, objectivity is still a penance for him.

Sutpen's experience haunts that of his children and they repeat various aspects of it, almost compulsively. Quentin, the figurative sibling of Henry and Bon, is no exception. Like Sutpen, he goes to a house that is part of another world. First he goes imaginatively, when he receives from Rosa "the quaint, stiffly formal request which was actually a summons out of another world almost" (p. 10). The equilibrium of his life is disturbed when, from Rosa, he hears the particulars of a theme which has been part of his inheritance:

> It was a part of his twenty years' heritage of breathing the same air and hearing his father talk about the man, Sutpen.... (p. 11)

As in Freud's account of the response of Jews to *der Mann*, *Moses*, Faulkner's novel reveals the need of a people, Southerners, to come to terms with a legend:

> or maybe Father and I are both Shreve, maybe it took Father and me both to make Shreve or Shreve and me both to make Father or maybe Thomas Sutpen to make all of us. (p. 202)

Certainly it is the last hypothesis that is most likely in this world where Sutpen remains still to be understood, as when Rosa speaks to Quentin, and out "of quiet thunderclap he would abrupt (man-horse-demon) ..." (p. 8). Indeed, the Gentile, Shreve, falls under the spell of the man-horse-demon totem himself. His sarcasms are not simply the signs of his distance from the material on which his imagination works, or a sign of his lack of depth:

> This was not flippancy either. It too was just that protective coloring of levity behind which the youthful shame of being moved hid itself, out of which Quentin also spoke.... (p. 250)

The Gentile even offers an ironic faith in the redeemer Son, the Jim Bond, who will "conquer the western hemisphere":

> '... and so in a few thousand years, I who regard you will also have sprung from the loins of African kings.' (p. 378)

As with the Christianity of Freud's own historical romance, of the Judaeo-Christian family, a son religion arises from a

religion of the father. But like Christianity, Shreve's para-
ble "has not escaped the fate of having to get rid of the
father." In his vision of the future, Egalitarianism is re-
gained by means of universal objectification. We all become
black, and await, perhaps, an implicit last judgment under the
ironic eyes of Pettibone.

Sutpen's heroic effort to close a circle and to make himself the seen-seeing, ends, as I have suggested, in Quentin's
effort to see: "'But I must see too now. I will have to.
Maybe I shall be sorry tomorrow, but I must see'" (p. 371).
The punishment for his sight of the emaciated, old Henry is
Clytie's destruction of the house, herself, and Henry. Quentin
is left with the heritage of a people chosen to watch this
drama, and of the South he can only say, "'I dont hate it!
I dont hate it! I dont hate it!'" And there is the terrible, ,
final opacity of the black avatar of Sutpen, Jim Bond, the
idiot who, like his grandfather, is a solitary. Only he has
no new house into which he can dream of access--his genes have
revealed him--no families left to allow a new drama of family
romance. Sutpen could not become a Pettibone, the Akhenaten
who, in this case, unwittingly revealed to Moses-Sutpen the
glories of a higher life. Yet Sutpen's own children do not
destroy him. They are too much like Sartre's Flaubert in relation to Flaubert's own Moses, Achille-Cléophas, mere "children
of the idea, invented before being engendered."[39]

The terrible father falls by the hand of a different kind
of son, a *coeval*, as befits the paradoxes of Sutpen's life.
This is, of course, Wash Jones. I suggested earlier that
Jones' idealized view of Sutpen makes the latter a surrogate
father to this poor white tenant of his land. Like Sutpen in
his own childhood, Jones lives on the land of an envied and
admired lord of the manor. In his abject poverty and his relation to Sutpen, he recalls, also, the situation of Sutpen's
own father on Pettibone's land. Like the first Sutpen (pp.
230-231) he suffers from the insolence of privileged slaves
("he walked always in mocking and jeering echoes of nigger
laughter" [p. 282]); like the boy, Sutpen, he finds in the
master of the estate "his own lonely apotheosis" (p. 282).
He is even denied access to the front door, by the slave-
daughter, Clytie, but accepts his rejection in order to spare
his "father" any embarrassment (pp. 281-282). After the war,
he and Sutpen drink together in the scuppernon arbor and recall to us, thereby, the discarded egalitarianism of the child
of the mountain men.

Jones even has a child who is "objectified"--by Sutpen.
This is not a son, however, but a granddaughter, Milly, on
whom Sutpen wishes to sire a son. When the experiment fails,
he says to the girl:

> 'Well, Milly; too bad you're not a mare too. Then I
> could give you a decent stall in the stable' and turned
> and went out. (p. 286)

Ironically, Sutpen turns, in his old age, to a low family,
one like his primary family, to create one more "child of the
idea." He creates a girl, and although Wash is not the father
who seeks to keep his "daughter" from the hero, he does demand
that she be recognized as a person. And he does what no other
of the sons of Sutpen could do. He *touches* the old Primal
Father who still believes he has access to all women, who has
"touched" a poor white girl who, in her poverty, reminds us
of the women from whose loins he himself came. Faulkner repeats the decisive words, "don't touch me," several times in
the course of the book:

> 'Stand back, Wash. Dont you touch me,' ... 'I'm going
> to tech you Kernel': and Sutpen again: 'Stand back,
> Wash!' sharp now, and then she ⌊the midwife⌋ heard the
> whip on Wash's face but she didn't know if she heard
> the scythe.... (p. 286)

The scythe falls on the old man who could no longer make men.
The family romance, the dream of autonomy, closes with Sutpen,
he who was himself, like every romancer, a child of his own
idea, falling, in 1869, at the feet of a man whose like he
had thought to have left behind him in 1820, in an old cabin,
on Pettibone's plantation.

NOTES

1. *The Myth of Southern History: Historical Consciousness
in Twentieth-Century Southern Literature* (Nashville, 1970),
p. 99.

2. *William Faulkner, From Jefferson to the World* (Lexington, 1966), p. 166.

3. *William Faulkner: the Yoknapatawpha Country* (New Haven,
1963), p. 298.

4. *Ibid.*, p. 306.

5. *Quest for Failure: A Study of William Faulkner* (Ithaca,
1960), p. 267.

6. *Ibid.*, p. 248.

7. Donald M. Kartiganer, "The Role of Myth in *Absalom,
Absalom!*," *Modern Fiction Studies*, 9 (1963-64), 362.

8. I am using the Modern Library edition of *Absalom, Absalom!*

9. New York, 1968, p. 75.

10. Sigmund Freud, "Family Romances," *The Standard Edition of the Complete Psychological Works of Sigmund Freud*, ed. James Strachey, IX (London, 1959), p. 237.

11. Holland, p. 310.

12. Otto Rank, "The Myth of the Birth of the Hero," in *The Myth of the Birth of the Hero and Other Writings*, ed. Philip Freund (New York, 1959), p. 69. *cf*. Freud, "Family Romances," p. 239.

13. Freud, p. 239.

14. Davenport, p. 97.

15. Quoted in Holland, p. 245.

16. Jean-Paul Sartre, *Being and Nothingness: An Essay in Phenomenological Ontology*, trans. Hazel F. Barnes (London, 1957), p. 222.

17. "Thus the Me-as-object-for myself is a Me which is *not* Me: that is, which does not have the characteristics of a consciousness. It is a *degraded* consciousness; objectivation is a radical metamorphosis." *Ibid.*, p. 273, Sartre's italics.

18. *Ibid.*, p. 267.

19. *Ibid.*, p. 421.

20. *Ibid.*, Sartre's italics.

21. *Ibid.*, pp. 421-422.

22. R.D. Laing, *The Politics of Experience* (Harmondsworth, 1967), p. 70.

23. Sartre, p. 275.

24. The effect of the slave's refusal upon Sutpen was a kind of desperate amazement: "... he seemed to kind of dissolve and part of him turn and rush back through the two years they had lived there...." (*Absalom, Absalom!*, pp. 229-230).

25. *The Ego and His Own*, trans. Steven T. Byington (London, 1915), p. 33.

26. Sartre, p. 290.

27. Sigmund Freud, "A Special Type of Choice of Object Made by Men," *Standard Edition*, XI, 172-173.

28. Brooks, pp. 298-299.

29. In addition to Kartiganer (*op. cit.*), see also Lennart Bjork, "Ancient Myths and the Moral Framework of Faulkner's

Absalom, Absalom!," *American Literature*, 35 (1963), 196–204.

30. Rank, p. 65.

31. *Ibid.*, p. 80.

32. *Ibid.*, p. 79.

33. Freud, "Moses and Monotheism," *Standard Edition*, XXIII, 109.

34. *Ibid.*, pp. 109–110.

35. *Ibid.*, p. 12.

36. Rank, p. 84.

37. *Ibid.*

38. *cf.* Cleanth Brooks, p. 317: "At all events, the whole logic of *Absalom, Absalom!* argues that *only* through the presence of Henry in the house was it possible for Quentin—and through Quentin his father and Shreve and those of us who read the book—to be made privy to the dark secret that underlay the Sutpen tragedy" [Brooks' underline]. Brooks' language and Quentin's anxious physical response to the sight of Henry (pp. 372–374) suggest another kind of visual trauma at work in the novel, the primal scene. As Holland puts it, "different possible responses to the primal scene [are]: curiosity, awe and wonder, fear" (p. 320). The distancing narrators of Faulkner's novel and the suspenseful curiosity they evoke, all leading up to Quentin's decision to enter the bedroom of the old house and his discovery of the last of the actors in the Sutpen incest drama, suggest the anxiety associated with the primal scene. Poor Sutpen, he becomes not only the object of the detectives in the novel but also of "those of us who read the book" and who are "made privy to the dark secret that underlay the Sutpen tragedy."

39. Jean-Paul Sartre, *L'Idiot de la Famille: Gustave Flaubert de 1821 à 1857.* 2 vols. (Paris, 1971). This incredible attempt to recreate the meaning of a life bears comparison to Faulkner's novel in its mixture of fact and conjecture, its spiral structure, and, not least important, its interminable sentences.

ABSALOM, ABSALOM!:
THE NOVEL AS HISTORIOGRAPHY

Carl E. Rollyson, Jr.

Though several critics have suggested that the interpretation of the past in *Absalom, Absalom!* has much in common with
the work of modern historians, no sustained and systematic
attempt has been made to view the novel in the context of
what historians and philosophers of history have actually
said about historical method.[1] To what extent do the character-
narrators approximate the strategies historians employ to obtain their knowledge of the past? And are we able to absorb
and articulate the pattern of historical interpretation in
such a way that the form of the novel can be compared with the
form of the historian's interpretation of the past? It seems
that as Quentin and Shreve scrutinize Sutpen's career and interact with each other, they simultaneously struggle toward
and sometimes achieve an interpretation of the past strikingly
similar to the historian's and great enough to measure Sutpen's
own ignorance of the past, which he fails to perceive as part
of the continuum of time and of his own and everyone's contemporary experience.

Sutpen provides the material for historical inquiry precisely because he is so innocent, so naive, so unconscious of
the parts of his story that do not cohere. His narrative
takes the form of specific scenes and episodes usually presented without any sense of continuity.[2] After describing to
General Compson his resolution to go to the West Indies, he
abruptly shifts to an "anecdote" of himself in the "besieged
Haitian room" trying to put down the slave insurrection, an
anecdote "called to his mind by the picture of the niggers
and torches" used to hunt down the French architect, whose
plight is obviously similar to Sutpen's own desperate circumstances when it appeared that he would be overrun and captured
(p. 246). One spectacle or "picture" stimulates in him the

From Literature and History, *No. 5 (Spring 1977), pp. 42-54.*
Reprinted by permission of the publisher.

memory of another without his being able to compare the two
situations or even link them chronologically. He lacks Quentin's consciousness of the burdens that the past places upon
the present: to him the slave uprising is a "spectacle" (p.
250) but not a stage in a developing history which includes
himself. In reading R.G. Collingwood's criticism of Arnold
Toynbee, it is apparent why Sutpen's way of perceiving past
experience is inimical to historical knowledge:

> he never reaches the conception of historical knowledge
> as the re-enactment of the past in this historian's
> mind. He regards history as a mere spectacle, something
> consisting of facts observed and recorded by the his-
> torian, phenomena presented externally to his gaze,
> not experiences into which he must enter and which he
> must make his own.[3]

Each of the narrators of Sutpen's career must face just this
problem: how to re-enact the past so that it becomes "experiences into which he must enter and which he must make
his own."

Quentin's impression of Miss Rosa's narrative reminds us
very much of Sutpen's pictorial imagination:

> Out of quiet thunderclap he would abrupt (man-horse-
> demon) upon a scene peaceful and decorous as a school-
> prize water color, faint sulphur-reek still in hair
> clothes and beard, with grouped behind him his band of
> wild niggers like beasts half tamed to walk upright like
> men, in attitudes wild and reposed, and manacled among
> them the French architect with his air grim, haggard,
> and tatter-ran. (p. 8)

She paints a child-like picture with no life-like dimension
to it; or rather, the picture is of a conventional type until
Sutpen crashes through with a dynamism that baffles and
astounds Miss Rosa. In her telling, events separated by long
intervals of time, such as Sutpen's first entrance into Jefferson and the architect's later escape, are telescoped into
a single image, just as Sutpen himself condenses into two
anecdotes the Haitian room and his original trip to Haiti six
years earlier.

From the very beginning of the novel the narrator himself
associates Miss Rosa with Sutpen. Sutpen's mansion, for example, is "unpainted and a little shabby, yet with an air, a
quality of grim endurance as though like her it had been
created to fit into and complement a world in all ways a little
smaller than the one in which it found itself" (p. 10). Miss
Rosa's narrative, like Sutpen's design, is too simple, in-
sufficiently commensurate with the complexity of the world

which she seeks to explain. Sutpen conceives of a design
which rejects anything that is not incremental to it. He
must keep faith only with himself in order to succeed. Rosa
Coldfield's story also has a narrow design which insists on
treating Sutpen exclusively as a demon. The way in which she
bases her whole story solely on her attitude toward Sutpen is
very like Sutpen's own obsession with his rejection at the
planter's front door.

But where Sutpen is simply ignorant of the fact that the
past has any special relevance to the present, Miss Rosa posi-
tively denies the possibility of any true historical knowledge.
Her concept of mind is as mechanical as Sutpen's, but it is
consciously expressed as a rejection of the accuracy of human
memory:

> *This is the substance of remembering--sense, sight,*
> *smell: the muscles with which we see and hear and feel--*
> *not mind, not thought: there is no such thing as memory:*
> *the brain recalls just what the muscles grope for: no*
> *more, no less; and its resultant sum is usually incorrect*
> *and false and worthy only of the name of dream.* (p. 143)

This is an excellent description of the way in which Sutpen's
mind works. In seeing the French architect being chased by
his wild Negroes, he is stimulated to recall a similar "sense,
sight, smell" experience in the past. Miss Rosa and Sutpen
both are automatons in this respect: as John Hagan puts it,
"each compulsively continues to respond to a single peculiar
stimulus with which his past history is crucially assorted--
the smell of wistaria in Rosa's case and the smell and taste
of sugar in Sutpen's.[4] For Sutpen the smell and taste of
sugar recalls the burning of the cane in Haiti during the
slave revolt. For Rosa the smell of wistaria recalls the
summer of her barren youth. But both the smell and the taste
do no more than summon up the past which itself remains in
stasis, blocking their consciousness of time as a process in
which past experiences are reinterpreted as well as recalled.

Miss Rosa's initial interpretation, however biased, sets
up the context in which we must perceive Sutpen, just as many
initial interpretations of historical figures and events establish the terms by which historians then pursue their interpretations of the past. As Herbert Butterfield points out:

> The starting-point for historical interpretation must
> lie in the ideas of the people who were living while
> the events in question were taking place. Their way of
> envisaging their struggles and formulating the issues
> of the time provides the historian with his initial
> framework. This version may continue to be reproduced

for a long period, yet it may actually have been devised
to serve as a weapon in the conflict which the historian
is trying to narrate.[5]

Miss Rosa, then, is the only narrator who can supply the
authenticity of a contemporary's attitude toward Sutpen. At
the same time, we know that her account is used as a weapon
against the man who corrupted her family and even seduced
Miss Rosa herself into abetting his design.

Just how much of the past's actual impact is felt through
Miss Rosa's narration is measured by Mr Compson's commentary
on what is to him the shadowy remoteness of the past. Immense
changes that have occurred in a relatively short period of time
seem to make the life of the past look incredibly simple, devoid of the complexity and ambiguity of modern life. Thus,
for different reasons, Mr Compson agrees with Miss Rosa that
historical knowledge may not be possible. To him the fact of
change itself suggests that all knowledge of the past is tenuous and insecure, and the growing instability of contemporary
consciousness makes it appear still more doubtful that past
and present can be integrated into a single narrative. He
reinforces Miss Rosa's reading of Sutpen in the sense that he
maintains that the characters are "not dwarfed and involved
but distinct, uncomplex" (p. 89).

But perhaps because of his bafflement, his feeling that
the present is estranged from the past, he feels a greater
need to explain that Sutpen was, in some respects, a rational
human being who confronted and, to some extent, succeeded in
mastering a difficult situation (p. 37). His view is much
more objective than Miss Rosa's, but it is considerably less
passionate, less attuned than hers to pick up any sense of
what it was like to live with Sutpen. At a greater distance
from the events he describes, Mr Compson takes note of all the
evidence he can scrape together and tries to reconcile the
divergent and contradictory reports of Sutpen's career. Yet
he acknowledges his failure to make sense of much of the evidence (pp. 100-101). Mr Compson errs, I think, in believing
that reconstructing the past is like a "chemical formula."
His materialism is not so crass or unsophisticated as Miss
Rosa's or Sutpen's, but he still tends to discount, as they
do, the interpretative processes of the mind. It is not the
relics of a bygone age, the meagre indications of what was
once a fully experienced life, that explains the past; rather
the past is made imaginable by the intricate connections such
as Mr Compson himself is able to make between the human thoughts
and activities suggested by this evidence. As R.G. Collingwood observes in his discussion of Hegel, history consists of
"empirical events" which are the "outward expressions of

thought, and it is the thought behind the events--not the events themselves" which make possible a "chain of logically connected concepts. When you look at the events and not at the thought behind them you see no necessary connexion at all."[6] Mr Compson has failed to make enough connections and, in his disappointment, he supposes that the very notion of reconstructing the past has been discredited.

Quentin and Shreve are greatly influenced by Mr Compson's initial presentation of the relationship between Henry and Bon. They retain, for example, Mr Compson's belief that Bon withdrew into a mysterious passivity after Henry had repudiated Sutpen, (p. 335) although they account for his seeming indifference by reconstructing a whole new set of motivations for him. He was, they imagine, not an urbane, detached observer of the blundering Sutpens (p. 93) but a son despairing over his father's refusal to acknowledge him (p. 333). Furthermore, Mr Compson's wonderfully detailed evocation of the intense friendship between Henry and Bon stimulates Quentin and Shreve to interpret the elusive meaning of the Sutpen story by concentrating on the meaning of the shadowy Bon's life and death.

However much in error he may be, then, Mr Compson's choice of episodes and his attempt to place human action into understandable contexts mark his narrative as a major advance towards Quentin's and Shreve's interpretation.[7] As W.B. Gallie says of historical explanations:

> not only do they enable the historian to classify and clarify and endorse facts which at first seem puzzling or improbable, they help him to enlarge his vision of the context and the potential relevance of particular actions and episodes. In fact, the quest for explanations is a main cause of the "outward drive" of historical interests--away from contemporary and parochial happenings to a large, a more complete and more complex presentation of the surrounding whole.[8]

Mr Compson's emphasis on Bon's role in the Sutpen story helpfully shifts attention from Miss Rosa's parochial obsession with Sutpen and leads to the discovery that Sutpen's story is linked to events that occurred far away from the immediate locality of Jefferson, Mississippi, from the South which Miss Rosa sees as doomed. Mr Compson's explanations inevitably enlarge the facts, making more of them than he himself is aware of, very much in line with Collingwood's emphasis upon history as "a kind of knowledge in which questions about ideas and questions about facts are not distinguishable,"[9] and with David Levin's view that interpretation itself becomes part of the historical evidence.[10] Once again, Mr Compson is clearly wrong to suppose that one is ever confronted with only "initials," "letters," "nicknames."

Confronted with this fusion and confusion of fact and interpretation, Quentin and Shreve bring to the Sutpen story a deeper understanding of human interaction than Sutpen, Miss Rosa, or Mr Compson have displayed. By boldly using their own sympathetic friendship as a guide to re-enacting the emotions and attitudes of the historical figures, they transcend the block of time that is separating them from the past. That they are talking to each other throughout their reconstruction of the past is of the utmost importance in explaining how they go beyond the other versions of the Sutpen story, and how they exceed the historian's normal reach and control over his subject matter. There is something inherently dramatic and life-giving in their portrayal of the relationship between Charles and Henry. We seem not only to gain knowledge about the past, but also to regain some of its actual experience. As Martin Duberman suggests, the historian cannot rival the verisimilitude of "the spoken word, which benefits from the direct confrontation of personality ... If we [as historians] could bring the spoken word's immediacy and emotion to the presentation of history, a new richness of response, a new measure of involvement with the past, would be possible."[11] All of *Absalom, Absalom!* enlivens history through the spoken words of the narrators, but the "direct confrontation of personality" between Quentin and Shreve brings to the story of Sutpen's career "a new richness of response, a new measure of involvement with the past."

But because the spoken word is so much the peculiar product of a particular speaker, it is often imprecise, unrefined, and sometimes unreflective, and therefore especially dangerous to invoke in attempted reconstructions of the past. In *Absalom, Absalom!*, however, the narrator clearly identifies those moments in which Quentin and Shreve do no more than project their own feelings into the historical figures. Similarly, Duberman recognizes that a call for immediacy and emotion in the presentation of the past often subverts the historian's traditional task of presenting facts rather than moral truths or philosophical statements or even past experience as such. Nevertheless, a more conventional historian like Herbert Butterfield agrees that in order to make sense of the "facts" the historian must take some risks. He should reach beyond the written documents and evidence of the historical figure's conscious intentions and drive below to the motivations which underlie human actions in the past:

> the historian may need to have a feeling--a sort of sympathetic sense--for areas of life and history where he knows that the evidence must be lacking. We may suspect

> that historical personages are like icebergs and though
> certain protruding parts of them are visible to posterity,
> the greater proportion of them is always submerged. The
> written evidence is inadequate, and if we take each piece
> of testimony, and draw a line from one point to another,
> we may produce a system or a picture but the result is
> liable to be a caricature.[12]

Butterfield cautions, however, that the historian must often
settle for a kind of knowledge different from that which Quentin
and Shreve eventually obtain:

> All of us will be able to realize on the one hand how
> easy it is for a man to cheat his biographer, and, on
> the other hand, how little the people around us at the
> present day can know or understand of our profounder
> internal life. A man like Martin Luther must have taken
> some of his fondest secrets with him to the grave; and
> certainly the historian must often be defeated—must
> expect to be defeated—on those issues of private feeling
> and ultimate motive which are a mystery even to intimate
> contemporary friends and which so often lie between a
> man and his Maker.[13]

Shreve and Quentin, nonetheless, do attempt to penetrate Bon's
fondest secrets, to determine his ultimate motives, whatever
we may think of their ultimate success. In this way they
resemble the novelist or historical novelist. Butterfield
would call their history romantic history, in the sense that
they desire "to touch the pulsing heart of men who toyed with
the world as we do, and left it long ago." This kind of history, Butterfield observes, is found only in novels, and it
represents the "quest for the most elusive thing in the world."[14]
He does not argue that this "quest" is any less valuable than
the historian's, but insists that it is a different "form" of
history.[15] History as the historian writes it "cannot come so
near to human hearts and human passions as a good novel can;
its very fidelity to facts makes it not perhaps less true to
life, but farther away from the heart of things."[16]
    Russel Nye, summarizing an example of the historical
imagination given by the Italian historian Gaetano Salvimini,
has furnished us with a useful insight into the limitations
the historian imposes upon himself in reconstructing the past:

> Suppose that we excavate a Roman statue with a missing
> head. The archaeologist and the historian agree that
> the head must have worn a helmet, perhaps even of a par-
> ticular design, and demonstrate proof of this in various
> ways—by reference to other statues of the period, from
> contemporary sculptors' styles, from detailed knowledge

of Roman military accoutrements. But at this point the
historical imagination must stop, while the artistic
imagination may continue. The sculptor who recreates
the missing head has much greater freedom in visualizing
and executing it; he must respect the style of the historical period in which it existed, of course, but the
face of the statue he may see as he wishes. Two sculp-
tors, in fact, might provide two quite different faces
for it without violating the rule of credibility. Thus
the historical and artistic imagination whose function
may be much the same, must operate under different conditions.

With Bon also, many vital facts are missing: if they are to be
established it cannot be by evidence alone but by an act of
the artistic imagination. Like the historian looking at the
Roman statue, Quentin and Shreve can follow the documentable
outlines of Bon's life, but these outlines would no more produce for them the "fact" of his Negro blood, or his feelings
toward that "fact," than a reconstruction of the helmet of the
statue would give the historian an image of the statue's head,
or of the expression on that face.

In *Absalom, Absalom!*, therefore, Faulkner is perhaps implying that there is a meaning in history which eludes a
logical, analytical approach. After all of the talking,
Quentin's and Shreve's abrupt submergence into the experience
of Henry and Charles appears to achieve a direct knowledge of
the past which resembles Bergson's "intuition," in that it is
not simply an emotion but a peculiar act of knowledge or,
rather, "a series of acts of direct participation in the immediacy of experience."[17] Of course their direct knowledge
is, in large part, based on antecedent speculations and discoveries, but the total of this earlier interpretative activity
does not of itself yield the actual experience of hearing and
seeing Sutpen, Henry, and Bon speak to each other: there is
an achieved imaginative whole which is discernibly if in-
definably greater than the sum of its factual parts. The
italicized scene in Chapter VIII (pp. 351-358) in which Sutpen
tells Henry that Charles Bon has Negro blood is designed to
compel our belief--better perhaps, our suspended disbelief--
in what Quentin and Shreve are presently doing, and it is
surely our impression that they have acquired something more
than relative knowledge. As Bergson says, "description, history, and analysis leave me here in the relative. Coincidence
with the person himself would alone give me the absolute."[18]

My point is not simply that Faulkner as a novelist is free
to have his characters imagine the past in ways which the historian may not attempt. Faulkner formulates a specifically

historical problem: what caused Henry to kill Charles Bon?
The ultimate clue to the killing is not so much a motivation
as it is a "fact," Bon's Negro blood. But this "fact" was
partially arrived at in ways contrary to the normal methods
of historical investigation; Quentin's contacts, for example,
with Clytie and Henry Sutpen--the two characters who might
have told him about Bon--are inconclusive, and indeed there
is no source, no document or testimony that could possibly
yield the conclusions which Quentin and Shreve reach.[19] Only
through their emotional and intellectual transactions do we
make the discovery that solves the riddle of the past. I take
it that this is one of the things that Waggoner means when he
says that *Absalom, Absalom!* "upsets our received notions of ...
history as an academic discipline":[20]

> Considered as an integral symbol the form of *Absalom*
> says that reality is unknowable in Sutpen's way, by
> weighing, measuring, and calculating. It says that
> without an "unscientific" act of imagination and even
> of faith--like Shreve's and Quentin's faith in Bon--we
> cannot know the things which are most worth knowing.[21]

Not only do Quentin and Shreve correct Sutpen's materialistic
ordering of reality, they also provide a comment on Mr Compson's
abstract conception of the past. What is needed, as Martin
Duberman points out, is the particularity of feeling that is
demonstrated when the historian openly involves himself in the
past he is interpreting.

    In taking a purely documentary approach to history in his
play, *In White America*, Duberman discovered:

> the past does not speak for itself, and the ordering
> intelligence that renders it, necessarily injects some
> degree of idiosyncrasy. The advantage of the documentary
> approach (if one is primarily interested in historical
> accuracy) is that it does at least minimize subjectivity
> and restrict invention. Its disadvantage (if one is
> primarily interested in making statements about experi-
> ence) is that it circumscribes reflection and generaliza-
> tion. Instead of confining myself, for example, to the
> actual words John Brown spoke at his trial, I might
> have invented words to represent what I guessed to be
> his thoughts and feelings during his speech. In not
> doing so, I suspect that what I gained in accuracy I
> lost in insight. Truth of fact has less durable rele-
> vance than truth of feeling, for a fact is rooted in a
> particular context, whereas a feeling, being universal,
> can cross time.[22]

Duberman's dissatisfaction with facts that are rooted in a particular context stems from his belief that the past must somehow

live now and be refocussed in terms of the present moment; it
must be a statement about current human experience. Of course
this is just what Quentin and Shreve are doing with the past
in their Harvard room. Duberman's dissatisfaction with facts
is expressed even more radically by Faulkner as a positive
distrust: "Fact is not too important and can be altered by
law, by circumstance, by too many qualities, economics, tempera-
ture, but truth is the constant thing."[23] Presentation of
fact, moreover, is not, as Duberman discovered, durable, because it depends not on insight and understanding, but on
accuracy. A fact, said Faulkner, has no depth: "you can't
stand a fact up, you've got to prop it up, and when you move
to one side a little and look at it from that angle, it's not
thick enough to cast a shadow in that direction."[24] Moving to
another angle of vision is the essence of Faulkner's method
in this novel; it provides the corrective to the stasis into
which Duberman felt he had trapped himself by remaining loyal
to the facts.

This constant circling around the so-called facts and
events, looking perhaps for a point of vantage but never set-
tling for the exclusivity of one's own vision, ensures that
interpretation is an unending process. This is perhaps emphasized in *Absalom, Absalom!* more than in Faulkner's other
works because the points of vantage are located not only in
individuals of varying temperaments and intellects, but also
in different places and periods of time. Sutpen, General
Compson, Miss Rosa, Quentin and Shreve encompass over a hundred years of experience. Different cultures and different
climates--the West Virginia mountains, Haiti, New Orleans,
Mississippi, Canada, and Cambridge Massachusetts--all figure
in the backgrounds of the characters and narrators.

The remarkable coherence of the Sutpen story (really quite
remarkable in spite of the considerable residuum of ambiguity)
is the product of a long historical process which relates past
and present, not through an agreement of all the facts which
are the ephemeral surface of a particular moment in time, but
through the human imagination (historical and artistic) which
constantly turns over the facts to see what significance they
now possess, whenever that "now" happens to be. The form of
Absalom, Absalom! remains true to the process of historical
interpretation, even though the place it accords to the artistic imagination is out of keeping with traditional concepts
of the historian's reconstruction of the past.

Thus it is possible to compare Herbert Butterfield's
description of the peculiar problems incurred in his study of
the historiographical literature of George III with Olga
Vickery's analysis of the form of *Absalom, Absalom!*:

As a student of the history of historiography, I have
long been interested not merely in the kaleidoscope of
changing views on the subject of George III, but also
in the causes of the changes, and, indeed, in the whole
curve of development which scholarship has taken. I
have tried to discover now the man responsible for the
initiation of a new idea or attitude, now the location
of the source of a myth or an error, now the forces and
factors which helped to determine the next turn that
would be given to the study of George III.[25]

The perspectives [of the various narrators] are no longer
self-contained and self-illuminating [as they were in
The Sound and the Fury]; as a result, we have a kaleidoscope instead of a juxtaposition of views. Each successive account of Sutpen is constantly being merged
with its predecessors. At every moment, there falls into
place yet another pattern which disavows some parts of
the earlier interpretations but never discards them.[26]

Both Herbert Butterfield and Ms Vickery employ the image of
the kaleidoscope to describe the dynamic fusion of points of
view which constitutes our perceptions of George III and Thomas
Sutpen as historical figures. So the historian is careful to
refer to the "subject" of George III, while the literary critic
envisages Sutpen as the "dynamic center" around which the
various interpretations are successively organized.[27]

Yet if no absolute knowledge of the historical figure
emerges from historical interpretation, an enlarging "curve"
or "pattern" seems to be its compensating product. Historical
interpretation has a form which exercises some control over
diverging views of George III and Thomas Sutpen. In particular,
Professor Vickery's account of the dynamics of interpretation
can be significantly compared with Hegel's historical dialectic:[28]

The power of the method lies in its inner dynamic and
universal applicability. One thought in an almost
literal sense, "gives" the next--thesis leading to
antithesis, and both to synthesis, the latter serving
as a new thesis for another train of thought encompassing
the first, and so on *ad infinitum*--until the whole world
and all things in it are caught in the chain of dialectic. This is possible, on the one hand, through the
complete formalism of the method, that is, its independence from any concrete fact; and, on the other hand,
its complete immersion in the concrete factuality of the
world.[29]

Miss Rosa's thesis might be said to give way to Mr Compson's
antithesis, for Miss Rosa's interpretation is interrupted by

Mr Compson's remarks in Chapter I. Then in Chapter II, III,
IV Mr Compson confronts and sometimes contradicts Miss Rosa
until she again explains and defends herself in Chapter V.
Finally both thesis and antithesis are absorbed by and sub-
sumed in the higher synthesis of Quentin and Shreve in Chapters
VI-IX. As Herbert Butterfield argues:

> the day may come ... when the historian, embracing both
> of the parties, or comprehending the issue at a higher
> altitude, will resurrect the forgotten aspects of the
> case, or see that all men were somewhat the victims of
> events--all of them struggling amid currents which they
> could not quite measure or understand. In such cases the
> history may have to be re-stratified and the narrative
> thoroughly recast.[30]

Quentin and Shreve, from the "higher altitude" of Cambridge
Massachusetts (and, in a way, of Canada), survey and resurrect
every aspect of Sutpen's career and find that it is much more
complex than either Miss Rosa or Mr Compson imagined. Yet
their joint account very much depends on the insights of their
predecessors.

This unique synthesis means that the truth inherent in the
Sutpen story had to be present right from the very beginning
of the story; that is, it had to exist within Miss Rosa's
first recital of events to Quentin, even though she did not
realize the implications of her recital. In the compassionate
rendering of Henry's agonizing struggles over the taboos of
incest and miscegenation, Bon's moving but desperate hope for
an acknowledgment from his father, and Judith's repudiation of
Sutpen's design by accepting and caring for Etienne Bon,
Quentin and Shreve expose the truth that, in trying to live
in accordance with his design, Sutpen refined away an awareness of life as an entity which demands from the individual
sacrifices which contradict his self image or threaten to harm
his self-interests. Sutpen demythologized, becomes something
like the demon Miss Rosa originally described. Appropriately
enough, Butterfield concludes:

> But, whatever new structure the story may require, the
> ideas of the men who were living at the time will be
> somehow comprised in the final version of the narrative.
> The ideas that men have about the events in which their
> life is involved are to be regarded as a dimension of
> the events themselves. The things that men think they
> are fighting about are an ingredient in the very conflict
> in which they are engaged.[31]

Put quite simply, the reason for the continuing influence of
Miss Rosa's demonizing--and perhaps the reason why the whole

novel has so often been described as Gothic when in fact only
Miss Rosa's narrative can be properly termed so--is that the
ideas she projects about Sutpen as a man with whom she had
become so deeply involved prove indeed to define one of his
main dimensions. Although she exaggerates the demonic in his
character, it remains to the end one of the essential ingredients in the conflict in which she and the readers of
Absalom, Absalom! have been engaged for so long.[32]

Our involvement as readers in Miss Rosa's problem needs
emphasizing because, like Hegel's historical dialectic, the
dialectic of Absalom, Absalom! might go on ad infinitum. It
is "independent from concrete fact"--that is, the "chain of
dialectic" is held together by something more than a linkage
of facts--yet we are immersed in superbly realized scenes. A
palpably specific and substantial world seems to grow out of
the process of interpretation;[33] as a result, we seem to participate in as well as observe the making of history.[34] As
Hegel himself affirmed: "We must hold that the narration of
history and historical deeds and events appear at the same time;
a common inner principle brings them forth together."[35] Eventually we see that man is both a product and an extension of
what he studies; so that no logical way can be found either to
enter into or exit from the historical world.[36]

This is true for both Butterfield's historical study of
George III and Faulkner's fictional history of Thomas Sutpen.
That the meaning of history and the direction of scholarship
are subtly changing, in response to each other, even as he
writes, is indicated by Butterfield's repeated use of "now" to
make clear that he has arbitrarily stopped the "curve of
development" at one of its "turns." And it is the "curve of
development" which has led him to the "now," or the present
moment of his study. In Absalom, Absalom! we are often plunged
into the midst of interpretation, as if to imply that we, no
less than the characters in the novel, are historical beings,
who must respond to history with provisional judgments: so
Professor Vickery, in the passage already quoted, attends to
"every moment" in which our view of Sutpen's career is slightly
modified.

In Absalom, Absalom! not only do Quentin and Shreve succeed
as narrators because they have learned to think historically
but also our awareness of history gradually expands as we
learn to assess their use of historical method and their attempts to go beyond it. In other words, our final reading of
the novel is largely a product of the historiographical experience which the novel itself has given us. Although this
claim could no doubt be made for other novels, a special case
has been made for Absalom, Absalom!'s unique insistence that
we do more than our normal share of historical thinking, that

we perpetually re-examine what we take to be a "fact." And by forcing us to put together so much of the Sutpen story, Faulkner demonstrates the difficulty of separating *what* we know about history from *how* we know it. For "we seldom reflect on the activities we perform quite easily. It is only the difficulties which we encounter that force upon us a consciousness of our own efforts to overcome them."[37]

NOTES

1. The following discussions come the closest to specific analyses of the interpretation of the past in *Absalom, Absalom!*: Ilse Lind, "The Design and Meaning of *Absalom, Absalom!*," in *William Faulkner: Three Decades of Criticism*, edited with an introduction by Frederick J. Hoffman and Olga W. Vickery (New York: Harcourt Brace, and World, 1963), pp. 278-304; Joshua McClennen, "*Absalom, Absalom!* and the Meaning of History," *Papers of the Michigan Academy of Science, Arts and Letters* 42 (1956): 357-369; Hyatt Waggoner, *William Faulkner: From Jefferson to the World* (Lexington: University of Kentucky Press, 1966), pp. 148-169; Hyatt Waggoner, "The Historical Novel and the Southern Past, The Case of *Absalom, Absalom!*," *Southern Literary Journal* 2 (1970), 69-85; Olga W. Vickery, *The Novels of William Faulkner: A Critical Interpretation, Revised Edition* (Baton Rouge: Louisiana State University Press, 1964), pp. 84-102; Cleanth Brooks, *William Faulkner: The Yoknapatawpha Country* (New Haven: Yale University Press, 1966), pp. 295-324, 424-443; David Levin, *In Defense of Historical Literature* (New York: Hill and Wang, 1967), pp. 118-139; F. Garven Davenport Jr., *The Myth of Southern History* (Nashville: Vanderbilt University Press, 1970), pp. 82-130; C. Hugh Holman, "*Absalom, Absalom!*: The Historian as Detective," *The Sewanee Review* 79 (1971), 542-553; Richard Poirier, "'Strange Gods' in Jefferson, Mississippi: Analysis of *Absalom, Absalom!*," *Twentieth Century Interpretations of Absalom, Absalom!*, ed. Arnold Goldman (Englewood Cliffs, New Jersey: Prentice-Hall, 1971), pp. 12-31; Patricia Tobin, "The Time of Myth and History in *Absalom, Absalom!*," *American Literature* 45 (1973): 252-270; Richard Gray, "The Meanings of History: William Faulkner's *Absalom, Absalom!*," *Dutch Quarterly Review* 3 (1973), 97-110; Harry B. Henderson III, *Versions of the Past* (New York: Oxford University Press, 1974), pp. 246-269.

2. William Faulkner, *Absalom, Absalom!* (New York: Random House, 1936), pp. 239-240, 244, 246. All references are to this first edition of the novel and are inserted in the text within parentheses.

3. R.G. Collingwood, *The Idea of History* (New York: Oxford University Press, 1956), p. 163.

4. John Hagan, "*Déjà vu* and the Effect of Timelessness in Faulkner's *Absalom, Absalom!*," *Bucknell Review* 11 (1963), 43.

5. Herbert Butterfield, *George III and the Historians* (New York: Macmillan, 1969), p. 41.

6. Collingwood, p. 118.

7. Lind, p. 292: "Nothing which is told or conjectured by the narrators, however distorted, is without thematic relevance." I would add that nothing they say is without historical relevance.

8. W.B. Gallie, *Philosophy and the Historical Understanding* (New York: Schocken Books, 1968), pp. 90-91.

9. Collingwood, p. 66.

10. Levin, p. 134.

11. Martin Duberman, *The Uncompleted Past* (New York: Random House, 1969), p. 26.

12. Butterfield, p. 250.

13. *Ibid.*, p. 34.

14. Herbert Butterfield, *The Historical Novel: An Essay* (Cambridge: At the University Press, 1924), p. 15.

15. *Ibid.*, p. 3.

16. *Ibid.*, p. 18.

17. Henri Bergson, *An Introduction to Metaphysics*, Authorized Translation by T.E. Hulme with an introduction by Thomas A. Goudge (Indianapolis: Bobbs-Merril, 1955), p. 12.

18. Bergson, p. 22.

19. For a close analysis of the ways in which Quentin and Shreve are indebted to the other character-narrators, especially Mr Compson, and of Chapter VIII, in which Quentin and Shreve reveal the "secret" of Bon's Negro blood, see my article "The Recreation of the Past in *Absalom, Absalom!*," in the Summer 1976 issue of *Mississippi Quarterly*.

20. Waggoner, "The Historical Novel," p. 70.

21. Waggoner, *William Faulkner*, pp. 166-167.

22. Duberman, p. 31.

23. James B. Meriwether and Michael Millgate, eds., *Lion in the Garden: Interviews with William Faulkner 1926-1962* (New York: Random House, 1968), p. 145.

24. Malcolm Cowley, *The Faulkner-Cowley File* (New York: The Viking Press, 1966), p. 89.

25. Butterfield, *George III*, p. 9.

26. Vickery, p. 84.

27. *Ibid.*, p. 84.

28. John Lewis Longley, Jr., *The Tragic Mask: A Study of Faulkner's Heroes* (Chapel Hill: University of North Carolina Press, 1963), p. 210, writes: "In some ways, the discovery of what Sutpen was follows the classic pattern of thesis, antithesis, synthesis." But he does not develop this observation.

29. G.W.F. Hegel, *Reason in History*, Translated by Robert S. Hartman (Indianapolis: Bobbs-Merril, 1953), pp. xi-xii.

30. Butterfield, *George III*, p. 41.

31. *Ibid.*, p. 41.

32. Elmond L. Volpe, *A Reader's Guide to William Faulkner* (New York: Farrar, Straus & Giroux, 1964), p. 195.

33. Robert H. Zoellner, "Faulkner's Prose Style in *Absalom, Absalom!*," *American Literature* 30 (1959), 499, has some interesting comments on the "abstract-as-most substantial" in Faulkner "which gives his prose the peculiar unreal quality so often criticized."

34. Waggoner, *William Faulkner*, p. 153.

35. Hegel, p. 75.

36. Conrad Aiken, "William Faulkner: The Novel as Form," in *William Faulkner: Three Decades of Criticism*, p. 140.

37. Collingwood, p. 4.

"WE HAVE WAITED LONG ENOUGH":
JUDITH SUTPEN AND CHARLES BON[1]

Elisabeth Muhlenfeld

Given the fact that *Absalom, Absalom!* is Thomas Sutpen's
novel, a very large proportion of the narrative is devoted to
the triangle between Judith, Bon, and Henry. Indeed, one way
of looking at the structure of the whole novel is to see it
as an examination followed (though never in strictly chronological order) by a recreation of the events surrounding the
shooting of Charles Bon and the motives which lay behind the
murder.[2] The author offers the reader several very different
interpretations of this event, culminating with that of Quentin
and Shreve. By all the laws governing the unraveling of detective stories, this last view should be the definitive one,
and, in fact, these imaginings of Quentin and Shreve, both
because of their placement at the end of the novel and because of the pulsing vitality of the imagined scenes, have
invariably been taken by readers to be far closer to the truth
than have the first-hand account of Rosa and the second-hand
or hearsay account of Mr. Compson.

However, in *Absalom, Absalom!* itself, Faulkner severely
undercuts the authority of the "final" version by showing both
of its authors to be somewhat unreliable--Quentin because he
is nearly destroyed by his emotional involvement with the
story; Shreve because he does not understand the reasons for
that involvement, and because he is so determined to make the
story dramatically satisfying. Further, in a remark made
more than twenty years after the publication of the novel,
Faulkner states clearly that the conclusions drawn by Quentin
and Shreve are not necessarily more correct than those of the
other narrators:

> nobody saw the truth intact.... But the old man was
> himself a little too big for people no greater in stature

Originally appeared in The Southern Review, *14, No. 1 (New
Series) (Winter 1978), pp. 66-80.*

> than Quentin and Miss Rosa and Mr. Compson to see all at
> once.... But the truth, I would like to think, comes
> out, that when the reader has read all these thirteen
> different ways of looking at the blackbird, the reader
> has his own fourteenth image of that blackbird which I
> would like to think is the truth.[3]

If the author's statement as to how Sutpen may be understood
can be extended to the other characters in the novel, then
certainly the reader must not accept the Harvard students'
version of the Judith-Bon-Henry triangle without carefully
assessing the evidence himself. We are asked, then, to arrive
at an understanding of Sutpen's children which, though it must
and should borrow the various narrators' best insights, also
transcends them.

One of the questions with which the narrator-characters
struggle is the precise nature of the relationship between
Judith and Bon. To Mr. Compson, it seems inexplicable.

> You see? there they are: this girl ... who sees a man
> for an average of one hour a day for twelve days during
> his life and that over a period of a year and a half,
> yet is bent on marrying him to the extent of forcing
> her brother to the last resort of homicide ... to pre-
> vent it, and that after a period of four years during
> which she could not have been always certain that he
> was still alive ... and this lover who apparently
> without volition or desire became involved in an engage-
> ment which he seems neither to have sought nor avoided,
> who took his dismissal in the same passive and sardonic
> spirit, yet four years later was apparently so bent upon
> the marriage ... as to force the brother who had cham-
> pioned it to kill him to prevent it.... It's just in-
> credible. It just does not explain.[4]

I do not wish to suggest that Judith and Bon are the central
characters in *Absalom*--though unquestionably their proposed
marriage is the deciding factor which leads inevitably to the
crumbling of Sutpen's design--but Mr. Compson is right to
consider this relationship one of the keys to the Sutpen story,
and the relationship is worth examining in far more detail
than has heretofore been given it: is it possible to determine,
from the evidence in the novel itself, what kind of people
Judith and Bon were and whether they did in fact love one
another? I intend to limit my investigation to an examination
of the *facts* which Faulkner provides, considering those remarks and events which are the products of the imaginations
of the narrator-characters only when such remarks or events
seem probable or shed light on the facts as we know them. If

there is sufficient evidence in the novel to come to a real
understanding of Judith and Bon apart from what is imagined
about them, then we can compare *our* findings with those of Mr.
Compson, Rosa, Shreve, and finally Quentin, and understand
these characters, too, more thoroughly. This examination,
then, attempts to discover if there may be yet another way to
read this rich, complex, and demanding novel.

Unfortunately, the task of separating fact from fiction,
the single most difficult and demanding critical problem in
the novel, makes any attempt to come to know and understand
one of the protagonists in *Absalom, Absalom!* frustrating at
best. The reader has no one whom he can trust implicitly--
even the narrative voice which begins the novel and intrudes
occasionally throughout is by no means omniscient. In the
first paragraph, for example, the narrative voice describes
Rosa as "in the eternal black which she had worn for forty-
three years now, *whether for sister, father, or nothusband
none knew*" (p. 7, italics mine), but the reader soon learns
that her "eternal black" dates from Sutpen's insult; she
grieves for herself. Thus we are alerted that the narrator
either does not *have* any final answers or will not *reveal* any,
and we come to take his later comments (as when he remarks
that Shreve's imagined Eulalia is "probably true enough" [p.
335]) as being based on a knowledge possibly not very much
greater than ours as readers.

Too, it is often difficult to determine exactly how much
of what the characters who act as narrators tell is fact.[5]
Further, they frequently make no attempt to document those
events which seem to be factual. A good example of a piece of
information which has the ring of truth but which stems from
an unknown source is the precise nature of Sutpen's insult
to Rosa. Rosa herself never makes it clear (pp. 168, 171),
but in the following chapter, Shreve delineates Sutpen's exact
proposal--undoubtedly learned from Quentin (p. 177). The
reader never discovers whether Quentin has been told or merely
intuits this. Similarly, we never know what Quentin learned
on his visit to Sutpen's Hundred or from whom he learned it.
Mr. Compson frequently mentions notes or letters which passed
between Henry or Bon and Judith, letters he says were destroyed,
but which in reality he or his father were unlikely to have
known about at all.[6] We should be wary of accepting information such as the existence of these letters as fact, for if
they are factual, then we must attribute Mr. Compson's knowledge of their existence to such people as General Compson and
his wife who heard about them from Sutpen or Judith. But, if
we attribute them thus, father and daughter would have to have
been a good deal less reticent than they seem to be in the
novel. Thus, if the reader wishes to find the fourteenth way

to look at the Judith-Bon blackbird, he must do a bit of detective work himself.

There is, however, a cluster of "givens" in the novel—facts and other pieces of evidence available to Quentin and Shreve—which ought not to be ignored. Foremost among these is Bon's letter, the only surviving document attributable to one of the key participants in the events. As we shall see, Mr. Compson gives considerable weight to the letter, finds it puzzling and has apparently pondered it at length.[7] Quentin and Shreve, on the other hand, do not speculate about it, indeed dismiss it, and there is no evidence in the novel that Rosa even knew of its existence. Except for the letter, almost everything we learn about Bon is exclusively the product of someone's imagination; thus it must be of crucial importance for our understanding of him. The only other documentary evidence in *Absalom* is that of the tombstones, and to these both Mr. Compson and Quentin attach significance as clues to the emotions and motives of Judith. Even armed with this set of givens, though, being objective about Judith and Bon requires constant care, for we are bombarded with highly stylized and colored descriptions of them before we understand the extent and nature of the biases of the narrators themselves. Judith, for example, is first mentioned by Rosa in mythic or biblical terms as being *"begot"* by Sutpen, *"without gentleness"* (p. 9), and our first view of her and her brother is rather horrifying: "the ogre-shape which ... resolved out of itself before Quentin's eyes the two half-ogre children" (p. 13).

In Chapter I, we learn from Rosa about two episodes in Judith's childhood: her wild delight at riding to church behind the runaway horses followed by her fury when deprived of this thrill (pp. 24-25), and her calm observance of her father's savage and ritualistic fight with the slave (pp. 29-30). Both these episodes may be accepted as fact: both were witnessed and seem to be common knowledge among the townspeople. Neither episode tells us much about the mature Judith, but together they indicate that, as a child, she was willful, passionate, and inclined to defy authority. Further, they bear witness to the close emotional ties she has with her father (in the horse-racing episode, she deliberately apes him) and to her intense determination to *experience* rather than retreat from life.

We know nothing more about Judith's upbringing, except that she occasionally saw Rosa and her grandfather, and as she entered adulthood, often went shopping and visiting with her mother, always seemingly uninterested, distracted. Mr. Compson describes her in very abstract terms and, because he could not have known first hand, his description must not be taken as necessarily true. Nevertheless, all of the townspeople

would have seen her at this time, and thus the passage suggests that, in fact, her behavior did change markedly between
childhood and adolescence. He says Judith had entered

> that transition stage ... that state where, though still
> visible, young girls appear as though seen through glass
> and where even the voice cannot reach them; where they
> exist (this the hoyden who could--and did--outrun and
> outclimb, and ride and fight both with and beside her
> brother) in a pearly lambence ... not in themselves
> floating and seeking but merely waiting, parasitic and
> potent and serene, drawing to themselves without effort
> the post-genitive upon and about which to shape, flow
> into back, breast; bosom, flank, thigh. (p. 67)

This description probably says more about Mr. Compson than
about Judith, but Richard Adams, in *Faulkner: Myth and Motion*,
suggests very plausibly that the passage represents "one of
Faulkner's earlier efforts to present a direct impression of
a young woman moving so harmoniously with the motion of life
that no motion can be seen."[8]   While in this waiting, serene
state, Judith first meets Charles Bon, a university friend of
her brother.
     The scant facts surrounding the courtship of Judith and
Bon[9] do not allow us to reach any conclusions regarding its
intensity. We know only that Bon visited at Christmas for two
weeks and again at the beginning of the summer for a few days.
Judith's mother, Ellen, apparently favored the match to the
extent that she bought a trousseau (p. 70) before any hint of
engagement had passed between the two. At some point Bon gave
Judith his picture (which Rosa saw, [p. 146]) and began to
write her regularly (p. 103). On the occasion of Bon's third
visit to Sutpen's Hundred, an interview between Henry and his
father terminated with Henry repudiating his birthright and
the two young men departing for New Orleans. Surely some
understanding existed between Judith and Bon at this time,
for she waited quite patiently for four years before she heard
from him again. Mr. Compson finds the "entire queerly placid
course of [the] courtship" (p. 97) very puzzling, and speculates
that the absence of any formal trappings of engagement indicates Bon's indifference. But it need not be so interpreted.
Earlier we have seen Sutpen, with a new hat and coat and a
"cornucopia of flowers" (p. 47), propose quite formally--but
without love.
     If Rosa and the townspeople know little about Bon, Quentin
and Mr. Compson know very little more. Bon is a fascinating
figure to Mr. Compson, who endows him with a Byronic personality.
Quentin apparently does not challenge his father's basic
premise that Bon was a fatalistic, doomed soul, but he and

Shreve do expand and modify the portrait. We as readers know
that he is Sutpen's son—a fact which Quentin apparently
learned at Sutpen's Hundred (p. 266), and which we can verify
by reference to Faulkner's appended chronology. Thus Bon,
son of a Haitian heiress and probably raised in New Orleans,
grew up knowing that he was fatherless. The evidence of the
octoroon's picture found on Bon's body,[10] and of Charles
Etienne's presence at Sutpen's Hundred, indicates that at some
point prior to his departure for the university, Bon "married,"
after the New Orleans fashion, an octoroon and had a son by
her. We know that at the time he studied with Henry, he was
considerably older than his classmates, and that he presented
a sophisticated, even elegant appearance. We know further
that he joined the university's regiment with Henry, that he
promptly received a commission, and that he was wounded. Finally we know that near the end of the war Henry had an interview
with his father (p. 276), and shortly thereafter Bon wrote a
long letter to Judith announcing his intention to return to
her. Outside the gates of Sutpen's Hundred, he was killed.

Mr. Compson finds these facts to be very suggestive, and
he devotes several pages of his narrative to probing beneath
them to find the "real" Bon. Particularly interesting to Mr.
Compson is the impression that Bon seemed always out of place,
"that mental and spiritual orphan whose fate it apparently
was to exist in some limbo halfway between where his corporeal-
ity was and his mentality and moral equipment desired to be"
(p. 124). He assumes, correctly I think, that Bon must have
had some motive for attending the university at Oxford—an
unlikely place for a wealthy, cosmopolitan young man to go:
"this man miscast for the time and knowing it, accepting it
for a reason obviously good enough to cause him to endure it
and apparently too serious or at least too private to be
divulged to what acquaintances he now possessed" (p. 98).

We do not know one very crucial thing: whether Bon was
aware that his father was Thomas Sutpen. Quentin and Shreve
imagine very moving scenes in which Bon longs for recognition
from Sutpen, and by the time the two Harvard students begin
their cold night of speculation. Quentin has already been to
Sutpen's Hundred with Rosa and has learned all he will ever
know—almost certainly he has been told by either Clytie or
Henry that Bon was Sutpen's son. Nevertheless, Quentin makes
a very curious statement to Shreve which suggests that he has
not been given any insight into Bon's motives for marrying
Judith: "nobody ever did know if Bon ever knew Sutpen was his
father or not, whether he was trying to revenge his mother or
not at first and only later fell in love"; then he adds
"whether Bon wanted revenge or was just caught and sunk and
doomed too, it was all the same" (p. 269).

Whether Bon sought revenge or merely fell in love may in the end be "all the same" in the sense that he died at Henry's hands in any case, but the distinction is an important one for the reader.[11] If Bon was merely using Judith to force recognition from his father, then all Judith's years of waiting, of devotion, of care for his son offer a very dark commentary on faith and love, and she becomes just one more victim—like so many others in the novel—of her own illusions. If, on the other hand, she and Bon do truly love one another, then her actions can be read as an affirmation of a powerful, real force—a human force antithetical to Sutpen's design.

All that we know about the adult Judith testifies to her devotion to duty as she sees it, and her conception of duty is neither meaningless nor rigid. Although not always successful, everything she does is constructive, aimed at alleviating human suffering. Apparently without knowing the reasons for her father's objection to her marriage (p. 120), she behaves toward Sutpen as if nothing had happened (p. 79). After her father goes off to war, she and Clytie live alone. Her mother, prostrate since the shock of the dissolved engagement, requires "the unremitting attention of a child" (p. 125), and Judith cares for her until her death, while doing the best she can to keep the plantation intact. With Clytie, she gardens, learns to catch and harness a mule (p. 126), and she does her part in town in a hospital for the wounded (p. 125). Although she hears nothing from Bon for four years, when she receives his letter, she and Clytie begin "at once to fashion a wedding dress and veil out of rags and scraps" (p. 101).[12] Mr. Compson, after brooding about this sequence of events, is forced to conclude that it bespeaks a deep love:

> Have you noticed how so often when we try to reconstruct the causes which lead up to the actions of men and women, how with a sort of astonishment we find ourselves now and then reduced to the belief, the only possible belief, that they stemmed from some of the old virtues?... Judith, giving implicit trust where she had given love, giving implicit love where she had derived breath and pride: that true pride ... which can say to itself without abasement *I love, I will accept no substitute; something has happened between him and my father; if my father was right, I will never see him again, if wrong he will come or send for me; if happy I can be I will, if suffer I must I can.* (p. 121)

Because of what we already know of Judith, Mr. Compson's portrait here seems true, and as Oliver Billingslea has suggested, it is "borne out by her subsequent responses throughout the book."[13]

Judith seems throughout the novel to be at the very least
a realistic, eminently sensible person; she does not romanti-
cize as does Rosa, nor does she flutter like her mother.
Therefore, her response to the letter, the making of a wedding
dress, probably represents a well-reasoned approach to Bon's
intentions. It is appropriate here, then, to examine the
letter in some detail, to see what kind of man the passionate
but sensible Judith intended to marry. Quentin thinks of the
letter as a "dead tongue speaking after the four years and
then after almost fifty more, gentle sardonic whimsical and
incurably pessimistic" (p. 129),[14] but the letter itself
affirms that he is wrong. It begins, "without date or saluta-
tion": *"You will notice how I insult neither of us by claiming
this to be a voice from the defeated even, let alone from the
dead"* (p. 129). This sentence does not offer apology for the
long silence, but bespeaks a firm, underlying understanding
between recipient and writer; it affirms that Bon is neither
defeated nor dead.[15] It is a sentence written by a proud man,
but one who knows that his reader shares his pride and his
love. Later in the letter he acknowledges Judith's love and
patience and indirectly affirms his own: *"I do not insult you
by saying that only I have waited"* (p. 131).

Bon goes on to note the ironic juxtaposition of the captured stove polish with which he writes on notepaper with *"the
best of French watermarks dated seventy years ago, salvaged
(stolen if you will) from the gutted mansion of a ruined aristocrat."* His words indicate that he is a man of taste and
discernment, that he regrets the fall of *"the old South which
is dead"* (p. 132) but considers that it was inevitable; and
he exhibits a grudging respect for the *"new North which has
conquered and which therefore, whether it likes it or not,
will have to survive"* (p. 132). Bon displays, in short, a
good sense of history; using the image of *"one fusillade four
years ago which sounded once and then was arrested, mesmerized
raised 'muzzle by raised muzzle, in the frozen attitude of its
own aghast amazement and never repeated and it now only the
loud aghast echo jarred by the dropped musket of a weary sentry
or by the fall of the spent body itself"* (p. 131), he asserts
that the outcome of the war has never been in doubt, and pre-
dicts that the world will be very little better for four years
of fighting. He is a realist.

Bon makes several observations in the letter which show
him to be a man very much aware of the human suffering that he
and Judith have shared with the whole South. Describing his
regiment, he writes *"I wont say hungry because to a woman ...
below Mason's and Dixon's in this year of grace 1865, that
word would be sheer redundancy, like saying that we were
breathing. And I wont say ragged or even shoeless, since we*

have been both long enough to have grown accustomed to it" (p.
129).

Writing just before dawn (p. 131) in a lonely encampment,
he gives thanks that man will not be defeated: "*thank God ...
that he really does not become inured to hardship and privation*" (p. 130). He observes that the endlessness and senselessness of war drugs the soul, but that the body, the living
flesh

> *with a sort of dismal and incorruptible fidelity which
> is incredibly admirable to me, is still immersed and
> obliviously bemused in recollections of old peace and
> contentment ... which ignores even the presence and
> threat of a torn arm or leg as though through some secretly
> incurred and infallible promise and conviction of immor-
> tality.* (p. 131)

It is the use of just such phrases as "dismal and incorruptible
fidelity" and "obliviously bemused" which strengthen Mr. Compson's contention that Bon is a world-weary aesthete, and it is
understandable that Mr. Compson, with his own tired nihilism,
would so interpret them. But we must remember that Bon writes
at the end of a war which he now sees to be hopeless, and for
four years he has lived with pain and death. That Bon finds
the fidelity of his body to life "incredibly admirable" is
therefore of the utmost significance; the letter is an affirmation of life, both in content and intent--to alert Judith to
his return.

Though the man who writes is exhausted from sleeplessness,
hunger, and privation, he devotes a good portion of the letter
to describing a humorous event: the capture of the stove
polish. His narrative shows him to be a man with a nice sense
of humor, who has the ability to take the defeats of life with
grace, and though he never draws attention to the fact, the
tale sheds light on Bon as officer when we realize that he must
have been the leader of the foraging party. He describes a
group of "*homogeneous scarecrows*"--not heterogeneous, but a
companionable group which fit well together. The plan of
attack, "*one of those concocted plans of scarecrow desperation which not only must but do work*" was brought off "*with a
great deal of elan, not to say noise.*" Bon pictures the men
madly struggling to open the boxes of what they hope will be
ammunition only to find "*Gallons and gallons and gallons of
the best stove polish ... doubtless still trying to overtake
General Sherman with some belated amended field order requiring
him to polish the stove before firing the house*" (p. 130).
The men respond to this discovery not with fury or despair,
but with good humor, and Bon notes that he has learned that
"*only when you are hungry or frightened do you extract some
ultimate essence out of laughing*" (p. 130).

After the four years which have left the South destitute
and her armies without even the barest essentials, food,
clothing, and ammunition, the North is vigorous, able to manu-
facture and to afford vast quantities of a comparative luxury--
stove polish. Bon sees the stove polish as an "augury," a
symbol of the inevitability of the South's defeat, and he
wants Judith to understand its import, too. He seems to have
full confidence that she will not only understand the implications of the anecdote, but also that she will enjoy the telling. He writes to make her smile, and he uses the opportunity
to reveal himself, to indicate that he has learned much about
himself and about human nature from his war experiences.
Further, the mere fact that he takes the time to relate the
adventure, aside from its symbolic import, shows Bon to be re-
laxed, unhurried. His letter is not the product of a moment
of passion or whim. (Indeed, his salvaging of the French
paper suggests that the letter has been long planned.) Rather,
Bon, a Southerner for whom the gallons of stove polish are a
ridiculous superfluity, has put the spoils of his abortive
foray for ammunition to positive use.

The inclusion of the anecdote, then, is far from irrelevant, and only after he has brought the incident to a close
does he move directly to the point of the letter: *"We have
waited long enough"* (p. 131). Apparently there has been a
mutual agreement, or at least acquiescence, to delay the marriage. Written to the accompaniment of enemy firing, Bon's
final words suggest that at least part of the reason for
waiting has been a reluctance to make of Judith an actual
widow: *"I now believe that you and I are, strangely enough,
included among those who are doomed to live"* (p. 132). I can
find no hint in the letter of any ulterior motives, of any
knowledge that he is about to commit incest or miscegenation;
if Bon knew about his parentage, the letter is that of a very
skillful and utterly despicable villain indeed.[16]

To my knowledge, critics have ignored the letter, or read
it through Mr. Compson's eyes, with one notable exception.
Virginia Hlavsa considers it a turning point in the novel:

> It is proof, after all, of a certain quality of man
> who existed, a man with depth, compassion and tenderness,
> but above all, a real man, who has experienced real
> hunger, fatigue, and suffering beyond the mind's compre-
> hension of that suffering, who, because he was a breathing
> man of flesh deserves respect, whose death is to be re-
> gretted.[17]

Quentin's father, who takes Bon to be a fatalist, and in-
vents him as a world-weary aesthete, postulates that he "loved
Judith after his fashion" but that he also loved Henry "in a

deeper sense" (pp. 107-108). He imagines that Henry worshipped
Bon, and used him to engage in a kind of mental incest (p. 119).
Quentin and Shreve fasten upon this possibility, and never return to the letter to test their hypothesis. But Mr. Compson
makes one supposition that seems to be borne out by the evidence
of the letter. He says:

> perhaps it was even more than Judith or Henry either:
> perhaps the life, the existence, which they represented.
> Because who knows what picture of peace he might have
> seen in that monotonous provincial backwater; what
> alleviation and escape for a parched traveler who had
> traveled too far at too young an age, in this granite-
> bound and simple country spring. (p. 108)[18]

Bon's own reference to "recollections of old peace and content-
ment," and the whole gentle and sure tone of the letter, suggest that he does indeed regard Judith--if not Sutpen's
Hundred in itself--as a kind of haven of sanity and peace in
a world which seems more than a little mad.

If the love which the letter seems to attest did exist,
then the one person who would have been most profoundly conscious of it was Sutpen's other son, Henry, and indeed the
single event in the novel to which the narrators repeatedly
turn is the moment in which Henry kills Bon. We have noted
earlier that the reader is not told (in fact Quentin asserts
that "nobody ever did know") whether Bon was aware at any time
of his relationship to Sutpen. However, we know fairly certainly that Henry knew of Bon's kinship to him, first because
he (or perhaps Clytie) must have told Quentin at Sutpen's
Hundred and second because, in a conversation reported by
General Compson, Sutpen decides that he is "forced to play
my last trump card" (p. 274)--if not a reference to Bon's
Negro blood, at least to his blood relationship--just before
his war-time interview with Henry. Only in Shreve and Quentin's re-creation does Henry reveal the truth to Bon. It
seems perfectly possible that Henry never told Bon. If he
really loved his brother, he might well have wished to spare
both him and Judith the pain of knowing: he may have murdered
out of mercy for Bon as well as for Judith.

In any case, after Bon returns and dies, Judith discovers
on his body the picture of the octoroon and when, several
hours later, Rosa arrives, she finds Judith calm: *"if there
had been grief or anguish she had put them too away ... along
with that unfinished wedding dress"* (p. 142). But Judith is
still holding the metal case--it has obviously affected her
profoundly. Mr. Compson assumes that this is a betrayal which
frees Judith from grief, and Shreve guesses that Bon had intentionally substituted the picture: "if [Henry] does mean what

he said, it will be the only way I will have to say to her,
I was no good; do not grieve for me" (p. 359).[19] If so,
Bon's message is ignored, for Judith obviously does grieve
for him: she oversees his burial and even tries to provide
him with a Catholic service; she places his body in the cedar
grove beside her mother and thus affirms that he is a member
of her family; and most significantly, she goes a week later
to Quentin's grandmother and, with a face "calm ... absolutely
serene," "comprehending ... not even bitter" (p. 128) seeks to
insure Bon's immortality by giving away the letter. When Mrs.
Compson indicates that she fears Judith will commit suicide,
Judith's reply affirms both her love for Bon and her dedication
to life, "Oh. I? No, not that. Because somebody will have to
take care of Clytie, and father, too, soon, who will want
something to eat after he comes home.... Women dont do that
for love. I dont even believe that men do. And not now, any-
way" (p. 128).

Judith cries only once for Bon (p. 159), but she erects
a tombstone for him, otherwise going about the business of
living and of sharing what she has; she gives food to passers-
by (p. 156) and periodically takes provisions to Rosa after
her return to Jefferson (p. 170). Her greatest and most sustained act of compassion, though, is her reaching out to the
octoroon and Bon's son. Inviting the woman and child to visit,
she offers them the best that she has (pp. 192-193), apparently with no condescension or bitterness. When she learns that
the boy is orphaned and Clytie leaves to bring him back to
Sutpen's Hundred, Judith goes to General Compson and orders a
tombstone for him to match his father's, paying a hundred
dollars, an immense sum for her to amass (pp. 191, 210).
This fact is extremely significant, and has for some reason
been completely ignored: Judith commits herself *before* he arrives to the lifelong care of her dead fiancé's son, knowing
he is Negro. And by insuring that he, too, will have the
formal recognition as a family member implicit in the grave-
stone, she in effect pledges to him the security and tradition
which she represents. When he arrives, he sleeps on a trundle
bed beside her (p. 197), the customary place for a child of
the time.

We cannot deny that Judith seems to fail rather spectacu-
larly with Charles Etienne, but almost without exception, all
that we are told about Judith's relationship to him is the
speculation of Mr. Compson, and his contention that Judith
treated the child coldly seems unlikely in view of her other
responses throughout the novel. We do know that at the time
Charles Etienne arrived at Sutpen's Hundred he was twelve
years old--his most formative years had been spent in the
isolation of an environment neither white nor Negro. His

subsequent fighting and his marriage to the black woman suggest that, like Joe Christmas in *Light in August*, he would have repudiated any warmth Judith showed him. Whether she fails with Charles Etienne because, as Mr. Compson suggests, she responds to him coldly, or whether the boy had already been ruined by Bon's rejection of him as Quentin and Shreve believe, we cannot question her continued concern for him. When his fighting finally results in arrest, she rushes to General Compson, her "face emanat[ing] a terrible urgency" (p. 201) for help. Her last act, that of nursing Charles Etienne, testifies to her devotion--if not to her love--even to the point of giving up her own life (p. 210).

In short, rather than interpreting the octoroon's picture as an indication that she should cease to love, Judith seems to have accepted it as a message, a commission to care for Bon's quasi wife and son. Is it not possible that the picture was intended to accomplish just what it did? Bon and Judith seem to have understood one another well (witness the letter), and Bon, who himself had to grow up without a father, may have made this gesture in an effort to break the pattern, to insure that his own son could have a father to acknowledge, and a family of which to be a part.

Absalom, Absalom! does not spell out for us the motives which move Judith, Bon, and Henry. It offers instead only a small group of facts, among them one letter and some gravestones. But when we realize that the evidence speaks so credibly for a very different interpretation of Sutpen's children than Quentin and Shreve develop, we must be profoundly moved by the utter complexity of the novel. The brilliance with which the novel chronicles each character's attempt to make sense of these bits of evidence has obscured for most readers the poignancy of the Judith-Bon story itself. Faulkner is surely not trying to delude the reader, but rather to impress upon him the ease with which love may be overlooked and the terrible isolation which wracks those who overlook it.

The world of *Absalom, Absalom!* is a dark world, both for the reader and for most of the characters who inhabit it. In a sense, the commanding presence of the cold, determined Thomas Sutpen almost blots out any considerations of love. At the beginning of the novel Rosa betrays her inability to associate marriage with human warmth and compassion, and Judith's own mother never even mentions love. Thus Quentin, himself a child of that world, cannot really be blamed for his assumption that since Judith showed no physical sign of grief at Bon's death, she felt none, but his conviction that she was a woman *"who, not bereaved, did not need to mourn"* (p. 193) is truly tragic. Of all the wrenching emotional

responses within *Absalom*, perhaps the most heartbreaking is
that of Quentin as he repeatedly interrupts Shreve's version
of Bon's courtship of Judith: "But it's love," "That's still
not love" (pp. 322, 328). That Quentin needed so badly to
see love, that he could not see it, intensifies the waste
which is Quentin; that the real possibility of love was there
all along if only he could have seen it adds immeasurably to
the richness of the novel. If the pain Quentin feels at its
end might be needless pain, the novel's world becomes darker.
But in another sense the possibility of Judith and Bon's love
brightens and strengthens *Absalom*, invests the doom of Sutpen's
world with a powerful and living alternative, and even en-
nobles Sutpen himself by giving us a glimpse of the strength
of his will and vitality when, through his children, these
elements within him are used in positive affirmation: to unite
instead of to dominate.

NOTES

    1. This essay owes much to the perceptive readings of
Professors Noel Polk, Stephen Meats, and James B. Meriwether.

    2. Virginia V. Hlavsa's "The Vision of the Advocate in
Absalom, Absalom!," *Novel*, 8 (Fall 1974), pp. 51-70, though
gimmick-ridden, studies the novel from this perspective.

    3. *Faulkner in the University: Class Conferences at the
University of Virginia 1957-1958*, F.L. Gwynn and J.L. Blotner,
eds. (Charlottesville: Univ. of Virginia Press, 1959; revised
ed., Vintage, 1965), pp. 273-274. At least every second
article relating to *Absalom* since the publication of *Faulkner
in the University* has utilized this quotation, but few
scholars have benefited from it, and moved beyond the accounts
--largely imaginary--given by Shreve and Quentin to a fresh
examination of the characters.

    4. William Faulkner, *Absalom, Absalom!* (New York: Random
House, 1936), pp. 99-100. Subsequent quotations from the
novel will be cited parenthetically.

    5. Duncan Aswell in "The Puzzling Design of *Absalom,
Absalom!*," *Kenyon Review*, 30 (1968), reprinted herein, observes
that the different narrators actually "obscure the *facts* of
Sutpen's life and hinder the reader from evaluating their
significance" (p. 68).

    6. See for example p. 128, where he characterizes Bon's
letters as "flowery indolent frequent and insincere," pp. 107
and 121, where he mentions wartime messages from Henry that

Bon was still alive, or p. 91 where he makes reference to a
note to Judith from Henry just before his departure with Bon
for New Orleans. Mr. Compson does make one rather cryptic
remark which seems to suggest he or his father had gone over
Judith's effects after her death: "you will see the letter,
not the first one he ever wrote to her but at least the first,
the only one she ever showed, as your grandmother knew then:
and, so we believe now that she is dead, the only one which
she kept unless of course Miss Rosa or Clytie destroyed the
others after she herself died" (p. 94).

7. Oliver LaFayette Billingslea, in his dissertation "The
Monument and the Plain: The Art of Mythic Consciousness in
William Faulkner's *Absalom, Absalom!*" (University of Wisconsin,
1971), finds it "ironic that Mr. Compson attaches so much
importance to the message of one letter" (p. 239), but clearly,
given the unique status of the letter within the novel, it
assumes extreme importance and deserves thorough study. It
is ironic, rather, that Quentin and Shreve, and that almost
every critic of the novel, attach so little importance to it.

8. Princeton University Press, 1968, p. 208.

9. Cleanth Brooks states in his notes (*William Faulkner:
The Yoknapatawpha Country*, Yale University Press, 1963, p.
429), that the facts surrounding the courtship are indeed
facts, and have General Compson as ultimate authority. He is
probably right, although apparently Quentin's grandmother is
also the source for some information (pp. 73, 76, 77, *Absalom*).
But there are several of these "facts" which, though they may
sound quite true, nevertheless seem to be hardly the sort of
thing that either Sutpen or Judith would discuss. Most
blatantly unlikely among these are Henry's role in "seducing"
Judith via his letters home (p. 97, *Absalom*) and Bon's character, since few townspeople got even a glimpse of him and none
would have had a chance to know him well.

10. This is apparently fact, and was presumably learned
from General Compson, but there is no proof in the novel that
the picture was indeed that of the octoroon; and Rosa, who
reached Sutpen's Hundred a few hours after the murder and remained for a year, apparently died convinced the picture was
of Judith.

11. Melvin Bradford makes this point very well in his
"Brother, Son, and Heir: The Structural Focus of Faulkner's
Absalom, Absalom!," *Sewanee Review*, 78 (Winter 1970), p. 81,
though he fails to do justice to the evidence, and thus does
a little "demonizing" about Bon. Bradford writes: "weigh and
judge him we (like Quentin) must. For upon that judgment will
depend what we make of Henry's decision to kill him."

12. See also p. 135 for Rosa's account.

13. Billingslea, p. 232.

14. See Gerald Langford, *Faulkner's Revision of* Absalom, Absalom! (Univ. of Texas Press, 1971), p. 146. Significantly, in the manuscript Faulkner originally ended Quentin's assessment here with the words "yet sincere," but subsequently canceled them; the passage is in *Quentin's* mind. For him to perceive Bon's words to Judith as sincere ones would be out of keeping with his conception of Bon's complicated motivation.

15. Adams (pp. 207-208) offers a good discussion of the letter and further notes the irony that "because he has written this letter Bon is doomed to die" (p. 208).

16. Of course, it is possible that the narrator-characters are right that Henry did tell Bon, but that the letter (which has no date) was written before Bon learned the truth.

17. Hlavsa, p. 60. Adams' discussion of the letter does not prompt him to analyze Bon in light of it.

18. Though Mr. Compson goes on to speculate about Bon and Henry in New Orleans, it is significant that up until this passage his narrative is presented largely as fact. But immediately following, as he begins to sketch the care with which Bon introduces Henry to New Orleans morality, Mr. Compson uses the phrase "I can imagine" or "I can see" seven times in the next paragraph (p. 108 ff.). The scene he paints is a convincing one precisely because he is engaged in convincing himself. He repeatedly refers to Bon as a fatalist, but we must remember that Mr. Compson himself is fatalistic, and much of what he has Bon tell Henry seems very close to his own philosophy. Significantly, Quentin and Shreve discount this scene (p. 336).

19. John W. Hunt in *William Faulkner: Art in Theological Tension* (Syracuse Univ. Press, 1965; reprinted by Haskell House Publishers, Ltd., 1973) discusses Bon's "capacity to love" (p. 133), suggesting that the substitution of the picture is his "greatest act of love." Hunt's discussion is based on the imagined scenes between Henry and Bon.

THE NARRATIVE VOICE AND FUNCTION OF SHREVE: REMARKS ON THE PRODUCTION OF MEANING IN *ABSALOM, ABSALOM!*

François Pitavy

The thirteen verses--at times as dense as haiku--of Wallace Stevens's poem, "Thirteen Ways of Looking at a Blackbird," speak of the elusive nature of reality, of which only misleading or illusory fragments can be discerned:

> He rode over Connecticut
> In a glass coach.
> Once, a fear pierced him,
> In that he mistook
> The shadow of his equipage
> For blackbirds.[1]

One understands why a Virginian student borrowed the title of this poem in order to draw Faulkner to define, in a declaration often quoted by critics, the function of the narrators in *Absalom, Absalom!*:

> I think that no one individual can look at truth. It blinds you. You look at it and you see one phase of it. Someone else looks at it and sees a slightly awry phase of it. But taken all together, the truth is in what they saw though nobody saw the truth intact.... It was, as you say, thirteen ways of looking at a blackbird. But the truth, I would like to think, comes out, that when the reader has read all these different thirteen ways of looking at the blackbird, the reader has his own fourteenth image of that blackbird which I would like to think is the truth.[2]

No one of the narrators would be able to see (or to tell) everything, nor to assume fully the visions (or the discourses) put forward by the others. The reader alone would be capable of seeing in this way, in whose eye the different perspectives superimpose (rather like some stereoscopic image) and take on meaning. Faulkner's reply, then, takes into consideration the reading of the text in the process resulting in the production of meaning, which thus does not solely ensue from the agency producing the discourse. (This was indeed a remarkable critical stance to adopt in the fifties.) However, Faulkner in no way undermines the narrators: Sutpen's story exists only in the narratives which tell it and *inform* it; the discourse of each narrator is, at one and the same time, utterance and utterance-act; that is, it remains inseparable from the conditions governing its own production, and from the personality of the speaker.

Of all the four narrators in *Absalom, Absalom!*, Shreve is perhaps the one who has been least--or the least well--examined in criticism. Of late, his function as co-creator in the narrative[3] has begun to be appreciated, though this role Faulkner himself had suggested to a Virginia audience in 1957: "Shreve was the commentator that held the [story] to something of reality."[4]

Within the space of fiction, but outside the narrative construct of Quentin and Shreve, this function is already recognized and defined by the anonymous narrator, in the Harvardian section of the narrative (chapters 6 to 9), in which the two young men are always perceived in relation to each other. Towards the end of chapter 8, after Shreve's speech about Charles Bon, and just before the *immediate* vision of Sutpen and his son on the battlefield at night, the anonymous narrator situates the two narrators in the *geography* of the novel and defines their reciprocal positions: "Shreve, the Canadian, the child of blizzards and of cold ...; Quentin, the Southerner, the morose and delicate offspring of rain and steamy heat."[5] An earlier intervention explains even better the nature of the bond uniting the narrators in spite of--or because of--the *polar* distance which separates them:

> both young, both born within the same year: the one in Alberta, the other in Mississippi; born half a continent apart yet joined, connected after a fashion in a sort of geographical transubstantiation by that Continental Trough, that River which runs not only through the physical land of which it is the geologic umbilical, ... but is very Environment itself which laughs at degrees of latitude and temperature. (p. 258)

Shreve and Quentin make up the two poles of the Harvardian narrative, but form one and the same axis which traverses it and gives it form and meaning, in the same way as the Mississippi River traverses North America. Or indeed, by shifting the image slightly, they can be seen as two opposite poles demarcating the same magnetic field. Just as these two poles cannot be disconnected and make sense independently of each other, so the narrators Shreve and Quentin can have a function and meaning only in their reciprocal relation. Despite seeming differences in voice and point of view, the two narrators are not only complementary, but become interchangeable as twins might be.[6] Or, more precisely, they are at once both complementary and interchangeable, for if they take up the Sutpen story indifferently, each one can only do so through the presence and agency of the other. So that their common point of view can be defined as an identification with its object and simultaneously a distancing from this object; and their relationship as one of difference and familiarity. Such is the concept, inferred by the anonymous narrator himself, which helps the reader understand Shreve's function.

Shreve's participation in the narrative is accomplished in two ways: on the one hand, he leads Quentin, through his insistent questions, to become embroiled in the narrative to the point where the investigation on Sutpen and his own quest for identity as a Southerner become one process which he can no longer choose not to pursue to the end; on the other hand, Shreve himself takes over a large portion of the narrative, now because Quentin is unable to do so in view of how painful such a process has become for him and how apprehensive he is regarding the consequences of such a commitment, now because Shreve himself feels implicated in an investigation to which he can no longer remain indifferent. In this manner, he comes to identify with Charles Bon in chapter 8 of the novel and to recreate the sufferings of the young Creole awaiting some gesture or sign of recognition from his father, which would allow him to define his identity--which would make him be. If then Shreve adopts Charles Bon's point of view in the investigation into Sutpen, it is because this Canadian living in New England--this Northerner who feels cut off from history (and says it), and who through his roommate finds himself in constant contact with a civilization which above all defines itself by and through the all-pervading presence of a past-- is perhaps better able than Quentin to understand and recreate the anguish of a son cut off from his father, of Absalom separated from David. For the quest of the father can also be seen in terms of the need to give oneself a history, to recognize oneself as its *effect*, and thus to learn to know oneself, which is what the Canadian from Alberta explains to the Southerner:

> Listen. I'm not trying to be funny, smart. I just want
> to understand it if I can and I dont know how to say it

better. Because it's something my people haven't got.
Or if we have got it, it all happened long ago across
the water and so now there aint anything to look at
every day to remind us of it. We dont live among defeated grandfathers and freed slaves (or have I got it
backward and was it your folks that are free and the
niggers that lost?) and bullets in the dining room table
and such, to be always reminding us to never forget.
What is it? something you live and breathe in like air?
... a kind of entailed birthright father and son and
father and son of never forgiving General Sherman? (p.
361)

It is important that in recreating this torrid story of
the South, Shreve should be the narrator from the North, that
is, a perfect stranger, who can provide a broader perspective
on the story and, steering the narrative by his questions,
can therefore introduce a logic or coherence into the investigation which it would not possess, had Quentin been left
alone to lead it. For all that, Shreve is so conscious of his
strangeness and therefore of the distance that separates him
from the South, that he asks Quentin repeatedly about the
specificity of the South, and even the possibility of its
existence, questions which occur at the beginning of practically every chapter in the second part of the novel,[7] as if
to point out the necessity of distance in the (re)construction
in which the two narrators are to become involved. Indeed,
Quentin himself can bring off such reconstruction only when
he has left the heat of the Mississippi summer for the New
England snows.

Shreve, then, has a function *in* the novel analogous to
that of the reader *of* the novel, capable of distancing, hence
of comprehension. He mirrors within the narrative certain
attitudes which the reader cannot fail to adopt vis-à-vis the
narrative structure; he mirrors, and anticipates, the latter's
questions: this is the case, for example, of the two interruptions in Quentin's narrative, when Shreve leads him to specify
that the information vital to the understanding of the Sutpen
story was not handed down from Mr Compson to his son, but
paradoxically passed up from son to father (pp. 266 and 274).
Thus implicated in the narrative process by Shreve's critical
attitude to this narrative (here it is not a case of his
judgment on the story), the reader becomes in a certain sense
co-narrator and co-narratee of the narrative—which is perhaps
what Faulkner meant when he explained that the reader's vision,
following that of the narrators, is the fourteenth way of
looking at the blackbird. Not, however, that the first
"thirteen" versions should be seen as equivalent, as this

image suggested to Faulkner and his own commentary on it may
lead one to think. Quentin and Shreve's version *tells* the
truth and the reader, for want of a better explanation, would
be unable to view the story with any other perspective than
that of the two narrators in their room at Harvard. Admittedly,
the reader has previously "heard" Miss Coldfield's and Mr
Compson's versions: even if he understands differently than
they, he will not be able to forget or disqualify totally
their "gothic" or "theatrical" visions, which represent a
short-sighted or, on the contrary, an over-distant perception
of Sutpen. But Quentin, and Shreve indirectly, have also
heard the first two narrators whose respective versions they
have retained so well that they often speak like Mr Compson
(which Quentin knows only too well, overwhelmed as he is by
the same obsessive storytelling), or like Miss Coldfield,
whose vocabulary Shreve mimics, to put to the test in some
way the vision it evokes, and not, contrary to appearances,
to reject it. Indeed, Rosa's vision of the *hubris* of Sutpen,
fascinated and bedazzled though she appears, is also profoundly
the vision shared by Quentin and Shreve in the dark room of
their imagination. To come back to the remarks spurred by
Stevens's poem, one might say that, of the "thirteen" versions
of the narrators, the thirteenth is the truest, the final
vision in which all obscurity is dissolved, even though it
may raise questions.

The reader's involvement in the narrative construction is
also facilitated by the attitude of Shreve, who plays the part
of any good reader of any good thriller, for every investigation is supposed to proceed along certain lines and to respect
certain conventions of the genre: this is the accepted price
for enjoyment in reading. Now Shreve obviously wants to
succeed in understanding and in relating a story which is
mysterious to him at the outset, but he will not have the
final revelation—the discovery of the "skeleton"—anticipate
all that this revelation finally explains, and which has to be
known previously, so that it may render the story completely
transparent. As long as he is not ready to hear the revelation, because he does not know yet all the factors in the
story, Shreve enjoys postponing until the end the moment of
comprehension.[8] So the suspense peculiar to any thriller-
type investigation is doubly justified here: by the presence
of narrators who are likely not to provide a piece of information so well known to them as not to warrant stating, and
which the reader lacks until the narrator is drawn by the
coherence of his investigation to speak about it; and by the
presence of Shreve in particular, who refuses to mar any
pleasure accorded to him in his investigator's role and who
defers the revelation so that it can coincide with the comprehension.

   In this way, Shreve can be seen at the end of chapter 6
almost bringing Quentin to the verge of disclosing what he
has discovered at Sutpen's Hundred (but Quentin has learned
nothing and is therefore unable to make any reply), and asking
him straightaway to put off the moment of discovery (is not
this also an example of the unpunished vice of the reader?):

> "And yet this old gal, this Aunt Rosa, told you that
> some one was hiding out there and you said it was Clytie
> or Jim Bond and she said No ... and so you went out
> there, drove the twelve miles at night in a buggy and
> you found Clytie and Jim Bond both in it and you said
> You see? and she (the Aunt Rosa) still said No and so
> you went on: and there was?"
> "Yes."
> "Wait then," Shreve said. "For God's sake wait."
> (p. 216)[9]

No wonder Quentin comments on this evident predilection of
Shreve's for delayed revelation: "I reckon Grandfather was
saying 'Wait, wait for God's sake wait' about like you are"
(p. 247). This predilection, after all, he also shares, since
on one occasion he interrupts Shreve, entreating him to wait
too (p. 277).
   So Shreve's function in the narrative is first and foremost one of distancing: in contrast to Quentin, in whose na-
rative both narration and story come to coincide, Shreve,
the Canadian, the man from the cold, refuses to let himself
be suffocated by this story, to which he remains, by virtue
of his environment, alien. Sutpen is not *his* story, not the
mark in his conscience of original sin, but the subject of
a story which he never forgets is a story,[10] and which he
asks his rommmate to relate right to the end. Whereas for
Quentin the investigation is confused with his own quest for
identity, it remains an investigation for Shreve, which enables
him to conduct it to some avail. Admittedly, Shreve will end
up like Quentin, identifying himself with the characters (in
Chapter 8), but without ridding himself in the process of his
awareness of distance.[11] So the *points of view* of the two
young men finally do not seem to me--in contrast to current
interpretations--to be radically different, but on the contrary to be superimposable. Both narrators finally see the
story of Sutpen from the same perspective, but at differing
distances. That is why, in the last analysis, the difference
between them is attributable to tone, or perhaps *accent*, as
the anonymous narrator remarks in chapter 8:

> It was Shreve speaking, though save for the slight dif-
> ference which the intervening degrees of latitude had

inculcated in them (differences not in tone or pitch
but of turns of phrase and usage of words), it might
have been either of them. (p. 303)

From the beginning of chapter 6, Shreve's first words reveal the distance which separates the narrator from his narrative: for him, the characters of this Southern tragedy
belong in some vague Middle Age, as lacking in relevance at
the beginning of the twentieth century as the real knight
Bayard or the mythical wife of King Arthur (p. 174).[12] At
the beginning in particular, Shreve creates and maintains
this distance by an almost systematic use of ironic language,
which frequently becomes derision. The techniques to which
he resorts most frequently are those of overstatement and
understatement, "inflation" and "deflation," often employed
together; so as not to let himself get caught in his attempt
at understanding the South, he pricks the balloons which he
himself has puffed up to bursting point. An example of "inflation," the rusty scythe which fells Sutpen becomes, beyond
death, the "symbolic laurel of a caesar's triumph" (p. 177).
On the other hand, the president of the Confederacy is
familiarly called "Jeff Davis" (p. 177), Miss Coldfield becomes "this old dame" or even "this old gal" (p. 176), the
first wife of Sutpen is generally referred to only with an
ironic phrase, "the old Sabine" (p. 303 ff.), and Clytie,
whom Rosa had transformed into the Cerberus of the Sutpen
hell, is stripped of her mythical aura: "a little dried-up
woman not much bigger than a monkey ..., her bare feet wrapped
around the chair rung like monkeys do" (p. 214). Wash Jones
is sometimes seen as the lowest of the poor whites and sometimes as the grave-digger in *Hamlet*, indeed Shakespeare himself coming on stage (but the exaggeration of what is here
basically Mr Compson's vision is such that the overstatement
bursts from its own excess[13]): "the voice of the faithful
grave-digger who opened the play and would close it, coming
out of the wings like Shakespeare's very self" (p. 280).

Subversion by means of derision is particularly effective
when Shreve repeats in order to undermine them the interpretations of the previous narrators, then frequently combining
"inflation" and "deflation" in the same breath, if one can
put it like this. By turning Clytie into the Cassandra of
the tragedy of Sutpen (p. 62), Mr Compson had implicitly con-
ferred upon the latter the stature of an Agamemnon; when
Shreve takes up the classical reference, Rosa does become the
Cassandra of the play, but simultaneously Shreve knocks the
heroes down from their mythical pedestals and makes them into
comic lovers, Pyramus and Thisbe (obviously the heroes of the
grotesque farce of the craftsmen in *A Midsummer Night's Dream*,

and not the highly literary elaboration on a myth in Ovid's
Metamorphoses): "[Rosa would] find instead of a widowed
Agamemnon to her Cassandra an ancient stiff-jointed Pyramus
to her eager though untried Thisbe" (p. 177).

Shreve even goes so far as to subvert Miss Coldfield's
vocabulary. Whereas the old lady had voiced her fears of
being betrayed by the flesh (irresistible by definition, and
thus ennobled by the real or imaginary fault), Shreve disrobes
desire, so to speak, and makes it a matter of joke: such is
the significance of the substitution of "meat" for "flesh":

> *To what deluded sewer-gush of dreaming does the in-
> corrigible flesh betray us.* (p. 165).

> betrayed by the old meat. (p. 177)

In this same way, the image of the dog used by Rosa is taken
up by Shreve, who then turns sexuality into mere bitchery,
lowering the characters to the level of animals (as he does
with Clytie):

> [I] *must come to him* [Sutpen] *like a whistled dog.*
> (p. 158; cf. pp. 167 and 168)

> he approached her and suggested they breed a couple of
> dogs together, inventing with fiendish cunning the
> thing which husbands and fiances have been trying to
> invent for ten million years. (p. 180)

Rosa's vision itself, and not just her vocabulary, is
blown up and at once punctured by Shreve. The demon becomes
Satan in person, and the man pursuing the insane dream of
making time stand still, an avatar of Faustus. But here
Beelzebub is merely an actor in a second-rate melodrama,
"who hid horns and tail beneath human raiment and beaver hat"
(p. 178),[14] or like the other characters in this "circus,"
he is reduced to the level of an animal: "this Faustus, this
demon, this Beelzebub fled ... hiding, scuttling into respectability like a jackal into a rockpile" (p. 178). Finally,
to top it all, this "ancient" Faustus is "varicose," (p. 182)
just as Pyramus has rheumatism.

These few examples, representative of the general tone
adopted by Shreve in his narrative, or more precisely at the
beginning (in fact, they all occur at the beginning of chapter
6), should allow one to conclude that the Canadian is the
detached, even scornful, observer of a story which would appear to be a spectacular show (not serious entertainment),
an elaborate joke, or a tall tale in the tradition of the
Southwestern humorists.[15] But, as a close reading of the
text demonstrates, Shreve's banter is only the reverse of his
desire to understand the South (and the means of achieving

this by guarding himself against emotion), his irony but the
mask of a sense of decency in a young man who prefers to appear sarcastic rather than sentimental--an attitude which he
comes to acknowledge to Quentin at the end of their long investigation: "Listen. I'm not trying to be funny, smart.
I just want to understand it if I can and I dont know how to
say it better" (p. 361). This remark would suffice in itself
to account for the Canadian's offhandedness. But to ensure
that no reader misses the point, the anonymous narrator interrupts Shreve's narrative twice to explain his attitude:

> His remark was not intended for flippancy nor even
> derogation. It was born (if from any source) of that
> incorrigible unsentimental sentimentality of the young
> which takes the form of hard and often crass levity--
> to which, by the way, Quentin paid no attention what-
> ever. (p. 275)

> This was not flippancy either. It too was just that
> protective coloring of levity behind which the youthful
> shame of being moved hid itself, out of which Quentin
> also spoke, the reason for Quentin's sullen bemusement,
> the (on both their parts) flipness, the strained clowning.
> (p. 280) .

Quentin's sullenness cannot be a defence from what touches
him deeply--himself. Shreve alone--a stranger to the South,
protecting himself by a mask of seeming *impertinence*, "unsentimental sentimentality"--succeeds at one and the same
time in identifying with the characters whom he recreates,
and in maintaining the distance necessary to understand what
they represent. Left to himself, Quentin would probably be
unable to recognize the implications to himself of Sutpen's
"mistake." Only in the last two pages of the novel does he
sense the imminent comprehension of the story he has recreated
with Shreve, and is he ready to accept the burden of this
heritage:

> he would be able to decipher the words soon, in a
> moment; even almost now, now, now.
>   "I am older at twenty than a lot of people who have
> died," Quentin said. (p. 377)

And the novel ends in the recognition and acceptance of the
love-hate bond which ties him to his land--to himself. But
such an increasing awareness has been made possible only
through the agency of Shreve, whose intuitions Quentin accepts
only with reluctance:

> "And so do you know what I think? ...
> "No," Quentin said.

"Do you want to know what I think?"

"No," Quentin said.

"Then I'll tell you. I think that in time the Jim Bonds
are going to conquer the western hemisphere. Of course
it won't quite be in our time and of course as they
spread toward the poles they will bleach out again like
the rabbits and the birds do, so they won't show up so
sharp against the snow. But it will still be Jim Bond;
and so in a few thousand years, I who regard you will
also have sprung from the loins of African kings. Now
I want you to tell me just one thing more. Why do you
hate the South?"

"I dont hate it," Quentin said. (p. 378)

That the Jim Bonds should cover the earth signifies the
inevitability in the long term of a mixing of the races
(which a Southerner is unable to accept in the short term,
as is demonstrated in the story by the attitude of Henry regarding Charles Bon, and in the narration by Quentin's sullenness through the Harvardian part of the narrative): the distinctions between the races should become blurred; between
men, the only *bond* (the idiot's name is ironically emblematic)
should be the one of their common humanity—which, short of
denying all his being, Quentin is finally brought to recognize,
painfully so.

Admittedly, it is the ambivalent attitude of Quentin
regarding the South, investing himself completely—an instance
of cathexis—in an investigation which he pursues unwillingly
and whose consequences he refuses to face, which has fascinated
Shreve and led him to invest himself in turn in this investigation, while keeping his mask of impertinence. But Quentin
would never have obtained such clear view of his past without
the aid of a stranger's view, so much the clearer for its
being distanced.[16] Therefore it was necessary for Shreve
McCannon to be Canadian, situated at a polar distance from
the young Mississippian and from the burden of the South.

So the narratives of Quentin and Shreve are to be distinguished (at the beginning above all, and even there intermittently), only by differences of tone. The two narrators
do not propose two different views of Sutpen's story, but two
complementary aspects of the same view, to the point where
their perspectives coincide in a single immediate vision,
at the end of chapter 8. To take up an earlier image, they
are the two poles of the same axis, as indeed Shreve the
Canadian feels involved in the Sutpen story, an involvement
which, however, he maintains at a distance, and as Quentin
the Southerner is capable of understanding his heritage only
at the other pole of the United States, in the snowy heart
of winter in New England—one might as well say in Canada.

Or, to use another image, Quentin and Shreve are, in the narration, heart and reason; but, with all due respect to Pascal,
they each know the reasons of the other because they know each
other at heart (perhaps in the mutual, but unconscious desire
which joins them): listening to them, one is aware of a con-
nivence of heart and reason, which need each other to function,
and know it. So, despite the initial differences in tone between the two narrators, their voices are gradually fused into
one composite voice, or an alternation, with no solution of
continuity, of voices which at times nothing allows to recognize specifically.

Indeed, the two voices gradually join harmoniously in a
homophonic structure, even integrating the voices of the two
previous narrators. Shreve takes up or mimics Miss Coldfield's
language, as has been shown, and even more frequently,
Mr Compson's, his periodical style, his taste for literary
allusions and sententious remarks, his overall "theatrical"
view of the tragedy of the South, to the point where again
and again Quentin finds himself thinking that Shreve's speech
reminds him of his own father's. But Quentin, too, resembles
his father (or even his grandfather), whose narrative he imi-
tates or integrates into his own, as it appears, for instance,
in a paradoxical comment on childhood innocence, "that frank
innocence which we call 'of a child' except that a human child
is the only living creature that is never either frank or
innocent" (p. 246), in a parenthesis on language and man's
inability to communicate (p. 251), or in the brilliant evocation of Haiti, that tropical heart of darkness, prodigiously
fertilized by the black blood of slaves (pp. 250-251).

The most remarkable instance of homophony, however, occurs
between Quentin and Shreve. They end up having the same verbal
mannerisms, the same feigned irritation when, for example,
Quentin answers "All right all right all right" to Shreve's
remarks on the secession of West Virginia from the Old Dominion
(pp. 220-221)--an answer which Shreve had previously thrown
out at Quentin who had insisted that Miss Coldfield was not
"Aunt Rosa" for him (p. 176). The anonymous narrator notes
that impertinence is not just Shreve's defence, but Quentin's
too--"that protecting coloring of levity ... out of which
Quentin also spoke" (p. 280). Thus, the brief summary given
by Quentin of the hunting of the architect is couched in what
could be Shreve's idiom, with its comic exaggerations and its
colloquialisms:

> "one day the architect couldn't stand it anymore or he
> was afraid he would starve or that the wild niggers
> (and maybe Colonel Sutpen too) would run out of grub

> and eat him or maybe he got homesick or maybe he just
> had to go--"
> ("Maybe he had a girl," Shreve said.) (p. 218)

In the last anaylsis, the fascination that Sutpen exercises on
them not only unites them in a common *passion*, but also fashions
their vision and language: Sutpen creates them as much as
they create him by their discourse: "*Maybe nothing ever happens
once and is finished.... maybe it took ... Thomas Sutpen to
make all of us*" (pp. 261-262). So much so that in chapter 8
they come to think and speak as one and the same person:

> it might have been either of them [speaking] and was in
> a sense both: both thinking as one, the voice which
> happened to be speaking the thought only the thinking
> become audible, vocal. (p. 303)

Such community of thinking renders useless the resolution
of possible ambiguities in personal pronouns, for, as the
anonymous narrator explains, the two young men think simultaneously of the same character without any need to name him:

> "and he"--(neither of them said 'Bon'. Never at any
> time did there seem to be any confusion between them
> as to whom Shreve meant by 'he') "--listening courteous
> and quiet." (pp. 310-311)[17]

Sometimes one foresees the intentions of the other *before* he
demonstrates them, such is their empathy with each other:

> "Wait," Shreve cried, though Quentin had not spoken:
> it had been merely some quality, some gathering of
> Quentin's still laxed and hunched figure which presaged
> speech, because Shreve said Wait. Wait. before Quentin
> could have begun to speak. (p. 321)

Sometimes, too, the relation becomes a case of telepathy, as
when Shreve interrupts Quentin, telling him: "Dont say it's
just me that sounds like your old man" (p. 261). Now Quentin
has not said it and never says it in the novel: he has only
thought of such a resemblance, which, it is true, haunts him.
Therefore the two young men can relay each other in a composite narrative, with no solution of continuity. In the last
part of chapter 7, Shreve is ready to take up another strand
of the story: "you wait. Let me play a while now. Now Wash."
And yet, it is Quentin who resumes the telling of the story,
"taking Shreve up in stride without comma or colon or paragraph" (p. 280). But quite often (especially in chapter 8)
the identity of the speaker is of no importance, as the anonymous narrator points out:

> it might have been either of them and was in a sense both.
> (p. 303)

> it did not matter to either of them which one did the
> talking. (p. 316)

> it did not matter (and possibly neither of them ·con-
> scious of the distinction) which one had been doing the
> talking. (p. 334)

Toward the end of chapter 8, before the joint vision of
Quentin and Shreve, the interchangeability of the narrators
makes it difficult to identify them (pp. 336-345). Admittedly
Shreve's rhetoric is recognizable, as is his specific imagery
("the old dame," "this nosegay of an afternoon, this ·scentless
prairie flower"), and it is clear that the speaker addresses
Quentin ("maybe your old man was right here too"). But at no
time has the speaker been identified here except in a parenthesis when Shreve, finally overtly named, suddenly interrupts
this (his own) discourse, *as if it had been someone else's*:
"(Listen,' Shreve said, cried. 'It would be while he would
be lying in a bedroom of that private house in Corinth after
Pittsburg Landing ...)'" (p. 339). By creating such a *possibility* of narrative confusion (the tone of the voice would
dispel any ambiguity), the narrator indicates once more that
Shreve and Quentin are indeed "thinking as one" (p. 303) and that
the modulations in the voice expressing this thinking are only
superficial signs, geographical accidents. The narrative
agency in the second part of the novel is, in a manner of
speaking, a narrator, or a poet, in two persons.

This may account for the dynamics of a narrative which,
considering only its aims and their realization, can be deemed
successful, unlike the one by Mr Compson--who comes to acknowledge his inability to account for the fall of the house of
Sutpen (p. 100). Such success is to be referred to the interchangeability of the functions of the narrator and the nar-
ratee, to their perfect "marriage": "it was not the talking
alone which did it, performed and accomplished the overpassing,
but some happy marriage of speaking and hearing wherein each
before the demand, the requirement, forgave condoned and forgot
the faulting of the other" (p. 316). This is no mere figure
of speech: the anonymous narrator repeatedly hints at the ·
existence of a relation of desire linking, even though con-
fusedly, the two young men--"twins" in the creative process.
Unconscious and imprecise though it is, even undifferentiated,
it is desire nevertheless, mirroring the relation of desire
between the half-brothers Henry Sutpen and Charles Bon, and
reduplicated, too, since the final identification of the
narrators is accomplished with both characters simultaneously:
"it was not even four now but compounded still further, since
now both of them were Henry Sutpen and both of them were Bon,
compounded each of both yet either neither" (p. 351).

Indeed, one cannot help noticing how feminine Shreve's
flesh appears, freshly out of adolescence, "his naked torso
pink-gleaming and baby-smooth, cherubic, almost hairless"
(p. 181). For these unexpected images do not just occur
at the beginning of the Harvardian sequence of the narrative,
but all through this long journey into the night, in which
time and again Quentin is seen looking at Shreve's soft, pink
flesh, like that of chubby angels in pictures[18] (nowhere do
these descriptions represent the explicit brooding of Quentin:
they are voiced by the anonymous narrator). One compound
adjective applied to Shreve is even more remarkable, "cupid-
fleshed" (p. 217), connoting less an actual desire than its
mythical representation, or possibly just some suggestion of
nudity: since Shreve is sitting at the table stripped to the
waist, "anyone entering the room would have taken him to be
stark naked" (p. 218). No suggestion, however, of any precise sexual desire, even homosexual, can be read in these
descriptions: it is a chaste desire, short of sex, or beyond
it--*pure* desire:

> There was something curious in the way they looked at
> one another, curious and quiet and profoundly intent,
> not at all as two young men might look at each other
> but almost as a youth and a very young girl might out
> of virginity itself--a sort of hushed and naked search-
> ing, each look burdened with youth's immemorial ob-
> session not with time's dragging weight which the old
> live with but with its fluidity: the bright heels of
> all the lost moments of fifteen and sixteen. (p. 299)

Such lack of specific relation to sexuality is also suggested
in the ambivalence of the two terms in the relation: at times,
Quentin appears to be the more delicate of the two, whereas
Shreve, taller and stronger, resembles "a disheveled bear"
(p. 293).[19] (Were it realized, the relation between the
"twins" would indeed be as incestuous as the one between
Henry and Charles, with or without the interposition of
Judith.)

By the agency of the anonymous narrator, Faulkner seems
here to have intended to point out the relation between
desire and creation. Miss Coldfield's vision, however warped
and biased, *apparently* inaccurate, *profoundly* revealed the
demiurge in Sutpen: indeed an ambivalent relation of desire
and terror linked her with Sutpen. Conversely, no relation
of desire came to exist between Mr Compson and "his" characters,
such was the deliberate distance he maintained between them
and himself. But by mirroring in the narration, even though
unwittingly and unconsciously, the dynamics of desire in the
story, Quentin and Shreve end up abolishing the gap between

narration and story. Culminating their investigation at the
end of chapter 8, their narrative breaks and becomes *immediate
vision* of the truth, since all *discourse* on the story implies
a narrative situation—that is, narration—and therefore the
consciousness of a gap between the two terms. Indeed, no
recognizable voice, not even the anonymous narrator's, tells
the confrontation of Sutpen and his son, then of the two half-
brothers, in the Carolinian night: it is *seen* immediately.

Thus the very possibility of a discourse on Sutpen required the presence of the Canadian Shreve in the dark "monastic" room of creation. His voice, at once strange and familiar,
allows and figures, in the narrative process, the implication
of the reader, who has to be taken into account in the production of meaning. Faulkner must have sensed this very inclina-
tion during the writing of *Absalom, Absalom!*: he had to in-
terrupt it, and then he resumed it in the detour of *Pylon* and
the Reporter, the narrator of contemporaneity; he must have
deemed insuperable the difficulty of creating a fiction which
he realized, while writing it, was also a metafiction.

NOTES

1. *The Collected Poems of Wallace Stevens*, London: Faber
and Faber, 1955, p. 94. Cf. the conclusion of the "still life"
by Stevens, "A Study of Two Pears": "The shadows of the pears/
Are blobs on the green cloth./ The pears are not seen/ As the
observer wills" (p. 197).

2. *Faulkner in the University: Class Conferences at the
University of Virginia, 1957-1958*, ed. Frederick L. Gwynn and
Joseph L. Blotner, Charlottesville: University of Virginia
Press, 1959, pp. 273-274.

3. For the now standard definitions of narrative, narration, and story, and for the distinction narrator-narratee,
see Gérard Genette, *Figures III*, Paris: Editions du Seuil,
1972; translated as *Narrative Discourse: An Essay in Method*,
Cornell University Press, 1979.

4. *Faulkner in the University*, p. 75.

5. *Absalom, Absalom!*, New York: Random House, 1936, p. 346.
Subsequent page references will be to this edition of the
novel and will be in parentheses in the text.

6. At the beginning of chapter 8, the anonymous narrator
refers to the two young men as "twins" (p. 294), thus recalling
the image of the umbilical cord.

7. See p. 174 (chapter 6), p. 217 (ch. 7), and for the last chapter Shreve's remarks quoted above. At the beginning of chapter 8, the anonymous narrator remarks on the somewhat incongruous gathering of the Northern "bear" and the frail Mississippian: "In the overcoat buttoned awry over the bathrobe he looked huge and shapeless like a disheveled bear as he stared at Quentin (the Southerner, whose blood ran quick to cool, ... perhaps merely nearer the surface) ..., looking somehow fragile and even wan in the lamplight" (pp. 293-294).

8. Cleanth Brooks has justly pointed out that in so doing Shreve is "the proper surrogate for the reader" (*William Faulkner: The Yoknapatawpha Country*, New Haven and London: Yale University Press, 1963, p. 323).

9. See also pp. 292, 321.

10. An interruption made by Shreve in Quentin's speech underlines the play element of the reconstruction in the former's eyes: "Let me play a while now" (p. 280).

11. A phrase of the anonymous narrator aptly defines Shreve's paradoxical attitude: "*intent detached* speculation" (p. 296, my italics).

12. Cf. this remark by the anonymous narrator or the Confederate generals, "as obsolete as Richard or Roland or du Guesclin" (p. 345).

13. The spectacle of the destruction of the South, which Mr Compson wanted to make into an analogue of ancient tragedy, is only a spectacular show, or even a "circus," in Shreve's eyes--*Ben Hur* rather than *Oresteia* (p. 217).

14. The juxtaposition of "raiment" and "beaver hat" stresses further this double action in Shreve's "method."

15. This view, widely accepted of late, is presented in an extreme form by Lynn Gartrell Levins, who sees an example of the tall tale in Shreve's narrative ("The Four Narrative Perspectives in *Absalom, Absalom!*," *PMLA*, 85 [Jan. 1970], 35-47). Cleanth Brooks discerns in Shreve "the attitude of the modern 'liberal,' twentieth-century reader, who is basically rational, skeptical, without any special concern for history, and pretty well emancipated from the ties of family, race, or section" (op. cit., p. 313). Brooks recognizes to a large extent that Shreve's involvement in his narrative is deeper than it appears, but he seems to let himself be influenced by Shreve's derisive tone in the last page of the novel: "we can see him drawing back from the tragic problem and becoming again the cheery, cynical, common-sense man of the present day" (*Ibid.*, p. 317). More recently, John Middleton has

shown, and rightly so (which is indeed evinced by a reading
of the novel with no preconceived ideas, without any hypothesis
to prove), that Shreve's banter is only a mask, and he has
stressed that only thanks to him does Quentin succeed in
contemplating lucidly his Southern heritage ("Shreve McCannon
and Sutpen's Legacy," *Southern Review*, 10 [Winter 1974], 115-
24). On Faulkner and Southwestern humor, one can read Cecil D.
Eby, "Faulkner and the Southwestern Humorists," *Shenandoah*, 11
(Autumn 1959), 13-21, and M. Thomas Inge, "William Faulkner
and George Washington Harris: In the Tradition of Southwestern
Humor," *Tennessee Studies in Literature*, 7 (1962), 47-59.

16. It is probably the recognition of this truth which
makes Judith confide to a stranger--the Compson grandmother--
Charles Bon's letter: "so maybe if you could go to someone,
the stranger the better, and give them something" (p. 127).

17. See also pp. 304 and 305. The attention suddenly
drawn to characters other than the one under discussion does
not require any shift of emphasis either: "'The letter which
he--' it was not Bon Shreve meant now, yet again Quentin
seemed to comprehend without difficulty or effort whom he
meant '--wrote maybe as soon as he finished that last entry
in the record'" (p. 314).

18. "pink bright-haired arms" (p. 217), "cherubic" (p.
256), "his pink naked almost hairless skin" (p. 275).

19. See also pp. 324, 346.

BIBLIOGRAPHY

SELECTIVE BIBLIOGRAPHY: 1936-1973

The following is a highly selective list of those books and
articles dealing with *Absalom, Absalom!* which were published
through 1973, the cut-off date for Thomas L. McHaney, *William
Faulkner: A Reference Guide* (Boston: G.K. Hall, 1976), the
standard secondary bibliography of Faulkner's works. All
items in the list which follows, except those reprinted in
this casebook, are annotated briefly. For convenience,
items are listed alphabetically by author; readers wishing
to review the scholarship chronologically may refer to the
number preceding each entry, keyed to McHaney (i.e., 68/B47
indicates an article listed in McHaney under the year 1968,
list B--shorter writings, item 47). The few items without
such a number do not appear in McHaney.

72/B1   Adamowski, T.H. "Dombey and Son and Sutpen and
              Son," *Studies in the Novel, North Texas State*,
              IV (Fall, 1972), 378-389. Both Dombey and
              Sutpen are isolated, interested in dynasty,
              and view their wives similarly.

68/A1   Adams, Richard P. *Faulkner: Myth and Motion.*
              Princeton, N.J.: Princeton University Press,
              1968, pp. 172-214. A thorough assessment of
              the novel, which emphasizes Rosa's Gothic
              vision, Mr. Gompson's classical vision, and
              Quentin's biblical language and association
              with the creation myth and the Fall. Discusses
              Sutpen as a "representative man."

59/B6   Arnavon, Cyrille. "*Absalon! Absalon! et l'histoire*,"
              Configuration Critique de William Faulkner II,
              La Revue des Lettres Modernes, V (Winter, 1959),
              250-270. Racial problems are the root of the
              evil in the novel. Quentin and Shreve, who
              begin by conducting a "police inquest" into
              Sutpen's life, enter upon a holy quest. Dis-
              cusses twentieth-century techniques and themes
              in the novel as well as its tragic and deter-
              ministic tone.

68/B4   Aswell, Duncan. "The Puzzling Design of *Absalom,*
           Absalom!" *Kenyon Review*, XXX (Issue I, 1968),
           67-84. Reprinted herein.

64/B5   Barth, J. Robert. "Faulkner and the Calvinist
           Tradition," *Thought*, XXXIX (Spring, 1964),
           100-120; reprinted in *Religious Perspectives
           in Faulkner's Fiction: Yoknapatawpha and Beyond*
           (Notre Dame, Ind.: Notre Dame University Press,
           1972), pp. 11-31. The curse on Sutpen, on a
           deeper level, is slavery—the curse on the
           South; on a deeper level still, it is the
           "curse over fallen mankind."

41/B4   Beck, Warren. "William Faulkner's Style,"
           American Prefaces, VI (Spring 1941), 195-211;
           frequently reprinted, included in *Faulkner:
           Essays* (Madison, Wisc.: University of Wisconsin
           Press, 1976), pp. 34-51. Uses numerous ex-
           amples from *Absalom* to discuss appreciatively
           Faulkner's elaborate "full style," diction,
           and his "persistent lyrical embroidering and
           coloring," which exists side by side with
           realistic colloquialism.

63/B5   Björk, Lennart. "Ancient Myths and the Moral
           Framework of Faulkner's *Absalom, Absalom!*"
           American Literature, XXXV (May, 1963), 196-
           204. Overview of myths drawn on by Faulkner
           in the novel, with particular attention paid
           to the stories of Agamemnon and King David
           which provide the reader with a moral frame-
           work against which Sutpen can be understood.

70/B11   Bradford, Melvin E. "Brother, Son, and Heir:
           The Structural Focus of Faulkner's *Absalom,
           Absalom!*" *Sewanee Review*, LXXVIII (Winter,
           1970), 76-98. Bon is his father's son, "single-
           minded and inflexible" and destructive of those
           he touches. Henry alone acts responsibly; he
           is the novel's hero. The novel cannot be fully
           understood without reference to *The Sound and
           the Fury*; it is Quentin who is weak and not
           the South.

51/B7   Breit, Harvey. "Introduction," *Absalom, Absalom!*
           New York: Modern Library, 1951, pp. v-xii.
           The novel has a personal quality, as though
           the father-son story is Faulkner's "objective
           correlative of a vision of the South."

51/B10   Brooks, Cleanth. "*Absalom, Absalom!*: The Definition
of Innocence," *Sewanee Review*, LIX (Autumn,
1951), 543-558. Discusses Sutpen's innocence
as tragic and Quentin's obsession with the
problem of tragedy.

64/B11   ————. "The American 'Innocence': in James,
Fitzgerald, Faulkner." *Shenandoah*, XVI
(Autumn 1964), 21-37; reprinted in *A Shaping
Joy: Studies in the Writer's Craft* (N.Y.:
Harcourt, Brace, Jovanovich, 1971). Sutpen
resembles Newman in *The Americans* and Gatsby in
The Great Gatsby; all are typical American
innocents who create themselves from ambigious
origins. Sutpen, oblivious to the concept
of sin, fails to take into account the community
of which he is a part.

72/B13   ————. "Faulkner and History." *Mississippi
Quarterly*, XXV (Spring 1972), supplement, pp.
3-14. Sutpen is a gnostic who finds history
meaningless; he has confidence that he can
change the present and create a future. Shreve
dismisses the past; Quentin is defeated by it.

63/A1   ————. "History and the Sense of the Tragic:
Absalom, Absalom!" In *William Faulkner: The
Yoknapatawpha Country* (New Haven: Yale University Press, 1963). See "History, Tragedy and
the Imagination in *Absalom, Absalom!*"

63/B13   ————. "History, Tragedy and the Imagination
in *Absalom, Absalom!*" *Yale Review*, LII
(March 1963), pp. 340-351; included in
William Faulkner: The Yoknapatawpha Country
(New Haven: Yale University Press, 1963),
pp. 295-324, 424-443. Overall analysis of
the novel, discussing its marriage of form
(which utilizes the detective story), content,
and theme. *Absalom* is a universal novel concerned with man's relationship to his past and
the way in which we apprehend meaning. Sutpen
is a tragic figure; Judith, who uses her great
strength and love in affirmation, is one of
Faulkner's noblest characters.

73/B16   ————. "On *Absalom, Absalom!*" *Mosaic*, VII
(Fall 1973), 159-183. Summarizes and contributes
to three critical debates: (1) the problem of
fact *vs.* speculation in the novel, and in

particular, the evidence that Bon is Sutpen's
son, (2) Sutpen as a "representative Southern
man" and (3) the nature of Sutpen's innocence.
Sutpen has absolute faith in his own will to
pursue the American dream. Revised version of
section 2 of this article is included in
*William Faulkner: Toward Yoknapatawpha and
Beyond* (New Haven: Yale University Press,
1978).

70/B13   ———. "The Poetry of Miss Rosa Canfield [sic]."
Shenandoah, XXI (Spring 1970), 199–206; included
in *William Faulkner: Toward Yoknapatwapha and
Beyond*. Rosa's monologue shows her to be a
geniune poet.

72/B18   Brumm, Ursula. "Forms and Functions of History in
the Novels of William Faulkner." *Archiv*,
CCIX (August 1972), 43–56. In *Absalom*,
Faulkner's "fullest exploration of the working
of a historic consciousness," Quentin exemplifies
that role.

69/B11   ———. "Thoughts on History and the Novel."
Comparative Literature Studies, VI (September
1969), 317–330. *Absalom* is an exploration of
the epistemological problem of history, and
marries "research" (truthful representation)
and "fiction" to demonstrate that history is
a product of the human mind.

68/A2   Brylowski, Walter. "Faulkner's Mythology."
Faulkner's Olympian Laugh: Myth in the Novels
(Detroit: Wayne State University Press, 1968),
pp. 17–42. Reprinted herein.

58/B17   Coanda, Richard. "*Absalom, Absalom!*: The Edge of
Infinity." *Renascence*, XI (Autumn, 1958),
3–9. Sympathetic effort to describe Faulkner's
style, especially in terms of its relationship
to baroque and Jacobean models.

63/B25   Connolly, Thomas E. "A Skeletal Outline of *Absalom,
Absalom!*" *College English*, XXV (November 1963),
110–114; reprinted in Arnold Goldman, ed.,
Twentieth Century Interpretations of Absalom,
Absalom! (Englewood Cliffs, N.J.: Prentice-
Hall, 1971). Title is explanatory. Does not
differentiate between characters with objective
fictional being and those invented by other
characters in the novel.

46/B2   Cowley, Malcolm. "Introduction." *Viking Portable Faulkner* (New York: Viking Press, 1946), i-xxiv; frequently reprinted. Cowley's most influential statement of his thesis that Faulkner's achievement is his construction of a saga of Yoknapatawpha County. *Absalom, Absalom!* is a metaphor for the decline of the Old South; Sutpen resembles Faust.

70/B21   Davenport, F. Garvin, Jr. "William Faulkner." *The Myth of Southern History: Historical Consciousness in Twentieth-Century Southern Literature* (Nashville: Vanderbilt University Press, 1970), 82-130. Faulkner's concern, best exemplified in *Absalom, Absalom!*, is with ideals and universal (not Southern or American) history. Sutpen's flaw is his inability to live in history. Relates Thomas Dixon's *The Sins of the Father* (1912) to *Absalom*.

72/B39   Garzilli, Enrico. "Myth and the Self: *Absalom, Absalom!*" *Circles Without Center: Paths to the Discovery and Creation of Self in Modern Literature* (Cambridge, Mass.: Harvard University Press, 1972), 52-60. Sutpen's aspirations are larger than the American Dream; he seeks "openness to infinity." Examines mythical analogues, mirrorings and parallels in the novel, particularly patterns of father/son and creator/creation.

73/B44   Gidley, Mark [Mick]. "Elements of the Detective Story in William Faulkner's Fiction." *Journal of Popular Culture*, VII (Summer 1973), 97-123; rpt. in Larry N. Landrum et al., eds., *Dimensions of Detective Fiction* (Bowling Green, Ohio: Popular Press, 1976). *Absalom* is only at its simplest level a detective story. The reader, who must weigh conjectures, becomes his own detective.

67/B36   Guetti, James. "*Absalom, Absalom!*: The Extended Simile." *The Limits of Metaphor: A Study of Melville, Conrad and Faulkner* (Ithaca: Cornell University Press, 1967), 69-108. Reprinted herein.

59/A1   Gwynn, Frederick L., and Joseph L. Blotner, eds. *Faulkner in the University: Class Conferences at the University of Virginia, 1957-1958* (Charlottesville, Va.: University of Virginia

Press, 1959). Contains several statements
about *Absalom, Absalom!*, usually made by
Faulkner in response to questions concerning
his characterization of Sutpen. Readers
should realize that Faulkner's answers suggest
that he does not remember the novel in detail.

63/B39   Hagan, John. "*Déjà Vu* and the Effect of Timelessness in Faulkner's *Absalom, Absalom!*" *Bucknell
Review*, XI (March 1963), 31-52; rpt. in H.R.
Garvin, ed., *Makers of the Twentieth-Century
Novel* (Lewisburg, Pa.: Bucknell University Press,
1977). Interesting study of interrelatedness
of imagery and structure. The novel is structured in three phases (Chs. 1-6, the Jefferson
phase; Chs. 7-8, the causes of Sutpen's ruin;
Ch. 9, the "hidden existence" of Henry). The
effect of this structure on the reader is a
sense of *déjà vu*, as described by Bergson.
Each revelation in chapters 7 and 8 has been
carefully prefigured by earlier images, motif
clusters and parallels, enabling Faulkner to
achieve a timeless stasis.

62/B58   Hagan, John. "Fact and Fancy in *Absalom, Absalom!*"
College English, XXIV (December 1962), 215-218.
First sustained look at what Quentin learned
at Sutpen's Hundred (that Bon is Sutpen's son)
and how he learned it.

73/B49   Hagopian, John V. "*Absalom, Absalom!* and the Negro
Question." *Modern Fiction Studies*, XIX (Summer
1973), 207-211. Examines the motives of the
central characters and concludes that the novel
"clearly repudiates Southern racism."

72/B45   Haury, Beth B. "The Influence of Robinson Jeffers'
'Tamar' on *Absalom, Absalom!*" *Mississippi
Quarterly*, XXV (Summer 1972), 356-358. Not
only do both Jeffers' 1924 poem and Faulkner's
novel use the Biblical Absalom/Amnon/Tamar
story, but Faulkner seems to have used elements
from the poem.

71/B41   Hodgson, John A. "'Logical Sequence and Continuity':
Some Observations on the Typographical and
Structural Consistency of *Absalom, Absalom!*"
American Literature, XLIII (1971), 97-107.
Proposes (unsuccessfully) to provide a key
to the various ways in which Faulkner uses

typographical indicators. Suggests that
because Chapter 3 has a different typographical
scheme than its frame chapters, it is actually
a conversation occurring later, after Quentin's
visit to Sutpen's Hundred.

71/B42   Holman, C. Hugh. *"Absalom, Absalom!*: The Historian
as Detective." *Sewanee Review,* LXXIX (October-
December, 1971), 542-553; rpt. in *The Roots
of Southern Writing: Essays on the Literature
of the American South* (Athens Ga.: University
of Georgia Press, 1972). The novel's detective-
story form insists upon interpretation of the
past. History, for Faulkner, "is always a means
toward an end...meaningful in what it says of
man rather than in what man says of it."

Hopper, Vincent F. "Faulkner's Paradise Lost."
Virginia Quarterly Review, XXIII (Summer 1947),
405-420. Sutpen, a Miltonic Satanic hero,
epitomizes man in conflict with nature.

52/A1   Howe, Irving. *"Absalom, Absalom!" William Faulkner:
A Critical Study* (New York: Random House, 1952),
53-59, 161-172; 2nd ed. (1962), 70-78, 221-232.
Absalom is a moral fable, in which the gothic
is used to 'freeze' his material and, thereby,
blunt its edge of feeling."

65/A2   Hunt, John W. "The Theological Center of *Absalom,
Absalom!" William Faulkner: Art in Theological
Tension* (Syracuse, N.Y.: Syracuse University
Press, 1965), 101-136; rpt. New York: Haskell
House, 1973; rpt. in J.R. Barth, ed., *Religious
Perspectives in Faulkner's Fiction* (Notre Dame,
Ind.: University of Notre Dame Press, 1972).
The final reality in the novel is far larger
than Quentin can see. Faulkner limits himself
by Quentin's role as narrator, but "implicitly
judges from...a Christian humanist point of
view" that Sutpen and the traditional world of
which he is a part fail because they cannot
recognize the work of Christian love.

63/B48   Isaacs, Neil D. "Götterdämmerung in Yoknapatawpha."
Tennessee Studies in Literature, VIII (1963),
47-55. Explores the identification between
Quentin and Wash; sees "Wash" as germ of the
novel.

62/B74   Justus, James H. "The Epic Design of *Absalom,
           Absalom!*" *Texas Studies in Literature and
           Language* IV (Summer 1962), 157–176. Reprinted
           herein.

71/B48   Kartiganer, Donald M. "Process and Product: A Study
           in Modern Literary Form, Part II." *Massachusetts
           Review* (Autumn 1971), 789–816. *Absalom, Absalom!*
           as a novel evolves a history of the mind. Its
           tragedy is the splitting apart of Quentin and
           Shreve at its end, which mirrors the split
           between Charles and Henry.

71/A4   Langford, Gerald. *Faulkner's Revision of* Absalom,
           Absalom!: *A Collation of the Manuscript and the
           Published Book* (Austin, Tex.: University of
           Texas Press, 1971). Compares the manuscript
           of the novel with the 1951 Modern Library print-
           ing, omitting reference to the typescript setting
           copy at the University of Virginia.

67/B60   Levin, David. "*Absalom, Absalom!*: The Problem of
           Recreating History." *In Defense of Historical
           Literature: Essays on American History, Auto-
           biography, Drama and Fiction* (New York: Hill
           and Wang, 1967), 118–139. Emphasizes the obvious
           (but seldom noted) point that Quentin is not just
           an observer but a participant in the drama.

70/B47   Levins, Lynn Gartrell. "The Four Narrative Perspec-
           tives in *Absalom, Absalom!*" *PMLA*, LXXXV (January
           1970), 35–47. Though all employ similar styles,
           each narrator has a different form: Rosa's
           Gothic mystery, Mr. Compson's Greek tragedy,
           Quentin's chivalric romance, Shreve's Old South-
           west tall tale.

55/B35   Lind, Ilse Dusoir. "The Design and Meaning of
           Absalom, Absalom!" *PMLA*, LXX (December 1955),
           887–912; rpt. in Linda Wagner, ed., *William
           Faulkner: Four Decades of Criticism* (East
           Lansing, Mich.: Michigan State University Press,
           1973). Frequently cited overview of the novel
           as a classic moral tragedy, of various characters
           as types of Southerners, of the failure of
           Sutpen's design as "the meaning of the decline
           of the South."

64/B48   Loughrey, Thomas F. "Aborted Sacrament in *Absalom,
           Absalom!*" *Four Quarters*, XIV (November 1964),
           13–21. Using imagery of stasis, ghostliness,

tombstones, funerals, the novel is about the
failure of love and the "lost meaning of sacrament."

66/A6   Millgate, Michael. "*Absalom, Absalom!*" *The Achievement of William Faulkner* (New York: Random House,
1966; rpt. Vintage, 1971; University of Nebraska
Press, 1978), 150-164. Excellent general essay
touching on the novel's genesis and publication.

72/B77   ————. "'The Firmament of Man's History': Faulkner's
Treatment of the Past." *Mississippi Quarterly*,
XXV (Spring 1972) supplement, 25-35. Compares
Scott's *Waverley* and *Absalom*. The latter is not
a historical novel as defined by Lukács, but is
concerned with "the act of historical interpretation in and of itself."

           Minter, David. "Apotheosis of the Form: Faulkner's
Absalom, Absalom!" *The Interpreted Design as
a Structural Principle in American Prose* (New
Haven, Conn.: Yale University Press, 1969), 191-
219. The novel is the highest example of the
jeremiad form in American prose. Other characters beside Sutpen have designs which mirror
his.

72/B83   Muhlenfeld, Elisabeth. "Shadows with Substance
and Ghosts Exhumed: The Women in *Absalom, Absalom!*"
Mississippi Quarterly, XXV (Summer 1972), 289-
304. A measure of Sutpen's inhumanity (and of
the tragedy of the novel) in his inability to
see the women in his life as human.

72/A6   Page, Sally R. *Faulkner's Women: Characterization
and Meaning* (Deland, Fla.: Everett/Edwards,
1972), 102-108 et passim. Examines the imagery
surrounding Rosa Coldfield but slights the
other women in the novel.

66/A7   Peper, Jürgen. "Die Sprache in *Absalom, Absalom!*"
*Bewusstseinslagen des Erzählens und Erzählte
Wirklichkeiten dargestellt an Amerikanischen
Romanen des 19. und 20. Jahrhunderts insbesondere
am Werk William Faulkners* (Leiden, Netherlands:
E.J. Brill, 1966). Focuses on language patterns
in the novel, especially subordinate clauses
which serve to downplay subject itself and
heighten imaginative construction.

51/B46   Poirier, William R. "'Strange Gods' in Jefferson,
          Mississippi: Analysis of *Absalom, Absalom!*"
          In F.J. Hoffman and O.W. Vickery, eds., *William
          Faulkner: Two Decades of Criticism* (East
          Lansing, Mich.: Michigan State College Press,
          1951) and elsewhere. Reprinted herein.

72/B93   Polk, Noel E. "The Manuscript of *Absalom, Absalom!*"
          Mississippi Quarterly, XXV (Summer 1972), 359-
          367. Langford's comparison of the holograph
          manuscript and the published book is inaccurate;
          more seriously, it ignores the typescript setting
          copy and therefore makes assumptions about
          authorial revisions which were, in fact, editor-
          ial.

71/B83   Putzel, Max. "What Is Gothic about *Absalom, Absalom!*"
          Southern Literary Journal, IV (Fall 1971),
          3-19. The novel is, among other things, an
          examination of the decay of chivalry.

71/B86   Raper, J.R. "Meaning Called to Life: Alogical
          Structure in *Absalom, Absalom!*" *Southern
          Humanities Review*, V (Winter 1971), 9-23.
          Chapter V owes much to Faulkner's "flirtation
          with the movies," especially to Eisenstein's
          montage technique.

73/A7   Reed, Joseph W., Jr. *Faulkner's Narrative* (New
          Haven, Conn.: Yale University Press, 1973),
          145-175. Especially useful on metaphor and
          metaphor chains in the novel. Appendices
          contain charts illustrating chronological
          sequences and the flow of images.

70/B66   Rinaldi, Nicholas M. "Game Imagery in Faulkner's
          Absalom, Absalom!" *American Quarterly*, VI
          (October 1970), 73-79. Sutpen assumes life
          is a contest; "to lose is the only evil."

54/B69   Scott, Arthur L. "The Myriad Perspectives of
          Absalom, Absalom!" *American Quarterly* VI
          (Fall 1954), 210-220. Reprinted herein.

59/B59   Sewall, Richard B. "*Absalom, Absalom!*" *The Vision
          of Tragedy* (New Haven: Conn.: Yale University
          Press, 1959), 133-147. Important early dis-
          cussion of *Absalom* as a tragedy. Uses Job,
          Oedipus, Faustus, Lear, *The Scarlet Letter*,
          Moby-Dick and *The Brothers Karamazov*.

67/B90   Singleton, Marvin K. "Personae at Law and in
            Equity: the Unity of Faulkner's *Absalom,*
            Absalom!" *Papers on Language and Literature,*
            III (Fall 1967), 354-370. Faulkner uses terms
            from English common law and chancery proceedings,
            and the frame of the novel itself corresponds
            to a "hearing on a Bill in Chancery before
            Quentin and Shreve as 'Chancery Masters.'"

61/B62   Slabey, Robert M. "Faulkner's 'Waste Land': Vision
            in *Absalom, Absalom!*" *Mississippi Quarterly,*
            XIV (Summer 1961), 153-161. Sutpen resembles
            Hawthorne's men of science; Quentin is his
            opposite--incapable of action but deeply empa-
            thetic. Faulkner's ethical affirmation resembles
            Eliot's.

60/A2   Slatoff, Walter J. *Quest for Failure: A Study of*
            William Faulkner (Ithaca, N.Y.: Cornell University
            Press, 1960), 198-203 *et passim*. A new critical
            approach especially interesting on the novel's
            ending.

46/B2   Sullivan, Walter. "The Tragic Design of *Absalom,*
            Absalom!" *South Atlantic Quarterly,* L (October
            1951), 552-556. Early assertion that the novel
            is a tragedy in the Hegelian sense.

63/A9   Thompson, Lawrance R. *William Faulkner: An Intro-*
            duction and Interpretation (New York: Holt,
            Reinhart and Winston, 1963), 53-65. The novel
            is organized around three tableaux: Quentin,
            in Rosa's parlor (thesis), on his father's
            porch (antithesis) and at Harvard (synthesis).
            Faulkner uses the Oresteia and the Old Testament
            to examine the theme of love and not-love.

            Tindall, William York. *The Literary Symbol* (Bloom-
            ington, Ind.: Indiana University Press, 1955),
            264-267. The novel's symbols are radiant.
            Sutpen's house is central; also of importance
            are the horseman, the tombstone, black and white,
            enclosures, wistaria--all of which help to
            create the feeling of nightmare.

73/B109   Tobin, Patricia. "The Time of Myth and History in
            Absalom, Absalom!" *American Literature,* XLV
            (May 1973), 252-270. The structure of the novel
            is an oscillation between historical (diachronic)
            time and mythical (synchronic) time. Judith,
            Charles, and Henry are all racist; all affirm
            Sutpen's design.

70/B79   Vande Kieft, Ruth M. "Faulkner's Defeat of Time
            in *Absalom, Absalom!*" *Southern Review*, VI,
            new series (Autumn 1970), 1100-1109. Time
            destroys Sutpen, but Rosa, Judith, and the
            novel itself defeat time.

59/A4   Vickery, Olga. "The Idols of the South: *Absalom,
            Absalom!*" *The Novels of William Faulkner: A
            Critical Interpretation* (Baton Rouge, La.:
            Louisiana State University Press, 1959; revised
            edition, 1964), 84-102. *Absalom, Absalom!*
            is an extension of the structure and themes of
            The Sound and the Fury, examining the ambiguity
            of "fact" and the multiplicity of subjective
            truths.

70/B82   Waggoner, Hyatt H. "The Historical Novel and the
            Southern Past: The Case of *Absalom, Absalom!*"
            Southern Literary Journal, II (Spring 1970),
            69-85. Although the novel respects the notion
            of the historical novel as a genre, it is not
            a historical novel but a work dealing with
            universal themes and with the American past
            as a whole.

59/A5   ————. "Past as Present: *Absalom, Absalom!*"
            William Faulkner: From Jefferson to the World
            (Lexington, Kentucky: University of Kentucky
            Press, 1959), 148-169. Sensible examination
            of the novel's structure, of the roles of
            Quentin and Shreve, and of their difficulty
            in making the leap from fact to truth. Each
            narrator contributes to "the accumulating
            past."

71/B103   Watkins, Floyd C. "Thirteen Ways of Talking about
            a Blackbird." *The Flesh and the Word:
            Eliot, Hemingway, Faulkner* (Nashville: Vander-
            bilt University Press, 1971), 216-233. *Absalom,
            Absalom!*, through silences and abstractions,
            dramatizes fully the failure of language.

67/B100   ————. "What Happens in *Absalom, Absalom!*?"
            Modern Fiction Studies, XIII (Spring, 1967),
            79-87. Reprinted herein.

67/B101   Weatherby, H.L. "Sutpen's Garden." *Georgia Review*,
            XXI (Fall 1967), 354-369. Compares Faulkner
            with Dante and discusses Christian imagery in
            Absalom, Absalom!

59/B81   Zoellner, Robert H.   "Faulkner's Prose Style in
          Absalom, Absalom!" American Literature, XXX
          (January 1959), 486-502. Faulkner's prose
          sytle reflects his philosophical conviction
          that all aspects of life (moral, temporal,
          historical, psychological) are a "massive
          continuum that cannot be compartmentalized
          without substantial loss of truth." This
          fine study is a precursor of John T. Irwin's
          Doubling and Incest/Repetition and Revenge
          (1975).

BIBLIOGRAPHY: 1974-1982

The following list includes all articles of which the author
is aware published between 1974 and 1982 that deal with
Absalom, Absalom! Items without annotation either were not
seen or not read by the author but are included because
they have been cited in a standard bibliography as containing
material on *Absalom, Absalom!*

Adamowski, T.H. "Children of the Idea: Heroes and Family
Romances in *Absalom, Absalom!*" *MOSAIC*, X (Fall 1976),
115-131. Reprinted herein.

Adams, Richard P. "Faulkner: The European Roots." In
George H. Wolfe, ed., *Faulkner: Fifty Years After* The
Marble Faun (University, Ala.: University of Alabama
Press, 1976), 21-41. Although this essay is not about
Absalom, Absalom!, Adams does comment at length on
Faulkner's November 1944 letter to Malcolm Cowley about
the novel.

Akiba, Yuji. "'Wash' Kara *Absalom, Absalom!* e: Quentin no
Katari ni tsuite." In *Bungaku to America: Ohashi Kenzaburo
Kyoju Kanreki Kinen Ronbunshu* (Tokyo: Nanundo, 1980),
185-197.

Beck, Warren. *Faulkner: Essays* (Madison: University of
Wisconsin Press, 1976). Difficult to use because it is
without an index, this book refers to *Absalom, Absalom!*
repeatedly though never in extended discussion. Readers
might wish to look particularly at Chapters 7 and 8, pp.
144-353, for isolated insightful comments.

Behrens, Ralph. "Collapse of Dynasty: The Thematic Center
of *Absalom, Absalom!*" *PMLA*, LXXXIX (January 1974), 24-33.
Why Sutpen's design failed is the basic problem of the
novel. Survey of critical answers: innocence, hubris,
the social evil (a patriarchal slave society), the doom
of Biblical dynasties.

Bellei, Sérgio Luiz Prado. "O Realismo Noturno de *Absalão, Absalão!*" *Minas Gerais, Supplemento Literario*, XIV (1981), 3.

Bennett, J.A.W. "Faulkner and A.E. Housman." *Notes and Queries*, N.S., XXVII (June 1980), 234. Three adaptations from *A Shropshire Lad*.

Berzon, Judith R. "Faulkner and the Mulatto Character: *Intruder in the Dust*, 'The Fire and the Hearth,' and *Absalom, Absalom!*" *Neither White Nor Black: The Mulatto Character in American Fiction* (New York: New York University Press, 1978), 87-94. Our fascination with Bon is emblematic of the South's racial history. This brief sociological article makes no distinction between real and imagined characters and events.

Bleikasten, André. "Fathers in Faulkner." Robert Con Davis, ed., *The Fictional Father: Laconian Readings of the Text* (Amherst: University of Massachusetts Press, 1981). Revision and translation of "Les maîtres fantômes, paternité et filiation dans les romans de Faulkner."

————. "Les maîtres fantômes, paternité et filiation dans les romans de Faulkner." *Revue Francaise d'Etudes Americaines*, VIII (October 1979), 157-181. Building on Irwin, a Freudian examination of father-son relationships in Faulkner's works. In the discussion of *Absalom*, examines the connections between the fictional structuring of the relationships and the language used to create such relationships. Sutpen's role as father is so egocentric as to "preclude the possibility of an act of recognition" for either son.

Blotner, Joseph. *Faulkner: A Biography* (New York: Random House, 1974). Scattered throughout the chapters dealing with 1934-36 period are facts dealing with the composition and publication of *Absalom*. First discussion in print of "Evangeline" and its relationship with *Absalom*.

————. *Selected Letters of William Faulkner* (New York: Random House, 1977). Contains selected letters from the period of composition of the novel. Indexed.

Bosha, Francis J. "A Source for the Names Charles and Wash in *Absalom, Absalom!*" *Notes on Modern American Literature*, IV (Spring 1980), Item 13. Charles and Wash were names of slaves sold by Col. W.C. Falkner in the 1850s.

Boswell, George. "Epic, Drama, and Faulkner's Fiction." *Kentucky Folklore Record*, XXV (January-June 1979), 16-27. Superficial summary of epic elements in Faulkner, citing *Absalom* as epic and dramatic in form.

Brodsky, Claudia. "The Working of Narrative in *Absalom, Absalom!*: A Textual Analysis." *Amerikastudien*, XXIII (1978), 240-259. An excellent reader-response analysis of the novel which stresses the importance of the listeners (Quentin and Shreve) in the novel. Plot development is of less importance than "circuitry of communication." Interesting discussion of the role of the lawyer invented by Shreve, and of the third-person narrator.

Brooks, Cleanth. "Faulkner's Ultimate Values." In Doreen Fowler and Ann J. Abadie, eds., *Faulkner and the Southern Renaissance* (Jackson, Miss.: University Press of Mississippi, 1982), 266-281. Reiteration of Judith's nobility.

————. "The Narrative Structure of *Absalom, Absalom!*" *Georgia Review*, XXIX (Summer 1975), 366-394. Discusses various narrative strata in the novel; debates Hershel Parker, "What Quentin Saw 'Out There'"; rpt. in *William Faulkner: Toward Yoknapatawpha and Beyond.*

————. The Sense of Community in Yoknapatawpha Fiction." *University of Mississippi Studies in English*, XV (1978), 3-18. Restatement of his contention that Sutpen's "very mixed and ambigicus" relationship with Jefferson is important to basic themes in the novel.

————. *William Faulkner: Toward Yoknapatawpha and Beyond* (New Haven, Conn.: Yale University Press, 1978). Includes Section 2, "On *Absalom, Absalom!*", "The Narrative Structure of *Absalom, Absalom!*," "The Poetry of Miss Rosa Canfield [sic]."

Brooks, Peter. "Incredulous Narration: *Absalom, Absalom!*" *Comparative Literature*, XXXIV (Summer 1982), 247-268. A confused "reflection" on narrative devices in the novel.

Broughton, Panthea Reid. *William Faulkner: The Abstract and the Actual* (Baton Rouge, La.: Louisiana State University Press, 1974), *passim*. Deals with *Absalom* throughout to illuminate the major thesis regarding Faulkner's idea of the human condition. Especially good on Judith Sutpen.

Brown, Calvin S. "Faulkner as Aphorist." *Revue de Littérature Comparée*, LIII (July-September 1979), 277-298. In *Absalom*, Faulkner's use of aphorism is mature.

Brown, May Cameron, and Esta Seaton. "William Faulkner's Unlikely Detective: Quentin Compson in *Absalom, Absalom!*" *Essays in Arts and Sciences*, VIII (May 1979), 27-33. Quentin is not a traditional detective.

Brown, William R. "Mr. Stark on Mr. Strawson on Referring."
    Language and Style, VII (Summer 1974), 219-224. Takes
    issue with John Stark, "The Implications for Stylistics
    of Strawson's 'On Referring,' with *Absalom, Absalom!* as
    an Example," *Language and Style*, VI (Fall 1973), 273-280.
    Stark oversimplifies. Faulkner's novel reads as if it
    were to be read not page by page but simultaneously,
    "like a painting."

Burns, Stuart L. "Sutpen's 'Incidental' Wives and the Question
    of Respectability." *Mississippi Quarterly*, XXX (Summer
    1977), 445-447. Sutpen is not motivated by a desire for
    respectability. Ellen is, in his eyes, a woman certain
    to be free of Negro taint (of a "good hue").

Campbell, Leslie Jean. "Exercises in Doom: Yoknapatawpha
    County Weddings." *Publications of the Arkansas Philological
    Association*, IV (1978), 2-7. Ellen Coldfield's wedding is
    one of several such "bizarre events" in Faulkner's fiction.

Canellas, Maria Isabel Jesus Costa. "Time in Faulkner's
    Absalom, Absalom! as Related to Film Technique." *Estudios
    Anglo-Americanos* (São Paulo, Brazil), II (1978), 33-44.

Canine, Karen McFarland. "The Case Hierarchy and Faulkner's
    Relatives in *Absalom, Absalom!*" *SECOL Bulletin: South-
    eastern Conference on Linguistics*, III (1979), 63-80.
    Absalom revals flaws in Edward Keenan's Case Hierarchy
    prediction model for relative clause formation.

————. "Faulkner's Theory of Relatively: Non-Restrictives
    in *Absalom, Absalom!*" *SECOL Review: Southeastern Con-
    ference on Linguistics*, V (Fall 1981), 118-134. Linguistic
    study of non-restrictive clauses in the novel.

Chabot, C. Barry. "Faulkner's Rescued Patrimony." *Review of
    Existential Psychology and Psychiatry*, XIII (1974), 274-
    286. Sutpen severs himself from a past he thinks is dead,
    thereby courting his fall.

Chavkin, Allan. "The Imagination as the Alternative to
    Sutpen's Design." *Arizona Quarterly*, XXXVII (Summer 1981),
    116-126. Outdated look at a novel the author sees as
    "romantic" in the extreme.

Clark, William Bedford. "The Serpent of Lust in the Southern
    Garden." *Southern Review*, X (Autumn 1974), 805-822.
    General essay on the theme of miscegenation and the
    "mulatto avenger." Joel Chandler Harris's "Where's
    Duncan" is a precursor of *Absalom, Absalom!*

Cleopatra, Sr. *"Absalom, Absalom!*: The Failure of the Sutpen
    Design." *Literary Half-Yearly*, XVI (1975), 74-93. The
    old story: Sutpen and sin.

Clifford, Paula M. "The American Novel and the French
    Nouveau Roman: Some Linguistic and Stylistic Comparisons."
    Comparative Literature Studies, XIII (December 1976),
    348-358. Compares works by Claude Simon and Faulkner,
    including Faulkner's *Absalom, Absalom!*

Conley, Timothy K. "Beardsley and Faulkner." *Journal of
    Modern Literature*, V (September 1976), 339-356. Refer-
    ences to Beardsley in *Absalom, Absalom!* suggest artist's
    influence on Faulkner's descriptions of Bon, his mistress,
    and child.

Connolly, Thomas E. "Point of View in Faulkner's *Absalom,
    Absalom!*" *Modern Fiction Studies*, XXVII (Summer 1981),
    255-272. Chapter by chapter examination of the five
    shifting points of view: Rosa, Mr. Compson (via General
    Compson), Quentin, Shreve, the third-person narrator.

Cook, Richard M. "Popeye, Flem and Sutpen: The Faulknerian
    Villain as Grotesque." *Studies in American Fiction*, III
    (Spring 1975), 3-14. Takes off from Wolfgang Kayser's
    The Grotesque in Art and Literature; only Quentin can
    see Sutpen, "the man in the monster."

Cowley, Malcolm. "Magic in Faulkner." In Evans Harrington
    and Ann J. Abadie, eds., *Faulkner, Modernism, and Film:
    Faulkner and Yoknapatawpha, 1978* (Jackson, Miss.: Univer-
    sity Press of Mississippi, 1979), 3-19. In an essay
    devoted primarily to "The Bear," takes Brooks to task
    for writing off the possibility of Sutpen's downfall as
    the myth of the South.

Davis, Robert Con. "The Symbolic Father in Yoknapatawpha
    County." *Journal of Narrative Technique*, X (Winter 1980),
    39-55. Rosa represents the "other" side of the symbolic
    father. As a structural concept, the father is "demonic"
    in Chapters 1 and 2, "mythic" in Chapters 3-5, and psycho-
    logical or speculative in Chapters 6-9.

Davis, Thadious M. "'Be Sutpen's Hundred': Imaginative Pro-
    jection of Landscape in *Absalom, Absalom!*" *Southern
    Literary Journal*, XIII (Spring 1981), 3-14. Physical
    landscapes are "noticably absent" in the novel; the
    setting is the interior landscapes of Rosa and Quentin.

─────. "The Yoking of 'Abstract Contradictions': Clytie's Meaning in *Absalom, Absalom!*" *Studies in American Fiction*, VII (Autumn 1979), 209-219. Clytie, more than Bon, "is the felt, mysterious black presence which pervades the South."

Dickerson, Lynn. "A Possible Source for the Title *Absalom, Absalom!*" *Mississippi Quarterly*, XXXI (Summer 1978), 423-424. The title may have come from Grace Lumpkin's *To Make My Bread* (1932), which Faulkner owned.

Donaldson, Laura E. "The Perpetual Conversation: The Process of Traditioning in *Absalom, Absalom!*" *Modernist Studies: Literature and Culture*, IV (1982), 176-194. Interdisciplinary examination of oral tradition. *Absalom* illustrates the traditioning process by presenting a core tradition (the basic Sutpen story) and examining various ways that tradition is appropriated and transmitted.

Doody, Terrence. "Quentin and Shreve, Sutpen and Bon." *Confession and Community in the Novel* (Baton Rouge: Louisiana State University Press, 1980), pp. 163-183. See "Shreve McCannon and the Confessions of *Absalom, Absalom!*" *Studies in the Novel*, VI (Winter 1974), 454-469.

─────. "Shreve McCannon and the Confessions of *Absalom, Absalom!*" *Notes on Contemporary Literature*, VIII (May 469. Shreve, Quentin's confessor, gives Bon "a place and an identity Bon never has in his own life." The novel posits community "as a higher value than art itself."

Doxey, W.S. "Father Time and the Grim Reaper in *Absalom, Absalom!*" *Notes on Contemporary Literature*, III (May 1978), 6-7. Wash is Sutpen's double.

Flynn, Peggy. "The Sister Figure and 'Little Sister Death' in the Fiction of William Faulkner." *University of Mississippi Studies in English*, XIV (1976), 99-117. Judith, like Caddy and Temple, is one of Faulkner's sister figures. The female is of importance only in the context of the male.

Ford, Daniel G. "Comments on William Faulkner's Temporal Vision in *Sanctuary, The Sound and the Fury, Light in August, Absalom, Absalom!*" *Southern Quarterly* (University of Southern Mississippi), XV (April 1977), 283-290. Brief discussion of *Absalom* and time in general terms.

————. "Maybe Happen Is Never Once: Some Critical Thought on Faulkner's Use of Time." *Publications of the Arkansas Philological Association*, V (1979), 9-15. Comments on the obsession with the past of several Faulkner characters, including Quentin and Rosa, and on the novel as structured by a "qualitative progression" of unfoldings of the past.

Forrer, Richard. "*Absalom, Absalom!*: Story-telling As a Mode of Transcendence." *Southern Literary Journal*, IX (Fall 1976), 22-46. Interesting discussion of the novel, focusing on the character-narrators' inability to reanscend their obsession with the past. Good discussion of the omniscient narrator, who "affirms a model of transcendence" which denies the fatalism of Mr. Compson.

Fujihira, Ikuko. "Beyond Closed Doors: Quentin Compson and Isaac McCaslin." *William Faulkner: Materials, Studies, and Criticism*, III (July 1980), 31-43. Another discussion of door imagery in *The Sound and the Fury*, *Absalom, Absalom!* and "The Bear."

Gallagher, Susan. "To Love and to Honor: Brothers and Sisters in Faulkner's Yoknapatawpha County." *Essays in Literature*, VII (Fall 1980), 213-244. Reminds us that there is no proof in the novel of incestuous feelings between Judith and Henry, and that Judith's love for Bon may be a moral norm.

Goldman, Arnold. "Faulkner's Images of the Past: From *Sartoris* to *The Unvanquished*." *Yearbook of English Studies*, VIII (1978), 109-124. Quentin's acts of questioning are a rebellion against his father.

Guerard, Albert J. "Faulkner the Innovator." In Evans Harrington and Ann J. Abadie, eds., *The Maker and the Myth: Faulkner and Yoknapatawpha, 1977* (Jackson, Miss.: University Press of Mississippi, 1978), 71-88. Contains a provocative examination of the different uses of italics in *Absalom, Absalom!*

————. "The Faulknerian Voice." In Evans Harrington and Ann J. Abadie, eds., *The Maker and the Myth: Faulkner and Yoknapatawpha, 1977* (Jackson, Miss.: University Press of Mississippi, 1978), 25-42. Discusses Jamesian, Miltonic, Shakespearean elements in Faulkner's voice, using many examples from *Absalom*.

————. "*Absalom, Absalom!*: The Novel as Impressionist Art." *The Triumph of the Novel: Dickens, Dostoevsky, Faulkner* (New York: Oxford University Press, 1976), 302-339. One of the finest essays on the novel of the 1970s, this

provides an overview of the novel with emphasis on moments
of high or deep drama, on Faulkner's "anti-realist impulse"
which gives rise to several crucial impossibilities (that,
even to save Judith or Henry, Sutpen would have refused
a nod of recognition to Bon; that either Clytie or Henry
would have revealed Bon's paternity and tainted blood;
that the emblematic murder at the gate occurred) and
which informs his language. The novel is a culmination
of Conradian impressionism; it is a "narration by
conjecture."

Hagopian, John V. "The Biblical Background of Faulkner's
Absalom, Absalom!" CEA Critic, XXXVI (January 1974),
22-24. Reprinted herein.

————. "Black Insight in *Absalom, Absalom!" Faulkner
Studies*, I (1980), 29-37. Notes the importance of the
murder scene to Quentin. Summarizes critical arguments
about what Quentin learned at Sutpen's Hundred and
votes in favor of a "flash of insight."

Henderson, Harry B., III. *Versions of the Past: The Historical
Imagination in American Fiction* (New York: Oxford University Press, 1974), 254-269 *et passim. Absalom, Absalom!*
is a holistic historical novel in the tradition of *The
House of the Seven Gables* and *The Grandissimes* (Charles Bon
derives from Cable's victims of miscegenation). Racism
corrupts Sutpen.

Herndon, Jerry A. "Faulkner: Meteor, Earthquake, and Sword."
In Glenn O. Carey, ed., *Faulkner: The Unappeased Imagination, A Collection of Critical Essays* (Troy, N.Y.: Whitstone,
1980), 175-193. Again, Sutpen's story is the rise and
fall of the Old South.

Hlavsa, Virginia V. "The Vision of the Advocate in *Absalom,
Absalom!" Novel*, VIII (Fall 1974), 51-70. *Absalom,
Absalom!* can be viewed as a nine-part trial. Some
interesting insights.

Holder, Alan. "The Doomed Design: William Faulkner's *Absalom,
Absalom!" The Imagined Past* (Lewisburg, Pa.: Bucknell
University Press, 1980), 53-72. The novel makes past
omnipresent.

Holman, C. Hugh. "To Grieve on Universal Bones': The Past
as Burden." *The Immoderate Past: The Southern Writer
and History* (Athens, Ga.: University of Georgia Press,
1977), 66-92. "Casual remarks" on several novels,
among them *Absalom, Absalom!* Shreve sees the story as
symbolic of the South, but for Faulkner, the story is a
fable to illuminate mankind.

Hunt, John W. "The Disappearance of Quentin Compson." In
Arthur F. Kinney, ed., *Critical Essays on William Faulkner:
The Compson Family* (Boston: G.K. Hall, 1982), 366-380.
Useful despite its primary focus on the short stories
narrated by Quentin or a Quentin-like narrator, especially
since several of these stories were written shortly before
or while Faulkner was working on *Absalom*.

————. "Keeping the Hoop Skirts Out: Historiography in
Faulkner's *Absalom, Absalom!*" *Faulkner Studies*, I (1980),
38-47. Quentin was Faulkner's device for evoking the
"full historical integrity" of the Sutpen story.

Ilacqua, Alma A. "Faulkner's *Absalom, Absalom!*: An Aesthetic
Projection of the Religious Sense of Beauty." *Ball State
University Forum*, XXI (Spring 1980), 34-41. The novel is
ultimately optimistic. Jim Bond himself is doomed, but
he "is alive...free...vocal...capable of begetting children."

Imbert, Henri-Francois. "Une Technique de la Fascination:
Faulkner (*Absalom, Absalom*) Giono (*Un roi sans divertis-
sement*)." *Revue de Littérature Comparée*, LIII (July-
September 1979), 323-337. Briefly examines influence
of Faulkner on Jean Giono and discusses parallels between
Langlois and Sutpen.

Irwin, John. "The Dead Father in Faulkner." In Robert Con
Davis, ed., *The Fictional Father: Laconian Readings of
the Text* (Amherst: University of Massachusetts Press,
1981), 147-168. See *Doubling and Incest/Repetition and
Revenge: A Speculative Reading of Faulkner*. The material
in this essay is drawn from Irwin's book.

————. *Doubling and Incest/Repetition and Revenge: A
Speculative Reading of Faulkner* (Baltimore: Johns Hopkins
University Press, 1975). Deals throughout with *The Sound
and the Fury* and *Absalom, Absalom!* and the patterns and
keys to meaning in the interstices between the two novels.
Irwin works imaginatively with psychoanalytical theory,
specifically repetitions and the death wish, and with the
philosophy of Nietzsche and recent critical theory. The
elements in the novel do not merely interact but "mutually
create one another" in a holistic structure.

Jackson, Blyden. "Faulkner's Depiction of the Negro."
University of Mississippi Studies in English, XV (1978),
33-47. Although he reads Quentin and Shreve's imaginative
recreation as fact, his comments on Bon and Jim Bond are
interesting. Sutpen's wild Negroes brought from Haiti
seem to spring from Faulkner's understanding of Reconstruction.

Jehlen, Myra. *Class and Character in Faulkner's South* (New York: Columbia University Press, 1976), 47-76 *et passim*. Marxist reading of the novel as "cavalier." Sutpen's career is initiated and doomed by the agrarian class conflict.

Jenkins, Lee. *Faulkner and Black-White Relations: A Psycho-analytic Approach* (New York: Columbia University Press, 1981), 177-219. Disappointing discussion of *Absalom, Absalom!* which, despite Jenkins' psychoanalytic approach, ignores the fact that much of the novel is the speculation of twentieth-century narrators. Draws on Irwin, *Doubling and Incest/Repetition and Revenge*, and on the author's own earlier article, "Faulkner, the Mythic Mind, and the Blacks."

————. "Faulkner, the Mythic Mind, and the Blacks." *Litera-ture and Psychology*, XXVII (1977), 74-91. See above, Black/white doubling in the novel (and in other novels) reveals "aspects of Faulkner's conceptual inheritance" of guilt and sexual jealousy.

Kanashiki, Tsutomu. "Bin no Kubi to Heso no o to: *Absalom, Absalom!* no Jikan." In *Bungaku to America: Ohashi Kenzaburo Kyojo Kanreki Kinen Ronbunshu* (Tokyo: Nanundo, 1980), 283-297.

Kantak, V.Y. "Faulkner's Technique." In Jagdish Chander and Narindar S. Pradhan, eds., *Studies in American Literature: Essays in Honour of William Mulder* (Delhi: Oxford Univ. Press, 1976), 77-96. General, outdated essay on technique in *The Sound and the Fury*, *Light in August*, and *Absalom, Absalom!*

Kartiganer, Donald M. *The Fragile Thread: The Meaning of Form in Faulkner's Novels* (Amherst: University of Massa-chusetts Press, 1979), 69-106. Excellent overview essay. The novel is about strategies of composition. Rosa resembles Quentin in *The Sound and the Fury*; Bon becomes, for Mr. Compson, a kind of "wish fulfillment."

————. "Quentin Compson and Faulkner's Drama of the Genera-tions." In Arthur Kinney, ed., *Critical Essays on William Faulkner: The Compson Family* (Boston: G.K. Hall, 1982), 381-401. Useful discussion of the relationship between Quentin and his father in *The Sound and the Fury* and *Absalom, Absalom!*; the dynamics of that relationship compel Quentin to struggle to recreate the past with tragic results.

Kawin, Bruce. "Faulkner's Film Career: The Years with Hawks."
In Evans Harrington and Ann J. Abadie, eds., *Faulkner,*
Modernism and Film: Faulkner and Yoknapatawpha, 1978
(Jackson, Miss.: University Press of Mississippi, 1979)
163-181. Relationship between Faulkner's movie script
Sutter's Gold and *Absalom, Absalom!*

————. "The Montage Element in Faulkner's Fiction." In
Evans Harrington and Ann J. Abadie, eds., *Faulkner,*
Modernism and Film: Faulkner and Yoknapatawpha, 1978
(Jackson, Miss.: University Press of Mississippi, 1979),
103-126. Montage techniques in *Absalom, Absalom!*;
parallels between the novel and *Citizen Kane.*

Kellner, R. Scott. "A Reconsideration of Character: Relationships in *Absalom, Absalom!*" *Notes on Mississippi Writers,*
VII (Fall 1974), 39-43. Quentin's emotional tie is
actually with Bon.

Kent, George E. "The Black Woman in Faulkner's Works, with
the Exclusion of Dilsey," part II. *Phylon,* XXXVI (March
1975), 55-67. Clytie, one of Faulkner's mammy-characters,
has extrasensory perception.

Kerr, Elizabeth M. "*Absalom, Absalom!*: Faust in Mississippi,
or, The Fall of the House of Sutpen." *University of*
Mississippi Studies in English, XV (1978), 61-82. Uses
Leslie Fiedler's definition of American Gothicism in
Love and Death in the American Novel. Both Sutpen's
Hundred and (in an inversion) Rosa's house are "haunted
castles"; each of the major characters is a variation
of typical Gothic characters.

————. *William Faulkner's Gothic Domain* (Port Washington,
N.Y.: Kennikat, 1979), 29-52. Includes revision of
"*Absalom, Absalom!*: Faust in Mississippi or, The Fall of
the House of Sutpen."

————. "The Evolution of Yoknapatawpha." *Univ. of Mississippi*
Studies in English, XIV (1976), 23-62. Briefly reiterates
Blotner's discussion of the genesis of *Absalom, Absalom!*
and mentions how many of the characters fit into the
history of Yoknapatawpha.

————. "The Women in Yoknapatawpha." *Univ. of Mississippi*
Studies in English, XV (1978), 83-100. In this general
essay, Judith, Rosa and Ellen are discussed as victims
of, among other things, a social system repressive of
women.

Kestner, Joseph A. *The Spatiality of the Novel* (Detroit: Wayne State University Press, 1978), 162-169. Uses *Absalom* as an example of a novel in which a "genidentic dynamic field of language" (Gerard Genette's term) absorbs the interpreter so that time and space are inseparable, and repetitions produce both simultaneity and negative motion.

Kikuchi, Akira. "The Nature of Thomas Sutpen's Tragedy in *Absalom, Absalom!*" *Review of Liberal Arts* (Japan, 1975), 27-41. Faulkner is concerned with the Southerner's loss of identity, of which the mulatto is the sharpest symbol. Sutpen feels that to have fathered Bon is to have tainted himself; therefore, he must convince himself that Bon does not exist.

King, Richard H. *A Southern Renaissance: The Cultural Awakening of the American South, 1930-1955* (New York: Oxford Univ. Press, 1980), 99-129. Heavily dependent on Irwin and Freudian family romance. "On one level, *Absalom, Absalom!* is about the failure to get the story (and history) right."

Kinney, Arthur F. "Faulkner's Fourteenth Image." *Paintbrush*, II (1974), 36-43. Faulkner's "operational structure," in *Absalom* as well as other novels, "always centers in the human process of *perceiving*, of *coming to understand*." Hence, the detective story is a natural form.

————. *Faulkner's Narrative Poetics: Style as Vision* (Amherst: University of Massachusetts Press, 1978), 194-215. Sutpen, the "generating image" in this novel composed of voices, is the original storyteller, leaving as legacy a form for understanding the past. Interesting examinations of Rosa (Sutpen's double), Mr. Compson and Shreve.

————. "Form and Function in *Absalom, Absalom!*" *Southern Review*, XIV (Autumn 1978), 677-691. A general article seeking to show influences on the novel other than the Bible and the Oresteia. Examines Col. W.C. Falkner's *The White Rose of Memphis* and several nineteenth- and early twentieth-century novels to show that the plots in *Absalom, Absalom!* come firmly out of a Southern tradition.

Korenman, Joan S. "Faulkner and 'That Undying Mark'." *Studies in American Fiction*, IV (Spring 1976), 81-91. Sutpen refuses to submit to change. He, Judith and Rosa all try to achieve immortality.

Kort, Wesley. "Social Time in Faulkner's Fiction." *Arizona Quarterly*, XXXVII (Summer 1981), 101-115. Social time is more important than natural time.

deLabriolle, J. "De Faulkner a Claude Simon." *Revue de Littérature Comparée*, LIII (July–September 1979), 358–388. Comparison of *Absalom, Absalom!* and *La Route des Flandres*, with particular attention to the demystification of war and the myth of the enternal feminine.

Landor, Mikhail. "*Absalom, Absalom!* in Russian." *Soviet Literature*, VII (1981) 164–172. Reception study of the Russian translation.

LaRocque, Geraldine E. "*A Tale of Two Cities* and *Absalom, Absalom!*" *Mississippi Quarterly*, XXXV (Summer 1982), 301–304. Suggests a source for Sutpen and Judith's love of wild driving and for the meeting of Henry and Quentin may be found in Dickens' novel.

Lensing, George S. "The Metaphor of Family in *Absalom, Absalom!*" *Southern Review*, XI (Winter 1975), 99–117. Draws on Faulkner's University of Virginia statement about "the human family" to examine families in *Absalom, Absalom!*, including Sutpen's boyhood family, the Coldfields, and Judith/Bon/Henry as the ideal family.

Lenson, David. *Achilles' Choice: Examples of Modern Tragedy* (Princeton, N.J.: Princeton University Press, 1975), 105–116. Faulkner's is an Emersonian view of history; "the reactions of those who study it are more important than the actual facts." The townspeople of Jefferson, Sutpen's slaves, and the narrators themselves function as a Nietzschean chorus.

Leroy, Gaylord C. "Mythopoeic Materials in *Absalom, Absalom!*: What Approach for the Marxist Critic?" *Minnesota Review*, No. 17 (Fall 1981), 79–95. The Marxist critic must "intervene" between the moral sensibility of the novel and the Marxist world view, to oppose the function of English departments as a "principal instrument of the State Ideological Apparatus."

Levins, Lynn G. *Faulkner's Heroic Design: The Yoknapatawpha Novels* (Athens, Ga.: University of Georgia Press, 1976). Chapter 2 is a revised version of "The Four Narrative Perspectives in *Absalom, Absalom!*" (*PMLA*, LXXXV, 1970, pp. 35–47) which goes on to consider the analogue with II Samuel and Greek tragedy.

Lubarsky, Jared. "The Highest Freedom: A Reconstruction of Faulkner on Race." *William Faulkner: Materials, Studies, and Criticism* (Tokyo), III (April 1981), 9–17.

MacKethan, Lucinda Hardwick. "Faulkner's Sins of the Fathers:
     How to Inherit the Past." *The Dream of Arcady: Place
     and Time in Southern Literature* (Baton Rouge, La.: Louisiana
     State University Press, 1980), 153-180. Each of the
     narrators sees Sutpen as a father figure; for Shreve and
     the reader, he is "the inscrutable force in the South
     itself."

Mălăneioiu, Ileana. "*Absalom, Absalom!* sau tragicul absolut."
     *România Literară: Săptăminal de Literatură si Artă Editat
     de Uniunea Scriitorilor din Republica Socialistă România*,
     XI (August 1977), 20-21.

Markowitz, Norman. "William Faulkner's 'Tragic Legend':
     Southern History and *Absalom, Absalom!*" *Minnesota Review*,
     No. 17 (Fall 1981), 104-117. Corrects, for the Marxist
     critic, *Absalom*'s picture of the South, which is histori-
     cally inaccurate.

Matlack, James H. "The Voices of Time: Narrative Structure
     in *Absalom, Absalom!*" *Southern Review*, XV (Spring 1979),
     333-354. Good discussion of the voices and the many
     temporal levels in the novel; especially useful discussion
     of complicated shifts in narration in the second half of
     the book. Uses Jan Vansina's *Oral Tradition* (trans.
     H.M. Wright, 1961).

Mathur, S.B. *American Fiction: The Technique of Point of
     View* (New Delhi, India: Arnold-Heinemann, 1975), 52-61.
     Plot Summary, relying heavily on Levins.

Matthews, John T. "The Marriage of Speaking and Hearing in
     Absalom, Absalom!" *ELH*, XLVII (1980), 575-594. Finest
     essay thus far in the decade of the 1980s and the single
     most important recent treatment of *Absalom, Absalom!*
     Deconstruction of the language of the novel using theories
     of Derrida and Barth to examine the novel as a brilliant
     meditation on "the act of fabricating meaning." Meaning
     in the novel entails endless language play of signifiers
     and is best explained using the metaphor of marriage
     (between speaker and listener, speaker and memory, creator
     and creation). Unlike most critics of the novel, Matthews
     attends carefully and sensitively to Rosa and Mr. Compson.

————. "Marriages of Speaking and Hearing in *Absalom, Absalom!*"
     The Play of Faulkner's Language (Ithaca, N.Y.: Cornell
     University Press, 1982), 115-161. Expanded version of
     above essay.

McClure, John. "The Syntax of Decadence in *Absalom, Absalom!*"
Minnesota Review, No. 17 (Fall 1981), 96-103. Faulkner
deliberately employs his narrative mode to portray a
"manifestation of decay."

Meindl, Dieter. "Bewusstsein als Schicksal: Zur Struktur
und Entwicklung von William Faulkners Generationen-
Romanen." *Amerikastudien* (Stuttgart), Bd. 30, 1974.
The dynamic of the novel is dialectic between two types
of narration, "Eindruck," a static tableau, and "Ausdruck,"
or narrative which makes the static comprehensively alive.

Middleton, John. "Shreve McCannon and Sutpen's Legacy."
Southern Review, X (Winter 1974), 115-124. Middleton
agrees with Shreve that the Jim Bonds will conquer the
western hemisphere. Only Shreve is capable of "bearing
the consequences of Sutpen's design."

Millgate, Michael. "'A Cosmos of My Own': The Evolution of
Yoknapatawpha." In Doreen Fowler and Ann J. Abadie, eds.,
*Fifty Years of Yoknapatawpha: Faulkner and Yoknapatawpha,
1979* (Jackson, Miss.: University Press of Mississippi,
1980), 23-43. This discussion of Quentin as hearer-
recorder in early related works sheds light on his role
in *Absalom, Absalom!*

————. "Faulkner and History." In Evans Harrington and
Ann J. Abadie, eds., *The South and Faulkner's Yoknapatawpha:
The Abstract and the Apocryphal* (Jackson, Miss.: University
Press of Mississippi, 1977), 22-39. Extends "'The Firma-
ment of Man's History': Faulkner's Treatment of the Past."
Mississippi Quarterly, XXV, supplement (1972), 25-35.

Milum, Richard A. "Faulkner and the Cavalier Tradition: The
French Bequest." *American Literature*, XLV (January 1974),
580-589. Brief mention of French and European influence
on Sutpen (through Haiti, New Orleans, the French architect).

Minter, David. "Family, Region, and Myth in Faulkner's Fiction."
In Doreen Fowler and Ann J. Abadie, eds., *Faulkner and
the Southern Renaissance* (Jackson, Miss.: University Press
of Mississippi, 1982), 182-203. The incessant remembering,
listening, talking in the novel are expressive of the only
way the human can come to know his community or his conscious self.

————. "'Truths More Intense than Knowledge': Notes on
Faulkner and Creativity." In Doreen Fowler and Ann J.
Abadie, eds., *Faulkner and the Southern Renaissance*
(Jackson, Miss.: University Press of Mississippi, 1982),
245-265. *Absalom* exemplifies the fact that for Faulkner
looking at the past opened up his creative genius.

————. "Three Trips to Babylon." *William Faulkner: His Life and Work* (Baltimore: Johns Hopkins Univ. Press, 1980), pp. 137-164. History of the novel's composition (which omits mention of "Evangeline") and critical evaluation.

Mortimer, Gail L. "Significant Absences: Faulkner's Rhetoric of Loss." *Novel*, XIV (Spring 1981), 232-256. *Absalom*, as well as other Faulkner novels, makes use of rhetorical gaps and absences, reflecting the author's "preoccupation with loss."

Muhlenfeld, Elisabeth. "'We have waited long enough': Judith Sutpen and Charles Bon." *Southern Review*, XIV (Winter 1978), 66-80. Reprinted herein.

Nelson, David W. "Two Novels of Speculation: William Faulkner's *Absalom, Absalom!* and Uwe Johnson's *Mutmassungen über Jakob.*" *Papers in Romance* (Seattle, Washington), II, supplement 1 (1980), 51-57. Brief comparative study with Johnson's 1959 novel.

Newby, Richard L. "Matthew Arnold, the North, and *Absalom, Absalom!*" *American Notes and Queries*, XVI (March 1978), 105. Presents slight evidence that two lines in the novel are allusions to Matthew Arnold's "The Function of Criticism at the Present Time."

Ohki, Masako. "The Technique of Handling Time in *Absalom, Absalom!*" *Kyushu American Literature* (Fukuoka, Japan), XV (1974), 89-94. Past, present and future are fused in the novel.

Onoe, Masaji. "Some T.S. Eliot Echoes in Faulkner." *William Faulkner: Materials, Studies and Criticism*, III (July 1980), 1-15. Includes discussion of a passage in Eliot's "Marina" which is echoed in *Absalom*.

Oriard, Michael. "The Ludic Vision of William Faulkner." *Modern Fiction Studies*, XXVIII (Summer 1982), 169-187. Includes *Absalom* in his discussion of tragic games in Faulkner's fiction.

Paddock, Lisa. "'Trifles with a tragic profundity'" The Importance of 'Mistral'." *Mississippi Quarterly*, XXXII (Summer 1978), 413-422. The short story foreshadows the novel in the use of increasingly involved narrators and enigmatic central figures.

Palumbo, Donald. "The Concept of God in Faulkner's *Light in August, The Sound and the Fury, As I Lay Dying*, and *Absalom, Absalom!*" *South Central Bulletin*, XXXIV (Winter, 1979), 142-146. Bon and Henry suffer loss of faith because the loss of the Civil War renders their suffering absurd.

Parker, Hershel. "What Quentin Saw 'Out There'." *Mississippi Quarterly*, XXVII (Summer 1974), 323-326. Quentin sees three Sutpen faces, Henry, Clytie and Bond, and concludes that Bon must have been a Sutpen.

Parkinson-Zamora, Lois. "The End of Innocence: Myth and Narrative Structure in Faulkner's *Absalom, Absalom!* and Garcia Marquez' *Cien años de soledad.*" *Hispanic Journal*, IV (Fall 1982), 23-40. Comparative study.

Parr, Susan Resneck. "The Fourteenth Image of the Blackbird: Another Look at Truth in *Absalom, Absalom!*" *Arizona Quarterly*, XXXV (1979), 153-164. Repetitive discussion of discrepancies between Chronology and Genealogy and text itself. Bon may never have existed at all. The omniscient narrator casts doubt on the speculations of the character-narrators.

Payne, Ladell. *Black Novelists and the Southern Literary Tradition* (Athens, Ga.: University of Georgia Press, 1981), *passim*. Brief mention of parallels between *Absalom* and James Weldon Johnson's *The Autobiography of an Ex-Coloured Man* and two novels by Charles W. Chesnutt.

Pearce, Richard. "Reeling through Faulkner: Pictures of Motion, Pictures in Motion." *Modern Fiction Studies*, XXIV (1979), 483-495. The image of Rosa at the beginning of the novel is not an image of arrested motion but of motion resisting arrest.

Piacentino, Edward J. "Another Possible Source for *Absalom, Absalom!*" *Notes on Mississippi Writers*, X (Winter 1977), 87-93. Parallels between Miltiades Vaiden, central character in T.S. Stribling's trilogy, and Sutpen.

Pikoulis, John. "Innocence and History." *The Art of William Faulkner* (London: Macmillan Press, 1982), 66-111. Outdated general essay, drawing upon T.S. Eliot but concluding that *Absalom* is the story of the South.

Pilkington, John. *The Heart of Yoknapatawpha* (Jackson, Miss.: University Press of Mississippi, 1981), 157-188. Drawing on Schoenberg, discusses *Absalom*'s composition, reception, relation to "Evangeline" and other Don-and-I stories, and various critical interpretations of the novel.

Pinsker, Sanford. "Thomas Sutpen and Milly Jones: A Note on Paternal Design in *Absalom, Absalom!*" *Notes on Modern American Literature*, I (Winter 1976), item 6. Suggests, on the basis of scant evidence, that Sutpen may have been the father of Milly Jones.

Pitavy, François. "The Gothicism of *Absalom, Absalom!*:
  Rosa Coldfield Revisited." In Doreen Fowler and Ann J.
  Abadie, eds., *A Cosmos of My Own: Faulkner and Yoknapatawpha, 1980* (Jackson, Miss.: University Press of Mississippi,
  1981), 199–226. *Absalom*, a "dream novel," has few traditional Gothic elements, but is a novel of darkness--the
  true essence of the genre. Rosa's narrative, a fine
  example of Gothic technique, is a means of questioning
  fiction and of showing the "recognition of the relation
  of the creative imagination to madness and divinity."

Polek, Fran James. "The Fourteenth Blackbird: Reflective
  Deflection in *Absalom, Absalom!*" *University of Portland
  Review*, XXVIII (Spring 1976), 23–24. Plot summary.
  There is no one "meaning" for the novel.

————. "From Renegade to Solid Citizen: The Extraordinary
  Individual and the Community." *South Dakota Review*, XV
  (Spring 1977), 61–72. Compares three 'renegades':
  Sutpen, Gatsby, and Corleone, Puzo's *The Godfather*.

————. "Tick-Tocks, Whirs, and Broken Gears: Time and
  Identity in Faulkner." *Renascence*, XXIX (Summer, 1977),
  193–200. Minimal effort which accords Eulalia the same
  reality and same space as Rosa.

Porter, Carolyn. "Faulkner and his Reader." In Glen O. Carey,
  ed., *Faulkner: The Unappeased Imagination, A Collection
  of Critical Essays* (Troy, N.Y.: Whitstone, 1980), 231–
  258. Reader-response approach. Shreve's summing up at
  the novel's end parodies the reader's similar attempt.

————. "William Faulkner: Innocence Historicized." *Seeing
  and Being: The Plight of the Participant Observer in
  Emerson, James, Adams and Faulkner* (Middletown, Conn.:
  Wesleyan University Press, 1981), 205–276. Examines
  Absalom first in light of Faulkner's own family history
  and of opposing views of the antebellum South in Cash and
  Genovese. Faulkner's view is more accurate. Sutpen embodies neither the capitalistic ideal (as Brooks holds)
  nor the paternalistic but tries to embody both; the
  contradictions have tragic results. Includes in revised
  form "Faulkner and his Reader."

Powers, Lyall H. "*Absalom, Absalom!*" *Faulkner's Yoknapatawpha
  Comedy* (Ann Arbor: University of Michigan Press, 1980),
  106–124. The novel is Faulkner's "most revealing exposure
  of the rot at the base of the Southern edifice."

Rimmon-Kenan, Shlomith. "From Reproduction to Production:
     The Status of Narration in Faulkner's *Absalom, Absalom!*"
     Degrés: Revue de Synthèse à Orientation Sémiologique,
     XVI (Winter 1978), f-f19. Examines the Chinese-box
     quality of who told who what and where they got it from
     and discusses signs of conjecture and creation from a
     semantic perspective.

Ringold, Francine. "The Metaphysics of Yoknapatawpha County:
     Airy Space and Scope for Your Delirium." *Hartford Studies
     in Literature*, VIII (1976), 223-240. Faulkner recreates
     Bergson's life force in the dynamic movements of the
     novel's prose line, and he exemplifies Einstein's relativity
     in his sense of infinite possibilities.

Rio-Jelliffe, R. "*Absalom, Absalom!* As Self-Reflexive Novel."
     Journal of Narrative Technique, XI (Spring 1981), 75-90.
     Tedious discussion of the novel's narrative strands.

Robbins, Deborah. "The Desperate Eloquence of *Absalom, Absalom!*"
     Mississippi Quarterly, XXXIV (Summer 1981), 315-324. The
     narrators' psychic survival depends upon their telling
     the story; each has a need to communicate with a world
     they are isolated from. The novel ends with "the failure
     of the search for coherence through speech."

Robin, Régine. "*Absalom, Absalom!*" In Viola Saches, ed., *Le
     Blanc et le Noir Chez Melville et Faulkner* (Paris:
     Mouton, 1974), 67-129. A long *explication de texte* of
     racial attitudes and relationships in the novel, which
     pays close attention to images, analogies, symbols, names,
     hidden structures, word etemologies, all of which are
     evidence of the racial attitudes and fantasies of the
     characters (and the author). Interesting discussion
     of Ellen.

Rodewald, F.A. "Faulkner's Possible Use of *The Great Gatsby*."
     Fitzgerald-Hemingway Annual (1975), 97-101. Discusses
     parallels between Gatsby and Sutpen without mentioning
     Brooks' work on the subject.

Rollyson, Carl E., Jr. "*Absalom, Absalom!*: The Novel as
     Historiography." *Literature and History*, No. 5 (Spring
     1977), 42-54. Reprinted herein.

————. "Faulkner and Historical Fiction: *Redgauntlet* and
     Absalom, Absalom!" *Dalhousie Review*, LVI (Winter 1976-77),
     671-681. Scott's *Redgauntlet* foreshadows Faulkner's
     "departure from the norms of historical fiction."
     Wandering Willie's tales work in much the same way as the
     French architect's story.

————. "Quentin Durward and Quentin Compson: The Romantic Standard-Bearers of Scott and Faulkner." *Massachusetts Studies in English*, VII (1980), 34-39. Faulkner may have borrowed Quentin's name and some of his characteristics from Scott.

————. "The Re-creation of the Past in *Absalom, Absalom!*" *Mississippi Quarterly*, XXIX (Summer 1976), 361-374. A sensible entry into the what-did-Quentin-learn-at-Sutpen's Hundred debate, paying close attention to Chapter 8.

Rose, Maxine. "Echoes of the King James Bible in the Prose Style of *Absalom, Absalom!*" *Arizona Quarterly*, XXXVII (Summer 1981), 137-148. Worth consulting for discussion of Biblical language, tone, and imagery in the novel. Faulkner's use of the Bible imparts to the novel a quality of timelessness, sacredness, mystery, and authority.

————. "From Genesis to Revelation: The Grand Design of William Faulkner's *Absalom, Absalom!*" *Studies in American Fiction*, VIII (Autumn 1980), 219-228. The novel's plot derives its skeletal framework from the Old and New Testaments.

Rosenman, John B. "Anderson's *Poor White* and Faulkner's *Absalom, Absalom!*" *Mississippi Quarterly*, XXIX (Summer 1976), 437-438. Wash's murder of Sutpen with the rusty scythe may have been inspired by image patterns associated with Joe Wainsworth in Anderson's novel, which Faulkner praised in 1925.

————. "A Matter of Choice: The Locked Door Theme in Faulkner." *South Atlantic Bulletin*, XLI (May 1976), 8-12. Brief discussion of similarities bewteen Dal Martin ("The Big Shot"), Wash and Sutpen.

Rosenzweig, Paul. "The Narrative Frames in *Absalom, Absalom!*: Faulkner's Involuted Commentary on Art." *Arizona Quarterly*, XXXV (1979), 135-152. Repeats unawares earlier discussions of the novel as a meditation on the process of the artist.

Ross, Stephen M. "Conrad's Influences on Faulkner's *Absalom, Absalom!*" *Studies in American Fiction*, II (1974), 199-209. Mr. Compson's narration (Chapters 2, 3, 4 and his letter to Quentin—which functions like Marlow's packet) resembles the rhetorical pattern in *Lord Jim*. Chapters 6-9 draw on the example of *Heart of Darkness*.

————. "The Evocation of Voice in *Absalom, Absalom!*" *Essays in Literature*, VIII (Fall 1981), 135-149. Draws on Freudian psychology and Derrida's technique to explore how the novel dramatizes narrators narrating. Pays particular attention to Judith's handling of Bon's letter to Mrs. Compson, which names "voice" as the power that can memorialize the past.

————. "Faulkner's *Absalom, Absalom!* and the David Story: A Speculative Contemplation." In Raymond-Jean Frontain and Jan Wojcik, eds., *The David Myth in Western Literature* (West Lafayette, Ind.: Purdue University Press, 1980), 136-153. A sound discussion of the ways in which *Absalom* draws upon the David stories, with particular attention paid to inversions, parallels, paradoxes.

Rouberol, Jean. "Faulkner et l'histoire." *RANAM: Recherches Anglaises et Américaines,* IX (1976), 7-17. Wide-ranging essay on Faulkner's interest in Southern history. *Absalom* is one of his many uses of the mythic view of history (chaos becomes cosmos becomes chaos again). Interesting discussion of the French architect's story as a small-scale recapitulation of this pervasive Faulknerian theme.

Roudiez, Leon S. "*Absalom, Absalom!*: The Significance of Contradiction." *Minnesota Review,* No. 17 (Fall 1981), 58-78. Whirlwind examination of many elements relating to *Absalom* (Faulkner's biography, race relations, Biblical parallels, class system, Depression history, etc.) which explores "contradictions" between Faulkner's insistence that this is Sutpen's story and the reader's fascination with Quentin's story.

Rubin, Louis D., Jr. "Looking Backward." *New Republic* (October 19, 1974), 20-22. Review essay of Henderson's *Versions of the Past* which takes issue with Henderson's reading of *Absalom*. At the end of the novel, Quentin is rejecting a way of thinking which will not allow him to be fully human.

————. "Scarlett O'Hara and the Two Quentin Compsons." In Evans Harrington and Ann J. Abadie, eds., *The South and Faulkner's Yoknapatawpha: The Actual and the Apocryphal* (Jackson, Miss.: University Press of Mississippi, 1977), 168-194; rpt. *A Gallery of Southerners* (Baton Rouge, La.: Louisiana State University Press, 1982), 26-48. Scarlett O'Hara also has a design.

————. "William Faulkner: The Discovery of a Man's Vocation." In George H. Wolfe, ed., *Faulkner: Fifty Years After The Marble Faun* (University, Ala.: University of Alabama Press, 1976), 43-68. Uses Quentin in *Absalom* as a yardstick · against which to measure the young Faulkner as he pursued his vocation to become a writer.

Rudich, Norman. "Faulkner and the Sin of Private Property."
    Minnesota Review No. 17 (Fall 1981), 55–57. Brief Marxist
    treatment of Faulkner's artistic use of property in
    Absalom, Absalom! and "The Bear."

Sabiston, Elizabeth. "Women, Blacks, and Thomas Sutpen's
    Mythopoetic Drive in *Absalom, Absalom!*" *Modernist
    Studies: Literature and Culture, 1920–1940*, I (1974–
    1975), 15–26. Masculine and feminine principles in the
    novel.

Samway, Patrick. "Storytelling and the Library Scene in
    Faulkner's *Absalom, Absalom!*" *William Faulkner: Materials,
    Studies, and Criticism*, II (December 1979), 1–20. Faulkner's
    respect for his characters prevents him from invading their
    deepest privacy. The central Christmas eve library scene
    remains elusive.

Scherer, Olga. "Faulkner et la fratricide: pour une théorie
    des titres dans la littérature." *Etudes Anglaises*, XXX
    (July–September 1977), 329–336. Argues for the importance
    of Faulkner's titles generally, and *Absalom, Absalom!* in
    particular, which contains clues not only to the concerns
    of the characters and narrators but also to Faulkner's
    relationship with his own text.

————. "La Contestation du jugement sur pieces chez Dostoievski
    et Faulkner." *Delta* (November 1976), 47–61. Interesting
    discussions of Bon's letter to Judith and Mr. Compson's
    to Quentin and of the ways in which the presentations of
    these written documents (Judith's speech to Mrs. Compson,
    Mr. Compson's letter lying on the table work upon the
    meanings of the documents themselves.

————. "Rosie Coldfield et Vanka Karamozov: Le diminutif au
    service de l'ambivalence." *Revue de Littérature Comparée*,
    LIII (July–September 1979), 311–322. In both novels,
    the diminutive form of the name appears only once, which
    leads Scherer to draw major conclusions about the narrative
    vision of Faulkner and Dostoyevski.

Schmidtberger, Loren F. "*Absalom, Absalom!*: What Clytie Knew."
    Mississippi Quarterly, XXXV (Summer 1982), 255–263. Sound
    character study of Clytie and how her access to apparently
    "secret" knowledge is quite plausible.

Schoenberg, Estalla. *Old Tales and Talking: Quentin Compson
    in William Faulkner's* Absalom, Absalom! *and Related Works*
    (Jackson, Miss.: University Press of Mississippi, 1977).
    Absalom, Absalom! is Faulkner's opportunity to rewrite a
    masterpiece, *The Sound and the Fury*, and lacks meaning for
    the reader without reference to the earlier novel. Traces

a Quentin-like character through Faulkner's works and
includes a good discussion of the relationship of
"Evangeline" to *Absalom*.

Schrank, Bernice. "Patterns of Reversal in *Absalom, Absalom!*"
   Dalhousie Review, LIV (1974-1975), 648-666. The novel
   is Sutpen's story and abounds in reversals. Sutpen's
   trouble was ignorance.

Schultz, William J. "Just Like Father: Mr. Compson as
   Cavalier Romancer in *Absalom, Absalom!*" *Kansas Quarterly*,
   XIV (Spring 1982), 115-123. Mr. Compson, whose cynicism
   is a mask, is fascinated with Charles Bon, and erects on
   slim evidence a chivalric tale of romance, which attracts
   him while intellectually he rejects it. Quentin shares
   his father's internal split.

Sederberg, Peter C. "Faulkner, Naipaul, and Zola: Violence
   and the Novel." In McGrath Barbor, ed., *The Artist and
   Political Vision* (New Brunswick, N.J.: Transaction, 1982),
   291-315. Briefly compares *Absalom* with Zola's *Germinal*
   and V.S. Naipaul's *Guerillas*, all of which exhibit dis-
   continuities of time, point of view, and meaning.

Shirley, William. "The Question of Sutpen's 'Innocence'."
   Southern Literary Messenger, I (Spring 1975), 31-37.
   We cannot deal with Sutpen's innocence as a fact but
   only as an interpretation by Mr. Compson and in turn by
   Quentin.

Singal, Daniel Joseph. *The War Within: From Victorian to
   Modernist Thought in the South, 1919-1945* (Chapel Hill,
   N.C.: University of North Carolina Press, 1982), pp. 187-
   195. *Absalom, Absalom!* is a social allegory. Sutpen's
   children represent small-town probity (Henry), backwoods
   vitality (Judith), cavalier identity (Bon).

Spivey, Ted R. "Lawrence and Faulkner: The Symbolist Novel
   and the Prophetic Song." *The Journey Beyond Tragedy:
   A Study of Myth and Modern Fiction* (Orlando, Fla.:
   University Presses of Florida, 1980), 72-93. Brief look
   at *Absalom*, seeing Sutpen as the "aristocratic spirit of
   the European white man all over the world."

Stafford, William T. "A Whale, an Heiress, and a Southern
   Demigod: Three Symbolic Americas," *College Literature*,
   I (1974), 100-112; included in *Books Speaking to Books:
   A Contextual Approach to American Fiction* (Chapel Hill,
   N.C.: University of North Carolina Press, 1981). Com-
   pares unprofitably Sutpen, Moby Dick and Milly Theale.

Stonum, Gary Lee. *Faulkner's Career: An Internal Literary
    History* (Ithaca, N.Y.: Cornell University Press, 1979).
    Standard overview of the novel. *Absalom* is Faulkner's
    study of arrested motion, of art. All the characters
    crave stasis. Interesting comments on Faulkner's
    "inherited body of material."

Strandberg, Victor. *A Faulkner Overview: Six Perspectives*
    (Port Washington, N.Y.: Kennikat, 1981), 48-53, 71-76.
    Brief musings on Sutpen as male principle and on psycho-
    analytic method in the novel.

Straumann, Heinrich. "Black and White in Faulkner's Fiction."
    English Studies, LX (August 1979), 462-470. Bon's
    relationship with Sutpen is "unconscious brotherly love...
    between White and Black" doomed by prejudice.

Suda, Minoru. "The Development of William Faulkner's Litera-
    ture: With Special Empahsis on *The Sound and the Fury*
    and *Absalom, Absalom!*" *Essays and Studies in English
    Language and Literature* (Sendai, Japan), LXX (1979), 23-40.

Sigiura, Ginsaku. "Nature, History, and Entropy: A Reading
    of Faulkner's *Absalom, Absalom!* in Comparison with
    Moby-Dick and *V.*" *William Faulkner: Materials, Studies,
    and Criticism*, II (December 1979(, 21-23. Compares Sutpen,
    Ahab and Herbert Stencil.

Sullivan, Walter. "The Decline of Myth in Southern Fiction."
    Southern Review, XII (Winter 1976), 16-31; rpt. *A Requiem
    for the Renaissance* (Athens, Ga.: University of Georgia
    Press, 1976). Thomas Sutpen is embodiment of the Southern
    myth. He desires a past; failing that, he desires to
    amass "the stuff of a past for future generations."

Sykes, S.W. "The Novel as Conjuration: *Absalom, Absalom!*
    and *La Route des Flandres.*" *Revue de Littérature Comparée*,
    LIII (July-September 1979), 348-357. Simon's 1960 novel
    owes much to *Absalom*, also a novel of failure.

Tobin, Patricia Drechsel. "The Shadowy Attenuation of Time:
    William Faulkner, *Absalom, Absalom!*" *Time and the Novel:
    The Genealogical Imperative* (Princeton, N.J.: Princeton
    University Press, 1978), 107-132. Builds on Irwin to
    examine in detail the metaphorical relationship between
    Sutpen and Quentin, who have many psychological elements
    in common.

Topuridse, Eteri. "Strukturaufbau des Romans *Absalom, Absalom!*
    von William Faulkner." In Helmut Brandt and Nodar Kakabadse,
    eds., *Erzählte Welt: Studien zur Epik des 20. Jahrhunderts*

(Berlin: Aufbau-Verlag, 1978), 337-358. Summarizes
American criticism before providing a general assessment
of the novel as in the tradition of the historical novel,
detective novel, social commentary, psychological inquiry,
and so on.

Tran, Qui-Phiet. *William Faulkner and the French New Novelists*
(Arlington, Va.: Carrollton Press, 1980). Misreadings
abound in this discussion of the influence of *The Sound
and the Fury* and *Absalom, Absalom!* on the "New Novelists."

Turner, Joseph W. "The Kinds of Historical Fiction." *Genre*,
XII (1979), 333-355. *Absalom* is a subgenre, the invented
historical novel. Quentin is concerned with the very
methodological issues which concern the historian.

Uroff, Margaret Dickie. "The Fictions of *Absalom, Absalom!*"
Studies in the Novel, XI (Winter 1979), 431-445. The
novel, which is full of imaginings or fictions, reveals
Faulkner's growing skepticism about his material. (After
Absalom, "Faulkner never wrote another novel about the
Civil War South nor another experimental novel.")

Vanderwerken, David L. "Who Killed Jay Gatsby." *Notes on
Modern American Literature*, III (Spring 1979), item 12.
Explores parallels between Sutpen and Gatsby, Wilson
and Wash.

Wagner, Linda Welshimer. *Hemingway and Faulkner: inventers/
masters* (Metuchen, N.Y.: Scarecrow, 1975), *passim*.
Sees echoes in *Absalom, Absalom!* of Clifton Cuthbert's
1933 *Thunder Without Rain*, which deals with incest.

Walters, P.S. "Hallowed Ground: Group Areas in the Structure
and Theme of *Absalom, Absalom!*" *Theoria*, XLVII (1976),
35-55. Follows Levins to examine space in the novel--
as literal setting, as settings through time, and as
symbolic.

Watkins, Evan. "The Fiction of Interpretation: Faulkner's
Absalom, Absalom!" *The Critical Act: Criticism and
Community* (New Haven, Conn.: Yale University Press, 1978),
188-212. Shreve's special function in the novel is to
assert that there was love between Bon and Judith and that
Henry's act was unnecessary, and hence, tragic.

————. "The Politics of Literary Criticism." *Boundary 2*,
VIII (Fall 1979), 31-38. Concerned with the "institution-
alized opposition" between artist and critic. *Absalom*
shows us the artist willing to commit himself to a creation
and yet also willing to let Shreve create a radically different novel.

Watson, James G.   "Faulkner: Short Story Structures and
     Reflexive Forms." *MOSAIC* XI (Summer 1978), 127-137.
     Relationship of "Wash" and "Evangeline" to *Absalom,
     Absalom!* Quentin, who grafts the stories, is an artist.

————.   "'If *Was* Existed': Faulkner's Prophets and the
     Patterns of History." *Modern Fiction Studies,* XXI
     (Winter 1975-1976), 499-507. As historicists, Rosa is
     subjective and Mr. Compson is objective. Quentin com-
     bines these two models and finds a prophecy for the
     future—his own "immanent *was*-ness."

Weinstein, Arnold L.   *Vision and Response in Modern Fiction*
     (Ithaca, N.Y.: Cornell University Press, 1974), 136-153.
     Excellent discussion of *Absalom* as primarily concerned
     with love. In a sound discussion of Rosa, notes sexual
     imagery in the scene in which Quentin and Rosa travel to
     Sutpen's Hundred.

Weinstein, Philip M.   "Precarious Sanctuaries: Protection and
     Exposure in Faulkner's Fiction." *Studies in American
     Fiction,* VI (1978), 173-191. Touch is a haunting motif
     in the novel; it destroys sanctuaries of "shibboleth and
     immunity."

Williams, J. Gary.   "Quentin finally sees Miss Rosa." *Criticism,*
     XXI (1979), 331-346. Quentin (not strictly speaking a
     narrator since he is usually listening) doesn't really
     "see" Rosa until the end of the novel. His response to
     her is more important than his response to Sutpen.

Wilson, Mary Ann T.   "Search for an Eternal Present: *Absalom,
     Absalom!* and *All the King's Men.*" *Connecticut Review,*
     VIII (1974), 95-100. Both novels share a Bergsonian view
     of time.

Wittenberg, Judith Bryant.   "Faulkner and Eugene O'Neill."
     Mississippi Quarterly, XXXIII (1980), 327-341. Striking
     similarities between *Mourning Becomes Electra* and *Absalom,
     Absalom!*

————.   *Faulkner: The Transfiguration of Biography* (Lincoln,
     Neb.: University of Nebraska Press, 1979), 130-156. *Absalom,
     Absalom!,* which springs from Faulkner's relationship with
     his own father, reveals positive psychological strides
     made by Faulkner in the years since the writing of *The
     Sound and the Fury.* Each narrator is an artist; the novel
     itself is a paean to the creative process.

Young, Thomas Daniel.   "Narration as Creative Act: The Role
     of Quentin Compson in *Absalom, Absalom!*" In Evans Harrington
     and Ann J. Abadie, eds., *Faulkner, Modernism and Film:*

Faulkner and Yoknapatawpha, 1978 (Jackson, Miss.:
University Press of Mississippi, 1979), 82-102; Rpt. Arthur
F. Kinney, ed., *Critical Essays on William Faulkner: The
Compson Family* (Boston: G.K. Hall, 1982). Another reading of
the novel with reference to *The Sound and the Fury.* Quentin
must meet psychological needs established in the earlier novel.